ınd Territories in the 21st Century

The 'tribes and territories' metaphor for the cultures of academic disciplines and their roots in different knowledge characteristics has been used by those interested in university life and work since the early 1990s. This book draws together research, data and theory to show how higher education has gone through major change since then and how social theory has evolved in parallel. Together these changes mean there is a need to re-theorise academic life in a way which reflects changed contexts in universities in the twenty-first century, and so a need for new metaphors.

Using a social practice approach, the editors and contributors argue that disciplines are alive and well, but that, in a turbulent environment where many other forces conditioning academic practices exist, their influence is generally weaker than before. However, the social practice approach adopted in the book highlights how this influence is contextually contingent – how disciplines are deployed in different ways for different purposes and with varying degrees of purchase.

This important book pulls together the latest thinking on the subject and offers a new framework for conceptualising the influences on academic practices in universities. It brings together a distinguished group of scholars from across the world to address questions such as:

- Have disciplines been displaced by interdisciplinarity, having outlived their usefulness?
- Have other forces acting on the academy pushed disciplines into the background as factors shaping the practices of academics and students there?
- How significant are disciplinary differences in teaching and research practices?
- What is their significance in other areas of work in universities?

This timely book addresses a pressing concern in modern education, and will be of great interest to university professionals, managers and policy-makers in the field of higher education.

Paul Trowler is Professor of Higher Education and Director of Research at the Centre for Higher Education Research and Evaluation in the Department of Educational Research, Lancaster University, UK.

Murray Saunders is Director of Evaluation at the Centre for Higher Education Research and Evaluation in the Department of Educational Research, Lancaster University, UK.

Veronica Bamber is Director of the Centre for Academic Practice at Queen Margaret University in Edinburgh.

International Studies in Higher Education

Series Editors:

David Palfreyman, OxCHEPS
Ted Tapper, OxCHEPS
Scott Thomas, Claremont Graduate University

The central purpose of this series is to see how different national and regional systems of higher education are responding to widely shared pressures for change. The most significant of these are: rapid expansion; reducing public funding; the increasing influence of market and global forces; and the widespread political desire to integrate higher education more closely into the wider needs of society and, more especially, the demands of the economic structure. The series will commence with an international overview of structural change in systems of higher education. It will then proceed to examine on a global front the change process in terms of topics that are both traditional (for example, institutional management and system governance) and emerging (for example, the growing influence of international organisations and the blending of academic and professional roles). At its conclusion the series will have presented, through an international perspective, both a composite overview of contemporary systems of higher education, along with the competing interpretations of the process of change.

Published titles

Structuring Mass Higher Education
The role of elite institutions
Edited by David Palfreyman and Ted Tapper

International Perspectives on the Governance of Higher Education
Alternative frameworks for coordination
Edited by Jeroen Huisman

International Organizations and Higher Education Policy
Thinking globally, acting locally?
Edited by Roberta Malee Bassett and Alma Maldonado

Academic and Professional Identities in Higher Education
The challenges of a diversifying workforce
Edited by Celia Whitchurch and George Gordon

International Research Collaborations
Much to be gained, many ways to get in trouble
Melissa S. Anderson and Nicholas H. Steneck

Cross-border Partnerships in Higher Education
Strategies and issues
Robin Sakamoto and David Chapman

Accountability in Higher Education
Global perspectives on trust and power
Bjorn Stensaker and Lee Harvey

The Engaged University
International perspectives on civic engagement
David Watson, Susan E. Stroud, Robert Hollister, and Elizabeth Babcock

Universities and the Public Sphere
Knowledge creation and state building in the era of globalization
Edited by Brian Pusser, Ken Kempner, Simon Marginson, and Imanol Ordorika

The Future University
Ideas and possibilities
Edited by Ronald Barnett

Universities in the Knowledge Economy
Higher education organisation and global change
Edited by Paul Temple

Tribes and Territories in the 21st Century
Rethinking the significance of disciplines in higher education
Edited by Paul Trowler, Murray Saunders and Veronica Bamber

Tribes and Territories in the 21st Century

Rethinking the significance of disciplines in higher education

Edited by
Paul Trowler,
Murray Saunders and
Veronica Bamber

Routledge
Taylor & Francis Group

LONDON AND NEW YORK

First published in paperback 2014

First published 2012
by Routledge
2 Park Square, Milton Park, Abingdon, Oxon OX14 4RN

and by Routledge
711 Third Avenue, New York, NY 10017

Routledge is an imprint of the Taylor & Francis Group, an informa business

British Library Cataloguing in Publication Data
A catalogue record for this book is available from the British Library

Library of Congress Cataloging in Publication Data
Tribes and territories in the 21st-century : rethinking the significance of disciplines in higher education / edited by Paul Trowler, Murray Saunders and Veronica Bamber.
    p. cm.
    1. Education, Higher–Cross-cultural studies. 2. Interdisciplinary approach in education. I. Trowler, Paul. II. Saunders, Murray. III. Bamber, Veronica.
    LB2322.2.T76 2012
    378.1'61–dc23
                2011030069

ISBN: 978-0-415-88062-8 (hbk)
ISBN: 978-1-138-02103-7 (pbk)
ISBN: 978-0-203-13693-5 (ebk)

Typeset in Minion
by Bookcraft Ltd, Stroud, Gloucestershire

Contents

List of Figures and Tables   x
List of Contributors   xi
Series Editors' Introduction   xvii

Introduction   1

PART 1
Theorising (Inter-)Disciplinarity and Social Practices   **3**

1   Disciplines and Interdisciplinarity: Conceptual Groundwork   5
    PAUL TROWLER

2   Disciplines and Academic Practices   30
    PAUL TROWLER

PART 2
Disciplinary Differences and Research Practices   **39**

3   Disciplines and Research: Key Themes   41
    PAUL TROWLER

4   Beyond Tribes and Territories: New Metaphors for New
    Times   44
    CATHERINE MANATHUNGA AND ANGELA BREW

5   Law, Research and the Academy   57
    FIONA COWNIE

6   Doing Research: the Case of Art and Design   68
    PAUL TROWLER

7   Research Strategies: 'Capital' and the Goods of Social Science
    Research   78
    NICOLA SPURLING

8 Theorising Disciplines and Research Practices   91
   PAUL TROWLER

PART 3
Disciplinary Differences and Learning and Teaching Practices   97

9 Learning and Teaching in the Disciplines: Challenging
   Knowledge, Ubiquitous Change   99
   VERONICA BAMBER

10 The Evolving Landscape of Nursing Science in the 21st
   Century: the Finnish Case   107
   ANNE LAIHO

11 The Pedagogic Device: Sociology, Knowledge Practices and
   Teaching–Learning Processes   118
   PAUL ASHWIN, ANDREA ABBAS AND MONICA MCLEAN

12 Scene Changes and Key Changes: Disciplines and Identities
   in HE Dance, Drama and Music   130
   PAUL KLEIMAN

13 'We're Engaged': Mechanical Engineering and the
   Community   142
   CHRISTINE WINBERG

14 Learning and Teaching, Disciplines and Social Practice
   Theory   156
   VERONICA BAMBER

PART 4
Catalysts for Changing Disciplinary Practices   167

15 Imperatives for Academic Practices: Catalysts for Sustained
   Change   169
   MURRAY SAUNDERS

16 Crossing Tribal Boundaries: Interdisciplinarity as a
   Threshold Concept   175
   RAY LAND

17 Change Vectors and Academic Identities: Evolving Tribes and
   Territories   186
   KERRI-LEE KRAUSE

18 Internationalisation: Troublesome Knowledge for the
   Disciplines   197
   VALERIE A. CLIFFORD

19 Teaching in an Age of 'Supercomplexity': Lecturer
   Conceptions in Context   208
   SUSAN J. LEA AND LYNNE CALLAGHAN

20 Technology and Change in Academic Practice   220
   MARTIN OLIVER

21 Transformations from without and within the Disciplines:
   the Emerging Practice Landscape   232
   MURRAY SAUNDERS

22 Conclusion: Academic Practices and the Disciplines in the
   21st Century   241
   PAUL TROWLER, MURRAY SAUNDERS, VERONICA BAMBER

   References   259
   Index   285

Figures and Tables

Figures

1.1   Conceptualising the relationship between disciplines and teaching,
      disciplines and research   16
1.2   Simplified set of positions on the three axes   16
13.1 Relationships between traditional teaching and learning practices,
      the academic discipline and professional practice in mechanical
      engineering   146
16.1 Perceived characteristics of the twenty-first century   181
20.1 Activity theory triangle   224

Tables

1.1   Summary of disciplinary differences in learning, teaching,
      assessment and curriculum   20
6.1   Conceptions of research   74
6.2   Conceptions of research as ideological   75
10.1 Institutionalisation of Nursing Science in Finnish universities   109
13.1 Dimensions of the epistemic and social relation in the mechanical
      engineering/community engagement project   155
19.1 Research design   211
19.2 Contextual issues identified by participants   212

Contributors

Andrea Abbas is Principal Lecturer in Sociology and a member of the Social Futures Institute at Teesside University. She is co-convener of the Unit for Social and Policy Research and co-investigator for the project Pedagogic Quality and Inequality in University First Degrees, which is funded by the Economic and Social Research Council. Andrea's research interests include: higher education; (in)equality and difference; consumption and higher education; social theory; cultural consumption; embodiment; and innovative qualitative research methods. Further information about Andrea can be found here: http://www.tees.ac.uk/sections/research/social_futures/staff_profile_details. cfm?staffprofileid=U0012180 and here: http://www.pedagogicequality.ac.uk/ project-team.php

Paul Ashwin is a Senior Lecturer in Higher Education at the Department of Educational Research, Lancaster University. His research focuses on examining different aspects of teaching, learning and assessment in higher education as well as the relations between theory and method in educational research. His recent book *Analysing Teaching–Learning Interactions in Higher Education: Accounting for Structure and Agency* (Continuum, 2009) critically examines different approaches to conceptualising the ways in which teaching–learning interactions in higher education are shaped by a range of personal, pedagogic, disciplinary and institutional processes.

Veronica Bamber is Director of the Centre for Academic Practice at Queen Margaret University, Edinburgh. Previously Roni was Director of Educational Development at Heriot-Watt University. The Centre for Academic Practice is responsible for enhancing learning, teaching and research at the university. She has worked as an educational developer for ten years, and has participated in numerous national initiatives, including the Scottish Enhancement Themes. Prior to this, Roni was a lecturer in Spanish for 18 years, teaching in four different universities around the UK. Roni's current research is in universities as organisations, the development of staff, and the evaluation of development programmes.

Angela Brew PhD is Professorial Fellow in the Learning and Teaching Centre at Macquarie University, Sydney, Australia. In 2009 she was awarded a National Teaching Fellowship from the Australian Learning and Teaching Council to enhance undergraduate engagement through involving them in research and inquiry. Before joining Macquarie, she worked at the University of Sydney where she led strategic projects on Research-enhanced Learning and Teaching and Research Higher Degree Supervision Development. Her recent research is focused on the nature of research and its relation to teaching, learning and scholarship, models of research-led teaching and undergraduate research. Her books include: *The Nature of Research: Inquiry in Academic Contexts*; *Research and Teaching: Beyond the Divide*; *Transforming a University: The Scholarship of Teaching and Learning in Practice* (with Sachs); and *Academic Research and Researchers* (with Lucas).

Lynne Callaghan is a postdoctoral Research Fellow in the Faculty of Health at the University of Plymouth. She has led and collaborated on a variety of pedagogic, health and community service projects and managed the research and evaluation unit of the Centre for Excellence in Professional Placement Learning. Current pedagogic research interests include the determinants of mobile learning behaviour; service user involvement in assessment; benefits and barriers of the scholarship of teaching and learning; perceptions of the supercomplexity of higher education; and pedagogic and community impact of student volunteering in a domestic abuse service.

Valerie A. Clifford is an Associate Professor who has held a number of key posts in higher education academic development centres including Oxford Brookes, UK; Monash, Australia; and the University of the South Pacific, Fiji. She was also the inaugural director of the Centre for International Curriculum Inquiry and Networking at Oxford Brookes. Her research is the areas of internationalisation of the curriculum for all students, global citizenship and reflective practice.

Fiona Cownie is Professor of Law at Keele University. Her research interests focus on legal education, and her published research includes work on values in higher education, on the place of women in the law school, an empirical study of teaching law to international students and *Legal Academics* (Hart Publishing, 2004), a monograph exploring the culture of law schools and the professional identities of academic lawyers. Her most recent book is '*A Great and Noble Occupation!' The History of the Society of Legal Scholars* (Hart Publishing, 2009), co-authored with Professor Ray Cocks (Keele). Fiona Cownie is a former President of the Society of Legal Scholars and a former Vice Chair of the Socio-Legal Studies Association. In 2011 she was elected as an Academician of the Academy of Social Sciences.

Paul Kleiman is the Higher Education Academy's (HEA) Discipline Lead for Dance, Drama and Music in the UK, and was previously – for eleven years – Deputy Director of PALATINE, the HEA's Subject Centre for those disciplines.

Trained as a theatre designer, Dr Kleiman spent the first part of his career as a designer and director, touring political and community theatre around the UK and Europe. In 1995, he became one of the founding tutors of the Liverpool Institute for Performing Arts (LIPA) which he left in 2001 to join PALATINE. His main research, writings, conference presentations and consultancies focus on creativity, curriculum design and assessment.

Kerri-Lee Krause is Chair in Higher Education and Prof-Vice Chancellor of Education, University of Western Sydney, Australia. Her research expertise spans broadly across higher education policy areas, with a focus on the quality and changing nature of the student experience, the changing nature of academic work and the implications of these changes for policy and practice. Professor Krause regularly provides advice to the sector on enhancing institutional quality, along with strategies for managing the changing student and academic staff experience in higher education.

Anne Laiho is a Lecturer in the Department of Education at the University of Turku, Finland. Her main research interests include the sociology of education, higher education and the education of healthcare professionals, as well as gender and education. Dr Laiho lectures in Pedagogical Studies for Teachers and in the Sociology of Education. Anne's most recent book is *Terveysalan ammatit ja koulutus* [Healthcare Professionals and Education] edited with Tarita Ruoholinna. She has also recently been involved in a survey in which Finnish university workers' experiences of the governance of university work were studied.

Ray Land is Professor of Higher Education and Director of the Centre for Academic Practice and Learning Enhancement at the University of Strathclyde. As part of his work within the centre he is Programme Director of the Certificate/Diploma in Advanced Academic Studies. He is a member and founding accreditor of the Higher Education Academy. His research interests include the theory and practice of educational development, threshold concepts and troublesome knowledge, and theoretical aspects of digital learning.

Susan J. Lea is Professor and Vice Dean (Education) at the Institute of Psychiatry. Susan joined King's in November 2010 from the University of Plymouth where she held a number of academic leadership positions including Acting Dean of the Faculty of Health, Associate Dean (learning and teaching) and Director of the Centre for Excellence in Professional Placement Learning. Susan's research interests are in the field of social justice. Her current psychological research focuses predominantly on sexual and domestic violence, while in the field of pedagogy she is interested in the supercomplexity of higher education and its implications for teaching and research. Some of her current projects involve the attrition of rape cases within the criminal justice system, rape survivors' experiences of sexual assault referral centres, and sexual and domestic violence and mental health. Susan works in partnership with the police in some of these areas.

Catherine Manathunga is Associate Professor in the Faculty of Education at Victoria University Wellington, Aotearoa New Zealand. Her research interests include doctoral supervision pedagogy, doctoral graduate outcomes and attributes, interdisciplinarity and the history of university teaching and learning in Australia and Aotearoa New Zealand. Prior to her recent move into the Faculty of Education, Catherine was an academic developer for 12 years at Queensland University of Technology and the University of Queensland in Australia. She has published widely on higher education and academic development and has acted as an educational consultant to many other universities in Australia and internationally.

Monica McLean is Associate Professor and Reader in Higher Education in the School of Education at the University of Nottingham. Her research draws on critical social theory and focuses on pedagogic quality and inequality in higher education policies and practice. Her book *Pedagogy and the University: Critical Theory and Practice* (2008) elaborates a theory of pedagogic justice for higher education drawing on the theories of Jurgen Habermas.

Martin Oliver is a Reader in ICT in Education at the London Knowledge Lab, a research centre in the Institute of Education, University of London. He is currently Chair of the Association for Learning Technology and edits the journal *Learning, Media and Technology*. His research focuses on uses of technology in Higher Education, with interests in theory and methodology.

Murray Saunders is Director of Evaluation at here@Lancaster, the higher education research and evaluation centre in the Department of Education at Lancaster University, UK. He holds a chair in the evaluation of education and work and has directed some 40 evaluations over a career of 30 years. He has been President of the European Evaluation Society and the UK Evaluation Society and was a founder member of the International Organisation for Cooperation in Evaluation. His interests are in the development of the theory and practice of evaluation and the evaluative research of policy and change.

Nicola Spurling has recently completed her PhD in Sociology at Lancaster University, UK. Her thesis entitled 'Authors of Our Own Lives? Institutions, Individuals and the Everyday Practice of Sociology' examines and develops theories of social reproduction and transformation by weaving together empirical data on individuals' everyday practices and careers with institutional and economic histories of UK universities and the discipline of sociology. Before commencing her PhD, she worked as Research Development Officer at the University of Salford, where she undertook research on the social situation of Chinese students in the UK. Whilst in this position, she played a key role in establishing the University's Learning and Teaching Research Network, Higher Education Research Centre and Education in a Changing Environment Conference.

Paul Trowler is Professor of Higher Education and Director of Research at here@Lancaster, the higher education research and evaluation centre in the Department of Education at Lancaster University, UK. His research interests include: planning and managing change in universities; the implementation of planned change particularly related to the enhancement of the curriculum, teaching, learning and assessment; higher education policymaking and environmental change; cultures in universities; academic 'tribes' and their disciplinary territories; approaches to evaluation. Paul's books, also edited with Murray Saunders and Roni Bamber, are *Reconceptualising Evaluative Practices in Higher Education: The Practice Turn* (2011) and *Enhancing Learning and Teaching in Higher Education: Theory, Cases, Practices* (Open University Press/SRHE, 2009). More details on Paul's work can be found at: http://www.lancs.ac.uk/staff/trowler/cv.html

Christine Winberg is Head of the Department of Academic Staff Development in the Fundani Centre for Higher Education Development at the Cape Peninsula University of Technology in Cape Town, South Africa. The Fundani Centre is responsible for enhancing teaching and learning and educational research at the institution. Chris' work involves academic development and programme evaluation. She is also the director of the Work-integrated Learning Research Unit, which is supported by the South African National Research Foundation. Her research focus is professional and vocational education and technical communication. Previously Professor Winberg lectured in applied linguistics and language education in South Africa and in Sweden. She is chairperson of the South African Association for Applied Linguistics.

Series Editors' Introduction

International Studies in Higher Education

This series is constructed around the premise that higher education systems are experiencing common pressures for fundamental change, reinforced by differing national and regional circumstances that also impact upon established institutional structures and procedures. There are four major dynamics for change that are of international significance:

1   Mass higher education is a universal phenomenon.
2   National systems find themselves located in an increasingly global marketplace that has particular significance for their more prestigious institutions.
3   Higher education institutions have acquired (or been obliged to acquire) a wider range of obligations, often under pressure from governments prepared to use state power to secure their policy goals.
4   The balance between the public and private financing of higher education has shifted – markedly in some cases – in favour of the latter.

Although higher education systems in all regions and nation states face their own particular pressures for change, these are especially severe in some cases: the collapse of the established economic and political structures of the former Soviet Union along with Central and Eastern Europe, the political revolution in South Africa, the pressures for economic development in India and China, and demographic pressure in Latin America.

Each volume in the series will examine how systems of higher education are responding to this new and demanding political and socio-economic environment. Although it is easy to overstate the uniqueness of the present situation, it is not an exaggeration to say that higher education is undergoing a fundamental shift in its character, and one that is truly international in scope. We are witnessing a major transition in the relationship of higher education to state and society. What makes the present circumstances particularly interesting is to see how different systems – a product of social, cultural, economic and political contexts that have interacted and evolved over time – respond in their own peculiar ways to the changing environment. There is no assumption that the pressures for change have set in motion the trend towards a converging model of higher education, but we do believe that in the present circumstances no understanding of 'the idea of the university' remains sacrosanct.

Although this is a series with an international focus it is not expected that each individual volume should cover every national system of higher education. This would be an impossible task. Whilst aiming for a broad range of case studies, with each volume addressing a particular theme, the focus will be upon the most important and interesting examples of responses to the pressures for change. Most of the individual volumes will bring together a range of comparative quantitative and qualitative information, but the primary aim of each volume will be to present differing interpretations of critical developments in key aspects of the experience of higher education. The dominant overarching objective is to explore the conflict of ideas and the political struggles that inevitably surround any significant policy development in higher education.

It can be expected that volume editors and their authors will adopt their own interpretations to explain the emerging patterns of development. There will be conflicting theoretical positions drawn from the multidisciplinary, and increasingly interdisciplinary, field of higher education research. Thus we can expect in most volumes to find an intermarriage of approaches drawn from sociology, economics, history, political science, cultural studies, and the administrative sciences. However, whilst there will be different approaches to understanding the process of change in higher education, each volume's editor(s) will impose a framework upon the volume inasmuch as chapter authors will be required to address common issues and concerns.

This volume in the series, edited by Paul Trowler, Murray Saunders and Roni Bamber, brings together a distinguished group of scholars from across the world to address the issue of the significance of disciplines and disciplinary difference in the contemporary global higher education environment. Have disciplines been displaced by interdisciplinarity, having outlived their usefulness? Have other forces acting on the academy pushed them into the background as forces shaping the practices of academics and students there? The editors conclude that in order to understand the continuing relevance of disciplines, it is time to reconceptualise what they are and how they are articulated in the day-to-day practices of the twenty-first-century university.

David Palfreyman
Director of OxCHEPS, New College, University of Oxford

Ted Tapper
OxCHEPS, New College, University of Oxford

Scott Thomas
Professor of Educational Studies, Claremont Graduate University, California

Introduction

The basic question this book addresses is: what is the significance of disciplines in contemporary higher education across the world? This is an important question because of the changes to higher education institutions and systems that have been happening. Some have argued that disciplines are dead or dying, replaced by interdisciplinary forms of organisation as higher education becomes more oriented to solving pressing real-world problems through multidisciplinary task-oriented formations that draw in expertise from beyond universities. The massification of higher education and its market focus, together with the entry into the university curriculum of vocational areas previously excluded, have meant that traditional disciplinary structures are being replaced by a modularised smorgasbord from which students choose, or by interdisciplinary approaches to an area of study – such as nursing or media studies. For others, however the continuing evaluation of disciplinary-based research by governments both reinforces and confirms the continued salience of disciplinary forms of organisation.

Meanwhile PhD students designing research studies tend to draw upon the classic book in the field when thinking about teaching and research in universities: Tony Becher's 1989 text *Academic Tribes and Territories* (with a second edition in 2001 by Becher and Paul Trowler, the lead editor of this volume). Drawing on empirical data collected in the mid-1980s in the US and the UK this book became a much-cited classic across the world. It set out a thesis which argued, in summary, that the knowledge structures of disciplines (the academic territories) strongly condition or even determine the behaviour and values of academics, who live in disciplinary tribes with common sets of practices – at least as far as research is concerned, although the argument has been extended beyond it by many other authors. More experienced academics draw on this book too, although they tend to be wary of some of its more essentialist claims and the somewhat crude disciplinary classificatory system, which was based on the work of Kolb and Biglan as well as incorporating Becher's own additions.

So the time has come to draw together the latest thinking which tries to answer that key question about the significance, relevance and power of disciplines today, and to offer a new framework for thinking about the drivers of academic practices. This book draws on the most important research into this issue by a range of authors from around the world who offer a short summary of their research and conclusions. The book is divided into four main sections. The first provides an overview of ways of seeing disciplines and of ways of understanding the academic practices in universities that they may, or may not, influence. The second and third sections drill down into two areas of those academic practices: research and learning, and teaching, with chapters by our contributors asking questions about the significance of disciplines in those areas. The fourth section takes a different tack, looking at the forces that have become more significant in recent decades influencing academic practices, perhaps replacing disciplinary power and the significance of disciplinary differences. The second, third and fourth sections each have a 'top' and 'tail' by the editors which first introduce the chapters in the section and, in the tail, discuss and situate them as a whole within the argument of the book. The final chapter offers an overview of the conclusions we have reached and sets out that argument in summary, showing how the social practice theory approach we have adopted throughout the book can offer an illuminating way of seeing the contemporary relationship between academic practices, broadly considered, and the factors that catalyse them.

1
Theorising (Inter-)Disciplinarity and Social Practices

1
Disciplines and Interdisciplinarity
Conceptual Groundwork

PAUL TROWLER

What Are 'Disciplines'?

It is difficult to pin down a common definition of 'disciplines' in the literature, and with good reason. The term, which derives from Latin roots meaning both pupil and teaching, carries multiple meanings. It has associations with the biblical 'disciple', which carries that Latin root, as well as submission to authority, punishment, being made to follow instructions, and rigorous self-control. Berger (1970) captures a few of these ideas when he defines a discipline as 'a specific body of teachable knowledge with its own background of education, training, procedures, methods and content areas'. This 40-year-old definition is attractive: it is broad enough to potentially cover any topic area yet sets clear boundaries between a discipline and a non-discipline.

But it has its problems. While often replicated in later definitions, it is important to recognise its limitations in the light of the contextual changes and more expansive thinking in the interim. These problems include the following. First, it fails to recognise that there are often internal disputes about procedures and content areas. Second, that definition conveys a static feel, yet disciplines are constantly evolving. Weingart and Stehr (2000) say that there are roughly 9,000 fields of knowledge, though no source is cited for this information. Most accounts argue that they are expanding all the time: Bourdieu (1998) argued that fields expand in a territorial way, though he did not give a motivation for this. Burton Clark (1998) describes the fragmentation of biological sciences in the mid-1990s and their reconfiguration into new disciplines, and how economics and psychology have similarly fragmented. Psychology has multiple associations at the national and international level representing its sub-specialisms, leading to the question of where the boundary is between being merely a sub-specialism and a new discipline entirely. Third, Berger's approach focuses on 'discipline as curriculum' – discipline as taught in educational institutions – not 'discipline as research'. I elaborate on this difference below. Fourth, his definition emphasises a specific body of knowledge as being the defining characteristic of a discipline, yet part of the role of a discipline is to develop new knowledge: knowledge-creation is one of the functions of a discipline. Finally, Berger omits the significant dimension of the organisational forms disciplines take within and beyond universities. Despite these lacunae similar definitions to Berger's are found in more recent literature, for example Donald (2002: 8) defines a discipline as: 'A body of knowledge with a reasonably logical taxonomy, a specialised vocabulary, an accepted body of theory, a systematic research strategy, and techniques for replication and validity.'

Another approach to understanding what disciplines are involves simply listing their characteristics. Krishnan (2009: 9), who provides a useful summary of how different disciplines approach how to understand 'discipline' as a concept, suggests that the following characteristics are common in such lists:

1 disciplines have a particular object of research ... though [this] ... may be shared with another discipline
2 disciplines have a body of accumulated specialist knowledge [referring to this object of research which is] ... not generally shared with another discipline
3 disciplines have theories and concepts that can organise the accumulated specialist knowledge effectively
4 disciplines use specific terminologies or ... technical language adjusted to their research object
5 disciplines have developed specific research methods according to their specific research requirements
6 disciplines must have some institutional manifestation in the form of subjects taught at universities or colleges, respective academic departments and professional associations.

But not all disciplines display these characteristics. For many there is no agreed body of accumulated specialist knowledge, nor even agreement on what the object of research is or what acceptable theoretical approaches are. This is most true of the 'restless disciplines' of the social sciences (Commission on the Social Sciences 2003: 24). Arguably those which tick all of these boxes are highest in the pecking order of disciplines – but sometimes intra-disciplinary wars break out and suddenly boxes are unticked and fundamental questions arise about what the discipline is, as happened in English literature. Parturition (Clark 1993), the splitting of disciplines into new forms, can sometimes occur, as has happened in the physical sciences.

Weingart and Stehr (2000) move away from the 'body of knowledge' approach to capturing the essence of disciplines and instead emphasise the functions of disciplines in relation to different aspects of knowledge. Unlike Berger they take into account the significance of organisational form:

> Disciplines are the intellectual structures in which transfer of knowledge from one generation to the next is cast ... [they] have a great impact on the structure of occupations – the world of practice ... Disciplines are not only

intellectual but also social structures, organizations made up of human beings with vested interests based on time investments, acquired reputations, and established social networks that shape and bias their views on the relative importance of their knowledge. ... Disciplines are diffuse types of social organization for the production of particular types of knowledge.

Weingart and Stehr, 2000: Introduction xi, xiv

In the Weingart and Stehr approach, compared to Berger's, we can see the depiction of disciplines taking on a more radical, poststructural feel. If Berger is a realist, taking the view that there are objective features of disciplines, Weingart and Stehr are clearly on the relativist side of the supposed divide between relativism and realism: for them particular social situations and motivations are significant in shaping the nature of disciplines. Turner goes further along the relativist road, seeing disciplines not in essentialist, objective terms but as socially constructed by people with agendas, reputations to defend and vested interests. 'Disciplines ... are cartels that organize markets for the production and employment of students by excluding those job-seekers who are not products of the cartel' (Turner 2000: 51). Disciplines in this view are essentially about organisational form – and in particular the degree-granting powers of universities to give named degrees, positions and power, to people who subsequently engage in the same practices. This is what Halsey (1992) called 'donnish dominion' – the power of academics over universities and their professional lives, now on the wane. From this point of view, the development of particular epistemic discourses, and of epistemic fluency in dealing with these, is a social product at least partly aimed at distinguishing insider from outsider. For Foucault (1975), similarly, a 'discipline' is a force and practice that brings about docile bodies, constrained discourses and compliant minds: it involves the operation of power.

There are echoes of Cardinal Newman (1853) in this understanding of disciplines as the terrain for the competitive playing out of careers, though Newman cast a rosier light on it. For Newman a university was

> ... an assemblage of learned men [sic] zealous for their own sciences, and rivals of each other, ... brought, by familiar intercourse and for the sake of intellectual peace, to adjust together the claims and relations of their respective subjects of investigation. They learn to respect, to consult, to aid each other. Thus is created a pure and clear atmosphere of thought, which the student also breathes.
>
> Newman 1853: 126

Despite taking a relativist approach at least in some of his thinking, Turner (2000: 46) also argues that 'departments in different universities in the same discipline are essentially interchangeable with one another', referring in particular to their 'problems, prospects and strategies'. Indeed, he says (2000: 46) that they take a 'more or less standard worldwide organizational form' and that they instil communicative competence – an interpretive community essentially, a group who share tacit knowledge about quality and are able to make judgements. So Turner to some extent also mixes a relativist social-constructionist model – disciplines as created by people, defending self-interest – and a realist essentialist one – disciplines objectively have a common set of problems, a common discourse and common procedures, a consistency that is driven by some underlying mechanism.

This mix of the social and the 'real' seems reasonable. Michael Young (2000) notes that it is now widely acknowledged both in sociology and philosophy that knowledge has both a social and an epistemological basis, so Turner's approach is not out of step with that. As we shall see in the next chapter, a critical realist practice approach such as Archer's (2000, 2007) also argues that both structure and agency are significant. Young cautions against going too far along the path of seeing disciplinary difference as only socially determined, as being completely relative. This 'voice' discourse (Moore and Muller 1999), rooted in postmodern theory, offers no criteria for judgement between 'good' and 'poor' knowledge, he says. Yet we need, and use, such criteria all the time, and have clear processes for making such distinctions. Young argues (2008: 28) that any useful theory of knowledge, and of disciplines, needs to see them as being to some extent socially constructed, but at the same time recognise that knowledge is objective in ways that transcend the historical conditions of its production. He proposes a social realist understanding of knowledge, and disciplines, which appreciates both their social and their epistemological dimensions:

A social realist approach ... recognizes the 'social' character of knowledge as intrinsic to its epistemological status because the logical reconstruction of truth is always a dialogue with others set within particular collective codes and values.

Young 2008: 34

Young argues that the grounds for objectivity – and therefore for claims to truth – are themselves sometimes social in nature: derived in part from the discourse, networks, gatekeeping practices and peer review safeguards built up by disciplinary specialists over a period of time. Klein (2000: 6) offers some further characteristics of a field of knowledge which contribute to guarantees of knowledge validity: 'general explanatory factors and goals, techniques and methods, and related concepts, laws and theories [used in tackling] a set of central problems [and] domains of related items for study'.

In some disciplines the grounds for objectivity are also physical in nature, and so the mix is different. There is not just one set of grounds for robust knowledge, but a number. However disciplines *must* have them: for Young, recognising the social nature of disciplines without acknowledging their essential character lapses into relativism, but a focus on its objective reality without acknowledging its sociality simply justifies the status quo – because as Weingart and Stehr's as well as Foucault's and Turner's approaches, above, highlight, disciplines can be used to gain relative advantage.

So how does all this help us in our search for a definition of 'discipline'? The discussion above leads us to reject one based on the 'voice' approach alone, despite its attractions. Such a definition might run:

A discipline comprises a set of different but clear narratives about a field of knowledge; its boundaries, procedures and purposes. These incorporate relative consensus about a disciplinary saga concerning key figures, conflicts and achievements. Disciplines take organisational form, have internal hierarchies and confer power differentially, to the advantage of a minority.

This does have merits: it allows room for the division and conflict we see within most disciplines, but also recognises that there is a degree of commonality. It highlights the sociality underpinning the construction of disciplines and their operation. Yet it falls into precisely the trap Moore and Muller (1999) warn us of: adopting a relativist 'voice' discourse without acknowledging the grounds needed to distinguish 'good' from 'bad' knowledge. A postmodern emphasis on narrativity loses the significance of the relative solidity of the social world, incorporated in recurrent practices and the organisational forms in which they occur, as well as the solidity of the epistemological basis, or at least the safeguards of knowledge built into organisational forms of which Young says we should not lose sight.

So, moving on from that definition, and attempting to build one on the social practice perspective that we adopt in this book and develop in Chapter 2, a second attempt is:

Reservoirs of knowledge resources shaping regularised behavioural practices, sets of discourses, ways of thinking, procedures, emotional responses and motivations. These provide structured dispositions for disciplinary practitioners who reshape them in different practice clusters into localised repertoires. While alternative recurrent practices may be in competition within a single discipline, there is common background knowledge about key figures, conflicts and achievements. Disciplines take organisational form, have internal hierarchies and bestow power differentially, conferring advantage and disadvantage.

This definition is defensible. Michael Young dismisses a social practice theory of knowledge and disciplines because it 'provides no grounds for distinguishing between curriculum knowledge and the knowledge we require in the course of our everday lives' (2008: 82). But Young is criticising social practice approaches that lack the structural elements included in our approach, ones that focus on the situated nature of experiential knowledge acquisition. He also criticises Paul Hirst for moving away (in 1993) from his early 'forms and fields of knowledge' realist thesis, which lent knowledge an absolute ontological status, and instead adopting what Young considers a relativist stance founded in what – for Hirst, at least – is a practice approach. But while Young's critique of Hirst's articulation of a practice-based approach may be justified, it is difficult to sustain in relation to the theoretical tradition generally. Reckwitz (2002: 249) briefly defines social practices as 'forms of bodily activities, forms of mental activities, "things" and their use, a background knowledge in the form of understanding, know-how, states of emotion and motivational knowledge'. A social practice approach recognises that knowledge tools vary between different fields of practice, and that they have a 'real' ontological solidity relatively free from social conditioning. Indeed, they can 'script' practices rather than being shaped by them. A social practice approach, then, can easily accommodate a social realist position like Young's. Such a position requires some criteria for discriminating between different kinds of knowledge generated and in use. We return to this discussion in Chapter 2.

One test of a good definition, even a working one, is that it must help us distinguish between what is and is not included under the heading of what is being defined. So, does our proposed definition distinguish, for example, between different candidates for the mantle of 'discipline'? Does it help answer common questions like: is nursing studies a discipline? Is medicine? Is art and design? If 'art and design' is too broad, what about fine art, or fashion design, or graphic design?

Unfortunately, even with the extended working definition offered above, a degree of judgement is still required in drawing those lines, but it at least helps draw broad boundaries. My response is that under the definition above nursing studies is a discipline, and so is medicine, but that art and design is indeed too broad to count because of differences between their fields of knowledge and the key differences in their background knowledge. Within that broad term some of the sub-areas of art and design, such as fine art, do count as disciplines but others, such as design for performance, are too young and restricted to yet have developed regularised sets of discourses, ways of thinking, procedures, emotional responses and motivations, all of which take time to develop.

Where disciplines do not (yet) exist, the concept of domains of study is helpful (Trist 1972). By contrast with 'discipline', this term can be used to refer to areas of study such as women's studies or education studies which are oriented around a particular subject matter and draw from a number of disciplines – as defined above – in the attempt to better understand it. Trist originally used the term to mean the study of a problem area, such as drug-taking. However, as Kogan and Henkel (1983) point out, this usually mutates into the study of a domain in the sense we are using it here.

Again, however, the lines are blurred. In his early work Hirst (1974) considered it relatively easy to objectively distinguish between a domain – a 'field' in his terms – and a discipline – a 'form' of knowledge. However that objectivist, realist account oversimplified the situation: the distinction is mainly a social one; one of convention, tradition and history. Domains can relatively easily become disciplines, and vice versa. Attempting to draw clear lines between particular domains and disciplines, or between one discipline and another in this way can be unhelpful. So can the imagery of 'fields', 'boundaries', 'territories', 'boundary crossing', 'cross-border raids', 'tribes' and so on – even discounting the colonialist heritage of the 'tribes' metaphor (see Chapter 4). More fluid metaphors are required, unless the purpose is to develop very simple heuristic categories for research or other purposes, in which case the reality of the model must not be confused with the model of reality (as Bourdieu says, 1977: 29). Moreover, what is made to count as a discipline varies according to context: in the UK, disciplines were constructed in one way for the quinquennial Research Assessment Exercise and in another for the purposes of developing the Higher Education Academy's Subject Centres, tasked with enhancing teaching and learning in their subject areas. In both substantive and social ways, fluidity characterises disciplinarity across the world:

> The organizational matrix of disciplines is beginning to dissolve ... disciplinary interests, boundaries, and constraints are dissolving; disciplines are merging in areas where their overlap forms a new field ...
> Weingart and Stehr, 2000: Introduction, xi, xiii

In fact the language used to describe disciplines reflects this. Evans (1995) uses the word 'subject' to mean the institutional enactment of disciplines in the shape of departments, which are largely concerned to give curricular shape to their discipline. This usefully helps us to distinguish between subject and discipline – the former is more concrete in form and more likely to be used in relation to teaching, while the latter is more likely to refer in the abstract to the field of study. So the Higher Education Academy's Subject Centres are well named – their role is to enhance teaching and learning practices in particular areas of university work. There is an argument (made by Parker 2002) that there is an increasing tendency to refer to subject rather than discipline and that this is part of a general trend towards deprofessionalising academics; effectively 'demoting' them to become 'merely' teachers or 'practitioners' (Sabri 2010):

> 'Subject' is reassuringly concrete – a subject can be defined, has a knowledge base which can be easily constructed into a programme of knowledge acquisition and, perhaps most importantly, of quantitative assessment. Subjects are inclusive – anyone studying on a subject programme belongs, whereas 'discipline' brings with it tricky questions about access and

boundaries: about inter- and multi-disciplinarity, about who can be said to be practising the discipline. However, subjects are also passive – they are taught, learned, delivered.

I suspect that this shift in discourse is part of the marketing practice of 'dissociation', whereby a product is progressively stripped of unwelcome associations. As the move from students to customers was designed to remind academics of the economic realities of the university structure, so 'subject' is designed to strip university departments of their sense of exclusivity and of inherent value: it is somehow easier to ask what use a 'subject' is in the real world than it is to ask the use of a 'discipline', 'profession' or 'calling' – words which, however unworldly, provide, by implication, the answer. For 'discipline' has Latinate, medieval, guild/religious community associations, overtones of vocation, of lifelong commitment, whereas 'subject' removes any mystique from academia (Parker 2002: 374).

'Subject', then, is about discipline as curriculum rather than discipline as research. Bernstein (1990, 2000) is right when he counsels us to pay careful attention to the *site of practice* of a discipline. He notes how a process of recontextualisation occurs as disciplines become translated into pedagogical practices and pedagogical discourses through the operation of three sets of rules: distribution rules; recontextualisation rules; and evaluative rules. The distribution and recontextualisation rules together provide an account of how disciplinary knowledge practices are situated differently in teaching–learning interactions than they are in research practices (Bernstein 2000; Ashwin 2009; Maton and Muller 2007). The distribution rules order the regulation and distribution of what counts as worthwhile knowledge in a society, determining for example what is and is not eligible to count as 'English Literature' and be included in syllabuses in that discipline. The recontextualisation rules render disciplinary knowledge into a form amenable to being taught, and learned, for example in textbooks. The evaluative rules offer different principles from those for research on which to judge these new pedagogical practices, setting out what is and what is not acceptable as an assessable piece of work, and what the standards are. Here, academic teachers in interaction with their students 'translate' the above rules into rules for the production of legitimate text by students and the evaluation of that text. This involves teachers and student interpreting the curriculum produced by the recontextualisation rules.

For Ashwin (2009) this is not just a technical-rational process of transformation: 'the pedagogic device is an area of struggle over how academics' and students' ways of thinking will be structured through pedagogic discourse, and whose interests will be served through this structuring' (Ashwin 2009: 91).

One important part of this struggle is around the distribution rules, which set out 'who may transmit what to whom and under what circumstances' (Bernstein 1990: 183). The 'what' here is a struggle within disciplines about what constitutes legitimate disciplinary knowledge. Many examples of this are given in Fiona Cownie's book *Legal Academics* (2004) in which she explores the struggle in the academy between, for example, black-letter law and critical legal studies approaches. Her chapter in this book (Chapter 5) elaborates on this. Later in the book we extend Bernstein's ideas about the recontextualisation of discipline in different sites of practice.

Then there is the struggle about *which* disciplinary knowledge practices should be the focus of the curriculum. There are other struggles about who may legitimately transmit knowledge to whom. Ashwin concludes: 'Thus differences in distribution rules can mean that in different institutions, the same disciplinary knowledge practices can be taught and studied under very different conditions and by students and academics with very different identities (Ashwin 2009: 93).

Meanwhile recontextualisation rules remove disciplinary knowledge practices from the site of practice and relocate them in a different context, re-configuring them. This is expressed rather neatly by Biggs (2003: 76): 'Teaching from lists is like sawing the branches off a tree, stacking them up in a neat pile and saying "There! See the tree?"'.

To further complicate matters, as Abbas and McLean (2010) and many others have shown, such processes of recontextualisation are heavily conditioned by institutional context – particularly by status issues associated with universities. This is explored in the chapters that follow. All this means, in short, that knowledge structures are not the same as curriculum structures. 'The same disciplinary knowledge practices may take on very different characteristics when … recontextualized into curriculum and … different disciplines may be subject to different forms of recontextualization' (Ashwin, 2009: 102). In postmodern conditions of complexity and turbulence, these static, nomothetic models that categorise into boxes and have simplistic causal links have lost much of their purchase on real conditions and challenges in higher education. They assume sets of regularities within disciplines, conditioned by knowledge structures, and take no account of the subtle 'interweaving of local, national and global processes which together give apparently the same disciplinary knowledge practices different structures in different institutions' (Ashwin 2009: 103). Yet despite the developing recognition of the deficiencies of epistemological essentialism and the elision of discipline-as-research and discipline-as-curriculum, the old ways of thinking about disciplines persist (Brew 2008; Kreber 2009; Malcolm and Zucas 2009; Whitchurch 2010a).

Conceptualising Interdisciplinarity

Interdisciplinarity can be seen, as Klein (2000) points out, as a methodological approach, a process, a way of thinking, a philosophy and/or as an ideology. It is often adopted as an attempt to solve problems and to avoid the partial, fragmented, understanding of the world that disciplinarity can involve. While multidisciplinarity involves conjoining two or more disciplines in a well-defined way using an aggregative logic that adds the findings from each discipline to those of others, interdisciplinarity and its slight variant transdisciplinarity are often portrayed as 'integrationist and consultative' (Ellis 2009: 7). A less positive view on that, however, is that interdisciplinarity is just as elitist as disciplinarity (Muller and Subotzky 2001: 171) and in pushing research towards a problem-solving mode it directs it away from critiquing the status quo, making it inherently more conservative (Muller and Subotzky 2001: 168). Because of this latter characteristic interdisciplinarity is reactionary in character, not progressive (Barry *et al.* 2008; Strathern 2007). Academics throughout the academy are admonished to adopt more interdisciplinary behaviours, to be more urban and less rural, as Becher and Trowler (2001) would put it. However, as Krishnan (2009: 6) indicates, a central problem with the notion of interdisciplinarity is that people using it do not make explicit what they understand by the term 'discipline', or when a disciplinary boundary is crossed, or with what consequences. As we noted above, simply listing recognised disciplines is not a satisfactory solution because disciplines are so dynamic and any listing provides a rough picture at best.

For the advocates of interdisciplinarity, disciplines operate to constrain ('discipline') knowledge in particular directions while interdisciplinarity frees knowledge production and transfer in ways more aligned with real need. Nowotny *et al.* (2001) describe a new and different mode of knowledge production, Mode 2, in which knowledge originates from tackling real-world problems, not those that arise from disciplines, as in the Mode 1 form. These can only be tackled by interdisciplinary teams, often operating outside the context of universities, bringing their various forms of expertise to bear in temporary coalitions that disperse after the problem has been solved. So for example the South African higher education curriculum was redesigned along Mode 2 lines to better equip it to focus on the economic, social and cultural transformation of the country after apartheid.

One can identify three distinct periods in the spread of alternatives to the discipline, at least in the UK. Period 1, from the 1960s into the 1970s saw the spread of domain-based 'studies' – for example American studies, modern studies. These were founded in critical movements of the time and an expanding higher education system that sought to offer a new, appetising, menu to a wider range of students. In some universities there was a genuine attempt at inter-disciplinarity in this curricular provision. Period 2, from the 1980s and into the early 1990s – saw a drive towards multidisciplinarity rather than interdisciplinarity, with curricular structures being driven by the search for economy, marketisation (particularly catering to student demand), the need for multi-disciplinarity in employment, plus a neo-liberal attack on the academic tribes – an attempt to break down 'producer capture' in universities. Parker (2002) argues that here we begin to see the shift from notions of 'discipline' to 'subject'. Period 3, from the later 1990s into the 2000s – now there is a call for interdisciplinarity, in particular Mode 2 forms of knowledge production (Nowotny *et al.* 2001) involving the triple helix of the state, business and academia. The drive now is towards performativity in students and among academics – the need to solve problems (usually identified by business) by short-term networks of specialists rather than the more critical driver of the 1960s and 70s. The state withdraws further from funding higher education, leaving it to rely on market-driven student fees and 'third leg' funding from research and consultancy.

The Power of Disciplines on Academic Practices

This section is a review of the literature on disciplines and their influence on academic practices. For the purposes of this section we are defining academic practices as the clusters of social practices that occur in higher education that are concerned, directly or indirectly, with the production, reproduction, circulation and use of knowledge in different forms. This will be elaborated in Chapter 2.

In examining the literature on the power of disciplines one can identify alternative positions along three dimensions describing the nature of the influence of discipline on practices in higher education. These are: a) cause; b) scope; and c) strength.

This framework is elaborated below and represented in the schema in Figure 1.1. This incorporates three axes along which can be placed the different perspectives on the relationship between disciplines on the one hand and practices on the other.[1] The three axes together offer a way of locating particular studies found in the literature with regard to the cause, the scope and the strength of the influence of disciplines on practices.

Simplifying, then, one can conceptualise this schema as 27 sub-boxes, as in Figure 1.2.

Axis A: Cause of Influence

Axis A addresses the causative mechanism in any link between disciplines and practices. These causes can be placed along a spectrum that moves from the structural to the agentic. The term *structural* is used to describe causal mechanisms that impose regularities and predictability on practices. One very significant structural factor found in the literature is the epistemological character of different disciplines: the nature of the knowledge structures found there. Under *agentic*, conversely, are included causal influences due to choices made by individual people. Here, more psychologistic explanations come to the fore; for example, self-selection by particular types of people into different disciplinary areas or the ideological resources individuals actively draw on in considering

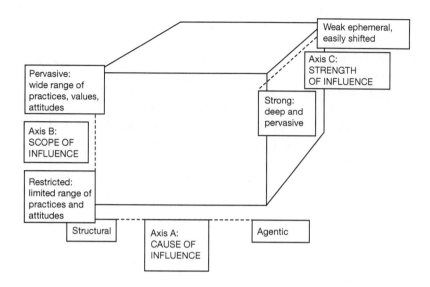

Figure 1.1 Conceptualising the relationship between disciplines and teaching, disciplines and research

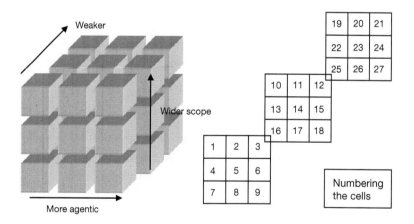

Figure 1.2 Simplified set of positions on the three axes

the nature and purposes of higher education (Trowler 1998a). Between these two poles come causal explanations that combine both structure and agency: for example, those that see disciplines as conditioning practices and attitudes but not totally determining them; room is left for agency or at the least multiple conditioning factors.

Axis B: Scope of Influence

This axis addresses the pervasiveness of the link between disciplines and practices. Under *pervasive*, the linkage is conceptualised as very extensive, moving beyond simple classroom practices, for example, into the everyday life and ways of seeing of academics and students. Under *restricted*, the linkage is conceptualised as much more limited: the restricted set of practices that occur only in particular places and underpinned by attitudes whose relevance and scope are limited to those contexts. Clearly there will be intermediate positions, this axis being a continuum rather than bipolar.

Axis C: Strength of Influence

The third axis addresses the strength of the linkage between disciplines and practices and attitudes. At the stronger end of the scale the linkage is not easily shifted, so that it is relatively impermeable to the influence of institutional context, local departmental cultures, national policies, technological change or other factors. At the weaker end of the scale the linkage, conversely, *is* easily displaced by other factors so that researchers find many exceptions to a hypothesised relationship between disciplines on the one hand and practices on the other.

So, putting this together, in the schema in Figure 1.2, cell 1 represents an exceptionally strong, essentialist position. There is very heavy structural determination of linkages between disciplines across a wide range of practices, extending across different contexts. From this position it would be possible to say that certain teaching and research practices, for example, are *always* found among specified disciplines. Conversely, cell 27 represents a situation where individual agency within disciplines means there is little regularity between a particular disciplinary context and practices, values and attitudes found there. Whatever linkage there is tends to be weak and to extend only to a limited range of practices and attitudes. Such a tenuous linkage is at the limits of any claims for *disciplinary* distinctiveness. Here there would be very few regularities identified across the same discipline in different contexts.

In the literature on the influence of disciplines on practices there is often some vagueness in describing the strength and range of effects. The same author can move between very different terms in their description of the linkage, using, for example, the words 'preferences', 'styles', 'rituals' and 'tendencies', 'conceptions', 'approaches' and 'practices'. This impression means that it is unclear, in some cases, precisely what claims are being made by an author, making it difficult to locate them on this grid, and enabling them to shift their truth claims as they see fit. Partly for this reason the following summary of key themes in the litera-ture will not mechanically explore each of these 27 boxes, but the multiple axes represent organising principles for analysing this literature.

Strong Epistemological-Essentialist Positions

A key central tradition in discussing the power of disciplines over academic cultures and practices argues that knowledge characteristics represent a key driving force of social life, with other factors being epiphenomenal (Clark 1987; Lodahl and Gordon 1972; Shinn 1982; Ruscio 1987; Davidson 1994; Gregg 1996). This is sometimes referred to as epistemological essentialism. In this view, the influence of academics' backgrounds is seen as insignificant compared to their socialisation into the knowledge characteristics of their discipline, their epistemological features:

> Characteristics imported into the academic profession by individual members from their personal background and prior experiences ... [are] ... the least important components of academic culture.
>
> Clark 1987: 107

'Essentialism' is often used as a derogatory term in social science, implying a simplistic and monocausal view of what is in fact a highly complex situation. Sayer makes the point that 'a strong, or deterministic essentialism is always wrong and often dangerously misleading' but that 'a moderate, non-determin-istic essentialism is necessary for explanation and for a social science' (Sayer 2008: 454). While he is right to point out the value of moderate essentialism in some cases, we would argue that perspectives that emphasise the determinant power of epistemological structures within disciplines represent a misplaced essentialism that wrongly posits a deterministic relation between the causal power of knowledge and a range of social practices.

Perhaps the most famous example of epistemological essentialism is Tony Becher's 1989 study *Academic Tribes and Territories*. The argument is that knowledge structures in different disciplines have significant different cogni-tive dimensions (a concept elaborated by Kolb 1981 and Biglan 1973) and social dimensions – whose characteristics were developed by Becher himself. The *cognitive* dimension divides disciplines into hard and soft, pure and applied, to give a four-cell matrix. Hard disciplines, according to their practitioners (Biglan 1973) have well-developed theory, universal laws, causal propositions, they are cumulative and have generalisable findings. Soft disciplines by contrast have unclear boundaries, relatively unspecified theoretical structure, are subject to fashions and have loosely defined problems. Pure disciplines are self-regulating and not directly applied to the professions or problems in the outside world, while applied disciplines are regulated by external influence to some extent – for example the Law Society – and are more applied within the professions and to problems.

The *social* dimension again offers a four-cell matrix. This time the axes run between convergent and divergent on the one hand and urban and rural on the other. Convergent disciplines have uniform standards and a relatively stable elite. Divergent disciplines sustain more intellectual deviance and frequently experience attempts to shift standards. Urban disciplines are characterised by intense interaction and a high people-to-problem ratio. Rural ones have bigger territories, less interaction and a lower people-to-problem ratio.

Combining these epistemic features it appears possible to say that physics, for example, is hard, pure, convergent and urban. Sociology is soft, pure, divergent and rural. Engineering is hard, applied, convergent and urban. Economics is hard, applied, convergent and rural.

Or not. The problem with this kind of categorisation is that while it seems to make sense when disciplines are viewed through the wrong end of a telescope, from a great distance, the distinctions begin to fall apart in the analytical hand when one looks at disciplines close up. The fractures within them become very apparent when the analyst steps out of the helicopter, as do the similarities between apparently very different sub-disciplinary areas. However, this is not the place for a critique of the validity or heuristic power of the Kolb/Biglan and Becher depiction of epistemological structure.

Becher himself (1989) and others have tended to tie in a very direct way the epistemological – and related social – characteristics of disciplines to academic practices of various sorts. Becher concentrated on the effect of knowledge differences on research practices and associated areas such as disciplinary discourse (Becher 1987a). Others have looked at their effects on learning, teaching and assessment practices. Thus Neumann *et al.* (2002) make claims for pedagogical differences between disciplines in different locations on the social and cognitive dimensions, offering the following sets of differences, set out in Table 1.1, using the disciplinary classification system mentioned above.

As is indicated by this nomothetic approach, Neumann *et al.* take a position that sees disciplines as having a strong, structural and pervasive influence on learning and teaching practices and so one that lies at or near cell 1 in Figure 1.2. As we shall see, other authors whose position lies elsewhere disagree, arguing that the significance of individual disciplines in pedagogical development has been overstated (for example, Young 2010).

Ylijoki's work (2000) on the *moral order of studying* in the disciplines of computer science, library science and informatics, public administration, and sociology and social psychology also stresses the central significance of discipline. She argues that disciplines have their own traditions and categories of thought, which provide the members of the field with shared concepts of

Table 1.1 Summary of disciplinary differences in learning, teaching, assessment and curriculum (after Neumann *et al.* 2002)

Learning, teaching and assessment dimension	Hard pure disciplines	Hard applied disciplines	Soft pure disciplines	Soft applied disciplines
Curricular structure	Cumulative, atomistic curriculum Linear programme design		Reiterative, holistic curriculum Spiral curriculum	
Purposes of higher education	Purpose to acquire subject knowledge and reasoning powers	Emphasis on acquisition of problem-solving and practical skills	Purpose to acquire a broad command of intellectual ideas, fluency of expression	Emphasis on vocationally related skills, but broadly defined, with intellectual breadth and personal growth
Teaching methods	Instructive (didactic) methods to 'deliver' fixed content. Small groups work on predetermined problems Teaching preparation is relatively quick Large lectures with class labs. ICT use extensive	Practical experience provided	Constructive (student-centred) methods to explore ideas. Small groups work discursively Teaching preparation is time-consuming Face-to-face teaching predominates, smaller class sizes. More limited use of ICT	Practical experience provided, but knowledge base acquired first
Learning	Students need to memorize facts and apply problem-solving skills. Logical reasoning	Practical competencies are needed in addition	Students need to think laterally, read copiously and have good powers of expression, critical thinking, fluency, creativity	The ability to solve open-ended problems is required in addition
Assessment	Outcomes of assessment objectively assessable Objective tests and examinations often used Assessment by teacher using model answers and guides		Outcomes of assessment require judgement Essays, short answers, continuous assessment often used Assessment by peers and self sometimes used. Assessment intuitive	

theories, methods, techniques and problems. They also have their own social and cultural characteristics: norms, values, beliefs, modes of interaction, life-style, pedagogical and ethical codes (2000: 339). The *moral order* concept captures this and forms the background ethos within the discipline. It operates as a form of social control, but is also significant in providing individual identity. Thus the disciplines studied by Ylijoki can be seen as tribes with different but very coherent moral orders, she argues. These give rise to distinctive practices; for example, learning by doing in computer science and, in library and information science, teaching and learning practices following the professional practices within libraries. Somewhat as a postscript, Ylijoki does recognise the multivocality within disciplines, the significance of context and the dynamism of moral orders. However, 'in spite of all these reservations ... it can be argued that disciplines still have a crucial role to play in the functioning of higher education' (2000: 358).

In this type of account of the power of disciplines, then, it is considered possible to make broad statements about whole disciplines, or about large categories (in the following example about academics in the sciences and humanities):

> Academics in the sciences perceive a connection primarily at the postgraduate level, whereas humanities academics are described as being divided on this issue.
>
> Jensen 1988, reported in Neumann 1996: 12

Donald (1995: 53–4), for example, argues that: 'Disciplines are the central source of identity for faculty ... The degree of coherence or structure within a discipline and the principal methods of enquiry affect the quality of learning.' And further:

> Psychology professors talked of developing students' capabilities through a series of courses which focus on different methods ... In education, case studies are seen as important instructional methods to aid students in making complex situations coherent. English literature professors paid attention to the analysis of text to determine the underlying assumptions ... and they were concerned with the development of argument in their courses.
>
> Donald 1995: 16

Many academics themselves adopt this position. For example van Heerden (2005: 95) says:

> I learned how to think like a chemist through nine years of education and three research positions. I thought about what that means, though, only

when I became a teacher. My discovery of how chemists think has evolved largely because of my interactions with students. I have come to believe that this discovery is absolutely critical for effective teaching; it has impacted on my courses, my relationships with students, my pedagogical approaches, and my assessments of students' performances.

Two things are notable about van Heerden's account, however: that his understanding of what it means to 'think like a chemist' was in some way occluded before his interactions with students; and that understanding has 'evolved' rather than being a realisation of a fixed thing. Both of these points would be used by social constructionists, with whom I deal next, to argue that 'thinking like a chemist' is more a creation than an absolute.

There are echoes of this strong position on the nature and power of disciplines throughout the literature describing higher education. One example is accounting where Jones talks about the 'culture of the discipline' in which students are taught (Jones 2010). Often such comments are left untheorised and unsupported.

Social-Constructionist Positions

Social-constructionist positions lie around the central part of Axis A. The basic argument is that, together, academics construct narratives about the nature of knowledge in their discipline, sharing and developing these narratives over time. Each discipline may have multiple narratives, and sometimes contrasting ones. This is close to the 'voice' approach, discussed above. Thus, for example, in academic law there are contrasts between black-letter law, which emphasises the transmission to students of legal knowledge, and critical legal studies, which emphasises the fostering of a critical perspective among law students.

Quinlan (1999) suggests that academic historians as a group can hold very different beliefs about the nature of the discipline, learning goals for students, teaching approaches and the nature of student difficulties. There are intergenerational tensions along these lines, with sets of beliefs shared among distinct groups of academic historians. She came to similar findings in her PhD study of Engineering (1996). Hers is a social, not a psychological explanation (1999: 462), with the departmental context seen as very significant. Brew (2003) and Robertson and Bond (2001: 10) agree. They state: 'We suggest that it is our participants' epistemological and ontological beliefs that shape their understandings of the research/teaching/learning experiential field and hence of the research/teaching relation.'

With regard to research practices, Latour and Woolgar (1979) and Gilbert and Mulkay (1984) argue that there may be a narrative of objective and rigorous research practices, especially in the natural sciences. However, the process of research is very much conditioned by social and psychological events and interactions in the laboratory or other context of research. It is a messy, social business, according to Brew (1999, 2001), which is only loosely linked to epistemological structures.

Many of the studies looking at the construction of such epistemological narratives tend to understate or occlude the significance of *multiple* narratives and *conflicting* narratives within the same discipline. Instead they characterise the situation as relatively monolithic.

This central position on Axis A leaves room for multiple influences on practices that interact with each other; for example, institutional context and epistemological structures. An example here is Lattuca and Stark (1995), who place emphasis on this interaction:

> Those who attempt to lead curricular reform may be more successful if they recognize both the strength of disciplinary culture and the campus contextual factors that make faculty redefine discipline cultures to meet local needs.
>
> Lattuca and Stark 1995: 340

Lindblom-Ylänne *et al.* (2006) used two inventories administered to over 300 academics in three institutions in two countries to establish links between teaching and learning practices, and discipline and teaching context. They found that teachers from 'hard' disciplines were more likely to report a more teacher-focused approach to teaching, whereas those teaching 'soft' disciplines were more student-focused, findings similar to those of Lueddeke (2003) and Trigwell (2002). The pure and applied categories were not significantly different, however. They also found, however, that teachers who have experienced different contexts or who change teaching context will sometimes adopt different approaches to teaching in those different contexts. Disappointingly, this study tells us only that teaching practices correlate with these two variables: *how* this happens can only be speculated upon. Kember and Leung (2011) note this lack of explanatory power in most studies exploring differences in learning and teaching across the disciplines, and suggest that some mix of 'real' epistemological differences and socially constructed stories about disciplines can explain differences in, for example, student ratings of teaching across the disciplines. In a study of two and a half thousand students Lindblom-Ylänne and others (Parpala *et al.* 2010) found that perceptions of the learning environment differed by discipline and by the approach to learning and teaching adopted in specific locales. Virtanen and Nevgi (2010) found *both* disciplinary and gender differences in self-regulated learning strategies. With a survey of almost 500 students, O'Siochru (2010) found differences in their epistemological beliefs that correlated with Biglan's hard/soft dimension, as used by Becher (1989), though there were also significant differences on this measure within the same discipline. Sampson and Komer (2010) also see the picture as a complex interaction of multiple factors: their study explores how different disciplinary differences in knowledge production are privileged or marginalised by national funding policy, in their case in New Zealand

Recent studies at the University of Edinburgh and elsewhere have suggested in some detail the ways in which the nature of disciplines might interact with more social factors. For example, *ways of thinking and practising* (WTP) (McCune and Hounsell 2005) is a concept designed to express the particular understandings, forms of discourse, values and ways of acting that are central to graduate-level mastery of a discipline or subject area. Similarly, the notions of *threshold concepts and troublesome knowledge* have come out of this research. Troublesome knowledge includes those ideas, techniques and concepts that create blockages to students, inhibiting academic progress. They tend to be counter-intuitive and so difficult to grasp. However, once mastered, troublesome knowledge can take students across the conceptual threshold:

> A threshold concept can be considered as a key to a portal, opening up a new and previously inaccessible way of thinking about something. It represents a transformed way of understanding, or interpreting, or viewing something without which the learner cannot progress. As a consequence of comprehending a threshold concept there may thus be a transformed internal view of subject matter, subject landscape or even world view.
>
> Meyer and Land 2003a: 1

The significance of such epistemological concepts of practices is that they guide what lecturers consider to be appropriate ways of helping students come to terms with them; for example, in media studies the use of shocking videos to challenge students' world view, or in electronic engineering ways of dealing with student difficulties in understanding the significance of circuit characteristics. However, the authors make it clear that there are multiple influences, including contextual influences, at work in conditioning practices: they are located around the middle of the axes in Figure 1.1, not at extreme positions. Specific contexts can offer both affordances and constraints in relation to different ways of thinking and practising. As with other studies that recognise multiple conditioning factors, the team suggest that particular contexts can evoke responses that may be muted elsewhere. This recognition is much stronger than, for example, in Ylijoki's approach (2000), with which it otherwise has some commonality. Chapter 17 explores this further.

The work of Shulman (2005a, b) on signature pedagogies and of Huber (2002) on disciplinary styles, both at the Carnegie Foundation for the Advancement of Teaching, bear many similarities to the approach adopted in the research just mentioned. Shulman argues that, in the professional disciplines at least, there are 'signature' approaches to teaching and learning; for example, the practice of doing clinical rounds with novice medics in medicine or the use of 'accountable talk' in law schools where case law is being taught and debated. Shulman writes:

What I mean by 'signature pedagogy' is a mode of teaching that has become inextricably identified with preparing people for a particular profession. This means it has three characteristics: One, it is distinctive in that profession. Second, it is pervasive within the curriculum. So that students learn that as they go from course to course, there are certain continuities that thread through the program that are part of what it means to learn to 'think like a lawyer,' or 'think like a physician,' or 'think like a priest.' There are certain kinds of thinking that are called for in the rules of engagement of each course, even as you go from subject to subject. The third feature is another aspect of pervasiveness, which cuts across institutions and not only courses. Signature pedagogies have become essential to general pedagogy of an entire profession, as elements of instruction and of socialization.

Shulman 2005b: 9

Signature pedagogies are not necessarily the 'best' way to teach and learn according to Shulman, and neither are they inevitable. However, they do work, at least for the purposes for which they were originally designed, and they have become established routines wherever a particular profession is taught. They are the product not only of disciplinary characteristics, but of 'complex sociological and political' factors (ibid: 15).

Disciplinary styles, meanwhile, apply more broadly than just the professions. They offer conceptions that guide enquiry, influencing the problems we choose, the methods we use, and the arguments we find persuasive. The disciplinary style also shapes – but does not determine – the teaching and learning methods used, giving academics:

a ready-made way to imagine projects and present their work – for example, metaphors such as the classroom as laboratory, as text, field site, or theater, might point you to different methods of inquiry and styles of analysis.

Huber 2002: 4

However, like the WTP approach, there is no singular driving mechanism at play here according to Huber. Disciplines are recognised to be divided and fissiparous: 'each discipline has its own intellectual history of agreement and dispute about subject matter and methods that influence what is taught, to whom, when, where, how, and why' (Huber 2002: 4).

Individual Agency Positions

In these positions, to the right of Axis A, the role of individual choice, action, beliefs and attitudes is the most significant variable. This understanding of the link between disciplines and practices is based on methodological individualism, which approaches the study of societies and organisations with the assumption that individuals' thoughts and decisions are more significant than the structures within which they operate. It is individuals' agency, their decisions and actions, which shape the institutions and social circumstances they operate within rather than vice versa.

Some studies suggest that self-selection into disciplines by particular sorts of personality types is a better explanation for any consistencies discovered within disciplines than, for example, the influence of epistemological structure. Greed (1991), looking at surveying as taught in universities, argues that personality and background are significant in determining the type of individual who goes into that profession. Stevenson and Sander (2002), whose title begins *Medical Students are from Mars*, argue that medical students arrive at university suspicious of student-centred learning methods and prefer more didactic ones. Their learning styles and general approach to studying as well as their experiences make them prefer what they see as more efficient and authoritative methods. As some of these students become lecturers they will tend to replicate their own preferred teaching styles, the argument runs, particularly as these are the ones still preferred by the types of students they find themselves teaching.

The outcome of student and staff choices is, again, regularities across the disciplines with regard to teaching, learning and assessment practices. Stevenson and Sander, for example, might agree with the depiction by Neumann *et al.* of disciplinary differences in relation to these practices (Table 1.1). However, the hypothesised causal mechanisms are very different – for Neumann *et al.* regularities and differences in practices across the disciplines are the result of structural determination by disciplinary knowledge differences. For Stevenson and Sander, by contrast, such regularities are the product of human choice of their preferred discipline and profession. Other positions that lie roughly in the same area of Axis A suggest that individuals develop narratives about their discipline, and take individual positions on teaching and learning as well as research.

Bain *et al.* (1998: 49) suggest that 'the educational context in which students learn is heavily influenced by the epistemological and educational assumptions of their academic teachers', a position that is replicated in much of the 'teachers' beliefs' literature, for example Hativa and Goodyear (2002). Taking three individual teachers as case studies (Joy, Frank and John) the authors draw on phenomenographic studies and concepts to explore the differences between the three with regard to their pedagogical and curriculum beliefs and the ways these relate to their practice. They conclude that:

> academics differ in their beliefs about which forms of knowledge are valuable, how knowledge should be organized for learning, and what should occur during teaching and learning, and these differences influence the methods which they and their students use.
>
> Hativa and Goodyear 2002: 56

Here the link to discipline is almost entirely lost. Indeed, these authors choose to dismiss that link by focusing on the different orientations towards teaching and learning that can be found within the same discipline, quoting (page 50) Quinlan's (1999) finding that two historians differed in thematically consistent ways. In this they choose to ignore Quinlan's major thesis that discipline does have a significant impact on learning, teaching, assessment and curriculum practices, and that fractures in the discipline are 'recapitulated' at the individual level. Quinlan (1999: 462) explicitly rejects an individualistic approach: 'this study has gone beyond most psychologically oriented studies of teacher thinking, by situating individual faculty members within the context of a department, a university and a discipline.'

Psychologically oriented approaches, such as phenomenographic ones, tend to lack an appreciation of context generally, and of the social context of teaching and learning practices, values and attitudes.

The Dissolution of Academic 'Tribes'

As disciplines are shifting and changing, so is the organisational and professional firmament in universities. Celia Whitchurch (2010b) helpfully summarises some of the changes in these two areas:

1   There is a changing disciplinary base, with the incorporation into universities of practice-based fields of study staffed by individuals with backgrounds as practitioners, not researchers, and with roots and links in other settings than the university.
2   There is a greater casualisation of the workforce, so that fixed term contracts of employment in universities are far more common than indefinite ones.
3   There are greater numbers of staff who work portfolios of short-term projects of different sorts: teaching; research; consultancy; evaluation.
4   Staff being appointed to posts that are very specific in terms of the specification of the person, rather than generic discipline-based criteria.
5   More staff are being appointed to support staff and students: learning developers and academic developers, technologists and career and counselling staff, for example. There is a tendency in at least some of these areas to develop distinctive professional characteristics with developing bodies of knowledge and professional associations.

In addition one can identify the increasing prevalence of academic staff being 'managed professionals' (Rhoades 1998, 2010) as well as the shift of some to become managerial professionals (Rhoades and Sporn 2002). Some commentators have identified a deliberate assault on academic autonomy and power, on the tribes and their territories, in order to displace them in the decision-making and agenda- and value-setting processes (see Trowler 1998a: 44–50). On top of all this a 'Third Space' has emerged between the professional and academic domains (Whitchurch 2010a, b) where blended roles occur with a mix of practices from both domains. There is:

> greater fluidity, and even instability, between academic disciplines, functional responsibilities, and institutional approaches to role definition, leading to concepts of professionals and professionalism that are 'borderless', in that they cannot be fixed in time and space.
>
> Whitchurch 2010b: 169

Scott (2006) analyses the changing role of the academic profession in a knowledge society and identifies three main changes in academic practice:

1 The massification of research, scholarship and university teaching itself due to the demand for knowledge workers. Knowledge production, reproduction and circulation are no longer the preserve of a small elite in a niche occupation.
2 There has been a tendency for teaching and research to become separated and at the same time to become more diversified roles. Teaching involves course design, quality management, sales and marketing as well as innovation using more sophisticated technologies. Research involves management and entrepreneurship.
3 Universities themselves have become more complex with multiple roles and evolving, bifurcating missions.

Turpin and Garrett-Jones (2000) show how research has moved from a 'donnish dominion' model to one driven by the need to demonstrate impact and useability as universities and research institutions are driven to 'corporatize'. The tensions and drivers of the 1990s are not only about the direction of scientific research – towards application and impact – but about the value placed upon different types of research. Commercial symbols and commercial strategies are at the heart of this, as Turpin and Garrett-Jones found from their interviews with 200 scientists of the Australian CSIRO (Commonwealth Scientific and Industrial Research Organization). At the heart of it is a struggle about *values*. Managerialism, enterprise culture and the fiscal crisis have shifted values in the direction of profit and use. Intellectual property is key in the knowledge economy.

Meanwhile the academic 'tribes' themselves are becoming multicultural, including new types of professional who are not on academic contracts, and perhaps have a background other than researching the discipline. As Whitchurch says:

> Since 2001, evidence has accumulated that rigid boundaries are becoming less sustainable, not only between academic disciplines, but also

between academic and other forms of professional activity. Increasingly, staff without academic contracts contribute to teaching activity (Rhoades, 2007), research spin-out (Allen-Collinson, 2007; Hockey and Allen-Collinson, 2009), and a range of institutional projects in quasi-academic areas such as widening participation, outreach, and regional partnership.

Whitchurch 2010a: 168

Conclusion: De-centering the Subject

These accounts exclude any developed appreciation that practices in universities exist within a much wider national and global network of influence. There is a tendency in these accounts to see academic practices as operating in a bubble, independent of the network of practices, forces and structures operating around the university. In reality higher education systems, universities and individual departments are open, natural systems, not the ivory towers of legend. They are strongly touched by outside forces and are conditioned in what they do, and how, by far more than the internal processes which are the focus of these accounts.

This is more the case than ever as the influence of the evaluative state, marketisation, new managerialism and the multiple effects of the 'global policy ensemble' (Ball 2008) impact on universities. In addition, universities are now 'media systems' (Friesen and Cressman 2010), intimately influenced by sets of practices associated with the interface between humans and technologies that permeate them. While the notion of the posthuman university (Hayles 1999: 2006) may be exaggerating the effect of this, it is clear that ubiquitous networked technologies have transformed the nature of practices in universities. It is arguable that there has been a qualitative break with the past under their influence, and representational practices have changed too (Lea and Stierer 2009).

The accounts in the pages that follow seek to rectify this and to offer a more nuanced understanding of the nature and extent of disciplinary influence on academic practices.

Note

1   Parts of this section were first available on the Higher Education Academy website and are derived from HEA-funded research.

2
Disciplines and Academic Practices

PAUL TROWLER

Only dead theories and dead practices celebrate their self-identity

Law 2004: 10

The theoretical stance we adopt in this book is social practice theory (SPT), drawing on Bourdieu (2000), Foucault (1984), Giddens (1979, 1984), Reckwitz (2002) and Schatzki *et al.* (2001). On the basis of previous empirically based research and evaluation studies we have conducted, we have come to consider this strand of theory the richest in terms of offering illuminative concepts, explanatory power and insights into probable outcomes of behaviour. SPT also offers value as a 'sensitising theory' – it gives fresh perspectives on habitual practices: rich ways of conceptualising the world (Sibeon 2007).

We take note of Law's warning that theories are dynamic and at best are flexible enough to accommodate novelty: they should remain theoretical and not slip into being doctrinal. Our use of SPT draws on a number of concepts and insights from a variety of related traditions that we consider powerful, including situated learning theory, activity systems theory and actor network theory. These lie within the broad category of 'cultural theory' which emphasises the significance of the symbolic structures of meaning in the social world, both their construction and their enactment by people. These symbolic structures condition behaviours, enabling and constraining them in particular ways.

Outlining actor network theory, Lefebvre suggests we should look beyond simply human agency, taking cognisance of the power of things and of conceptualisation:

> The fields we are concerned with are, first, the *physical* – nature, the Cosmos; secondly, the *mental*, including logical and formal abstractions; and thirdly, the *social*. In other words, we are concerned with logico-epistemological space, the space of social practices, the space occupied by sensory phenomena, including products of the imagination such as projects and projections, symbols and utopia.
>
> Lefebvre 1984: 11–12

So SPT is also a version of socio-material theory, that is, it is interested in the relationships between humans and artefacts and how the two co-exist and 'use' each other in the enactment of practices. Artefacts, objects, things or tools – the language differs according to theoretical strain – can configure human behaviours, scripting them, but at the same time recurrent practices shape the way artefacts are deployed. Social practices always consist of patterned relations between humans and things, including those things that together create the physical context of practice: buildings, furniture and spatial organisation. Spatiality theories explore the latter aspects in detail (see for example Löw 2008; Tissen and Deprez 2008). So, as I suggested at the end of the previous chapter, the single human agent is 'de-centred' in this view. Rather each of us is part of a network of things and other people that operate relationally, and do so as part of a temporal flow. However, we do not go as far as actor network theory, which gives equal a priori analytical weighting to things and humans; we consider human agency to be very significant in the areas we are examining in this book.

For SPT specifically the significant unit of analysis lies in *practices*, what is enacted, not in texts, not in the heads and hearts of individuals, and not in interactions, as is the case in some other versions of cultural theory. Reckwitz defines social practices as follows:

> forms of bodily activities, forms of mental activities, 'things' and their use, a background knowledge in the form of understanding, know-how, states of emotion and motivational knowledge. A practice – a way of cooking, of consuming, of working, of investigating, of taking care of oneself or of others, etc. – forms so to speak a 'block' whose existence necessarily depends on the existence and specific interconnectedness of these elements, and which cannot be reduced to any one of these single elements.
>
> Reckwitz 2002: 249

Because of this focus on practices, knowledge is also seen in a particular way in SPT. Knowing, or knowledgeability, is situated in practices, so that knowledgeability – and emotionality – is a constituent of a practice. Intentionality, knowing, desiring and behaving are all tied into social practices. They are situationally contingent, therefore, and are distributed among the people and things engaged in the relations which make up the practice. Again, the individual is de-centred in this view: knowledge lies not in a single person's head, but is distributed and situated.

So, to illustrate this with some examples. One might criticise Shulman's notion of signature pedagogies, elaborated in the previous chapter, by saying that actually there is very little that is unique if we compare, for example, clinical rounds at the teaching hospital, case dialogues in a law department and the 'crit' in an art and design department. Each involves a small group of students discussing a particular 'case' under the leadership of a tutor who may ask them questions to lead their thinking in desired ways. But from an SPT perspective these are all quite different examples of practices. Although perhaps similar on the surface, each has a very different configuration of relations, different understandings of how to 'go on' in that practice, different emotions, knowledgeability and different intentionality. They are actually configured as practices very differently, the one from the other, in ways which are more important than simply the fact that one deals with a patient (or 'case'), another with an artwork or designed object and a third with another form of case, this time a legal one. Nespor (2003: 95) writes:

> The meanings of an event are constituted by hooking it up to moving networks of people moving with, through, and by virtue of their entanglements with durable artefacts, structures and materials. Into these networks of action are woven so many identities, commitments and interests.

Pulling these comments together, for us the key characteristics of a social practice approach to understanding universities and change that we want to emphasise and draw on are as follows:

1 People are carriers of practices: they enact in specific ways a reservoir of ways of behaving, understanding and responding in ways which are to a certain extent particular to them in a social field (Bernstein, 1999, distinguishes between 'reservoir' and 'repertoire' to describe this process of individuation from structural characteristics). Individuals thus articulate repertoires of recognisable practices: 'patterns of bodily behaviour and routinized ways of understanding, knowing and desiring' (Reckwitz 2002: 250). The focus on analysis is therefore best located in the practices, not the individuals involved.

2 People in universities, departments and work groups engage in clusters of practices in different locales, and in so doing develop partly unique sets of recurrent behaviours and meanings about the world they are dealing with, ones that are particular to their location. Universities end up with a *multiple cultural configuration*, with different clusters of social practices in different locales within them – usually departments – as well as many commonalities.

3 In their practice clusters – perhaps in developing a new syllabus, teaching face-to-face in a lecture, or researching in a laboratory, doing bedside rounds in a teaching hospital or a 'crit' in an art studio – human agents use artefacts and tools of various sorts which themselves influence the social reality in particular ways. Patterns of understanding, feeling and wanting are involved in this, it is not simply a technical tool use. The use and manipulation of artefacts to achieve goals involves 'knowing' those

artefacts in specific ways, interpreting rather than just using them. They are cultural symbols. Meanwhile the process of contextualisation shapes the ways in which tools and artefacts are used. New initiatives such as those aimed at sustainability often involve changes in tool use, and so this interaction is significant for them. Another way of putting this is that artefacts can configure activity, inscribing relations between people (Latour 2000; Harman 2009), but usually there is co-adaptation between people and artefacts: the reproduction of everyday life involves *actively* and effectively configuring complex assemblies of material objects, often in new ways. Thus, for example, the use of PowerPoint can shape the way classes are taught and content is presented (Adams 2006), but there is space too for active manipulation of the technologies involved.

4   Discourses – the particular forms of production of 'text' (talk, writing, etc.) which are mediated by reservoirs of deeper, historical, social forces and social structures – express social reality and also operate to constrain and delimit it. Discursive practices and the social construction of reality work together. Thus 'managerialist' discourse expresses a particular view of the nature of universities and works to bracket out other views and other discourses. There is an interplay between discursive and other practices. However, from an SPT perspective discourse is not privileged above other forms of practice: it is simply one among many.

5   Individual identity, or subjectivity, is intimately involved in the process of contextualisation both shaping and being shaped. People and things operate to shape and reshape context, and each other. There is a process of contextualising, decontextualising and recontextualising (Nespor 2003) in which identity is intimately involved. As people engage in social practices they shape their own identities and those of others, though they may also defend their identities from this process. However, identity is a lifetime project and people bring with them relatively permanent aspects of identities as they follow their lifecourse. This is one source of difference, even conflict, within sites of social practice.

6   So, the historical background of individuals and also of the group is important. History, and narratives about history, have significant influences on social life in the present. These may be stories about academics' disciplines, about the institution, about other institutions or about the higher education system as a whole. Whatever they are, these histories and stories about the past will impact on change initiatives such as sustainability in the present: practices have an evolving trajectory, rarely a revolutionary one. However, narrativity is not privileged to the extent that 'voice' theories foreground it (see Chapter 1). There are semiotic trajectories too, trajectories of evoked meanings. Additionally the temporality of practices, and differing temporalities for different actors in the same practice, are significant in affecting the trajectories of practices (Nespor 2007).

7   A corollary of all of the above is that the process of context generation, with the particularities it creates, is a very significant factor in changing organisations. There are special features in every university, and every university department, every discipline, that mean that initiatives will be received, understood and implemented in ways which are, partly at least, unique. So, any attempt to generalise advice on how to change things is fraught with danger. Leaders on the ground need to understand their own situation well, and what will work and not work there. This needs good ways of seeing.

8   The social practice perspective we are using in this book stresses the significance of the *knowledge resources* individuals and groups access in order to engage in routine or emergent practices. These resources are of different kinds and can include examples such as the following: self knowledge; knowledge of tools and artefacts and their interactions; 'readings' of prevailing pressures and strategic imperatives historically derived but contemporaneously experienced; the way the cultures of disciplines help structure our activities and behaviours. Knowledge and interpretations of these imperatives and their implications help reconstruct new configurations or 'repertoires' of practices. They may result, for example, in new emphases in the way curricular designs evolve, the discourses in use develop and professional identities change.

9   Finally, we view practices as conditioned by the operation of power in various ways. We understand 'power' to have both a solid and a fluid character: power is located in structures and in positions – for example in university governing bodies such as Senate and Council, or in committees as well as in people who occupy senior roles – and it has a moment-by-moment character in which it ebbs and flows between social actors and things – for example within committee meetings. These different articulations of power, the 'faced' and the 'de-faced' (Hayward 2000), can constrain agendas, limit actions, imbue preferred readings and actions in situations and, of course, punish and reward in different ways.

The key point about conceptualising disciplines from a social practice perspective is that disciplines are not singular in character, and are not 'things'. Disciplines are enacted as social practices are performed and as micropolitics are played out: teaching; research; conference attendance; departmental meetings; collaborative writing; mixed-disciplinary meetings of a political nature – for example where resource allocation is at stake; funding applications, etc. In each area of practice different identities, discourses and contextual concerns (Archer 2007) are mobilised. To consider a discipline as having a unitary character is a mistake. Similarly it is a mistake to suggest that 'context' is a thing, and that the articulation of disciplines is conditioned by – departmental, university – context. Rather than formulating the relationship in this way, we consider disciplinary articulation to be one aspect of a dynamic process of 'contextualisation', that is that active creation and recreation of context. Thus it is necessary to expand Bernstein's (1990, 2000) concepts of discipline as research and discipline as curriculum into many different areas of social practice. To discipline as research and discipline as curriculum one can add, for example, 'discipline as bastion' – a basis on which to defend the status quo – and 'discipline as warrant' – as a kind of surety of expertise and capability and as 'carrying' social value (as exemplified in some being privileged through being state funded, others not).

Following from Bernstein's analysis of the transformation processes from research to teaching, we can assume that a form of transformation will take place too into these other incarnations of discipline. So the bodily activities, forms of mental activities, forms of understanding, knowledge, states of emotion and sets of motivations are very differently configured and mobilised in, for example, teaching, research or university meetings – of different sorts. 'Discipline' is often an important factor, but it is recontextualised in each case.

So, in SPT individuals are not cultural dopes who simply enact social roles, they are active in the world, interacting with objects and other people in a knowing, intentional, way. They are knowledgeable about the world and about themselves precisely because they carry, and carry out, a multitude of routines, practices – even though some are derived from social structures and are simply enacted – and so can gain a perspective upon them. 'The individual is the unique crossing point of practices, of bodily-mental routines' (Reckwitz 2002: 256). Texts of all sorts are manipulated by literate individuals who 'read situations and understand what is required to participate effectively in particular practices' (Wolfe and Flewitt 2010: 389). Moving from situation to situation, from task to task, academics actively configure the concept of 'discipline' in different ways.

SPT as we interpret it is not a theory of 'social hydraulics' (Archer 2007: 6) which discounts the individual and their internal conversations, reflections and agency in favour of 'context', interpreted as either social structure or in terms of the collective construction of the social world. In this we depart from some interpretations of, for example, communities of practice theory. Processes within workgroups are very significant, as are broader structural forces, but the individual is capable of autonomous reflection and decision-making, even though much of the social world goes on in the form of routinised recurrent practices for much of the time. At a slightly less determined level than unreflective practices based upon taken-for-granted sets of assumptions we can also identify *structured dispositions*: tendencies to act and respond in particular ways which are broadly conditioned by factors external to the individual.

Archer goes further than our position on this when she says:

our personal powers are exercised through reflexive inner dialogue and that internal conversation is responsible for the delineation of our concerns, the definition of our projects and, ultimately, the determination of our practices in society. It is agential reflexivity which actively mediates between our structurally shaped circumstances and what we deliberately make of them.

Archer 2007: 16

For Archer (2007: 17) the social world can be considered in terms of a three-stage model:

1   Structural and cultural properties objectively shape the situations that agents confront involuntarily, and *inter alia* possess generative powers of constraint and enablement in relation to subjective properties imputed to agents and assumed to govern their actions.
2   Subjects' own constellations of concerns, as *subjectively* defined in relation to the three orders of natural reality: nature, practice and social.
3   Courses of action are produced through the *reflexive deliberations* of subjects who subjectively determine their practical projects in relation to their objective circumstances.

While we agree that reflexive deliberations are important, and in particular the definition of the situation in relation to projects – especially change projects, which move people away from 'auto-pilot' and stimulate reflection – we also consider such characterisations as often externally structured, especially within workgroups. In situations of stasis we tend to operate on auto-pilot, because this is simply easier and makes life flow, as the *Centipede's Dilemma* poem (author-ship contested) suggests:

> A centipede was happy quite,
> Until a frog in fun
> Said, 'Pray, which leg comes after which?'
> This raised her mind to such a pitch,
> She lay distracted in the ditch
> Considering how to run.

However, in some circumstances agency and reflectivity are 'activated' and the hegemony of structural constraints is recognised and perhaps challenged. We can, for example, surface and then resist discursive capture (as I argued in Trowler 2001) but this takes effort: it involves work. Rather than necessarily causing us to 'lay distracted in a ditch', such times can free us. These times happen when 'the deep layer of foreclosed decisions is … forced up to the level of decision making' (Beck and Beck-Gernsheim 2002: 6). For some writers such as Anthony Giddens, Scott Lash and Ulrich Beck, modernity itself forces more and more of this to happen – a process called reflexive modernisation leading to 'individualisation'.

Again, for us this goes too far. For one thing environments such as universities and departments generate a series of concerns for individuals which are largely outside their power to change or shape. This agenda-setting power (one of Lukes' three forms of power, 2005) has not undergone any weakening in recent decades, indeed arguably the reverse. For those who work in them the weight of contextual concerns is considerable and the supposed 'individualisation' of society very weak in comparison. One of the motives behind my developing the concept of teaching and learning regimes (TLRs) was to highlight this fact. While TLRs tend to lack consensual norms and values, each has a series of concerns that are very influential on individuals' behaviour, cognition and emotions. Again, for Archer, the individual can engage in reinforcement, redefinition and revision of these concerns according to how they receive them, resulting in a *modus vivendi* being established – some accommodation being reached between the individual and the properties and powers of their context (2007: 151). Once more, we think this goes too far, for most people at least, in universities.

For SPT social interaction and the development of meaning, ways of seeing and ways of doing are key drivers of both social order and – sometimes – social change. As Warde (2005: 141) says:

> practices also contain the seeds of constant change. They are dynamic by virtue of their own internal logic of operation, as people in myriad situations adapt, improvise and experiment. … In addition, practices are not hermetically sealed off from other adjacent and parallel practices, from which lessons are learnt, innovations borrowed, procedures copied.

The trajectories of practices are inherently unstable because they depend upon the recurrent assembly and integration of artefacts, meanings and forms of competence by groups of practitioners who 'carry' practices.

SPT sees people as carriers of routinised bodily behaviours that are underpinned by socially situated and acquired knowledge, ways of understanding, feeling and wanting. They 'carry out' practices which are recurrent, often taken-for-granted and founded in socially acquired sets of meanings developed and learned through social interaction. These practices can be both quite distinct and – as in a university – interconnect in institutional complexes: a nexus of practices or a 'social field' in Bourdieu's language. The focus of our book in the chapters that follow is to establish the changed and changing power of disciplinary differences in conditioning these practices. Any changes to disciplinary significance may be internal to the discipline or come from external sources and they sometimes prompt new academic practices.

But which are the most significant sites of social interaction for the areas of academic practice we are interested in? Much of the literature focuses on the 'invisible college' (Crane 1972) of the discipline, on the significance of academic tribes and their territories, but we believe this is less relevant now. Instead more localised factors are salient, especially in fields of study and a stress on interdisciplinarity in research as against distinct disciplines. It is the debate between the tribes thesis and other types of explanation of regularities in social practices that this book concentrates on. The decline of the significance of discipline may represent a challenge to the Enlightenment project and a fundamental shift in the nature and role of universities. However, at the same time, countervailing forces and structures, such as national evaluations of research excellence, operate to sustain the relevance of disciplines: seismic shifts are not all in one direction.

2
Disciplinary Differences and Research Practices

3
Disciplines and Research
Key Themes

PAUL TROWLER

The four chapters in this part come at the issue of disciplines and research practices in very different ways and with very different foci. Fiona Cownie looks
at the development of research in law departments around the world, and the
alternative approaches to that. Angela Brew and Catherine Manathunga question the contemporary salience of disciplines globally as organising structures
for knowledge and research, and hence question the continued purchase of the
'tribes and territories' metaphor. Nicola Spurling examines the drivers of practices in sociology departments in the UK, while Paul Trowler looks at research
as practised in four disciplines in the art and design area in a specialist university also in the UK. The editors wanted to achieve as many different 'takes' on
the issue as possible within the constraints of these four chapters, and we think
we have achieved that. Some key themes, though, emerge from this diversity.
There are five.

First is the critical question of the salience, in the twenty-first century, of
disciplines as an organising device in research practices. For different reasons
and from different perspectives both Spurling's chapter and Manathunga and
Brew's suggest that disciplinary boundaries and distinctions are no longer of
great significance. For Spurling, departmental strategy and culture set in institutional contexts within the frame of higher education systems and policy
frameworks are more important now than disciplinary distinctions in conditioning what people do. Likewise for Manathunga and Brew other drivers have
taken over and interdisciplinarity has become the dominant leitmotif of this
century. Territorial boundaries have largely gone – insofar as they ever really
existed – and the tribal metaphor, always suspect for these authors, is no longer
of value. For Manathunga and Brew (citing Smith 1999) the rise of interdisciplinarity that they describe is a liberating force, one which frees academics
from the confines of the disciplinary cages which have been used to regulate
and control them. As Chapter 1 described, though, there are other takes on
that issue, ones which see interdisciplinarity as essentially a conservative force
which pushes research and other academic practices in directions preferred by
capitalist interests.

Cownie's chapter on legal academics demonstrates the fundamental internal divisions that exist, or can exist, within a single discipline; the lack of agreement on what research and teaching are for, how they should be practised and what the goal of higher education in that discipline is. Doctrinal, liberal, socio-legal, critical legal studies and feminist positions are articulated in law departments in universities across the world, and paradigm wars sometimes break out.

This illustrates the point that Manathunga and Brew make in pursuing their critique of the salience of disciplines – that there are sometimes more divisions within disciplines than between them. But it also highlights the second common theme: the importance of differences in educational ideology in the academy. Trowler's chapter on research in art and design disciplines makes the point explicitly – that practices are highly conditioned by local articulations of structured educational ideologies which practitioners deploy as they reach for understandings of what research is and how it should be practised.

Other structural features condition research practices too, ones beyond the discipline and, sometimes, imposing homogeneity upon diverse disciplines. The UK Research Assessment Exercise (now called the Research Excellence Framework) is one such that is mentioned by Cownie, Spurling and Trowler, though all agree from their data that there are mixed views on exactly what the direction of influence has been. Regulatory frameworks such as those are often accompanied by new managerialist practices, especially when deployed in a low-trust environment. This is the third of the five themes and it is one we return to in the last part of the book: extra-disciplinary structural forces.

The fourth common theme across this part relates to the impact of the financial context in which universities operate. The UK higher education context has been severely hit by the government's spending review and by changes in the funding structures for research – as well as teaching. The amount available for distribution from research funding bodies, the way those bodies make decisions, the increasing conditionality of funding and the drying up of other funding streams has hit universities hard there. The same is true in many other European and North American contexts, though less so in Australia, South Africa and a few other countries with developed higher education provision. For Cownie, such shared contextual concerns (Archer 2007) bring about a certain degree of commonality across the disciplines. Spurling makes a much stronger point – that the drive to accumulate capital (both of a financial sort and in other forms) is actually a more powerful influence on practices than are disciplinary differences.

The final issue that surfaces across this section, and elsewhere in the book, is that of identity. With the projected decline in the significance of disciplinary differences has come a diminution of the significance of professional identity associated with a particular discipline. Brew's work has noted that few academics unproblematically associate themselves with a specific discipline, and Manathunga and Brew see this as explicable in terms of the decline in the relevance of distinct disciplinary knowledge in research and other academic practices. Spurling uses the concept of 'role array' to suggest, further, that identities are protean in character, dynamic and multiple rather than singular and fixed, tied to the stake of discipline as captured in the phrase 'I am a sociologist'. Trowler's data also shows how academic researchers in art and design sometimes look across to other disciplines to describe what they do, or see themselves more in terms of being a practitioner rather than an exponent of a particular discipline.

There is a further issue that appears across the book and is not specific to research. It relates to what Clark (1993) calls 'program affiliation' and the 'dignification' of disciplines. That latter, rather pompous, word is perhaps not the most appropriate one to describe what he means – the increasing academicisation of professions or fields of enquiry as they move into the academy. Cownie's account shows us that this began to happen in law towards the end of the nineteenth century. The chapter by Laiho in the next section gives us an account of nursing science moving into the academy and its 'dignification' in Finland much more recently. This account sees disciplines moving in the opposite direction to that described by Manathunga and Brew; becoming more distinctive and delineated rather than less so. This depiction raises again the question of the salience of disciplinary difference in modern times: perhaps these processes occur, only to fade into merged, hybridised sets of knowledge and knowledge practices as they reach maturity.

We hope that this book will help the reader make their own decision on Manathunga and Brew's contention that:

> the metaphors of tribes and territories first coined by Becher (1989) and reinforced by Becher and Trowler (2001) in their second edition are no longer applicable or helpful in understanding contemporary research practices and epistemologies.

4
Beyond Tribes and Territories
New Metaphors for New Times

CATHERINE MANATHUNGA AND ANGELA BREW

Introduction

The notion of 'academic tribes' from Becher's 1989 'landmark work' (Bayer 1991: 224) has passed into the discourse of higher education research to such an extent that it is often used without reference to the original text (for example Davies 2006). It was a 'colourful' metaphor that was taken up with such acclaim that it has come to dominate discourses around disciplines, disciplinary knowledge, disciplinary affiliation; indeed, everything to do with the ways in which knowledge is defined and organised within universities. The use of the 'tribes' metaphor has extended well beyond those who have read the text, to permeate academic practice and policy across the globe. Becher's book provided a way of thinking about disciplines and about the people who inhabit them which appeared to be intuitively 'correct' and provided a framework for further thinking at the time. However, universities have substantially changed since the publication of *Tribes and Territories*. Notions of knowledge have undergone radical shifts. Research is increasingly called upon to address multidisciplinary questions and modular course structures mean that university study has become more interdisciplinary. There are reasons to suppose that these trends will continue.

The question that we set out to explore in this chapter is: what other metaphors might be more appropriate? We first examine theories of the changing context of higher education and their implications for disciplines and disciplinary thinking. Specifically we argue that there is a need to fundamentally rethink the ways in which we talk about disciplinary knowledge. Then we explore in more detail, and from a post-colonial perspective, why the metaphors of tribes and territories are not only no longer helpful but have become highly problematic. We then examine some alternatives that have been suggested and critically examine the usefulness of these.

The assumption that there are distinct disciplines that can be classified affects the ways in which academic culture is subsequently interpreted. As Klein (1996: 6) says: 'As a dominant principle, disciplinarity has the force of necessity, implying that the academic institution could hardly be structured otherwise'. In academia there are different kinds of problems and questions, different epistemologies and different ways of thinking and acting which have their expression in a range of different kinds of formal and informal communities, groupings and networks. A focus on discipline as the main or the key way of understanding academic work and organisation is in tension with the constantly changing dynamic disciplinary and interdisciplinary areas of the contemporary university.

It seems fair to say that during much of the nineteenth and twentieth centuries, disciplinarity was mainstream. Degrees tended to focus on a single discipline, or a limited range of disciplines. Researchers tended to work within disciplinary boundaries and tended not to venture into questions requiring knowledge from different areas. Work that crossed disciplinary boundaries was regarded as deviant, problematic or risky. With the advent of modular degrees and a recognition of the interdisciplinary nature of problems and issues requiring research – and the demand within the knowledge economy for Mode 2 knowledge – the rapid pace of change in the postmodern world has forced researchers increasingly to venture out into the quest for interdisciplinary knowledge (Brew and Lucas 2009).

Various theories have been advanced to explain the changes within the nature of knowledge and its relationship to society. Prevalent among these has been the work of Gibbons and colleagues (1994) who coined the terms Mode 1 and Mode 2 knowledge to characterise the shift from a situation where knowledge was principally defined within universities by academics within well-defined disciplinary domains, to the multitude of ways in which the public interacts with scientific findings. In Mode 2, governments intervene in dictating research agendas through, for example, their funding and evaluation mechanisms requiring researchers to focus on short-term clearly defined project outcomes that have economic benefits. There is critical questioning by an informed public of the practical and ethical implications of particular discoveries and programmes, and public debates about what kinds of research should be pursued, all of which have made problematic the relationship between research and society (Nowotny et al. 2001).

It is clear, as Fuller (2002) has argued, that both modes of knowledge have operated simultaneously for a long time and that the distinction between Mode 1 and Mode 2 knowledge production is an artificial divide. Nevertheless, the greater contextualisation of knowledge within society has had consequences for the ways in which research problems and issues now emerge. Nowotny and colleagues suggest that negotiations among interested individuals and organisations, within what they call 'transaction spaces', may grope towards a concept of what is to be explored – for example, the Human Genome Project – or where a chance discovery defines a new field of investigation – for example, the discovery of superconductivity. They call this a Mode 2 object and suggest that it cannot be decided in advance, but once it has been conceptualised, research, and especially funding attention can coalesce around it. In such contexts, discipline, for the purpose of defining a problem or question to be explored, is now completely ignored. It is no longer of relevance. Multidisciplinary teams of experts are likely to be needed to work on these Mode 2 objects and these are likely to come from many different organisations and countries.

Another way of conceptualising the changes in knowledge derives from theories of neo-liberalism. Here the notion of disciplinary tribes sits uneasily within a neo-liberal context where goods are traded in a market economy; knowledge being viewed as one of those goods. Hence there is talk of the knowledge economy. Possessing knowledge is an important element of international trade and commerce. In this view, what becomes important is knowledge that will benefit the economy. How and whether it fits notions of disciplinary understanding is less important than whether the ideas are tradable, for example, in the form of patents and products. Knowledge has to be of use.

There is within such thinking the recognition of the speed of change. Giddens (1999) referring to global interdependency suggests we are in a 'runaway world' and Bauman (2000, 2006) talks of life being 'liquid'. This suggests that the rate of change is faster than structures can be formed. Before new ideas have been integrated into habits and routines, further change has taken place. The static ways in which disciplinary structures are traditionally conceived leave no room for the speed of change in understanding and knowledge. Academic departments are relatively enduring and this has given the illusion that disciplines are too. Indeed, disciplines and departments have been frequently confused or conflated. Attempts, for example, in newer universities to define new disciplines by setting up departments that crossed disciplinary boundaries, such as those that Keele and Essex universities set up in the 1960s, never became commonplace. Yet we now know that there is as much variation within disciplines as there is between some disciplines (Klein 1996). A focus on disciplines as distinct tribes tends to bleach out the complexity and variety of different ways of thinking about knowledge.

From an analysis of disciplines as tribes, assumptions can be deduced about the ways in which academics might think about their disciplinary identity. Indeed, there is a substantial literature that differentiates a range of different academic practices and these are attributed to differences in 'tribes'. However, this does not tell us how academics actually experience the disciplinary groupings in which they are situated and how they conceptualise the problems and issues that they are researching and teaching. Recent work exploring the problematic nature of disciplines as 'tribes' therefore focuses on the ways in which academic researchers and teachers think about the work they are doing. For example, we now know that, contrary to popular belief, many, if not most, academics do not identify as being affiliated to one particular discipline. Brew (2008) highlights some of the difficulty academics can experience in assigning themselves to a particular discipline, suggesting that academics discuss the use of different disciplinary labels at different levels in different contexts. Indeed, they may need to negotiate an acceptable answer when questioned about their disciplinary affiliation. Brew suggests that while some disciplines do appear to have a strong academic affiliation, for example biology and geography, more generally academics' affiliations take on a much more complex pattern. Some academics view the subjects they are researching and teaching in a nested way with one area being viewed as inside another, which is, in turn, inside another. Other academics see their work as at the confluence of two or more disciplinary areas. Brew also found that for many academics the whole notion of a discipline was problematic:

> The subject that the researcher studied for their first degree, for their masters and PhD, the associations they belonged to and the discussions about the nature of the discipline that are taking place in conferences of these associations combine with the actual research and writing projects that are the current focus of attention to create a complex picture of disciplines as shifting and changing over time.
>
> Brew 2008: 132

So too, Manathunga's (2009) study demonstrates the potency of interdisciplinary identity formation for some researchers. In particular, her work investigates the deconstructive possibilities and unhomely tensions involved in constructing interdisciplinary researcher identities that forsake comforting but illusory identifications with disciplinary communities.

Pinch (1990) suggests that given the diversity of contexts within which research and teaching are practised, it is problematic to generalise about disciplinary culture. He argues that different perceptions, descriptions and uses of disciplines are at the heart of the discipline and that the day-to-day reflexive discourse of academics is focused on questions about the nature of the discipline and disciplinarity. Some labels, which are acceptable to describe teaching, are not acceptable when describing research. Pinch refers to all of this as the rhetorical work that goes on in the usage of disciplinary labels: 'the rhetoric of disciplinary talk' (p. 300), or the 'rhetoric of disciplinary identities' (p. 302).

This rhetorical work tended until very recently to focus on the nature of a particular disciplinary area or areas. There tend to be only limited or absent mechanisms within universities for discussions across departments of disciplinary variation. There is evidence to suggest that academics can be somewhat naïve in their views of what people in other academic areas do (Wareing 2006). This can create problems when collaborative interdisciplinary work is undertaken (Rambur 2009).

Problematising Tribes and Territories

While Becher's (1989) original text has been subject to some critique (Bayer 1991), the selection of the tribal metaphor does not appear to have been questioned. However, from a post-colonial perspective, the general use of the term 'tribes' has been roundly critiqued as a 'pejorative' classification intimately entangled with the forces of colonialism and white imperialism (Southall 1996: 1332). Southall traces the history of the term 'tribes' from ancient Roman times and demonstrates how the term has been used in European colonial discourses since the eighteenth century to signal distinctions between savagery and civilisation. In a particularly telling example, he describes how British colonialists were happy to label groups such as the untouchables in India as tribes, but never used that classification for maharajahs (Southall 1996).

In order to establish control over colonial territories, it was necessary to engage in a process of categorisation and naming of indigenous peoples (Southall 1996). So colonialists around the globe tried to classify people into tribes based on significant 'mistranslation and misunderstandings of local social structure, geography and history' (Southall 1996: 1331). The term tribe then came to signify 'primitive peoples' who shared a 'common language and culture, with uniform rules of social organisation, a common name, contiguous territory and tradition of common descent' (Southall 1996: 1334–5). As a result, the vague and often inaccurate differentiations between colonised peoples came to be essentialised and solidified into false tribal labels. In many – although not all – cases, indigenous peoples around the world seek to avoid the term 'tribes' and may use words such as 'people' (Southall 1996) or, in the Australian context, 'clan', or 'skin group' (ATSI Commission 1992).

So, when Becher (1989) first coined the phrase 'academic tribes', he was drawing upon a term that signified to his largely western readership notions of primitivism and savagery. Although this seems bizarre given that he was so intrigued by and personally invested and implicated in conceptions of academic disciplines, a close reading of his original text appears to confirm this. He includes a quote from Bailey's (1977: 212) work, which is subtitled 'the folklore of academic politics', in his preface:

> each tribe has a name and a territory, settles its own affairs, goes to war with the others, has a distinct language or at least a distinct dialect and a variety of ways of demonstrating its apartness from others.

He then draws upon Evelyn Waugh's (1956, quoted in Becher 1989: 22) description of the pre-World War II English aristocracy as 'a complex of tribes, each with its chief and elders and witch-doctors and braves, each with its own dialect and deity, each strongly xenophobic'. There are obvious colonial overtones in this construction of 'chiefs', 'witch-doctors' and 'braves' that reinforce populist notions of savagery and 'primitive' social roles and behaviour. As Southall (1996) points out in the case of chiefs, colonial authorities often created 'chiefs' as a basis of their administration even if they did not exist in indigenous societies, or they invested traditional chiefs with political powers that went well beyond their pre-existing ritual powers.

Becher (1989: 22) suggests that 'a crowd of witnesses attests' that academic cultures operate in a similarly 'tribal' way. From this 'crowd' he selects a quotation from Burton Clark (1963, quoted in Becher 1989: 23) about academic sub-cultures:

> men [sic] of the sociological tribe rarely visit the land of the physicists ... If the sociologists were to step into the building occupied by the English department they would encounter the cold stares if not the slingshots of the hostile natives.

Again this quote clearly reverberates with colonial connotations embedded in terms like 'natives', who are constructed as likely to be 'cold' if not outwardly 'hostile' and to use 'primitive' weapons like 'slingshots'. All of these quotes illustrate western stereotypes of tribes as insular, isolated and aggressive to outsiders. Becher (1989: 24) similarly suggests academics are just as likely to 'defend their own patches of intellectual ground by employing a variety of devices geared to the exclusion of illegal immigrants'.

The second edition of this text, co-authored by Becher and Trowler and published in 2001, seeks to address some of the dramatic contextual and epistemological changes to higher education during the late 1980s and 1990s. In particular, it explores the impact of Mode 2 knowledge – applied, transdisciplinary, problem-orientated knowledge – and new triple helix linkages between universities, the state and industry on academic tribes and territories. The second edition gestures towards interdisciplinarity only in the first chapter, but does not substantially address its impact upon disciplinarity. Significantly, the co-authors do not problematise the adoption of the term 'tribes', although there appear to be more references to 'academic cultures' in this edition. While the original quote about academic tribes from Bailey has been deleted, the extended quotes from Waugh and Clark remain.

Indigenous authors such as Linda Tuhiwai Smith (1999: 65, 67) have shown that, although western academic disciplines have sought to insulate themselves from each other and develop mythologies about their 'separate and "pure" identities', they are actually 'deeply implicated in each other'. She outlines how they 'share genealogical foundations in classical and Enlightenment philosophy' and demonstrates how these traditional disciplines have been 'implicated in colonialism' and totally ignore or are 'antagonistic to other belief systems' (Smith 1999: 65). Indeed, as Smith illustrates, many western academic disciplines 'derived their methods ... or ... tested their ideas in the colonies ... new colonies were the laboratories of western science' (1999: 65). There was also a great deal of destructiveness embedded in western Enlightenment forms of investigation, where it was thought necessary to destroy an object or living creature, to open it up, to dissect it and pin it to a board, in order to study it. In particular, western researchers' measurement, categorisation and desecration of indigenous people's remains were a gruesome and hideous manifestation of this atomistic and destructive approach to knowledge. The ongoing pain and outrage caused by these practices reverberates through Smith's (1999: 1) description of scientists 'filling the skulls of our ancestors with millet seeds … to [determine] the capacity for mental thought'. So, academic disciplines cannot deny their troubled, entangled history in colonialism.

That having been said, why was it that Becher's concept of academic 'tribes' resonated so strongly with the academic community? Perhaps it was because academics desired a stable, fixed cultural identity and sense of belonging to a particular knowledge community. They resonated with a metaphor that would capture the particular discourses, rituals, practices and artefacts that came to be associated with their discipline. They adhered to the separation and compartmentalisation of knowledge that was a feature of Enlightenment thinking, as Smith (1999) suggests. They wanted to maintain boundaries around knowledge to exclude Others. Rather than reflecting western pejorative interpretations of primitivism and savagery, Becher's use of the term academic 'tribes' was read as a way of reifying perceptions of disciplinary identity formation.

Ultimately, these disciplinary classifications proved to be as false and illusory as western constructions of indigenous 'tribes', based on misunderstandings and mistranslations of disciplinary social structure, conceptual geography and history. Although this falsity has become more obvious with the increased recognition of the need for interdisciplinary research, Smith's (1999) analysis reminds us that disciplinary boundaries were always illusory.

Perhaps the academic 'tribes' metaphor worked as well because it reflected university managers' and administrators' desire to classify and categorise academics, who are often regarded as an unruly and idiosyncratic group. The invention of disciplinary categories of knowledge was a way of establishing control and ongoing domination over academics just as the classification of indigenous peoples into 'tribes' allowed colonial administrators to subjugate and manage colonial territories. By corralling academics into fixed and bounded territories and encouraging them to defend and protect their borders, they could divide and rule. Although Becher (1989) highlighted the differing strengths of these boundaries between disciplines, with some clearly more porous and open than others, the territory metaphor was also something that resonated with many academics. In particular, some academic groups inhabited their 'territories' with a type of jingoistic pride that disciplined members into strict adherence to disciplinary norms and worked against creativity, growth and the (re)generation of ideas. The links between notions of disciplinarity and the act of discipline – control, punishment, government – become clear. Indeed, Smith (1999) reminds us of Foucault's analysis of the links between the organisation of bodies of knowledge into disciplines and the organisation of actual bodies. Adequate supervision and control can be maintained over academics by separating them and the conceptual and physical territories or spaces within which they work into disciplinary compartments (Smith 1999).

Alternative Metaphors: Oceans of Knowledge

If the metaphors of tribes and territories are no longer tenable, how are we to understand the spaces that now define disciplinarity and interdisciplinarity? What metaphors can be used instead? In some of our earlier work (Brew 2008; Manathunga 2009), it was found that a number of academics described their work as being at the confluence of two or more disciplines. This idea has led us to eschew land-based metaphors such as 'territories' and to explore disciplinarity in terms of oceans and to see knowledge domains in terms of fluidity. A critical question has been: what is gained and what is lost by changing the metaphors we use?

As mentioned earlier, notions of distinct disciplines arise from the tendency of Enlightenment thinking to fragment, separating one idea, entity or system from another. The notion of separate and distinct disciplines also embodied hierarchies, with some disciplines, such as the pure sciences, being considered more fundamental than others and, in consequence, having more power to define what counted as knowledge. Once we shift to metaphors of fluidity we open up possibilities for more holistic ways of examining academic knowledge. Traditional hierarchies have little relevance. For example, using the notion of an *ocean* of possibilities, disciplinary and interdisciplinary spaces can be considered in an infinite variety of combinations. Such spaces 'flow' into each other, merging to form different kinds of knowledge groupings as problems and needs arise. This gives expression to disciplinary discussions about the nature of particular subject areas that Pinch (1990) talks about.

Oceans have tides, displaying tendencies for different aspects to dominate at different times. Academics may see themselves, as in the study by Brew (2008), as at the confluence of different disciplinary spaces. This is similar to Nowotny *et al.*'s (2001) notion of Mode 2 society, which they argue is similar to Mode 2 knowledge production and expresses the ambiguity that emerges from a co-evolutionary process with the growth of complexity and uncertainty in various aspects of society, including politics and the economy.

'Mode-2ishness' arises not through the existence of any one causal dimension of late modernity such as the dominance of the 'market', or through the pervasive use of communication technologies, or globalisation. It arises, the authors argue, through a number of processes underlying any or all of these dimensions: the generation of uncertainties, new kinds of economic rationality (for example, what is likely to be funded) the role of expectations (the future being viewed as an extension of the present) and what they call the 'flexibilisation' of distance (both physical and social). A fifth important co-evolutionary process is the development of increasingly flexible and permeable social structures with a capacity for self-organisation.

Brew 2002: 353

So knowledge viewed as an ocean is as an eco-system not merely a conduit or facilitator of international trade and commerce as is the case with notions of a knowledge economy

The rapid pace of change that is a basic condition of our super-complex world (Barnett 2000a) is also a driver of moves towards an interdisciplinary ocean. Watery metaphors also pick up on Bauman's (2000) notions of liquid modernity which describe a society where, he argues, practices change faster than the time it takes to consolidate them into habits and routines. Clearly the growth of new specialisations, the emergence of problems requiring interdisciplinary teams for their solutions, the development of a multitude of different orientations of students who have studied modular courses with varying subjects, all point to a fluidity of disciplinary spaces that are not tied to routines or to organisational structures. Indeed, organisational structures tend, as we argued earlier, to fossilise outdated disciplinary boundaries.

Rivers run into the ocean at which point they may constitute estuaries where several rivers join, marsh land, wetland, swamps which may be boggy, and inlets where the water is cut off from other tributaries. Using these metaphors we can similarly describe researchers as traditionally fishing in well-defined rivers and not venturing out into the unknown ocean where knowledge streams blend and merge. Interdisciplinarity or fishing in the ocean of knowledge used to be regarded as somewhat deviant, problematic or highly risky. There was a danger that problems would become too complex, that researchers would get 'bogged down' in troublesome swamps. However, the demand for Mode 2 knowledge and the rapid pace of change has forced researchers to venture out into interdisciplinary oceans of knowledge and to meet the challenges of joining together. Rip (2004) uses the metaphor of a 'reservoir' to describe a body of transdisciplinary knowledge in which researchers from public and private sector organisations 'fish ... to create new understandings, technologies and options' (Rip 2004: 156, 159). However, this does not capture the wildness and unpredictability of interdisciplinary knowledge in the way that an ocean does.

The use of watery metaphors does not deny the solidity of disciplinary and interdisciplinary spaces. There is, after all, a solid surface underneath the ocean and from time to time, the ocean floor rises to form an island, which might be a kind of new territory; previously unknown. This is similar to the way in which Mode 2 objects emerge for Nowotny and others (2001). They talk about knowledge as taking place in what they call the 'agora' which is a kind of marketplace where ideas are traded in what they call 'transaction spaces' where academics, experts, government advisors and members of parliament as well as the public come together in a transaction space to trade ideas. For example, the idea of drawing up a catalogue of the entire genetic make-up of humans arose through numerous interactions in different countries and scientific and political organisations. No single person, group or organisation was in control but over time, interests and funding coalesced around a global programme of research now known as the Human Genome Project.

By and large, an ocean is constantly moving. Seen as an ocean, knowledge is wild, vast, unpredictable, treacherous, deep, windy, becalming, life-giving, fluid, liquid, powerful, invigorating. It has slipstreams, currents, waves and travel routes. New research specialisations that emerge and then form part of the larger whole flow into it like rivers. Academics both individually and collectively bring together disciplinary spaces converging, merging, changing and challenging previous structures.

The idea of tribes and territories traps us in the past. If disciplines are viewed as fluid this is, we suggest, a more sustainable way to think of the ecology of academia. It allows us to respect what is, rather than forcing academic work into artificial structures. In this sense, it is like the ways in which indigenous peoples do not make distinctions between the spirit world and the natural world and between the natural world and themselves, so enabling them to preserve a natural interconnectedness.

Without the safety of disciplinary rivers, academic and researcher identities can be all at sea. Harvesting ideas and approaches from the sea of knowledge can be a risky venture because there are no knowledge borders or boundaries; no hierarchies of knowledge; and no order. Just as medieval maps depicted unspeakable monsters lurking in the oceans at the edges of a flat world – 'here be dragons' – interdisciplinary research is full of uncertainties and risks. Voyaging across knowledge oceans can be an uncomfortable experience. Post-colonial theorists used the term 'unhomeliness' to capture the sense of ambivalence and displacement experienced by migrant workers forced to travel the world in search of work (Bhabha 1994). Unhomeliness could also be an effective term to describe the interdisciplinary researcher's restless search for knowledge in the knowledge ocean (Manathunga 2009). It is also a useful concept because it encapsulates both the destabilising and uncomfortable effects of searching for knowledge but also the productive, deconstructive possibilities of creating new knowledge and understandings.

Implications

If we are to adopt more holistic, life-affirming and respectful approaches to knowledge creation, then huge changes will need to be made to existing research and knowledge production systems. As mentioned above, these systems were largely developed during the eighteenth, nineteenth and twentieth centuries and remain dominated by western Enlightenment, individualistic, atomistic, competitive and masculinist thinking. This section of our chapter explores the implications of these new, more fluid, respectful and open metaphors for undergraduate research experiences, research training, the mentoring of early career researchers and the ongoing professional development of experienced researchers. They also have major ramifications for research assessment and funding exercises.

As the trend increases to include more research experiences in under-graduate programmes, there will be an even greater need to make explicit to students the epistemologies they are grappling with and the interdisciplinarity implicit in many courses. Many undergraduate degrees are – and in some cases have always been – multidisciplinary, but have rarely been taught as if they were. For example, education has always incorporated paradigms, approaches and methodologies from both psychology and sociology but this is rarely made explicit to students, who may be penalised for not intuiting how oppositional these knowledges can sometimes be. Undergraduates are increasingly engaging in 'capstone' courses where there is a requirement to integrate their study from often quite disparate areas. As a result, increasingly undergraduate programmes will need to engage explicitly with their disciplinary histories, philosophies and roots and incorporate more inquiry-led learning that actively exposes students to interdisciplinary research questions, practices and approaches.

There are even greater implications for research higher degree programmes. Students are increasingly intrigued by interdisciplinary research projects and, in many fields, the truly original, cutting-edge research is located on the boundaries and cracks between disciplines. However, the research training system continues to be designed for disciplinary-based research and identity formation. The best solution arrived at to date seems to be just to increase the numbers of supervisors that research students are required to work with. This has the effect of shifting the burden of interdisciplinary research to the students themselves as they seek to wrestle with conflicting advice and disciplinary socialisation strategies. They can also suffer penalties in terms of publication, access to additional grant money and prizes, thesis examination and future employment prospects associated with working outside disciplinary cultural norms. In order to equalise the burden of responding to a more fluid world of knowledge creation and interdisciplinary research, the focus needs to shift away from students onto supervisors and universities. In particular, universities should provide supervisors with additional professional development on interdisciplinary supervision and team work and opportunities to engage in interdisciplinary research themselves.

So too, all research higher degree students, including those engaged in disci-plinary-based research, should be encouraged to develop a critical knowledge about their field(s)' underlying epistemologies, philosophies and histories so that they understand the common genealogies among disciplines. This, we suggest, should be a key part of the development of a reflexive critique that Glassick *et al.* (1997) argue is a key component of the way in which research is evaluated. They should be encouraged to remain alert to the possibility of Mode 2 knowledge objects emerging from their existing research projects. At the same time, greater efforts need to be made to recruit, support and reward indigenous and culturally diverse research higher degree students.

All of these implications are also important for early career researchers. In particular, systematic mentoring programmes that encourage early career researchers to question and transgress the existing boundaries of the discipline should be established. Similarly, more indigenous and culturally diverse researchers need to be actively recruited and supported in universities and other research organisations. More authentic and respectful intercultural and international research collaboration, which genuinely incorporates western, eastern and indigenous ways of thinking and knowing, also needs to be encouraged and facilitated. There also need to be greater professional development opportunities available to experienced researchers to facilitate their involvement in interdisciplinary research teams and to encourage them, as leaders in their fields, to legitimate disciplinary boundary-crossing and support it in their roles as academic gatekeepers, peer reviewers, editors and employers of new researchers.

Finally, existing evaluation and funding of research through research assessment exercises becomes highly problematic if these metaphors of research and knowledge ecology are to become actualised. Scholars have demonstrated how the UK Research Assessment Exercise reinforces and rewards disciplinary boundaries (Lucas 2006; McNay 2009). This pattern seems to be replicated in other research quality measurement systems like the Performance Based Research Fund in New Zealand and the forthcoming Excellence in Research Assessment process in Australia. Instead, real energy and ingenuity will be required to systematically rethink how the quality of interdisciplinary, holistic, sustainable and life-affirming research could be recognised and rewarded. This would also require more authentic understanding, funding, rewarding of and respect for eastern and indigenous knowledge systems.

Conclusion

We have argued that for a range of interdisciplinary and post-colonial reasons, the metaphors of tribes and territories first coined by Becher (1989) and reinforced by Becher and Trowler (2001) in their second edition are no longer applicable or helpful in understanding contemporary research practices and epistemologies. In particular, we have drawn attention to ways in which 'liquid modernity' (Bauman 2000) and its complex and multi-layered problems require interdisciplinary research approaches and ways of thinking and being. Drawing upon the work of Southall (1996) and Smith (1999), we have shown how the term 'tribes' has always been deeply implicated in the projects of colonialism and white imperialism, as have the disciplines that began emerging during the Enlightenment. We have also demonstrated how the separation and atomisation of western knowledge into disciplines and territories has long denied their common origins and interconnectedness.

Instead we propose the alternative metaphor of oceans of knowledge as being more generative, holistic and fluid for our new times. We suggest that knowledge, research and researcher identities in current times can be just as wild, vast, unpredictable, unhomely, life-giving, powerful, and invigorating as the oceans of the world. Finally, we consider some of the implications this new metaphor has for research training, early career researcher development, the ongoing professional development of experienced researchers and the evaluation and funding of research. Thinking about knowledge and research in this ecological way might allow us to grapple with our world's complex and intertwined problems and work towards more interconnected, holistic and life-affirming solutions.

5

Law, Research and the Academy

FIONA COWNIE

The nature and purpose of academic research in law has been controversial ever since law began to be established as a discipline in the English universities during the second half of the nineteenth century. There have been long-running debates about whether the purpose of legal research should be to produce commentaries and other analyses which are primarily of use for practising lawyers, providing 'a house of intellect for the professions' as suggested by Savage and Watt (1996) or whether academic legal research should share the intellectual and theoretical objectives of other disciplines in the academy. This academic/vocational debate has another related aspect: whether law should be analysed using a doctrinal approach – focusing almost exclusively on legal materials such as reported cases and statutes – which would be the approach of the majority of practising lawyers (Goff 1983: 171), or whether academic lawyers should draw on other disciplines – anything from economics and politics to literature and media studies – to analyse legal phenomena from a purely academic perspective (Bradney 1998: passim).

These debates, which therefore apply not only to the nature of legal research, but also to the way in which law is taught in universities, have frequently been couched in terms of the nature of the legal education which university law schools should be offering: should it be a liberal education, or one which is vocational in nature (Cownie 2010: 2–4)? Commentators such as Brownsword and Bradney have put forward strong arguments in favour of a liberal education (Brownsword 1999; Bradney 2003) while Hepple and Twining have argued strongly for some sort of middle ground (Hepple 1996; Twining 1998) and others, such as Brayne and Maharg, urge in different ways, that legal education should focus on the vocational (Brayne 2000; Maharg 2007). To understand these debates, and their influence on the nature of academic legal research, it is helpful to have a brief look at some of the main themes that have emerged, starting with the establishment of English law as a university discipline, when it was immediately faced with the question of whether it was vocational or academic.

Doctrinalism and the Textbook Tradition

The story of the establishment of law in English universities is relatively short, and, for the most part, somewhat depressing. Although the Vinerian Chair was created at Oxford in 1750, and the Downing Chair at Cambridge in 1800, law failed to become established in the academy until well into the twentieth century (Twining 1994: 24). In 1846, the House of Commons Select Committee on Legal Education reported that 'No legal education worthy of the name is at this moment to be had in either England or Ireland' (Select Committee on Legal Education 1846: 8). In the second half of the nineteenth century, a series of dedicated legal academics worked hard to gain recognition for law as a serious academic enterprise (Lawson 1968). However, even by the time that one of the most famous of these, Professor A.V. Dicey, gave his inaugural lecture as the Vinerian Professor at Oxford in 1883, law remained marginal within the academy.

Dicey's lecture was entitled 'Can English Law be Taught at the University?' (Dicey 1883). The rhetorical nature of this question referred to the debate between legal practitioners – who thought that apprenticeship was the best way to train lawyers – and the newly-established breed of legal academics – who were struggling to persuade not only legal practitioners, but equally sceptical university dons, that law as a discipline was worthy of a place in the academy (Sugarman 1991: 38). To the practitioners, Dicey pointed out that it was unacceptable to educate lawyers by allowing them, on a haphazard basis, merely to learn about those areas of law which happened to pass across the desk of the lawyer to whom they were apprenticed (Dicey 1883: 10–12). To the dons he argued that law must be taught in universities, where it would be the job of the new law dons to teach law in a logical and coherent manner, enabling students to gain a firm grounding in legal principles. It would also be the task of legal academics to 'create a legal literature' (Dicey 1883: 18–22).

However, in pursuing their task of creating a legal literature, academic lawyers did not engage in the same type of intellectual pursuits as those members of the academy researching other areas of the arts and humanities. The focus of academic lawyers was on the doctrinal analysis of law, and, as one of Becher and Trowler's respondents commented critically, the main concern of doctrinal lawyers is 'with ordering a corpus of knowledge: it is largely a descriptive pursuit' (Becher and Trowler 2001: 31). The doctrinal or 'black letter' tradition assumes that the law is an internally coherent and unified body of rules, which are derived from a small number of general principles. It is the job of the (doctrinal) academic lawyer to describe and explain these general principles. Consequently, as compared with research in other disciplines, doctrinal law was open to the charge of being narrow, atheoretical and unimaginative. Surveying the early history of academic law, Duxbury comments that throughout the early part of the twentieth century '[a]cademic law remained a fairly moribund, amateurish profession ...' He goes on to quote from a letter written in 1929 by Harold Laski to the distinguished American judge, Mr Justice Holmes:

> [o]utside one or two posts like the Vinerian professorship, the law teachers are a very inferior set of people who mainly teach because they cannot make a success of the Bar ... and who regard research as a merely professional by-product instead of being central to the profession and its organisation.
>
> Duxbury 2001: 71

Despite its obvious difficulties, there have been some stalwart defences of doctrinal analysis, with Twining – far from a doctrinal lawyer himself – arguing that 'If one considers the greatest achievements of the expository tradition, none fits the picture of mere description and arrangement' (Twining 1994: 131) and Birks, sometime Regius Professor of Civil Law at the University of Oxford, criticising those who seek to detach the study of law from 'the world of legal practice and adjudication' (Birks 1998: 406). However, the doctrinal approach has also been subjected to sustained criticism. Thornton, for example, has referred to the 'technocentrism' of the doctrinal tradition, in which law is seen as autonomous, with discernible boundaries between law and morality, as well as between law and other academic disciplines. The pedagogical practice which is found in law schools, she notes, 'focuses primarily on legal rules [and] creates a law school environment in which the technocratic is normalized' (Thornton 1998: 372). Thornton's criticisms are part of a series of challenges to the doctrinal tradition which have become ever more vociferous over the decades. Goodrich, for example, writes of the way in which traditional legal education produces '"the reasonable man", the "black-letter" lawyer, the dull white face with one less thought each year' while law schools value 'not thought, but rather prestige, publication, the circulation of texts and the manipulative repetition of standard argumentative forms' (Goodrich, 1996: 59). Similarly, Collier writes of the need to 'transcend the restricted and inadequate positivist framework' (Collier 1991: 42).

Doctrinal legal scholarship has also faced the criticism that it is far too closely tied to the needs of the legal profession. Its orientation towards the needs of practising lawyers has profoundly affected the nature of academic legal research, encouraging the production of textbooks and other items of utility to practitioners, such as case notes and commentaries on statutes, while inhibiting the production of the kind of original theoretical research which the academy in general would value. As a result, academic law has struggled to forge its own identity separate from that of the legal profession, despite repeated calls for academic lawyers to take a more mainstream place in the intellectual life of the academy. As early as 1950, Gower, giving his inaugural lecture at the London School of Economics, called for 'a clear separation between preliminary theoretical training, which should be left to the universities, and subsequent practical training ... which should be controlled by practitioners ...' (Gower 1950: 162). However, change, if any, was incremental, and when new universities were established in the 1960s, in the wake of the Robbins Report, few of them were interested in having a law department. As Abel-Smith and Stevens note, 'at least some of the younger academic lawyers did not hesitate to explain the exclusion' (Abel-Smith and Stevens 1967: 373):

> The programmes of the new Universities are avowedly liberal. We cannot hope to encourage them to look sympathetically on law as part of liberal education as long as the existing Faculties present a public image of isolated technicalities and professional single-mindedness. We should be more welcome in Sussex if we educated instead of trained; more acceptable in York or Canterbury if we taught about the contemporary problems of law rather than merely analyzed a text-book full of rules.
>
> Milner 1963: 192, quoted in Abel-Smith and Stevens 1967: 373

Torn between the academic and the vocational, the legal profession and the university, during most of the twentieth century law sat uncomfortably on the sidelines of the academy, largely untouched by the intellectual currents that swirled around the universities.

Challenges to Doctrinalism

The doctrinal tradition remained the dominant mode of law teaching and research until well into the twentieth century. In the early years of the century most law graduates came from the 'golden triangle' of Oxford, Cambridge and London universities, where the use of classic textbooks ensured that the legal education offered was doctrinal in nature. Since it was graduates of these universities who became law teachers, they continued to foster the doctrinal approach to law. In addition, many provincial law schools were founded as a result of the activities of local Law Societies and, as a result, they were highly sensitive to the needs of the legal profession (Sugarman 1991: 54). The pre-eminence of doctrinalism was also reinforced because, until the major expansion cemented by the Robbins Report, many law school staff were part-time practitioners, whose orientation also tended to be towards practice. It was not until after the mid-1960s that law schools began to employ young lecturers who were full-time academics, whose allegiance was to the development of law as an academic discipline, rather than to law as a vocational subject (Campbell and Wiles 1975: 560). The influence of the doctrinal approach on both research and teaching remained strong, much to the dissatisfaction of those academic lawyers who wished to engage in legal research of a similar nature to the research emanating from other, more overtly intellectual parts of the academy. As late as 1987, Professor Geoffrey Wilson characterised research in law in the following terms:

The words 'English legal scholarship', though high-sounding, have a similar function to the words 'disposable plastic cup'. Each adjective strengthens the message that one cannot expect much in terms of quality or long-term utility from it.

Wilson 1987: 819

However, during the latter part of the twentieth century, a number of alternative approaches to the study of law emerged to challenge the supremacy of doctrinal law. Scholars working within these traditions did not accept that law is composed of an autonomous body of rules, nor that it is 'neutral' or 'value-free' (Campbell and Wiles 1975: 547).

Of the various critiques that emerged, the one which has arguably gained the widest following among legal academics has been the socio-legal or 'law in context' approach (Bradney and Cownie 2000: 6). Socio-legal studies is hard to define, because of the diverse range of scholarship carried out under that name; like other movements, it is not confined neatly within well-defined boundaries, and the term 'socio-legal' can be used to include feminist work and critical legal studies, two of the other significant approaches which have emerged to challenge doctrinal law. However, a useful working definition can be found in the review of socio-legal studies carried out by the Economic and Social Research Council in 1994, which characterised socio-legal studies as 'an *approach* to the study of law and legal processes' which 'covers the theoretical and empirical analysis of law as a social phenomenon' (ESRC 1994: 1, emphasis in original). Interest in socio-legal studies has been characterised as 'the emergence of a new legal paradigm' (Thomas 1997: 19) and socio-legal scholarship as 'the most important scholarship currently being undertaken in the legal world' (Cotterell 1995: 314). While the strength of socio-legal studies may remain a matter of debate (see, for example, Collier 2005), its existence gives an insight into a fundamental difference between academic lawyers regarding their approach to research. The establishment of socio-legal professional associations, not just in the UK, but also in the USA and other parts of the Common Law world – where socio-legal studies is referred to as 'Law and Society' – is a further indication of the way in which this challenge to the doctrinal paradigm has become firmly entrenched within academic legal studies.

During the latter part of the twentieth century, both critical legal studies and feminism also emerged as alternatives to the dominant doctrinal paradigm within academic law. The application of feminist ideas to law arose in the wake of the feminist movement of the 1960s. Early work tended to analyse areas of law of particular concern to women, such as domestic and sexual violence, pointing out the ways in which legal rules, though apparently neutral, excluded or disadvantaged women (see for example, Atkins and Hoggett 1984). New ideas about the social construction of gender were reflected in published research such as O'Donovan's *Sexual Divisions in Law* (1985), and since then feminist legal academics in the UK have gone on to develop a significant body of work, ably documented by Conaghan, in her useful review of the state of feminist legal studies (Conaghan 2002).

Critical legal studies (CLS) originated in the USA in the late 1970s and rapidly spread to a number of other countries, including the UK, where the first critical legal conference took place in 1984 (Fitzpatrick and Hunt 1987: 1). Critical legal scholars are self-consciously radical and, while there are disparate views about the nature of CLS, a useful definition can be found in Hunt's characterisation of critical legal scholars as 'reacting against features of the prevailing orthodoxies in legal scholarship, against the conservatism of law schools and against many features of the role played by law and legal institutions in modern society' (Hunt 1987: 5). CLS shares many features with socio-legal studies, and membership of the two movements is not necessarily mutually exclusive (Cownie 2004: 51–2). Equally, the relationship between CLS and other critical movements in law, such as critical race theory and feminism, is complex. As Naffine has commented:

> To many critical theorists, it would seem that feminists represent the intellectual vanguard of legal theory ... But all is not harmonious. Certain feminists have openly taken issue with the critical theorists, regarding them as masculine in their orientation and concerns ... Other feminists regard critical scholars as 'fellow travellers'.
>
> Naffine 1993: 79

One thing that all these approaches do have in common, however, is that they offer alternative paradigms to the doctrinal one with which legal research was for so long exclusively associated, and which was clearly reflected in the comments made by the respondents in both editions of *Tribes and Territories*.

A Discipline in Transition

The existence of these different approaches to legal scholarship means that legal academics can draw upon a range of theoretical and philosophical perspectives when researching legal phenomena. However, until recently, there was little evidence on the relative strength of the alternative approaches. Many people – myself included – assumed that doctrinal analysis retained its dominance over legal education and legal research. Indeed, I had expressed reservations about the arguments put forward by some commentators, particularly Bradney (1998: 73), that doctrinalism was 'now entering its final death throes' (Cownie 2000: 72). However, in 2002, stimulated by reading *Tribes and Territories*, I embarked upon an empirical study of English legal academics (Cownie 2004), which was to lead me to change my views.

One of the main purposes of the empirical study I undertook was to make a contribution to what Becher (1989), following Geertz (1976), called 'an ethnography of the disciplines'. Law features as one of the disciplines examined in both editions of *Tribes and Territories*, but the additional data included in the second edition does not seem to have greatly added to the insights about law that were put forward in the first edition. Indeed, the authors comment 'with the exception of an interesting discussion by Campbell and Wiles (1975) the attempt at a literature search drew a complete blank' (Becher and Trowler 2001: 53). The fact that two expert and experienced researchers could uncover virtually none of the extensive literature on various aspects of legal education and research speaks volumes about the opacity of law as a discipline to those outside it. One reason for this may be that much of this literature is labelled 'legal education', which may make it appear to relate only to teaching. In fact, there is a range of material that can throw light upon many aspects of the discipline; this includes writing about law teaching and pedagogy, through inaugural lectures and analyses of the nature of academic law, to empirical studies of the legal academy (Cownie 2004: chapter 2). For those interested in learning about the tribe of academic lawyers, however, much of this literature is about the 'public' life of academic law, as opposed to the 'private life' of law schools and academic lawyers. It was in an attempt to fill that gap in our knowledge that in 2002–3 I interviewed 54 legal academics, all involved in teaching academic – as opposed to vocational – undergraduate law courses. They were located in seven English universities of varying missions, included men and women who had differing amounts of experience as academics, and who occupied the whole range of academic grades, from lecturer to professor.

Awareness of the different paradigms which can be adopted to analyse legal phenomena led me to ask: 'How would you describe your approach to teaching and researching law, on a scale from doctrinal [generally referred to by academic lawyers as 'black-letter'] through socio-legal to critical legal studies (CLS) and feminist?' A few described themselves as adopting a CLS/socio-legal approach, nearly half as socio-legal and the other half as black-letter. Respondents were evenly distributed across gender and experience, although those describing themselves as socio-legal were slightly more likely to be situated in a pre-1992 university (Cownie 2004: 54). However, it rapidly became apparent that the differences between the socio-legal and the black-letter lawyers were less stark than might have been anticipated. Several socio-legal respondents stressed that in order to be a good socio-legal lawyer, it is imperative to have a good grasp of traditional legal reasoning:

> So far as I'm concerned, you must be accurate about the law, but it's completely useless unless you have a critique or politics around it … equally, it's completely useless to have a view if you don't know the law.
>
> Principal lecturer, mid-career, female, post-1992 university

> I honestly don't think you can be a critical lawyer unless you've got a firm grasp of the black-letter, that's crucial.
>> Senior lecturer, mid-career, male, post-1992 university

Equally, only a very small minority of those who described themselves as black-letter lawyers described themselves, without qualification, as adopting a doctrinal approach. Most of them qualified their description, saying that describing themselves as black-letter did not mean that they focused exclusively on legal rules. They thought it was equally important to introduce contextual issues – social, political, economic and so on – into their analyses. These respondents came from both parts of the sector, both genders and all stages of experience.

> [My approach is] predominantly black-letter, but law can only be understood in the context in which it exists. So bearing in mind that I teach contract, there are a lot of relevant economic points and a lot of purely policy decisions ... so I'm quite law in context really ...
>> Professor, experienced, male, post-1992 university

> I'm not right at the black-letter end. In fact, I've become less black-letter than I once was ... I try to give more attention to the political context in which rules are being formulated and applied.
>> Professor, mid-career, male, pre-1992 university

Comments like these not only throw light on the fluidity of the terms 'black-letter' and 'socio-legal'. They also indicate the way in which doctrinal law has changed in nature, with many doctrinal lawyers combining the traditional approach with an analysis of policy objectives or other social phenomena in a way that would have been unthinkable to legal academics at the beginning of the twentieth century (Cownie 2004: 56). Self-ascription as 'black-letter' or 'socio-legal' may therefore have more to do with a matter of emphasis, or a desire to indicate a particular political viewpoint, than with actual differences in approach to the analysis of legal phenomena. It also has to do with widespread assumptions about what being 'socio-legal' actually entails. There were strong indications from my respondents that many held the view that 'socio-legal' research was exclusively empirical, and that since they did not do that kind of research, they could not describe themselves as 'socio-legal', even if they were uncomfortable with describing themselves as 'black-letter' (Cownie 2004: 57). This narrow definition of socio-legal research was clearly not the definition used in the ESRC's review of socio-legal studies, which regarded library-based research drawing on concepts from other disciplines as equally worthy of the name 'socio-legal' (ESRC 1994: 1). Quite apart from the niceties of definitions, the data I collected suggest that, whatever they call themselves, the majority of academic lawyers occupy the middle ground between the two extremes of pure doctrinal analysis and a highly theoretical feminist or CLS approach to the study of law.

The existence of these different paradigms brings with it the possibility of conflict between adherents of different theoretical positions. Certainly this was the case with the introduction of CLS into American law schools, and the resulting struggles have been well documented in the literature (for an informative overview see Austin 1998). Based on the data I collected, there was little evidence that ideological conflicts played a significant role in English law school culture, with most respondents describing their departments as 'pluralistic', though in one institution differences had clearly risen to the surface, with an attempt being made to marginalise socio-legal scholars (Cownie 2004: 59). There was also evidence that the work of feminist lawyers was not universally respected, with about half my respondents reflecting the negative attitudes which Clare McGlynn had alluded to when reporting the results of her empirical survey of gender/feminist issues in law schools in 1998 (McGlynn 1998: 50). However, negative attitudes were balanced by just as many positive comments about feminist work, such as the male professor in a department which did not have a particularly strong feminist culture describing feminist research without hesitation as 'highly regarded' (Cownie 2004: 62). Overall, the penetration of the socio-legal approach, combined with the fact that most doctrinal lawyers were including in their teaching and research materials which would arguably be regarded as socio-legal, led me to conclude that law is a discipline in transition, moving away from its exclusively doctrinal roots to a much more pluralistic culture, in which academic lawyers routinely adopt a variety of approaches to the study of law (Cownie 2004: 72).

The Limits of Choice in Legal Research

The existence of a variety of approaches that can be used to analyse legal phenomena means that academic lawyers have significantly more choices available to them at the beginning of the twenty-first century than they did a hundred years ago, when law was just establishing itself as a discipline in the academy. No longer must they adhere to a strict doctrinal paradigm. Now, they can choose to draw on a range of theoretical perspectives and can follow several different paradigms. Of course, their choice is not unconstrained – like other disciplines, they are subject to the structural pressures experienced by all academic researchers, in particular the regular audit of research in the UK's Research Assessment Exercise and more recent Research Excellence Framework (RAE/REF). When I asked my respondents whether the RAE had affected their research at all and, if so, in what ways, nearly all of those working in post-1992 universities said that it had, together with about half of those working in pre-1992 institutions. Women and early-career academics were particularly likely to agree that their research had been affected by the existence of the RAE. Most people described the RAE as an ever-present consideration when they were thinking about their research, affecting where they published, the type of work they published and providing an ever-present pressure to publish (Cownie 2004: 135–6). One of the interesting effects of the RAE is that it may have contributed to the movement away from doctrinalism that I noted above (Hicks 1995). Vick *et al.* (1998) noted on the basis of their empirical survey that there is a widespread belief among academic lawyers that the RAE has made writing for practitioners 'a second rank activity' and that 'there is a general perception that the law panel's [research] assessment procedures are weighted against professional and practice publications' (Vick *et al.* 1998: 558).

Overall, there were mixed views on the RAE. Those for and against it were very evenly split, with some respondents forcefully pointing out the negative aspects of the audit culture, such as its tendency to cause divisions within law schools, leading to considerable unhappiness for individuals not entered for assessment, as well as to a constant pressure to publish and the growth of another form of 'managerialism' within the academy. However, others pointed to effects that they regarded as positive, such as its capacity to encourage the production of much more research, and to make research much more highly valued within the legal academy than had previously been the case (Cownie 2004: 138–40). This effect of the RAE provides further evidence of the academic drift currently affecting legal research, and the way in which the discipline as a whole is moving significantly nearer to the heart of the academy in the twenty-first century than it was when Dicey raised the issue of law in the university just before the beginning of the twentieth century.

Increased choice about the way in which to research law has not resolved all the doubts that academic lawyers have about their discipline. Empirical researchers, in particular, are worried about the capacity of the discipline to continue to produce empirical research about law. Since undergraduate law degrees do not generally include any significant study of the theories or methods which are regarded as fundamental by most disciplines within the social sciences, the socio-legal community relies upon highly motivated individuals who undertake postgraduate training, or experienced researchers who decide to teach themselves the relevant skills and become familiar with theoretical perspectives from outside their discipline. The recent Nuffield Enquiry, *Law in the Real World* concluded that there is a developing crisis in the capacity of UK universities to undertake empirical legal research, which presents a number of challenges if this type of socio-legal research is to continue to make an effective contribution to legal scholarship (Genn *et al.* 2006: 39). However, such views are not universal, and others are considerably more optimistic about this growing field. For instance, Mulcahy – a former chair of the Socio-Legal Studies Association – published a robust response to the Nuffield Enquiry, commenting that she saw 'no shortage of really excellent multi-disciplinary work being undertaken' in the UK and that perhaps one reason for the lack of legal scholars applying to funding bodies to carry out empirical research was simply due to 'a lack of interest amongst socio-legal scholars in carrying out this type of project' (Mulcahy 2007: 3).

Nevertheless, other legal scholars have expressed doubts about the future of theoretical – as opposed to empirical – socio-legal research, worrying that it does not fit in with government policy agendas for higher education, and that it therefore has an uncertain future. Collier argues that the current socio-political climate results in a political economy for academic research that is directed towards wealth creation. Academics are positioned as 'knowledge workers' who will see knowledge not as something of value in and of itself, but as 'a commodity; a resource to help create wealth and competitive advantage' (Collier 2003: 4). In this context, he raises concerns about the future of legal research, and its ability to resist being confined to an atheoretical empiricism aimed at meeting the needs of business or government (Collier 2003: 4). Similar concerns are expressed by Bibbings in her examination of the 2003 White Paper on the future of higher education:

> Doctrinal lawyers, socio-legal academics, historians, archaeologists, philosophers, post-modern theorists, political critics and, of course, medi-aevalists, together face the prospect of a precarious future in an environment in which universities rely less upon state funding and more upon income from students, business and exploitable knowledge.
>
> Bibbings 2003: 3

Paradoxically, the existence of such concerns, which are shared by many academics in arts and humanities disciplines, as well as some social scientists, serve to underline the way in which law has become integrated into the academy, reflecting the fact that legal academics now participate in the same debates – and same concerns – as their peers in other disciplines. In doing so, they provide a vivid illustration of the extent to which the discipline of law has developed since Dicey sought to persuade a disbelieving world that law did indeed deserve a place in the academy.

6

Doing Research
The Case of Art and Design

PAUL TROWLER

Introduction

The following chapter is based on research into the 'teaching-research nexus' funded by the Higher Education Academy (Trowler and Wareham 2007, 2008). It draws on data from semi-structured interviews conducted with 16 academic staff across the four disciplines of Graphic Design, Design for Performance, Fine Art and Fashion Design and across each of the six institutions that make up the University of the Arts, London (UAL). The scope of these interviews focused on research practices. Other interviews on teaching practices were conducted with a different sample of 18 staff in that institution (described in Shreeve *et al.* 2010), but those are not used for this chapter.

This focus on art and design and on the UAL needs some explanation. Elsewhere I have found that an examination of an unusual example of a particular phenomenon has yielded insights and raised important questions about more mainstream versions of that phenomenon (for example in Trowler and Turner 2002). Of course this is not a new observation: Freud's psychiatric work using case studies of his patients, for example, shows how detailed examination of atypical cases can shed light on the 'normal'. The various fields within art and design face tensions over what counts as 'research' as they move further into the mainstream of higher education because traditionally they have had very distinctive approaches to it. Studying these fields has the potential to unsettle usual conceptions of what 'research' is, and to make us think anew about its character and the practices associated with it.

A second characteristic that I considered important in designing this research project is that UAL is a relatively new institutional structure, and thus institutional influences on perceptions of research and research activity would be more apparent and less part of the tacit understandings of staff than in longer-established institutions. UAL comprises six pre-existing institutions with a diverse array of missions and cultures: Central Saint Martin's College of Art and Design, Camberwell College of Arts, Chelsea College of Art and Design, London College of Communication, London College of Fashion and Wimbledon College of Art. Interviewing staff from all of these would, we hoped, give us an insight into the significance of different institutional backgrounds in the context of attempts to forge a single entity from them.

Problematising 'Research' and its Trajectory

The nature and definition of the term 'research' continues to be a subject of ongoing debate in the creative disciplines. Historically, research in the creative arts has referred to that set of practices which supports the creative process. Respondents described the way that this form of research is continuous, often unconscious, eclectic, visual and tactile rather than verbal and unlikely to be goal-oriented in the same way that, say, scientific research might be designed with clear research questions, a literature review, methodology and reporting processes. In this sense, research in art and design has been understood to be organic, creative and quite ad hoc in its nature. Notions of rigour, reliability, validity and so on do not apply here: the key criterion of good research in art and design, understood in this way, is the end result, the artwork or artefact. One respondent said:

> When I'm doing research I'm thinking and looking and painting. It involves all the same things that practice involves: [the difference is] where the emphasis lies – [that] depends on your overview. A second strand of research is to do with series of projects called Past into the Present. We're looking at ways in which all of us look at other artwork and then reinvent out of that looking process. [It's] a bit like a standard that a jazz musician will take and invent a new contemporary vision of that original piece of music. That reinvention and fluidity of thinking is very much what I see as the grounding to which my practice orientates.
>
> Senior Fine Art Researcher

Another distinctive feature of that approach to research is its playfulness and uninhibited activity that seeks to challenge orthodoxies. Respondents from the areas of fashion design and graphics referred to the importance of play in relation to the creation of new work, talking about techniques to stimulate creativity and playfulness both in their own work and that of their students.

Not all research in art and design has this character though. A minority of respondents had research specialisms of a sort more familiar to academics in the humanities especially. An art historian, for example, noted that research in his field was quite different from that of the fine art practitioners in his department; it followed the conventional practices of the discipline of history generally.

> My own? It is completely conventional. The production of scholarly monographs or essays, or it might be being involved in an exhibition which

provides new information or new insights [and so a] ... re-thinking of historical work. It contributes to a notion of the subject moving forward – so there's always a sense of where the research fits in terms of issues and debates.

Professor of Art History

Many of the respondents, however, expressed a sense that research in art and design as a whole was becoming more formalised, in fact more like 'research' as understood in the social sciences or humanities. There was a change in the modality, so that the written form was becoming important: ideas and creativity needed to be expressed in text as well as – or instead of – through artworks and artefacts. There was less of an emphasis on the product itself, the arte-fact, the work of art, and less emphasis on its power to affect the audience or observer, on affective or illuminative power. There was more emphasis on the reliable demonstration of analytical and textual skills of researchers and emer-gent researchers, on the quality of the processes leading to the artefact. Some respondents felt defensive about their own approach to research, others though were clear that their own approach had intrinsic value in its own right. This quote exemplifies the former:

My research is just story-telling about objects – explaining why something is like it is. I take that not to be coincidental. Things are produced in a particular way at a particular moment. My research has been to uncover how some of those forces are related to each other. It's a very simple approach. I sometimes feel an amazing fraud.

Senior Researcher, Graphic Design

A variety of forces were at work in shaping this change, according to respondents. It was partly happening through the growth of PhDs in the creative disciplines. As indicated above, an important dimension of the specific character of research in art and design was the nature of the language through which research is conducted and presented. Several respondents alluded to the fact that the language of their work was predominantly visual and that learning about their discipline was essentially learning a visual language; one that expresses ideas and emotions as well as alluding to influ-ences and contexts beyond the immediate piece. One respondent explained that at undergraduate level students were striving to develop a visual means of expression.

The growing significance of the PhD was seen by some respondents as increasingly defining appropriate training for academic work in at least some of the areas of art and design where previously the indicators of esteem would have been more likely to professional or artistic recognition within the particular field. While 'alternative route' PhDs are available in many institutions, allowing an only-partly textual work to be submitted for examination, the dominant form was the long, written, thesis. Concerns about needing to demonstrate quality meant that there was a push in this direction in art and design. Some worried that the need to use verbal language about work that, in their view, came out of a process of research might somehow undermine the legitimacy and value of the visual statement.

As well as the growing perceived significance of the need for a PhD in departments of art and design, respondents also referred to the strong influence of the five-yearly Research Assessment Exercise (RAE) and of the policies of research funding councils in reshaping the traditional concept of research in their fields. Definitions of research for the 2008 RAE for art and design, it was agreed, were quite broad, incorporating exhibited work, publications, curation of exhibitions, performance, and so on as admissible submissions. Nonetheless, even the act of explicitly framing what was and was not defined as research appeared to have a constraining effect on some of the respondents. One said:

> We've adopted a research model that has been defined by other subjects and is now caught up with how we present work for the RAE return in terms of being able to say up front what your research question is and what the process is, and how you've explored it and the rigour of that investigation and testing and so on. That seems to me to be a model that doesn't fit happily with what many practitioners [in art and design] count as a research activity within their practice.
>
> Senior Academic, Graphic Design

The perceived influence of the RAE was not homogeneous across the set of respondents though. For a minority the increasing influence of the RAE and more formalised focus on research had served to support new work, giving it a legitimacy and, in many cases, additional resources that it would otherwise not have. One respondent referred to the way in which the funding for research which flowed from good performance in the successive RAEs had meant that artists were freer to be creative as they had been liberated from market demand which required them to produce certain types of artefacts. One fine art lecturer felt she could only produce excellent work if free to pursue her own line of enquiry and creativity:

> [My work is] intensely personal. I can't see the point in making work that doesn't have integrity – that isn't exploring – I can't make work that is done say for commission, or because it fits in a particular research project. It wouldn't be good work – it would be done for different reasons. It's a personal research as well.
>
> Junior Lecturer, Fine Art

Although not mentioned by respondents because the replacement for the Research Assessment Exercise, the Research Excellence Framework (REF), had not yet been instituted, the increasing need to measure the 'impact' of research is likely to push research in art and design in particular directions. One respondent noted:

> a conference is an organised activity where the proceedings are published or on a web site. But in a gallery you don't necessarily know who is going to see [the exhibition] and what their response is. It's not controlled and organised in the same way.
>
> Senior Academic, Graphic Design

Potentially, then, there will be pressure towards research practices that have more measureable outcomes. A series of workshops about 'impact' in the new exercise that involved both researchers and 'users' in the creative arts (PALATINE 2010: 2) concluded that:

> [T]here was ... a perception that the introduction of impact in the REF may encourage researchers to focus more on popular topics or applied research that could potentially achieve a 'quick impact'. The REF will need to avoid creating a disincentive for longer-term, basic and curiosity-driven research – which have more profound long-term impacts.

However, participants at that workshop thought that the emphasis on 'impact' may allow a broader recognition of all types of excellent research, some of which were seen as being discouraged by traditional, academically focused peer review processes. Again, then, there was no clear uni-directional influence of research assessment instruments and only time will tell what behavioural consequences will follow from the application of the REF methodology – the first exercise will conclude in 2014.

Institutional context was also important. As noted above, the interviews within the four selected disciplinary areas were conducted across all six of the constituent institutions of UAL and it was evident that institutional context was a powerful factor in how individuals viewed their disciplinary research, even where they were from the same or similar disciplinary backgrounds. The causality of this was less clear – it was evident that some individuals had actively selected a particular institution because of its perceived values. In other cases it appeared that the research approach was in part shaped by factors at play within the institution, such as institutional or school research strategies or funding council opportunities that might, for example, emphasise collaborative or cross-disciplinary work.

Also of considerable importance in the shaping of research approaches was the personal biography of the individual: professional background, long-held personal philosophy, idiosyncratic opportunities, family history and current responsibilities were particular dimensions of this that became apparent. Some respondents talked explicitly about their sense of discipline, frequently qualifying the definition of graphic designer, or art historian, for example, by reference to either creative or academic practices that brought them into a different disciplinary domain. The graphic artist might, for example, indicate influences from historical studies; the fashion designer might make reference to critical studies. So while the disciplinary context clearly provided a framework within which research practices and philosophies were located there was considerable variation within that framework. The overall picture presented was of a kind of Venn diagram of overlapping and interacting research approaches.

Explaining Academics' Responses to Changing Conceptions of Research

Angela Brew has usefully set out four types of orientation to research that she draws from research on both new and senior academics. She calls these respectively the domino, trading, layer and journey orientations. They have the following characteristics:

Domino orientation: 'Research is viewed as a series (often a list) of separate tasks, events, things, activities, problems, techniques, experiments, issues, ideas or questions, each of which is presented as distinct' (Brew 2001: 276). The domino metaphor describes the ways in which these separate tasks can be configured in a variety of patterns. The domino effect (sequential tumbling) also applies – other problems may be solved after one has been cracked.

Trading orientation: In the foreground here are 'products of research: publications, grants, and social networks. These are created and then exchanged in a social situation for money, prestige or simply recognition' (ibid: 277).

Layer orientation: 'It is helpful to think of this variation as describing two or more layers. Data, previous theories or ideas are initially in the foreground. There is an internal orientation, where the researcher is bringing to light the ideas, explanations and truths lying in the background by illuminating or uncovering the underlying layer. The researcher is absent from the focus of awareness' (ibid: 278).

Journey orientation: 'Encounters with the data are viewed holistically as transforming theoretical and experiential understandings of the issues which are the focus of interest. The researcher grows or is transformed by this. The content or topic of the investigation is less important than the issues or underlying questions posed, or the ways in which they dovetail with the researcher's life or career. The researcher is central to the focus of awareness' (ibid: 279).

Table 6.1 (overleaf) summarises this account.

We offered this table to our respondents and asked them where they felt their own approach lay. While most felt that different conceptions came into play at

Table 6.1 Conceptions of research (Adapted from Brew 2001: 280)

Conception	Characteristics	Processes
Domino conception	Sets (lists) of atomistic things: techniques, problems, etc. These separate elements are viewed as linking together in a linear fashion.	A process of synthesising separate elements so that problems are solved, questions answered or opened up.
Layer conception	Data containing ideas together with (linked to) hidden meanings.	The process of discovering, uncovering or creating underlying meanings.
Trading conception	Products, endpoints, publications, grants and social networks. These are linked together in relationships of personal recognition and reward.	A kind of social marketplace where the exchange of products takes place.
Journey conception	The personal existential issues and dilemmas. They are linked through an awareness of the career of the researcher and viewed as having been explored for a long time.	A personal journey of discovery, possibly leading to transformation.

different moments, the two most congruent conceptions with their own were *layer* and *journey*, with respondents most likely to describe their own research in these terms. However, there was a resigned recognition that the trading conception was the one increasingly required in an academic research context as opposed to creative practice outside the academy.

Their response to these different understandings of research can be understood as conditioned by ideological viewpoints that they articulate. *Educational* ideologies primarily revolve around three axes: the *aim* of higher education – Newmanite or vocational; the important content – discipline-based propositional knowledge or general transferable skills; and the important functions taking place within it – research or teaching. At their most fundamental level, then, they answer the three essential questions about education: 'What exactly should we do?' 'Why should we do this?' and 'How should we do it?' The literature in this area usually identifies four distinct educational ideologies, which can be referred to, in shorthand, as traditionalism, progressivism, enterprise and social reconstructionism. Traditionalism focuses on transmission of the content of the discipline and induction of students into it. Progressivism focuses on the development of thinking and other skills in the student, on their capabilities. Enterprise sees higher education as concerning the world of work and the preparation of students for that. Social reconstructionism foregrounds the critical evaluation of the status quo and the capacity of research and teaching students to effect change.

Table 6.2 Conceptions of research as ideological

Ideological perspective	Research process/Approach/Type	Criteria of value in research	Key ideas
Traditionalism	Disciplinary focus, empirically-based, peer review, clear boundaries between research and other activities (eg scholarship). Often positivist	'RAE-able' Of 'tradeable' value among the community of scholars (Brew 2001) Development of propositional knowledge ('knowing that': Ryle 1949)	Development of robust new knowledge Propagation to a wider community Agglomeration of knowledge towards 'capturing' truth
Progressivism	Can include the above also likely to use interpretive inquiry, critical thinking. There may be fuzzy boundaries between research and other activities	Development of the mind 'Journey' conception of research (Brew 2001) Development not only of 'knowing that' or 'knowing how' (Ryle 1949) but of 'knowing' itself: new ways of seeing, new concepts and theories, ways of thinking.	Conceptual and personal development Personal enlightenment Illumination of a field of enquiry or practice
Social Reconstructionism	Critique, making questions not taking them. Thinking differently, challenging. Clear boundaries between research and other activities	Power for social change Development not primarily of 'knowing that' or 'knowing how' (Ryle 1949) but of 'knowing' itself for change: new, critical, ways of seeing, challenging concepts and theories, new discourses and tools for deconstruction	Deconstruction Challenging established practices and relations Critique
Enterprise	Integrative, Mode 2 knowledge, action research, research skills important, research and business very close, practice-based research. Fuzzy boundaries between research and other activities (eg professional practice)	Value to enterprise economy Development of 'knowing how' (Ryle 1949): performative knowledge	Value Global competition Knowledge economy Knowledge transfer

Table 6.2 sets out the implications of each of these as far as research is concerned.

Again, this account was offered to our respondents and they were asked where they felt their own position was most accurately described. What they said about that was compared with both what they said in the interviews generally and the discourse in which they articulated those statements. There was a clear correspondence between each of those forms of data across the interviews. There was also a clear congruence between the conception of research espoused (Table 6.1) and espoused ideological position (Table 6.2): a progressivist stance tended to evoke a journey or layer approach to research.

In terms of explicit statements, respondents predominantly articulated a 'progressivist' position, a finding replicated elsewhere in relation to teaching (Shreeve *et al.* 2010). Virtually all the respondents spoke about the purpose of their research being to offer insights and critical perspectives both to the research community, the informed lay person and to the wider context of society. There was reference to those aspects of traditionalism that emphasised the mastery of techniques, but there was a sense that this was only ever a means to support the progressivist approach. Similarly some respondents said that there was an element of social reconstructionism, but this might be a by-product of the critical approach in the progressivist ideology. There was quite strong resistance among some respondents to the notion that social reconstructionism should be an explicit element of their teaching approach even if it guided their own research and professional practice.

Implications for Conceptualising Disciplines and Research

As social practice theory would indicate, when academic staff develop orientations to research they do not do so *ab initio*. Rather they draw on knowledge resources that can be described as ideological, that is they deploy an already-present framework of values and beliefs about social arrangements and the distribution and ordering of resources (Hartley 1983). This framework provides a guide to and justification for practices in work contexts, including practices to do with research. The different backgrounds of staff are significant in conditioning their attitudes to research, and particularly in terms of the purposes of research and its relationship with, for example, 'users' such as relevant industries. This gets folded into an ideological orientation and a tendency to draw on particular ways of expressing purposes and priorities in research, conceptions of ideal research practices and attitudes to institutional context and national policies and pressures.

It is evident, however, that conceptions of research within the creative disciplines have been changing substantially over the past few years, influenced to a considerable extent by the requirements of the RAE and the rise of both traditional and alternative format PhDs within creative subjects. These factors have brought about a situation where practitioner research that results in an art or performance work is required to have a written aspect, offering a critical, analytical account of the work for scrutiny and judgement. Together these two points – the significance of presage and the trajectory of pressures shaping research practices – potentially signify that some staff will increasingly feel marginalised in terms of their research practices while others will feel validated. This 'loss of plurality' (Churchman and King 2009) is neither monolithic nor complete, but in disciplines within art and design and related fields it represents a real threat for the future.

'Research' has a different set of resonances within the creative disciplines than it has elsewhere in the academy. Here research may well be intuitive, playful, experimental, unconscious, eclectic and sensory rather than verbal and goal-oriented in the way that, say, scientific research may be designed with clear research questions, literature review, methodology and reporting processes. For a scientist or even a social scientist what is described as 'research' in, say, fine art would be a completely inaccurate description of what was going on. For the wider public too the word 'research' has a wider set of associations, rooted in positivist methodology, that sit awkwardly with descriptions of some of the research that goes on in art and design disciplines. One could say that the word 'research' has been captured by a particular set of practices that marginalises others. Discursively it is doing important work, and work that is at least potentially damaging to those alternative sets of research practices.

For those who wish to challenge the pressures towards imposing one orientation towards research a possible implication of this is that alternative discursive repertoires should be deployed to make space for the full range of what 'research can be'.

7

Research Strategies
'Capital' and the Goods of Social Science Research

NICOLA SPURLING

There is a tension in the working lives of academics which lies at the intersection of personal commitments, everyday practices and departmental strategy and culture. That is to say, in navigating their way through their everyday work, there is both alignment and discrepancy between what individual academics are committed to, what they actually do, and the priorities of the departments in which they work. Henkel (2000) characterises these tensions as a reflection of changing relationships of academic identities to disciplines and institutions in new higher education contexts. Deem *et al.* (2007) suggest that new managerialism has reshaped academic work by increasing levels of bureaucracy, placing a new emphasis on finance in decision-making and decreasing discretion and trust in everyday academic work. Strathern (2000) and Shore and Wright (1999) argue that audit mechanisms such as those of the Quality Assurance Agency and the Research Assessment Exercise (RAE) have profoundly changed the work and lives of academics, as individuals internalise the norms of audit and regulate their own activities in new ways. Although these studies reveal important dynamics of academic work, and provide useful accounts of why tensions and struggles between individuals and institutions exist, we are still left wondering exactly what it is that individuals and institutions are struggling for.

In this chapter I seek to answer this question. I draw on qualitative data from in-depth interviews with five academics in sociology departments at a large civic and a post-1992 university. The data are drawn from a larger study – which also informs this chapter – concerned with the reproduction and transformation of everyday practices in sociology departments and the processes of change revealed at the intersections of interviewees' daily activities, their careers, institutions and policy in different combinations. (For example, how does daily activity intersect with department and institution? How do individuals' careers intersect with changing policy contexts?) The related empirical work took place between October 2007 and June 2008, and was a comparative study of the everyday practices and career biographies of academics in sociology departments at four different kinds of university – large civic, small civic, post-1992 and ex-College of Advanced Technology.

Rather than supporting the idea that the discipline is the organising principle of academic life (Becher and Trowler 2001: 23), my comparative analysis illustrates how departmental strategy and culture, situated in institutions and the field of UK universities, have strong implications for what academics do. 'Sociology' – as the cumulative sum of these everyday activities – is a situated practice that takes different form in different places, as the tensions of personal commitments, everyday practices and departmental priorities are negotiated in everyday work.

This chapter specifically focuses on the post-1992 and the large civic university, and on data related to 'research work', as within my interviews these discussions above all others exemplified the alignments, tensions and struggles in question. I make comparisons between departmental research strategies, the meaning of research work for new lecturers, mid-career academics and professors at the two study sites, and the deliberations and decisions they encounter. I suggest that tensions in the relationship between individuals and institutions persist because both are variously concerned with accumulating capital (economic and symbolic capital, Bourdieu 1986) and with accessing valued practices and ways of life – in a broad sense with accessing the 'goods' (MacIntyre 1981) of research work.

More specifically, I show that sociology departments and their institutions are first and foremost concerned with accumulating the material resources – or economic capital – that they need to exist at all. An institution's position in the field means these financial resources are mediated into departmental and institutional strategies in different ways. In particular, those high up in the field can focus on research income as a key source of funding, those lower down cannot. This dispersal of economic capital across the field, mediated in departmental research strategies, affects the role array at the institutions (Archer 2000). That is to say, the availability and valuing of research practice per se affects what research is or can be, for a new lecturer, mid-career academic or professor.

Individual academics are concerned with accumulating capital too – they seek recognition and prestige, as well as requiring an income – money – to live. However, the deliberations they face in their everyday work cannot be reduced to these struggles. Academics also strive for access to valued practices and ways of life. They seek the intrinsic satisfactions that come from doing research, and are often driven by their commitment to reveal something new about the world. Focusing on capitals – as institutions often do – undermines this aspect of research work.

To begin, I compare the roles of 'Departmental Research Director' at the large civic and post-1992 universities.

The Direction of Research

Being Research Director at the Large Civic University

At the large civic university Professor A has accepted the role of 'Department Research Director' as a 30 per cent allocation in her workload and in return for a double sabbatical after three years. The role has been created centrally, as part of the institutional structure, to strategically steer research nationally and internationally. There are equivalent posts in each department across the university, with a formal reporting structure in which departmental directors form a faculty-level committee that reports to Senior Management Boards.

The role involves leading RAE preparation, coordinating the department's response to RAE framework developments, head-hunting new chairs and presenting the case for research investment within the department and faculty. At the time of interview a key aspect of the role was to establish, with the research directors from other departments, the thematic priorities of the faculty via an internal review. The professor explains:

> there [are] seven research themes, and we're reviewing whether we stay with them. What should we be thinking about longer term, in terms of developing the strengths we have and picking up on issues which are big bucks for the social sciences at the moment?

The review is an opportunity to 'identify existing strengths', to 'notice links' in research between different departments, to 'link strengths to future research income' and to formally 'bring on' newer members of staff, for example, by encouraging them to lead research bids in 'strong' areas.

So, within this department, the research director role is very closely linked to the development of research strategy, which is itself linked to research income. For example, one of the immediate effects of the review will be to put small pots of institutional money into initiatives that strengthen and develop the newly identified themes – for example, by holding cross-department seminars. The themes identified will inform future appointments, with the possibility of new chairs within the faculty, thus affecting the kinds of research expertise that is bought in. Further, the strategy has the explicit objective of securing future research funding, in particular by developing mechanisms that enable 'systematic' responses to Economic and Social Research Council (ESRC) funding calls.

The strategy has other aims too: there is a particular concern with accumulating material resources – economic capital – to ensure that research can continue to form a substantial proportion of the everyday work of the department. This accumulation requires individual academics to engage with multiple forms of research funding which all have different criteria and methods of allocation, and themes and purposes which are partly shaped by funders.

Accumulation of material resources is not only important for the ongoing funding of research. It also strengthens the research capital of the sociology department and institution – acting as a symbolic good that contributes to league table status and converts to further economic capital by adding to the reputation of the department, and the individuals that work there.

The university is also concerned with performing well in the RAE – this acts as a source of economic and symbolic capital at the same time – it brings in money and adds to the kudos of the department and institution, strengthening bids to external funders as well as affecting the institution's success more generally in terms of league table position. This adds complexity to the institutional and departmental strategy, as different things are important depending on which source of funding is prioritised. For example, with its key measure of publication, the RAE requires different provisions to be made for individuals in their everyday work. I expand this point further in a moment, first though, I want to compare the discussion of this Department Research Director to her equivalent at the post-1992 university.

Being Research Director at the Post-1992 University

At face value Professor B at the post-1992 institution has the same role as Professor A. However, our discussions reveal some big differences. In contrast to the institutionalised role at the large civic university, Professor B has taken the Research Director role upon himself: 'When I came there wasn't one [a research strategy]. So I created one'. As such he has developed a strategy and structure for research in sociology that is localised with no connections to broader institutional goals.

The aim of the strategy is to create a 'research culture' so that those who wish to research have a 'vehicle' to do so. He has a particular concern for new lecturers who might fail to undertake research due to the lack of emphasis on research in the department and thus damage their future career prospects. Rather than setting targets to apply for large funding bids, his aim is to encourage individuals to write; within sociology, publishing research is an achievable way for individuals to accumulate research capital. This department's lack of experience and 'track record' of externally funded projects makes it difficult to compete with other universities in this arena.

Here, individuals are positioned quite differently in terms of research, depending on the amount of 'research capital' they have prior to joining the department. Those academics who already have an established publications record and external networks can flourish. The professor is an example of this phenomenon; because he can confidently author papers without the support of immediate colleagues, and because he has a track record that means he receives invitations to participate in seminars and conferences elsewhere, he finds a way to weave his research into his everyday activities.

The new lecturers are positioned differently. With no established publications record or area of research, and little time to get something 'off the ground' they find themselves permanently deferring research work. In other words, those with higher research capital have reputations that outweigh the reputation of the department and institution. Those with low research capital can become 'type-cast' as teachers not researchers, whether this is their long-term intention or not.

Resuming my discussion of how institutions prioritise capitals and my question of what it is that institutions are struggling for, material resources once again take priority here. However, in this case, rather than coming from research funding, the department's main financial resources come from teaching sociology and related subjects. This explains why there is a lack of a centrally coordinated research strategy, even though individuals are encouraged to research in their own time and submit to the RAE if they wish. Research is viewed as 'nice to have', because of the kudos it gives the department and institution – it is recognised to an extent that having some form of research capital is important. However, the lack of money that it provides means that, from the institution's point of view, it is not worth a great deal of investment.

In the preceding discussion I have shown that material resources – or economic capital – are the primary – though not the only – concern for institutions across the field. Such resources exist as positional goods, that is, universities and departments focus their attentions on particular economic resources depending on their position in the field. The large civic university, which has existing accumulations of economic and research capital, focuses its attention on more of the same, institutionalising and investing in the development of research strategy. Those institutions without such accumulations focus their attentions on other areas. In the next section I describe and discuss the role array at the two universities to consider the implications of these mediations of capital at department level for the research practices of sociologists at the two study sites.

The Role Array

The 'elasticity' of roles in sociology departments, and the place of research within these roles varies across the study sites. By this I mean that what it is to be a new lecturer, senior lecturer or professor in practice has different possibilities in different places. I found that at the large civic university there are lots of 'niches' that co-exist as legitimate formulations of the sociology academic role. At the post-1992 university this is not the case, and what it is to be a sociology academic in this department is relatively homogeneous.

Archer's concept of 'role array' (2000) is useful when considering this point. Archer suggests that individuals do not just passively 'take' roles but subjectively personify them, that is, they actively make them via human qualities of creativity and reflexivity (Archer 2000: 288). In this sense roles are 'elastic' – in practice their boundaries and requirements are flexible. Though Archer introduces the concept of role array to theorise the process by which 'agents' become 'social actors', here I draw upon the idea with a different purpose in mind. Given my discussion of institutional struggles for capital in the previous section, I want to consider how and why the role array, and seeming 'elasticity' of roles, varies across the study sites.

The Role Array at the Large Civic University

In addition to being Departmental Research Director, Professor A also directs a research centre. The professor is committed to her research area and very successful at securing research funding, resulting in high allocations of research time via buy-out. At the same time, she spends a large proportion of her research time writing funding bids. The department has come to expect her to draw in large amounts of external funding to contribute to strategic targets of income generation, and strengthen RAE submissions. She is also committed to her PhD students and contract researchers, and feels obligated to keep them in employment. Further, her involvement and status beyond the department in various European and policy networks means lots of research 'comes her way'. Not wishing to damage these relationships and the future funding they might bring, she is always keen to accept this work. This continuous stream of new projects limits the time she can spend on publishing academic articles or developing new areas of research. As such, she describes herself as being 'locked-in' to a pattern of work that makes her feel she is 'rewriting her PhD' over again – that her academic ideas are not developing.

That she can occupy her role as 'Professor' in this manner is because the department provides a niche for her. As shown earlier, the department has a broad research strategy that values both prospective (for example, ESRC) and retrospective (for example, RAE) funding. That this professor contributes more strongly to the former than the latter is not a problem – though it might be at other universities. She was submitted to the RAE with an unconventional publications record – one sole-authored chapter, an edited collection and two co-authored journal papers where she was not the lead author. She has also been promoted to professor 'even though' she has not authored a book.

I also interviewed another professor at this university (meet Professor C). His research career has focused on the development of academic ideas via funded projects from the ESRC. Like Professor A he also directs a research centre, though his is funded by the Research Council. This contrasts with the research centre of Professor A, which has been created within the university to house and develop projects around a theme. Whereas Professor A's research is oriented outwards towards funders, project partners and policymakers, this professor orientates his research towards developing and making new contributions to social science knowledge; his contributions to policy are secondary: 'We work for policymakers to some extent but it's not our main role.'

That a 'niche' exists for this professor is no surprise. In terms of strategy, he 'ticks all the boxes', drawing down high-status ESRC funding, creating research and PhD posts within the department, and producing a steady stream of academic publications highly ranked in terms of the RAE. Whereas Professor A experiences some tensions between her personal commitments, everyday practice and her 'niche' in the department, this professor shows little experience of such conflict. The capitals that he accumulates in his everyday work are very closely aligned with those identified in departmental strategy.

In addition to the 'niches' occupied by these professors, the senior lecturer I interviewed has a different understanding and practice of 'research work'. Rather than bidding for large amounts of research funding to 'buy out' time for empirical research, it is sole-authored books that comprise his research profile. He described a working week as one in which he spent two days on campus, undertaking teaching and administrative duties, with the rest of the time spent writing at home. This academic explains that he writes books partly because that has been his lifelong ambition; however, he also mentions there are institutional pressures which shape the publication deadlines of his work:

> The book I just published was written in a hurry because we were told to write stuff. I wanted to get promoted and I knew that to do that I needed to write a book. So I did, and I got promoted, but now I feel that I've sold my soul away … it became more and more instrumental as it went on.

Given the previous discussions, it is quite obvious that this academic's research makes no direct contribution to the economic capital of the department. Instead, he occupies a niche which directly contributes to the retrospective funding from the RAE and, as such, he can only be accommodated in the department as long as he publishes.

The senior lecturer then, has found an 'elasticity' in the role array which enables him to practice being an academic in the manner he desires – for now at least. It is likely that such a niche would be impossible in other institutions, as its existence depends on the economic resources of the department to support his research time – meaning others are teaching and undertaking departmental duties to support this writing post. Institutionally, this is justified at this university because of the strength that his publications add to RAE returns, though it is likely that such privilege might be the cause of discontent among colleagues.

To summarise, these qualitative accounts suggest that role arrays at the large civic university are broad and flexible; these three academics have occupied their roles in quite different ways, yet all are valued by the department. This is due to the multiple objectives of the department's research strategy which is concerned with both retrospective and prospective funding, and the strong position of the institution and department within the field, which means both economic and research capital are relatively high. Nevertheless, some tensions exist in alignments between personal commitments, practices of everyday work, and the department's research aims. Further, the dynamics of these tensions are likely to change as the new research strategy is developed.

For example, I have noted above that securing economic resources is a key aim. It is therefore likely that as research policy and funding change, institutional and departmental aims will be mediated to ensure the continued accumulation of economic capital. The direction of the current strategy, described earlier in the chapter, attempts to pre-empt the future direction of prospective funding at the same time as keeping a check on the criteria of the RAE. This suggests that whereas the niches of the two professors might be relatively secure, that of the senior lecturer might be placed in tension in the near future – for example, he might experience increasing pressure to bid for and secure external funding for his work.

The Role Array at the Post-1992 University

At the large civic university my interviewees develop departmental niches as they occupy their roles, but this is not the case at the post-1992 university. The professor's position – as a professor – means that he has a small reduction in other activities – eight hours teaching a week instead of 11 – to undertake research, but he must still engage in all the usual teaching-related and administrative duties, like everyone else in the department.

This requirement to engage in departmental activity places limitations on the potential shape his research can take. Rather than having the option of 'big funding' and 'buy-out' that is available at the large civic university, his research is arranged via consolidation of activities, and progressed – in terms of ideas, and in terms of his career – via sole-authored publication. Being tied to the everyday rhythms of the institution, and without the finances to employ research assistants, the empirical studies he can develop are small scale, and in fact he has developed a style of research not found in the large civic university – an ongoing ethnographic study, which runs alongside his academic enterprise work with local community organisations.

The semi-retired reader at the post-1992 university that I interviewed also engages in research. However, once again, it is peripheral to teaching and administrative duties, and mainly undertaken in addition to his contracted hours. Financial limitations mean he has adapted his research, from an initial interest in African society – in his PhD and the early stages of his career – to an interest in the city where the university is located. This makes empirical work much cheaper and pragmatically possible. For academics in sociology departments, such modifications of research area and design are possible, and in this case were a necessity.

These limitations on the flexibility of roles, and the subsequent impact on research work can be understood if we consider the position of research in this department and institution. Engaging in research work does not contribute to the institution's economic income in any direct sense, and while the research of these individuals might strengthen an RAE submission, the marginal research culture of the department means such a strengthening will still have little economic impact – that is, overall the submission would still receive a low grade that would probably remain unfunded. There is a realisation that research has the potential to raise the kudos of the university and the department, and in this sense it is viewed as 'nice to have', but a lack of material resources mean the niches which develop at the large civic university do not exist here. Academics are free to pursue their research interests, as long as it does not interfere with their everyday work.

Capitals and the Role Array

The discussion in the preceding sections suggests a relationship between the capitals an institution seeks to accumulate and the flexibility of the role array at the study sites. At the large civic university research income is a key source of economic capital. The department's research aims are broad, as the institution attempts to harness the different sources of money available. Such a strategy both requires and accommodates broad and flexible role arrays. This diversity of research work is not only valued for the economic capital it secures, but also for related accumulations of research capital that improve league table status, as well as 'feeding back' into economic income. However, the primary aim of bringing in money can be seen in the current revision of strategy that attempts to predict where future funding will be channelled.

At the post-1992 university the key source of economic capital is teaching activity. Here there is no institutional direction to the research strategy – rather, it is because of the commitment of a professor that a strategy exists at all. At this university, the small amount of support for research that exists is channelled towards academics with established research profiles – for example the slight reduction in teaching hours for the professor – however, the requirement to continue engaging in teaching and administrative duties remains. The flexibility of roles is more limited, and the main value of research within departmental goals is the kudos that might be gained from having some research taking place.

This not only leads to a difference in the elasticity of the role array, it also limits the kinds of social science research it is possible to engage in. So, for example, the professor and reader develop and engage with research methods and areas that can be investigated despite the institutional rhythms and commitments that dominate their lives. Although subject to these – mainly financial – limitations, in many ways their research is less vulnerable to changes in research policy and funding than at the large civic university. The 'niches' at the large civic university are likely to wax and wane as changes in funding criteria are mediated into the department's research strategy; those who find a way to research at the post-1992 university can continue to do so unaffected by such policy shifts and the related economic concerns of the institution.

The concept of capitals goes some way to explaining the research strategies and role arrays at the study sites, as well as throwing light on what it is that individuals and institutions are struggling for. However, if we draw solely on these concepts, many of my interviewees' deliberations and decisions simply do not make sense. Such deliberations and choices form the focus of the final section of this chapter, as I seek a more adequate understanding of the struggles of the individuals and institutions found in my empirical study.

The 'Goods' of Research Work

The nature of the struggles characteristic of academic life can be further illuminated by referring to MacIntyre's (1981) distinction between internal and external goods.[1] Though MacIntyre introduces this distinction in his critique of modernity, the concepts are useful here to offer further understanding of what it is that individuals are seeking when it comes to research work, and why this can be in tension with departmental and institutional aims.

Internal goods are those that are unique to a practice in which one participates, including both the products of the practice, as well as the 'goods' achieved by being a practice participant. For example the specific achievements and satisfactions of doing complex skilled work well, the development of specific technical skills that come from continued practice and refinement over long periods of time, or a particular way of life '… the painter's living out of a greater or lesser part of his or her life as a *painter*' (MacIntyre 1981: 190). Internal goods like these can be found in activities such as music and the arts, carpentry and other crafts, and academic study. As Sayer (2005: 112) notes, all these activities allow learning and the development of complex skills.

The same activities that offer internal goods may also provide external goods such as fame, approbation, prestige and money to participants. Whereas internal goods are unique to the practice – for example, the complex skills and knowledge required to play a musical instrument are quite different from those learned and used by a novelist – external goods are ubiquitous, especially money which can be obtained in infinite ways and once accumulated bears no trace of its raison d'être.

In MacIntyre's particular definition of practices, it is the practice's standards that define what are 'good' or 'bad' instances of internal goods and, since they can be achieved in no other manner, participation in the practice is essential to be able to produce the goods and to identify them. Further, those participating in the practice desire and seek the recognition of those who are 'experts' in the field (Sayer 2005: 114). This does not mean that all the participants of a practice are in agreement all of the time, as contestation and reflection upon standards may be intrinsic to the practice's vigour. This distinctive definition of practices and goods provides a useful alternative perspective with which to view the deliberations that accompany discussions of research work in my data.

Referring to the examples in this chapter, there is the case of Professor A at the large civic university, who had a large proportion of allocated research time, and had 'made it' to professor but expressed frustration at feeling 'locked in' to a particular pattern of work. She had achieved many of the 'external goods' of academic work, yet was still troubled and dissatisfied.

The senior lecturer was concerned that writing his latest book had become 'more and more instrumental' as he went along. He felt that the pressure to publish had undermined the contribution to knowledge he had wanted to make – an internal good. In the end he had to forgo his commitments so the book could be published and he could apply for promotion – an external good – leaving him feeling he had 'sold his soul'.

Another interviewee – this time a new lecturer – expressed similar sentiments in relation to his first authored book:

> I was struggling with it for quite a while, just thinking well what's the value of doing this, and I couldn't tell you how many people said to me 'yeah, just get it out, try and get it right in the second one'. I was thinking, what a strange sort of thing to say, you know? I was thinking, yeah but you're just adding to all this, aren't you?

Across the study sites, my data are rich in dilemmas like these. What these examples suggest is that rather than merely being concerned with accumulating research capital – in the form of external funding, journal articles and books – my interviewees are committed to 'goods' that are internal to the practice of social science research, such as developing knowledge and new ideas. These may be compatible with the accumulation of external goods – in the form of research capitals – or not.

Further, my interviewees have a desire to be recognised for the particular skills and excellences of their practice. As Sayer suggests:

> We are social beings and we need the recognition of others: the question is what the recognition is for, or, to put it provocatively, whether there is any problem with having unearned income and status unrelated to any genuine internal goods.
>
> Sayer 2005: 114

This is the exact deliberation that the senior and new lecturers are engaged in when they reflect on the books they have recently authored. There is no doubt that the publications are good for their CVs, in one case leading to promotion, but both are left feeling this has missed the point. What really mattered – and what has possibly been undermined – was the opportunity to fully develop the contribution to knowledge they hoped to make.

In addition to generating ideas, my interviewees acknowledge an intrinsic worth and enjoyment of research practice and its 'goods'. The academics in my study do not just seek to undertake research so they are freed from institutional rhythms – for example, via buy-out, or reduced teaching loads – though that probably comes into it for some. They also get inherent enjoyment from undertaking research, and believe that it has value in the world – that it is, or can do, good. For many academics, being committed to these 'goods' is synonymous with their commitment to being an academic, as this researcher explains:

> research isn't just reducible to the RAE, you know there is some value around research that involves contributing to discussions and engaging with important issues, doing work that you think is of value, or trying to do work that's of value, and I think that I always try to hold on to that, and try not to be driven by externalised pressures. Perhaps it comes down to doing what you think is good and important. Answering questions that you think are interesting.

Conclusion

My analysis suggests that, when it comes to research work, the 'practice of sociology' as the cumulative sum of individuals' everyday activities is highly situated, and so varies substantially across the field of UK universities: what 'research practice in sociology' actually means varies according to context. As such, my findings contrast with Becher and Trowler's (2001) observation that disciplinary cultures 'lend coherence and relative permanence to academics' social practices, values and attitudes across time and space' (2001: 23). Rather than coherence, I have found great variance between the everyday research practices of individuals in different sociology departments. Further I have shown that what is possible in research work is shaped by departmental and institutional research strategies that mediate economic and symbolic capitals and subsequent role arrays in different ways – depending on their position in the 'field' of universities.

Having highlighted this variance in practice, the realm where coherence might be identified is in relation to the 'goods' of research work. All the individuals in my study at some time had experienced dilemmas, or made decisions in their everyday work, which could not be understood in terms of capital accumulation. MacIntyre's concepts of internal goods provide a more useful interpretation of these aspects of the data, which illustrate that individual academics across the study sites are committed to generating ideas and revealing something new about the world, as well as finding inherent enjoyment and satisfaction in such projects. Whether such commitments to a research area should be interpreted as allegiance to the discipline is questionable. Few of my interviewees described themselves as 'sociologists' and such commitments might be viewed as characteristic of all academics.

Acknowledgement

My thanks to Elizabeth Shove, Andrew Sayer and Paul Trowler for their comments on earlier versions of this chapter.

Note

1   Chapter 5 in Sayer's (2005) *Moral Significance of Class* alerted me to the analytic power of drawing together these conceptual schemes.

8

Theorising Disciplines and Research Practices

PAUL TROWLER

These end-pieces to sections are designed to locate the section chapters within the theoretical frame we use in this book and to raise issues to which we return in the final chapter.

In Chapter 2 we said that social practice theory (SPT) offers richness ...

> in terms of offering illuminative concepts, explanatory power and insights into probable outcomes of behaviour. SPT also offers value as a 'sensitising theory' – it gives fresh perspectives on habitual practices: rich ways of conceptualising the world.

This short chapter considers what SPT has to offer in reflecting on the four substantive chapters in this section and what those chapters bring to SPT. In doing this I hope to substantiate that claim.

Identity Work

While much of the literature on the topic of disciplines focuses on individuals, a shift to looking at *practices* takes the focus off the individual and the work they do to construct or enact their discipline. Identity issues in relation to the discipline are very significant: academics may count themselves in or out of a discipline or field of study, or part of it, and at least implicitly draw boundaries between 'us' and 'them'. This sounds agentic and person-centred, yet identities – or subject positions – are made available to people by the practices in which they participate (Mouffe 1992) so subject positionings have a specificity which is contextually contingent because a particular assemblage of practices is situated in the local, in particular social conditions (Schatzki 1996: 8). While within that assemblage the politics of identity is the subject of negotiation (Lingard *et al.* 2007), it is important to see the operation of power in identity work. Stanley makes the point that power is differentially distributed in questions of what a discipline is, and should be, and what shape it should take (Stanley 2005: 1.1). Schatzki sums up this viewpoint:

A person is not a substance or inner kernel. ... individuality is a socially constructed and achieved status. Personhood is an *effect* of social practices, in that expressive bodies, life conditions, and ascriptions/comprehension of these conditions exist (for the most part) only within practices ... an individual's 'coherence' or lack thereof is staged entirely in the play of his or her life conditions and bodily states. As a result, identity, in the sense of continuity and self-identity, is a tendentious affair. There can be no presumption of unity in the play of conditions and states, and whatever coherences are sustained there go unanchored in an abiding, substantial self.

Schatzki 1996: 35

So, in sociology departments we find academics 'navigating' their way through their everyday work. These processes do not take place in a bubble however, and Spurling's chapter illuminates the significance of the policy and fiscal context as well as the historical trajectory that brought academics in sociology departments to where they currently are. This is not just in terms of the operation of sanctions and rewards but relates more closely to issues of meaning and understanding: sociology academics can and do internalise norms and understandings and then regulate their own practices. For Henkel (2005) academics are able to resist such pressures and the internalisation of meaning: her study of researchers in biological sciences shows that they have largely managed to maintain sets of values based in their disciplinary heritage against the pressures of changing policies and contexts. Other empirically based studies have reached similar conclusions (for example, Anderson 2008).

Situating 'Research'

Akerlind's useful review of the literature on academics' views of research (Akerlind 2008) suggests that authors examining this question all identify academics' views which can be located in one or more of four categories:

• Research intentions – who is affected by the research
• Research outcomes – the anticipated impact of the research
• Research questions – the nature of the object of study
• Research process – how research is undertaken.

The literature reviewed does not, however, address how academics come to take up one position rather than another along these axes. Moreover it predominantly adopts a methodological individualism, as does Akerlind herself in her empirical study in the same article. By contrast we argue that the very meaning of key ideas in academic life in general and research in particular becomes shaped and reshaped contextually. Trowler's chapter illustrates the different ways in which the meaning of 'research' is shaped as academics come to terms with, resist, or navigate a path between trends in university priorities, policy and fiscal contexts and their personal biographies and trajectories of identity. Elsewhere Fanghanel (2009) has used the concept of a 'filter' to describe how academics reshape and operationalise contextual factors through their own ideological and personal predispositions, and Trowler's analysis of the factors influencing predispositions in art and design is very similar. Arguably, though, both these positions still adopt a subject-centred approach, one that fails to properly situate the individual person within the assemblage of practices in which they operate.

Disciplines, like identity, come to be shaped by the configuration of sets of practices in particular locales. While they undoubtedly have an epistemological nature, they are also socially constructed in an active process of creation (Young 2008). In tackling the relationship between the real and the social, Baldwin (2010) talks about the *relationship* that students and academics have with knowledge: relationships with knowledge concern the way in which academic knowledge becomes meaningful to people in and through their practices. This rendering does not lose the significance of the epistemological ground (Muller 2007), but rather sees it as the material that is shaped and re-shaped in the context of practice.

Recurrent Practices and Structures

Post-structuralists and anti-positivists respond to the positivist celebration of identification of regularities in social life with the rejoinder that only the most mundane dimensions are so identified: the fact that people mostly stop at red traffic lights or wear the same sorts of clothes. However, there are patterned sets of significant practices that can be determined. Tight's careful study of co-citations across articles in journals of higher education research suggests to him:

> that, within the somewhat porous territory of higher education research, there are two major clusters or groups of researchers and research activity. These groups might equally be termed tribes or communities of practice. One of the groups has Clark as a key member, and might be, given his research interests, labelled organisation/structure: interest here is primarily directed to the national, system and international levels of operation. The second group has Ramsden as a key member, and might be labelled teaching/learning: interest here focuses on the course and institutional levels.
>
> Tight 2008: 603

How did these groups come to be? Meaning is not just constructed on the hoof, rather it is almost always received and subsequently re-constructed, because the meanings and associations have already been made when the object carrying them comes to us. This structural characteristic lends regularity to social life, even where meaning-reconstruction does occur. To give an example (from Aikenhead 2007) the question 'is it really science?' invokes pre-formed associations about what 'science' is. They are questionable and challengeable, but they already exist and they have important implications for practices. Similar issues about whether students using calculators constitutes them 'really' doing maths, or whether a new kind of pole means that pole vaulters are 'really' doing pole vaulting have been discussed in the now-classic literature on SPT (Wertsch *et al.* 1995).

Likewise it is possible to identify consistent, structural, disciplinary genres of writing within particular disciplines: writing practices are not invented *ab initio*. Reynolds (2010) illustrates this in her study of writing within anthropology, but there are many other examples in the literature on academic literacies. It is very significant, though, that there are multiple genres within each discipline, they are dynamic and, in some cases, they are contested by exponents of other genres within the same discipline. Again, these reservoirs of meaning lend regularity to social practice, and we can see these regularities in the four chapters of this section: regularities in debates about the very nature of academic law, art and design and sociology.

Metaphors and Disciplines

Manathunga and Brew follow a line of thinking which has tried to move away from metaphors that impose a fixed and singular model on a social world that is 'ineffable and imminent' (Fenwick and Edwards 2010: 16). Mol and Law (1994), for example, have also used the liquid metaphor of 'fluid spaces' to approach the complexity of the socio-material world, as has Bauman (2000) in his conceptualisation of 'liquid modernity', attempting to capture the 'liquefaction' of contemporary society.

Conclusion

SPT indicates that nomothetic and essentialist positions, which see disciplines as driving regularised practices right across the academic social field, are misconceived. Instead what we see is different practices in the 'same' discipline as it is articulated in different locations and by different individuals. This is because there are multiple structural factors which come into play differentially, and because of the agency of actors as they operate in different areas of professional life and so 'field' the different pressures upon their actions. 'Real' conditions have also changed: in postmodern conditions of complexity and turbulence, the old static, nomothetic models have lost much of their purchase on real conditions and challenges in higher education (Knight and Yorke 2004; Ylijoki 2000).

What these chapters show us is fluidity, narrativity, discursive differences and dynamic social processes within disciplines. This is in line with much of the other recent literature on research practices (for example, Brew 2008; Krause 2009a; Malcolm and Zukas 2009; Gordon and Whitchurch 2010). As Reckwitz indicates (2002: 258) a social practice perspective leads us to direct our interest towards how a *nexus* of practices – understood as body/knowledge/things-complexes – reconstruct how 'research' is produced in a particular locale. Within academic law, as Cownie shows, we certainly see this, as individuals and groups differentially operationalise ideological repertoires in research and teaching contexts.

3

Disciplinary Differences and Learning and Teaching Practices

Learning and Teaching in the Disciplines
Challenging Knowledge, Ubiquitous Change

VERONICA BAMBER

[Disciplines are] a normative structure, exerting a strong pull. [S/he] who leaves it for another will experience the opprobrium of the inmates. [S/he] will be left in no doubt that [s/he] has sold out. Even if the move was only temporary, to see the world from another viewpoint, [s/he] should not expect a warm welcome back since [his/her] ease in transcending frameworks will be troubling to those of a narrower faith. That ability to hold in view more than one framework at a time will be sensed as a form of contamination in and of the purity of the tribe's collective beliefs. The academic world allows critique, but, again, within limits.

Barnett 1994: 120

This section of the book is about the influence of discipline on the learning and teaching aspects of academic practice. Much of what has been written about learning and teaching and disciplines is predicated on Biglan's (1973), Kolb's (1984) and Becher's (1989) essentialist position regarding disciplines and epistemology. There is value in that position. But as indicated in Chapter 1, the epistemological take on disciplines is not the whole story. This section offers views from authors who are writing from within specific disciplinary bases, but who bring different ideas to the debate on disciplines. This introductory chapter will pick out key themes raised by these authors. The two major themes challenge Barnett's (1994) statement (above); rather than staying within some kind of inflexible disciplinary framework, academics seem to be constantly reworking disciplinary norms. The themes raised by the four contributing authors relate to what constitutes knowledge, and the changing nature of disciplines over time. The final chapter of this section will take another look at what the authors say, this time from the perspective of social practice theory.

What may surprise the reader is that the four authors did not all immediately delve into the pedagogical issues mentioned in Chapter 1, for example of 'signature pedagogy' (Shulman 2005b) or 'ways of thinking and practising' (McCune and Hounsell 2005) or threshold concepts (Meyer and Land 2003a). Pedagogy does figure in the chapters – Chris Winberg talks about the ways in which learning and teaching is conducted in engineering, and Ashwin *et al.*

consider learning and teaching in sociology. Ashwin *et al.* look at the relations between disciplinary knowledge practices and learning and teaching processes in first year students' experience of sociology, and suggest that Bernstein's (2000) notion of the pedagogic device provides a better tool than the tribes and territories metaphor for understanding that student experience. They suggest – and this book concurs with their view – that disciplinary knowledge forms are only part of the student experience jigsaw. Ashwin *et al.* reflect on what kinds of knowledge are produced, who has access to these different kinds of knowledge, and how different groups in society gain access to particular kinds of knowledge.

In contrast, in Laiho's chapter about nursing science, learning and teaching issues do not figure highly. Of most concern to her is the question of what makes a discipline what it is, and how its place in universities mutates over time in response to a number of influences. In the case of nursing, the argument even extends to whether the subject should be taught in higher education (HE): are nurses born or made? Is nursing a subject to be learned by scholarship or practice?

Kleiman's analysis of the performing arts subjects of dance, music and drama problematises the deceptively simple brush stroke of 'performing arts' and explains how the trajectories of these subjects in higher education over time have shaped both their place in higher education and the identities of the academics involved.

The remainder of this chapter will explore the key themes of what constitutes knowledge, and the changing nature of disciplines over time, which emerge from these four writers.

What Constitutes Knowledge

The question of what constitutes knowledge in the disciplines, and how that knowledge and conceptions of knowledge are expressed in pedagogy, is fairly well researched. In Chapter 1 we acknowledged Biglan's (1973) work on epistemological paradigms, and subsequent elaborations of Biglan's work; for example, Neumann *et al.* (2002) map Biglan's categories onto learning and teaching dimensions, but notes that there are exceptions to the Biglan configuration – such as disciplines that straddle both hard pure and soft pure categories – and disciplines which change categories over time. Lattuca and Stark (1995) also root their ideas in Biglan, finding 'unequivocal' patterns in knowledge conceptions and practices. Nelson Laird *et al.* (2008) found that deep approaches to learning were more common in Biglan's soft, pure fields than among students, for example, in engineering and physical sciences. In their large-scale study, Kember and Leung (2011) found significant differences in teaching ratings according to discipline. While there were common perceptions of what constitutes an effective learning and teaching environment, variations in how the different elements were brought into play in different subjects suggested epistemological influences; greater didacticism in the hard sciences is one example. So it would seem that epistemology matters. However, Kember and Leung (2011: 297) suggest that 'socially-constructed stories' might play as big a part as real disciplinary differences.

So, if we take Biglan's epistemological essentialism at one end of the spectrum, and a much more eclectic interpretation at the other, later writers could be placed at different points on that spectrum. Most of these writers treat epistemology as only one element in the mix: for Shulman (2005b), signature pedagogies, for instance, are the product not only of disciplinary characteristics, but also of complex sociological and political factors. Meyer and Land's (2003a) threshold concepts also acknowledge contextual factors, as do McCune and Hounsell's (2005) ways of thinking and practising in the disciplines. For a number of writers in recent decades, teachers' conceptions of learning and teaching are fundamental to their teaching approaches (for example, Trigwell and Prosser 1996; Trigwell *et al.*, 1999; Bruce and Gerber 1995; Dunkin and Precians 1992; Entwistle and Walker 2000; Gow and Kember 1993; Kember and Kwan 2000). Henkel (2000) also emphasises epistemological differences that lead to differing conceptions of learning and teaching, academic identities and career trajectories.

The question of what constitutes knowledge in the disciplines takes on different guises in each of the four chapters in this section. Chris Winberg's chapter considers the relationship between academic knowledge and professional knowledge. She indicates that when engineering faculty and students work with users of engineering knowledge, they have to develop new forms of knowledge and adapt existing practices. Winberg looks at the relationship of knowledge claims between and across fields, along epistemic and social axes. In the academic world, not surprisingly, the epistemic relation – for example, knowledge of mathematics or physics – is dominant, while in professional practice the social relation – for example, interpersonal communication, or the ability to mediate technical information for particular clients – comes to the fore.

In this different conceptualisation of knowledge between professional and academic contexts, there is also different attribution of value to learning and teaching activities; community engagement via student projects, for example, is seen by some academics to lack intellectual rigour, so the relationship between pedagogical practices and practices in the professional field is a site of dissent, as academics attempt to translate engineering problems into academic activity. The translation is never exact – translations never are – and, inevitably, the college project translates into a mini, probably mono-dimensional, version of a real engineering project. While the learning and teaching activity simulates professional practice as far as possible, the cracks in the simulation become apparent as the project work progresses. Simulacra are not the same as the real thing; practising engineering knowledge is not the same as engineering practice.

What constitutes knowledge in academia and in the professional field is part of a whole web of differences in practices, related to identities. Two manifestations of these differences are apparent in Winberg's chapter. The first concerns the identity of engineering academics, and the differences between them and engineers in the field. The second is reflected in the fragmented identities visible between engineering academics with different specialisations, and even between academics in the same area of engineering. In nursing, in contrast, the divide between the professional field and academe is usually smaller, since nursing educators are always also nursing practitioners. Identity gaps in Anne Laiho's chapter are more evident between nursing lecturers and other medically related academics, reminding us that the tribes concept does still have value.

In the performing arts, the pull towards generic skills and employability eats away at the development of subject-specific skills, leading to identity drift for those academics who are trying to respond to these external drivers. Paul Kleiman also speaks of student identities, which are being constructed and reconstructed in higher education generally, and which could be put under special strain in the performing arts as the place and value of the arts and humanities in higher education is questioned.

Ashwin et al. also ask fundamental questions about the nature of knowledge, how this links to discipline, and what the outcomes are for learning and teaching in sociology. They highlight three different forms of disciplinary knowledge: discipline-as-research, discipline-as-curriculum, and discipline-as-pedagogic-text. While epistemology certainly figures in the relationships between the three forms, other factors, such as local context and national position, exert a strong influence. For example, in Bernsteinian (2000) terms, some universities offer 'singulars' – single discipline forms of sociology – while others, often less elite institutions, offer 'regions' or combinations of disciplines. This influences the focus of what is taught, and how it is taught, with a greater focus on research in universities offering singulars, and on employability in those that offer regions. However, as with all good theory, the research conducted by Ashwin et al. both confirms and challenges Bernstein's ideas. Their findings underline the contingent nature of knowledge in higher education, since some of Bernstein's theoretical take does apply in their four institutions of study, but the understandings, practices and purposes of sociology learning and teaching in each institution are not easily categorised along theoretical lines. Ashwin et al. also point out the distinctions between knowledge, curriculum and pedagogic practices. There is a huge gap, for example, between what academics do in their work, and what first year students do, although in theory they are all working within the discipline of sociology. Again, other factors, such as personal identities, mediate what goes on in sociology learning and teaching.

The Changing Nature of Disciplines over Time

Another key theme in this section is that disciplines change over time, and these changes affect learning and teaching practices. The changes are of various types. For Fulton (1996: 159) an accelerating process of knowledge specialisation and fragmentation of academia leads to 'constant disciplinary fission'. For other writers, change comes less from knowledge practices and structures, and more from external influences (for example, Barnett 1994).

Anne Laiho's chapter explains how the historical background and current university context of nursing science have influenced the identity of the discipline. Nursing is subject not only to change forces from within the discipline, but also to national science and professional policy, and institutional strategies regarding subject groupings. Nursing science has changed on a number of dimensions: chronologically, geographically, in terms of where different nursing specialisms are taught and in relation to practices, for example in the presence or not of research. In addition the agents of the discipline have diversified to include professors in some places, for example, as well as in terms of the extent of links to other subject disciplines and whether the discipline has an international, national or local profile. Academics may be cosmopolitans or locals (Gouldner 1957; Becher 1987b; Fulton 1996), operating within 'an asymmetrical and incommensurate framework of influences' (Henkel 2002: 138) and with an ensuing focus on either teaching or research. In nursing science, the trajectory of the discipline over time has led to greater emphasis on research and on legitimising nursing as an academic subject. All of the changes that have taken place in nursing science raise an interesting question: at which stage along the continuum of its development does a discipline cease to be what it was and become something quite different? Over time, nursing has splintered, realigned itself with other subjects, found itself located in different universities and in different departments, and gone from being a teaching-only subject to a teaching-and-research subject. What is not clear is whether the status of the discipline has changed, and Laiho asks the question of whether this is related to the subject being seen as 'a science of nice girls'. Another interpretation is that, rather than gender, the status of nursing comes from its vocational rather than academic association, and from its relative youth as an academic subject. Nonetheless, Laiho convinces us that nursing does still have its own strong identity, partly emanating from the clinical nature of research.

Paul Kleiman gives us the example of dance, which has matured as a discipline in terms of research and academic robustness, and which now enjoys more acceptance of the diversity of what the discipline covers. But, like nursing, dance suffers from its relative youth as an academic discipline and from possible (inter)dependencies with other subjects. In times of change, disciplines with shallow roots may be more susceptible than long-standing ones. Boundary crossing between subjects takes vulnerable new shoots into contested territories.

This is less of an issue in settings where the ethos has been steady, but change is described by one of Kleiman's respondents as 'scary'.

Engineering, nursing and performing arts can all be seen through the lens of where they sit in relation to other disciplines – they are subjects at intersections. Nursing sits at the intersection of the academic and professional worlds, and nurse educators have at least one foot in both camps. Laiho tells us that nursing science also straddles a number of other boundaries: it is multidisciplinary, multiprofessional, methodologically diverse, and diverse in its range of research topics. This boundary position is sufficient to ensure that the discipline will continue to evolve in response to pressures from all sides.

Similarly, in performing arts, Kleiman notes the 'dual identity' of performing arts academics, working in both academic and practice-based disciplines. Kleiman notes the 'broad spectrum' of themes, subjects and methodological approaches now covered in the discipline of drama/theatre studies, and in dance; each of these 'disciplines' is a splintered combination of academic identities, discourses and practices. Drama is a 'hybrid' discipline, whose discourses and practices draw on many other influences, leading to 'multiple, metamorphosing identities'. However, 'de-centering' – the extent to which a discipline becomes detached from its core discourses and practices – is more extreme in drama than in music or dance. Yet again we see the impossibility of generalising across 'disciplinary tribes'.

A recurrent theme within this issue of change over time is the legitimacy of disciplines as subjects within higher education. For Kleiman and Laiho the question has been whether these subjects are appropriate for undergraduate – not to mention postgraduate – study. There are tensions between training and education, often expressed in strains between academic norms and discourses, and professional practice. The process of moving from vocational qualification to what Kleiman calls 'bona fide academic subjects' is not a straightforward one. The intellectual hierarchy of academe may recognise the legitimacy of some parts of the discipline group – for example, music – but not the more 'arriviste' subjects.

Conclusions

This chapter has sought to depict two key themes that echo through the next four chapters. The disciplines of nursing, sociology, performing arts and engineering might seem a fairly wide spectrum of the subjects taught in universities, and yet the issues they raise have much in common. We see academics struggling in different subject areas with the intersections of academic and professional work; with the status of their discipline; and with the nature of the discipline in different institutions and departments. The question of what constitutes knowledge in higher education is also up for discussion. Each of the chapters describes fluid situations, demanding adaptability from all involved: no ivory towers around here.

In reading the next four chapters, you may want to consider how useful the 'tribes and territories' metaphor is for capturing these dynamics. This is especially the case when considering learning and teaching, since Becher and Trowler paid little attention to this aspect of academic activity. I have argued in this introductory chapter to the section that the tribes frame is restrictive, and that we will be better able to understand what is really going on in learning and teaching if we step out of that frame.

Seeing learning and teaching as a disciplinary transaction between a teacher and students doesn't bear any relationship to the challenges of today's higher education environment. Working within 'epistemological complexity' (Baxter Magolda 2008: 17) is challenging, and certainly to be coveted, but the other factors mentioned in this chapter – socio-cultural mixes, crossing disciplinary and professional divides, ubiquitously changing environments, policy initiatives, institutional and departmental differences – turn that complexity into something even bigger.

Trowler and Cooper's (2002) notion of teaching and learning regimes (TLRs) is useful, since it describes individuals in interaction, who both construct and enact culture. Trowler and Cooper acknowledge the power of implicit epistemologies, but add a strong sociological dimension, related to communities of practice, departmental and institutional context, and power relations. Barnett (1994) also pulls away from disciplinary explanations for academic differences, although for him the driving force comes from policy initiatives such as enterprise, competence, modular programmes, and credit accumulation, which are 'eroding disciplines as the dominant subculture of the curriculum' (Barnett 1994: 136). Becher and Trowler's (2001) update of the tribes and territories concept placed more emphasis on social context than Becher's original (1989) work had done, and this book goes further: epistemology is important, but the chapters in this section will demonstrate that disciplinary knowledge systems are fluid, dynamic and constantly nudged by non-disciplinary policies, initiatives, contexts and higher education trajectories.

This, again, puts a question mark over the value of the 'tribes' metaphor, and its usefulness for helping us understand what is going on in university learning and teaching situations. If not 'tribes and territories', which metaphor might we use – shifting sands? sliding doors? Catherine Manathunga and Angela Brew's 'oceans of knowledge' in Chapter 4? Paul Kleiman's notion of 'splintering' or 'trajectories'? Whichever metaphor you prefer, I think you will find that we have moved beyond Becher and Trowler's useful 2001 concept. Fanghanel (2009: 565) offers other useful metaphors: discipline is only one of the filters that affect pedagogical constructs – that is, the ways in which academics conceptualise and approach their learning and teaching, and how they position themselves towards the learning and teaching context. The reality is that ideologies overlap and a lecturer's ideology may contain 'several competing *stances*' (Fanghanel 2009: 574). In fact, the disciplinary dimension could be '*back-staged*' (ibid.), especially if contextual factors require teachers to be pragmatic. Fanghanel urges a nuanced view of disciplines, since context and personal ideology affect practices.

Perhaps the question of which metaphor might be most evocative of the realities of academic life, and learning and teaching practices on the ground, is Paul Kleiman's reference to 'the DNA of the discipline' in performing arts; crucially, while that DNA is made up of hereditary material, Kleiman feels it is also characterised by shifting identities and permeable boundaries. The four chapters that follow will demonstrate that, as well as having that hereditary core, academic disciplines, identities and practices do, indeed, shift and mutate. An individual's own characteristics, as well as many other contextual factors, work with the DNA of the discipline to constantly reshape what goes on in academic work.

10

The Evolving Landscape of Nursing Science in the 21st Century

The Finnish Case

ANNE LAIHO

Introduction

In this chapter I present some perspectives on Finnish nursing science (NS). There are a number of issues concerning nursing as a university education and as a discipline. My enquiry into the nature of the linkages between the academic culture of NS and disciplinary knowledge focuses on the following themes: how the historical background and current university context of NS explains the identity of the discipline; NS as a discipline with a professional orientation and female dominance; and theory–practice distinctions challenging NS. I conclude by discussing what it means to NS that it is working at the intersection of different influences. This chapter highlights, in particular, the changing nature of disciplinary cultures associated with vocational or professionally oriented higher education practice.

The national higher education system and the history of the discipline have given NS a different position and identity in Finland than, for example, in the UK. NS as an academic discipline is a relatively young field of research and education in Finnish universities. Teaching in NS was started at the end of the 1970s. Currently, five universities offer degree programmes in NS, as well as conducting research in the field. Academic education is the further education of healthcare professionals for administrative tasks – for example, chief nurse – for teaching nursing, for researching and for clinical nursing expertise.

By contrast, initial nursing education is carried out in the polytechnics,[1] where nursing education was transferred from post-basic secondary institutions after higher education reforms in the 1990s (Laiho 2005). The introduction of the binary system was almost the opposite of the reforms generally carried out in other countries at that time (Rinne 2004). Finnish registered nurses are trained separately from NS departments, unlike in many other western European countries (Nieminen 2008; Spitzer and Perrenoud 2006).

As the international evaluation group (Academy of Finland 2003a) states: 'Nursing is a large and essential profession, and a costly one, and its contribution to any 21st century healthcare system must be evidence-based.' Science is not the only source of evidence, but, arguably, it is the most powerful. So the key question is: what kind of science is nursing science?

Nursing Science in Finland – Historical Background

While the institutional history of NS and nurses' academic education began in 1979, NS as an intellectual tradition originates in the first decades of the twentieth century when nurses began to promote nursing and education in the field (Laiho 2005, 2010; Tuomi 1997).

The professorship closely connected to NS – the professorship in Nursing and Health Care Management Science (nowadays Health Management) – was started at the University of Kuopio in 1979. The professorship has had great importance for developing health management science as well as NS. The first three proper chairs in NS were established in the universities of Helsinki, Kuopio and Tampere in 1985. The development of university education was rapid and was then launched in Tampere (1981), Helsinki (1983), Oulu (1986), Turku (1986) and Åbo Akademi University (1987). Research education (PhDs) began in 1981. Since the 1990s, professors in nursing departments have also had subsidiary posts in university hospitals. The newer universities took a more positive stance on NS than the older ones, to widen their territories (see also Elzinga 1990), starting with Kuopio and Tampere. Kuopio is also the Finnish version of a 'health science university' (see Table 10.1).

The current profile and research areas of NS have been influenced by several disciplines, for example behavioural and social sciences as well as health management sScience. The first professorship in Health Management Science at the University of Kuopio is a breeding ground for NS and the first MA nursing administration degree programmes have directed research in nursing administration. Three of the first professors of NS received their academic merits in educational science. The close collaboration with educational science originated in the 1960s when the first cooperation agreements were concluded between Nursing Colleges and universities to educate nurse teachers (Laiho 2005). Finnish NS has had strong contacts with educational science, which in turn has directed research in nursing education.

Nursing Science in the Current University Context

NS departments are mostly administered in medical or other – for example, social science – faculties (Table 10.1). Most NS departments are small units representing a discipline that is not very well known, even in its own faculty (Academy of Finland 2003a; Laiho 2005). The current international trend is that NS and other health sciences are merged within a single academic unit in higher education. The structural development of the higher education system in Finland also emphasises bigger units, including NS, as at the University of

Table 10.1 Institutionalisation of nursing science in Finnish universities

University	Starting education MA degree	First professorships	First associate professorships[1]	First posts in hospital	Faculty	Number of professorships in nursing science in 2010
Kuopio	1979	1979,[2] 1985[3]	1981	1990	Social Sciences (1979–2009) Health Sciences (2010–)	4
Tampere	1981	1985	1983	1995	Medicine	3
Helsinki	1983	1985[4]			Medicine	–
Åbo Akademi/ Vaasa	1987	1986	1989	1996	Education (1987–1992) Social and Caring Sciences (1992–2009) Social Sciences (2010–)	2
Turku	1986	1986	1993	1991	Medicine	4
Oulu	1986	1986	1991	1994	Medicine	2
Jyväskylä	1984	1992[5]			Sport and Health Sciences	–

Source: Laiho 2005; Academy of Finland 2003a: 5

Notes

1 Associate professorships were changed to professorships in 1997.
2 Professorship in Nursing and Health Care Administration
3 Professorship in Nursing Science
4 Closed in 1998
5 Donation professorship. Closed in 1997

Oulu. The impact of such institutional changes on NS will certainly shape the future trajectory of NS.

At the beginning of the twenty-first century the academic and social context of NS is quite different from its expansion period in the 1980s and 1990s. As Becher and Trowler (2001) note, the changes in the higher education system mean a growth in the strength and number of forces acting on academic cultures, enhancing the externalist rather than internalist character of influence on the sciences. The changes in the university environment are interpreted and responded to differently in different disciplinary and organisational cultures (Slaughter and Leslie 1997; Ylijoki 2008).

During the past 15–20 years, neoliberal policy shifts and the doctrines of new public management have gained hegemony in Finland, as elsewhere (Koivula *et al.* 2009; Ylijoki 2008). Several re-constructions and reforms have been carried out in legislation, administration, budgeting and the steering mechanism of higher education (Jauhiainen *et al.* 2009). Compared with many Western countries, Finland's market orientation in higher education is still minimal, but clearly growing (Koivula *et al.* 2009).

Finnish science and research have developed rapidly in the twenty-first century, with a strong emphasis on international competitiveness. In 2002, the Academy of Finland launched an evaluation of NS by an international panel of experts, who looked at the strengths and weaknesses of NS, and its significance to Finnish society, as well as the extent of international activity and collaboration in the field (Academy of Finland 2003a). Research is essential to the discipline's identity, and nursing research has steadily increased. Research has followed in the footsteps of international developments, starting with professionalism and education, and then clinical research. In the 1990s, research was internationalised and started to focus on more comprehensive projects, with more international publications and international conferences (Laiho 2005). In Finland the volume of international publishing has increased significantly in all fields of science, and especially in medicine and health sciences (Ahonen *et al.* 2009).

The research goals of NS departments currently include the enhancement of health and quality of life, developing NS as an autonomous discipline, analysing and developing nursing theories and practical models for clinical practice and human health promotion, analysing and developing nursing education and nursing administration (University of Kuopio; University of Oulu; University of Tampere; University of Turku; University of Åbo Akademi).

The definition of NS in Finland has not been unambiguous and views on the essence of the discipline have varied among nursing academics (Academy of Finland 2003a; Laiho 2005; Tuomi 1997). Two scientific orientations are distinguishable: nursing science and caring science. The Department of Caring Science at the University of Åbo Akademi has a humanistically oriented caring science tradition and an ethos of reverence for human dignity (Academy of Finland 2003a; University of Åbo Akademi).

By the late 1990s, the staff in NS departments had taken doctoral degrees (227 between 2000 and 2009) or were taking their scientific postgraduate degree (Perälä and Ponkala 1999). Finnish nursing departments have a strong local and national infrastructure supporting the training of nurse researchers, and high productivity in terms of researcher training in relation to the relatively limited level of resource (University of Kuopio; University of Oulu; University of Tampere; University of Turku; University of Åbo Akademi). The productivity of NS as a field of research and education is high, given that nurse students are mostly women with families and are working in healthcare during their studies. They enter the scientific domain at a mature age because a professional degree is a prerequisite. These factors influence the development possibilities of the scientific domain.

All the evaluations of NS in Finland have highlighted how the discipline is one of the least-resourced areas of science, and that official positions in departments are focused on teaching posts – affecting the possibilities for conducting research (Academy of Finland 2009, 2003a, 2003b, 2000, 1997; Perälä and Ponkala 1999). As a result of these evaluations, the Research Council for Health of the Academy of Finland allocated 600,000 euros of special funding to nursing research in 2005, and an evaluation of the effectiveness of that funding was carried out in 2010 (Academy of Finland 2009).

NS has been criticised for the scarcity of clinical research. The growing demands on prioritisation and rationalisation of nursing, and the impact of medical technological development on the holistic nursing of patients and nursing practices, have received little research attention (see, for example, Kinnunen 1999). The international panel highlighted NS as 'a clinical science linked intimately to clinical practice' and underlined that there should be greater emphasis on NS being seen as a means to an end – the improvement of nursing – rather than as an end in itself (Academy of Finland 2003a).

Nursing academics themselves have expressed concern about the lack of clinical research. However, unanimity about what, in fact, constitutes clinical research does not exist, even among scholars (Laiho 2005). Tuomi (1997: 173–4) indeed criticises Leino-Kilpi and Suominen's (1997) research classification in which all patient-directed studies have been classified as clinical research, even though the source of information is often nursing staff.

The desire of nursing scientists to prove that their research is clinical can be explained by its importance to the discipline. Clinical research provides a distinctive identity to NS because it is nearest to the substance – nursing and the patient. Research on education, administration and management of healthcare does not provide an equivalent identity, because the issues can also be investigated in other domains of science, such as educational or administrative sciences. Highlighting clinical research is also a double-edged sword – it creates an identity as a professional science, the essential criterion of which is that the knowledge it produces can be put into practice. Clinically orientated research also maximises the opportunity for interested clinical colleagues to collaborate actively with nursing research being conducted in NS departments. Cooperation between academics and practitioners can bridge the theory–practice gap described by nursing scholars (see for example, Gallagher 2004). On the other hand, the danger is that research becomes separated from the needs of practitioners on the ground.

Nursing Science – a Professional Science of Women

While arguing for their 'own discipline', nurses have stressed the pragmatic nature of the discipline, offering a holistic view of the patient as a counterweight to differentiated medicine (Laiho 2005). The domination of nursing by the medical profession is highly significant (Davies 1995; Grindle and Dallat 2000). The fact that NS is usually placed under the Faculty of Medicine speaks of the physicians' desire to act as 'big brother' and to supervise the scientific efforts of the nurse profession. Placing NS in the Faculty of Medicine has strengthened its identity as a 'professional science' and close vicinity to medicine has also created a masculine model of science (Laiho 2005). The close faculty connection has not, however, meant cooperation in research and education with medicine (Academy of Finland 2003a). One reason for the low level of cooperation is probably the starting point of NS – a holistic ideology of nursing. Cooperation could have created plausibility problems in the establishment phase of NS.

NS is a professionally oriented field of science. In Finland, the official view has been that NS is a common science for nurses and neighbouring professionals alike. Professorships in NS have been held by nurses from the outset. This has made the development of the substance of NS problematic, because it has been considered to be the common knowledge base of nurses and other occupational groups, who have not necessarily experienced NS as a relevant field from a vocational/professional point of view (Laiho 2005). Physiotherapists have been most successful in Finland in pursuing a scientific domain of their own in terms of founding professorships. Even though the statute regulating degrees in NS has made it possible to study the field without a professional degree in healthcare, most universities have limited the selection of students by special regulations so that in practice the discipline has stayed only within the reach of healthcare professionals (Laiho 2005; SA 794/2004).

However, Nieminen (2008: 140) asks an important question: 'Can any science claim a monopoly as the science of a professional field?' Also Tuomi (1997: 190) reminds us that if interest is restricted only to the professional part of caring, the subjects of the discipline have already been limited. Kuuppelomäki and Tuomi (2005) indicated that NS should not be approached from the vantage point of one single professional group, but as one discipline among many others. The knowledge produced by NS can also be used by other professional groups, such as physicians, psychologists, etc. However, in Finland it is still widely thought that NS is a discipline that primarily benefits nurses (Kuuppelomäki and Tuomi 2005). Also the international panel (Academy of Finland 2003a) emphasised that NS needs to be articulated more clearly – in ways that are likely to be more meaningful to practitioners, consumers, research funders and the scientific community.

Female prevalence is characteristic of health sciences and especially of NS. In 2008, the share of female professors in health sciences was 62 per cent, although 84 per cent of students were women (Brunila 2009: 72–5). NS, as one of the health sciences, is women's science and a fully segregated study field if examined from the perspective of staff and students. In 2010, all 15 professors in NS were women and more than 90 per cent of students were females. Only 10 of the 227 nursing scientists who took doctoral degrees between 2000 and 2009 were males.

Establishing NS in Finland took place during the same decades as the second wave of the feminist movement and the institutionalisation of the principles of equality. Despite the predominance of women in NS and nursing, neither the feminist movement nor politics have had any great influence on nursing research in Finland. Nursing scientists have chosen the traditional model of doing science (Laiho 2005; Ryttyläinen 2003). Perhaps the suspicion with which the first nursing academics were met made them cautious of endangering the status of NS by close connections with the burgeoning tradition of women's studies, which was itself experiencing distrust.

Within the international NS community, the gender perspective has been a matter for debate for several decades, for example, in ethics and the philosophy of science. In Finnish research, gender has been put to use as an analytical instrument since the beginning of the twenty-first century (Lahtinen and Heikkinen 2003). Ryttyläinen (2003) urges nurse scientists to reflect upon and organise their own research fundamentals and provocatively calls NS 'a science of nice girls'. NS has the potential to influence women's social status, both as a producer and user of nursing and services (Lahtinen and Heikkinen 2003). The gender perspective brings out interesting questions about the identity of NS. How does the predominance of women in NS affect the framing of research questions and scientific approaches? Can female researchers understand men's health and illness? Is knowledge gendered in NS?

The Pull between Scholarship and Profession

NS and the academic education of nurses have had to fight for their position in universities, like other new sciences and fields of education. Research has highlighted the tensions facing NS, nurses and nursing due to academicisation (for example, Becher 1990; Grindle and Dallat 2000; Laiho 2005; Miers 2002). The necessity of higher education for nurses and the status of nursing as an academic discipline have been questioned, and nurse academics worry about nursing's lack of status within higher education. Nursing has traditionally been viewed as a non-academic domain in which it was believed that nurses are born, not made (Mackay 1990). NS has also met with doubts from the nursing profession, which is not unanimous in accepting that nursing should be in the university.

The theory–practice distinction is an expression of the issues and problems that arise in connection with the expectations of the professional fields toward 'their' sciences (Becher 1990). Nursing scholars talk about a theory–practice gap, which is firmly established in nursing research (for example, Corlett 2000; Cheek and Jones 2003; Gallagher 2004). The theory–practice gap can be defined as a mismatch between nursing as taught and nursing as practice or as the rejection of theoreticality (Gallagher 2004).

The debate on the need for nursing to have a scientific knowledge base seems to be alive in the twenty-first century. Finnish research reveals that there is resistance to NS and nursing research among nurses and students (for example, Kuuppelomäki and Tuomi 2006; Kilpiäinen 2003; Nieminen 2008; Laiho 2005; Laiho and Ruoholinna 2008).

The development of NS and its institutionalisation in universities has meant that NS is defined as the core of nursing education and as the basis for all nursing practice. NS has created new substances in nursing education curricula and students in polytechnics are being closely tied with NS (Laiho and Ruoholinna 2008). However, according to Kilpiäinen (2003), nursing students in polytechnics have experienced scientific activities as too abstract and divorced from the practical work of healthcare professionals. Occupational activities were more important for students themselves, but those activities were not clearly emphasised in the level of teaching (Kilpiäinen 2003).

Kuuppelomäki and Tuomi (2006) have studied what Finnish registered nurses think about nursing research and its relation with nursing practice. Attitudes to nursing research were generally quite positive. Nonetheless, 55 per cent felt that NS had remained distant and almost half of respondents said that research in the field is completely detached from the practice of nursing. Doing research is not regarded as an integral part of nursing practice. According to Kuupelomäki and Tuomi (2006), part of the explanation why NS is experienced as unfamiliar lies in the fact that nurse education in Finland is not yet organised on the university level but in the polytechnics.

When Nieminen (2008) analysed rhetorical discussions concerning NS on a Finnish internet discussion platform for healthcare professionals, she generated the science narrative, the wage-earner narrative, and the calling narrative. Some professionals in discussions identify with NS. They believe that the academicisation of nursing promotes the status of nursing and see NS as the source of professional development. In the wage-earner narrative, nursing is seen as craft-based professional work that does not require 'scientification'. The wage-earner nurse constructs him/herself as hardworking, non-reflective and non-academic. For the wage-earner nurse, polytechnic nursing education is not progress. The wage-earner nurse – often male nurses in Nieminen's research – do not reject science in general, only NS. From their perspective NS lacks practical contribution (Nieminen 2008).

Laiho and Ruoholinna (2008), who have studied healthcare professionals' and students' educational accounts, say NS was seen as 'humbug science' and theories and research results offered by it are considered unsuitable for nursing. This anti-academic discourse created one of the strongest tensions in the educational accounts they analysed. Anti-academic discourse is characterised by views that NS is a way to avoid 'bedside work', 'real nursing'. NS was also seen as a servant of administration and as an ideology that has to be supported by healthcare professionals (Laiho and Ruoholinna 2008).

Although academicisation holds a special promise for nurses, at the same time it presents a major challenge in the identity formation of the profession and the discipline. Academicisation is not just an educational phenomenon, but a multidimensional cultural phenomenon that challenges old myths and shared ways of knowing (Nieminen 2008: 127). The anti-academic attitude manifested in research downgrades the intellectual requirements of nursing and reveals conflicts between healthcare professionals' education based on NS and clinical practice (Mackay 1990). The anti-academic attitude can also be seen as defending the essence and ethos of nursing in the context of effectiveness and economic cuts, especially when nurses identify NS as a servant of administration (Laiho and Ruoholinna 2008).

A nurse scientist is always also a practitioner in the field of her/his background. This double position creates challenges for academic socialisation and identity work. On the one hand, the professional background keeps you close to practice and helps to ponder the relevance of the research from the practical viewpoint. On the other hand, the professional background socialises you strongly to the professional culture, in which case openness and innovativeness may suffer. Professional culture may also be transferred to be part of academic culture. For example, nursing scholars have seen the lack of critical discussion as an internal NS problem (Laiho 2005; Vuolanto 2004). One reason for the lack of critical discussion has been presented as the attitude – firmly established in nurses' professional culture – which emphasises the acceptance and understanding of people (Laiho 2005). This attitude also is reflected to some extent in NS within the academy.

Discussion: Nursing Science Working at the Intersection

The discipline and university as institution are the key communities in which academics have built their identities (Henkel 2005). Finnish NS can be characterised as at an intersection. NS is placed somewhere between different sciences and various scientific traditions. In addition, NS is defined as the common basis of healthcare professionals and it combines a scientific domain and profession as well as university and polytechnic education. On the one hand, the science is always characterised by having an international scientific community, on the other hand by challenges of the national context: the global versus the local. NS at an intersection creates many contradictory demands for nursing academics and the discipline.

Nonetheless, Finnish NS has established its place in the twenty-first-century university. NS is multidisciplinary, multiprofessional, theoretical and methodologically diverse, and covers a broad range of research topics. The history of NS is different in various countries and different institutional environments, with healthcare professionals who direct the development of the discipline in different ways. Carrying out initial nursing education in the polytechnics and placing NS departments in the universities has provided Finnish NS with an opportunity to concentrate on academic education and research, unlike in many other countries.

Finnish nursing academics live amid change – changes in higher education policy and science policy as well as university developments. What do these changes mean to academic practices – to research, teaching and service? Changes can be possibilities but also threats to the disciplines. The central technique of new public management – evaluation – emphasises NS as a clinical applied science that should be useful for healthcare practice. Is the trend shown by higher education and science policy relevant? Even though highlighting clinical research is important to the identity of NS, it can also be an obstacle for developing the still relatively young NS as an autonomous discipline. Higher education and science policies permeate science domains, often without paying attention to their special characteristics, history or essential nature. It is crucial for the future of NS how its self-understanding and own logic succeed in reacting to external demands. Also the structural development of Finnish universities can be a threat for NS as an independent science and thus to its special nature. The institutional context connects, integrates and coordinates disciplines and thus creates or sets limits, for example in interdisciplinary cooperation.

New higher education policy encourages universities to become more entrepreneurial, to seek funding from a diversity of sources. As Rinne and Koivula (2007) note, academics become intellectual workers who are forced to redirect the loyalty previously held towards their discipline to the source of funding. The differentiation of NS into an orientation toward 'caring' and one toward 'nursing' can become an obstacle, for example, when seeking research funding.

Evaluations have emphasised the improvement in the international visibility of research and the integration of NS into the international scientific community. Also globalisation creates new opportunities as well as dangers for disciplines (Becher and Trowler 2001). In different countries and cultures the research questions of NS can be quite different, due to the prevalent illnesses of the population, health policy, health services, education of healthcare profes-sionals and professional culture of the field. The relationship with the interna-tional scientific community is important, but in such a way that it is reflexive with Finnish practice.

Academic practice in NS is influenced by vocational culture. One can even claim that 'tribe' thinking is strong in NS because nursing academics have already dedicated themselves to the tribe – healthcare – in their vocational education. Academic socialisation and academic identity can become challenges to university teaching in this kind of situation. On the other hand, research has verified theory–practice distinctions in NS. Must nursing academics keep a distance from vocational practice, because applied and especially vocational applied knowledge has a lower status in academia than the more disciplinary traditions? The current relationship of NS to practitioners and to other poten-tial users of knowledge generates one of the central future challenges within the discipline – in research and teaching. The theory–practice distinction creates major tensions between nursing academics and the nurse profession. As Nieminen (2008: 140) asks: 'What happens if the contribution of an academic discipline is rejected or it is perceived to have little to offer to those who are supposed to embrace it?'

The current changes in universities can also mean a shift in balance. As Ylijoki notes in comparing Snow's classic thesis of a split between literary intel-lectuals and applied sciences, the power relations between the two cultures are changing: the former are losing their elite position in defining the core academic values and the latter are gaining a more dominant role (Ylijoki 2008: 77–8). The forms of service are an integral part of academic practice. The service to larger community – the social relevance of knowledge and the possibility of applying it – has become increasingly important. As an applied science, NS has excellent opportunities to produce knowledge that increases human well-being, dimin-ishes suffering, improves the quality of nursing and develops cost-effective care.

Notes

1   Nurses and their neighbouring professionals – public health nurses, midwives, paramedics, physiotherapists, medical laboratory technologists, radiographers, etc. – qualify through poly-technic education in Finland. Completing polytechnic health studies lasts from 3½ to 4½ years (210–270 ECTS credits).

11

The Pedagogic Device
Sociology, Knowledge Practices and Teaching–Learning Processes

PAUL ASHWIN, ANDREA ABBAS AND MONICA MCLEAN

Bernstein's (2000) notion of the pedagogic device provides an alternative to the 'academic tribes and territories' thesis (Becher 1989; Becher and Trowler 2001) for conceptualising the relations between disciplinary knowledge practices and teaching–learning processes in higher education (Ashwin 2009). Whereas the academic tribes and territories thesis emphasises the centrality of disciplinary knowledge practices in producing curricula and shaping the kinds of work that students produce for assessment, the pedagogic device suggests that these are just one set of the many factors that shape the students' experiences of studying at university. In this chapter, we use material from our ESRC-funded Pedagogic Quality and Inequality in University First Degrees Project[1] to present a case study of how disciplinary knowledge practices are turned into curricula, and how these curricula relate to the sociological knowledge that first year under-graduate students develop in four departments teaching sociology and related disciplines in UK universities.

The Pedagogic Quality and Inequality in University First Degrees Project

The Pedagogic Quality and Inequality in University First Degrees project is a three-year ESRC-funded research project, which focuses on ways of assessing the quality of teaching, learning and curricula in undergraduate sociology and allied subjects for students in four universities that are differently positioned in university league tables for sociology. *Selective* and *Prestige* can be seen as 'elite'[2] universities which have a strong focus on research, whereas *Community* and *Diversity* are non-elite universities that have a less strong research profile. For example, the departments in *Selective* and *Prestige* were in the top third of submissions in the 2008 Research Assessment Exercise, while *Community* and *Diversity* were either not submitted or were in the bottom third. Similarly, in an average of the 2010 *Guardian* and *Times* league tables for sociology, *Selective* and *Prestige* were in the top 25 per cent of institutions and *Community* and *Diversity* were in the bottom 25 per cent of institutions.

Sources of Data

In this chapter we draw on data relating to the first year student experience in our four departments, that we have generated from a variety of sources and analysed as part of our project. These include analyses of departmental websites, programme and module handbooks, analyses of videos of a first year seminar in each institution, interviews with 96 (24 per institution) students about their first year experience, and a focus-group discussion involving four lecturers, one from each institution, in which examples of first year student assessed work from each institution were compared and contrasted.

The Pedagogic Device

The pedagogic device is a way of conceptualising the process by which access to knowledge is stratified within society. It consists of three sets of rules which determine which kinds of knowledge are produced, who has access to these different kinds of knowledge, and the different ways in which different groups in society are given access to particular kinds of knowledge. Maton and Muller (2007: 19) summarise the pedagogic device as follows:

> the ordered regulation and distribution of a society's worthwhile store of knowledge, ordered by a specifiable set of *distribution rules*; the transformation of this store into a pedagogic discourse, a form amenable to pedagogic transmission, ordered by a specifiable set of *recontextualising rules*; and the further transformation of this pedagogic discourse into a set of evaluative criteria to be attained, ordered by a specifiable set of *evaluative rules* (emphasis in the original).

Thus, as Singh (2002) argues, the pedagogic device brings together the contexts in which knowledge is produced (distribution rules), made ready for transmission through the recontextualising of that knowledge into curriculum (recontextualising rules), and is reproduced through teaching–learning practices (evaluation rules). As higher education can involve all three of these contexts within the same departments, the pedagogic device seems particularly useful for understanding the relations between disciplinary knowledge practices and teaching–learning processes in higher education. This is because in separating the ways in which knowledge is produced, the ways this knowledge is transformed into curriculum, and the ways in which students' understanding of this knowledge is assessed, the pedagogic device highlights three different forms of disciplinary knowledge: discipline-as-research, discipline-as-curriculum, and discipline-as-pedagogic-text.

There are two further aspects of the pedagogic device that are worth emphasising. First, the three sets of rules are organised hierarchically, so that the distribution rules, by setting limits on what counts as knowledge, limit what can be turned into curriculum, and the curricula established by the recontextualising rules limit the kinds of pedagogic texts that can be produced according to the evaluation rules (Bernstein 1999, 2000). Second, it is important to recognise that the pedagogic device is an area of struggle over how academics' and students' ways of thinking will be structured through pedagogic discourse and whose interests will be served through this structuring (Bernstein 1990, 2000; Singh 2002; Maton and Muller 2007). Within this struggle disciplinary knowledge practices are one voice but there are others related to national and institutional discussions about teaching–learning processes that also seek to shape what counts as worthwhile knowledge, curriculum and pedagogic texts (for further discussion see Ashwin 2009). In this way, the pedagogic device suggests that the relationships between these three forms of discipline are complex and contingent because it emphasises how they involve the interweaving of local, national and global processes.

Bernstein (2000) argues that one of the most crucial factors that will shape the relations between knowledge, curriculum and assessment in a university is its position in the field of higher education. At the level of the distribution rules, he predicts that elite universities, such as *Selective* and *Prestige*, will use their international reputation to focus on research, whereas non-elite universities, such as *Community* and *Diversity*, will focus on recruiting students. At the level of the recontextualisation rules, the elite university will focus on 'singulars', single disciplines, such as sociology, whereas non-elite universities will recontextualise their disciplines as 'regions', combinations of disciplines, such as criminology and social policy, in order to create new packages of knowledge that are attractive to prospective students and employers. Finally, in relation to the evaluation rules, Bernstein predicts that curricula that are focused on singulars will lead to identities that are focused on the discipline whereas those based on regions will focus on the application of knowledge within the world of employment. For Bernstein (2000) this would suggest that there is inequality in the provision for the students in our four institutions, with students at *Selective* and *Prestige* given access to a 'pure' version of sociology which offers them a way of thinking beyond the current ways in which the world is constructed, whereas students at *Community* and *Diversity* will be given access to a sociology that is mainly focused on preparing them for employment and does not give them the resources to think beyond this.

These predictions are in stark contrast to the tribes and territories thesis which suggests that there will be a direct relation between these three aspects of sociological knowledge, as the knowledge structure and practices of the discipline will shape the curriculum and assessment. Thus while the tribes and territories thesis predicts that students will have access to the same kinds of knowledge, the pedagogic device suggests that there will be inequalities between what is offered at the elite and non-elite institutions. In this chapter we examine how sociological knowledge is transformed into curriculum and pedagogic practice in the first year of undergraduate degrees in sociology and related disciplines in four institutions. In doing so, we assess the extent to which the rival predictions of the tribes and territories thesis and the pedagogic device are supported or challenged by our case study.

A Case Study of the First Year of Undergraduate Sociology in Four Institutions

Distribution Rules

The distribution rules of the pedagogic device govern 'who may transmit what to whom, and under what conditions' (Bernstein 1990: 183). In relation to higher education, the distribution rules represent a site of struggle over *what* can legitimately be taught in universities, *who* may legitimately take on the role of a 'teacher' or 'learner' and the *conditions* under which teaching–learning processes take place.

For sociology degrees in the UK, struggles over the '*what*' of higher education are related to what counts as sociology in higher education. This has been charted in a number of histories of sociology in Britain (Bulmer 1985; Halsey 2004 ; Halsey and Runciman 2005). For example, Halsey (2004, 2005) identifies the battle between the qualitative interpretation of the *social* and the quantitative *science* of empirical fact finding that have come from sociology's origins in literature and science. Looking at the way that the research conducted is presented on the websites of our four departments, there is a clear difference in the number of approaches taken to sociological research in the departments in the elite and non-elite universities. In the elite universities, *Selective* and *Prestige*, there are at least four different study groups in each institution that vary both in the topics that they examine and the theoretical and methodological approaches that they take. In the departments in the non-elite institutions, *Community* and *Diversity*, there are fewer research groups and less variety in the theoretical and methodological approaches taken. These research groups are also smaller and more likely to be faculty-wide rather than based in a single department. Given their different positions in the 2008 Research Assessment Exercise, these differences are not surprising, but they do emphasise that there is a greater focus on researching sociology in the elite universities.

In relation to '*who* can teach *whom*', there are clear differences between who teaches and who can be a student in our four institutions. Based on analysis of the staff profiles in the departments, academics at the elite universities are more likely to hold doctorates. At *Prestige* and *Selective* virtually all of the academic staff hold doctorates, compared to around 60 per cent of academic staff for *Diversity* and *Community*. This may not tell the whole story, as there may be greater teaching by postgraduate students at the elite universities, but it does suggest that to be considered a fully established academic in the elite universities requires a professional training as a researcher. In relation to who can be taught, there are again differences with the equivalent of BBC at A level needed to gain entry to *Selective* and *Prestige*, and CCD required for *Community* and *Diversity*.

In terms of the *conditions* under which programmes are taught, while the size of the courses are similar, the staff:student ratios are lower at the elite universities – *Selective* and *Prestige* have around one staff member for 15 students – than the non-elite universities – *Community* and *Diversity* have around one staff member for 20 students. Again this cannot be assumed to actually result in smaller class sizes in the elite institutions, because it will depend on how much of an academic's time is actually spent on teaching. The differences in entry requirements mean that the non-elite universities have the more diverse student populations, with more first generation and working class students. *Diversity* has the most diverse student body with by far the largest proportion of students from minority ethnic backgrounds, and the highest proportions of students with disabilities and part-time students. In all cases the students are predominately female – ranging from 70–80 per cent of the students. *Prestige* has a much higher proportion of overseas students than the other three programmes.

So at the level of the distribution rules we can see clear differences between our four institutions. *Selective* and *Prestige* have more approaches to sociology taken in their academic research, have more academics who have completed a traditional research training, are more selective of students and have less diverse student bodies than *Diversity* and *Community*. We now turn to look at whether these differences are reflected in the production of curriculum and student texts, as predicted by Bernstein (2000).

Recontextualising Rules

For Bernstein (1990, 2000) recontextualising rules govern the transformation of legitimate knowledge into pedagogic discourse, that is to say the transformation of disciplinary knowledge practices into 'teachable' material. In this process Bernstein argues that the knowledge is removed from the principles of practice through which it was developed and transformed into a 'virtual practice' (Bernstein 1990:184). There are two elements to the recontextualisation of disciplinary knowledge practices: the extent to which disciplinary knowledge practices maintain their specialised voices, what Bernstein (1990, 2000) refers to as 'classification', and the processes by which these recontextualised voices are transformed into the messages of curriculum, which Bernstein (1990, 2000) refers to as 'framing'.

In relation to classification, Bernstein (2000) predicts that in the elite universities disciplinary knowledge will be recontextualised as singulars, such as sociology, whereas in the non-elite universities it will be recontextualised as regions such as criminology or social policy. At a broad level, this is not quite the case in our four institutions. The two elite institutions, *Selective* and *Prestige*, do focus on sociology as a singular, but so does *Diversity*. *Community* is the only one of our institutions that offers sociology only in the form of a region, and *Selective* offers a regional form of sociology as well as a singular form.

The framing element of recontextualisation focuses on the processes through which disciplinary knowledge practices are transformed into the higher education curriculum. For Bernstein (1990, 2000) decisions about the framing of curriculum – that is the selection, sequencing, pacing, criteria for assessment of learning, and the relations between academics and students within the curriculum – are not simply based on the logic of the disciplinary discourse. Rather framing is again an area of struggle over the way in which the discipline is recontextualised. We will look at two aspects of framing, the aspects of sociology that are selected as part of the first year curriculum and the student identities that are promoted within the curriculum documents.

Within our four institutions there are differences in the aspects of sociology that are selected as part of the first year curriculum, but again these are not simply along 'elite/non-elite' lines, as predicted by Bernstein. In this case it is *Prestige* that stands out, as it is the only institution in which first year students are introduced to the canon of 'classical sociology'. They start learning sociology with ten weeks' introduction to the 'founding fathers' of sociology (Durkheim, Weber and Marx) for which the textbook is an introduction to 'classical' sociology. The commentary in the module guide shows how week by week the classical, historical approach allows the lecturer to convey to the students the 'inescapability' (in handbook) in sociology of a variety of concepts and theories. At *Diversity*, *Community* and *Selective*, students are instead introduced to what could be called 'political' and 'critical' sociology. Political sociology is based on UK sociology's strong focus on the link between social critique and social reform (Halsey 2004; and Halsey and Runciman 2005). All three departments have modules that spend several weeks looking at inequalities and social justice. 'Critical sociology' is particularly strong in these three institutions. Each department has a one- (*Community*) or two-term (*Selective* and *Diversity*) module looking at issues of social identities and cultures. The emphasis is on the social practices of human individuals and humans grouped in many different ways.

In terms of the student identities promoted in the curriculum documents, in all four institutions students are constructed as moral, critical citizens. However there are differences in the identities promoted that are consistent with the differences in the aspects of sociology selected as part of the first year curriculum. In line with its focus on classical sociology, *Prestige* positions students as sociologists who are told that doing sociology is an 'intensely moral activity [because] our subject matter is human beings [and] we [...] serve to set a social agenda'. At *Diversity*, *Community* and *Selective*, in line with their focus on political and critical sociology, the aims of modules and the questions that frame seminars or assessments direct students to challenge and to consider and produce alternative ways of seeing social issues or problems. For example, *Community*'s core module about crime calls for 'critical engagement with dominant ideological depictions' and a 'challenge to commonsense explanations', while *Selective* exhorts students to think of nothing as 'self-evident' and to believe that anything can be explained and changed.

Overall, in relation to the recontextualisation rules, there are differences in the content of the degrees and the pedagogic identities that the curricula produce. However, these are not split straightforwardly down elite/non-elite lines. In one of the elite universities, the students are introduced to the classical canon of sociology, which is seen as a way for them to act upon the world. In the other, as with the non-elite universities, there is a tendency for sociology to be seen as a way of transforming the individual student by supporting a movement from accepting taken-for-granted, common sense perspectives about social issues and problems towards challenging them. So at the level of the recontextualising rules, we find some evidence for the hierarchical nature of the pedagogic device in the curricula at *Prestige*, *Diversity* and *Community* but also some evidence against it in the curriculum at *Selective*. We now turn to look at what happens at the level of the evaluation rules.

Evaluation Rules

The evaluation rules are focused on the transformation of pedagogic discourse into pedagogic practice. From Bernstein's (2000) perspective, the key to pedagogic practice is the continuous evaluation, or assessment, of whether students are creating the legitimate 'texts' demanded by the pedagogic discourse. By 'text' Bernstein is referring to forms of evidence that the aspect of curriculum has been acquired, which may not necessarily be a physical text. It is evaluation rules that govern the production of these texts (Bernstein 1990) and they regulate pedagogic practice because they define the standards that the students must reach in their studies. In our project we have access to pedagogic practices and texts in first year sociology through three data sets: our videos of first year seminars, our interviews with first year students and our focus group discussion of first year assignments.

While, unsurprisingly, the four seminars we videoed focused on different and distinct topics – researching sensitive topics (*Diversity*); documentary and secondary data analysis (*Community*); theorising and conceptualising the growth of cities (Nilesbrough); and Marxist theory (*Prestige*) – in terms of practices there were striking similarities. In each of the seminars our analysis suggests that students were being encouraged to integrate three primary types of knowledge: *sociological theories and concepts* which were discussed and alluded to; *empirical data* which may have been created by sociological knowledge – for example, research about the number of rape convictions, *Diversity* – or by other forms of social research – for example, maps of city populations, Nilesbrough – but were not theoretical or conceptual in and of themselves, at least at the point they are discussed in the seminar; and *illustrative examples* which were hypothetical scenarios or are taken from the daily lives of the participants in the seminar or people they know or have heard of. While the boundaries between these three types were not always clear, they are distinct enough that the videos could be coded using these distinctions. All three types of knowledge were present in all of the seminars and appeared to be important to teachers and students for the legitimate enactment of sociological knowledge. In the seminars, the tutors appeared to enact their competency in the integration of these types of knowledge: interpreting examples; presenting theoretical and conceptual knowledge; and integrating empirical data. They tried to encourage these integrative practices in their students, so that they would be able to: draw upon the multiple languages and perspectives of sociology, including those through which research methods are constituted; use these to understand and evaluate existing empirical data – sociological and other research; and apply both of these to understanding novel situations in their own research or daily lives in order to develop a 'sociological gaze' (Bernstein 2000: 164).

In relation to the texts that students produced in their interviews about the purposes of sociology, there was variation but this did not appear to be related to the students' institutions. In the interviews with students from each institution, we found evidence of four different ways in which students expressed the purpose of sociology in the first year of study. These were: to allow them to develop their opinions; to develop their understanding of other people; to understand the world; and finally to challenge and develop knowledge about the world.

In the first, sociology was seen as a way in which students could develop their opinions about issues by drawing on a greater range of sources on the topic:

> For me sociology is … to be open to other people's views and then making an opinion of my own after that, so just to get as much knowledge as I can.
>
> *Prestige* student

The second was similar, but the focus shifted so that it was less about developing the student's opinion and more about developing a better understanding of other people:

> I am interested in people I guess, knowing what is going on in people's minds. Studying different groups I guess.
>
> *Community* student

The third way of seeing sociology among the first year students, rather than focusing on understanding other people, was more focused on using sociology to develop an understanding of the world:

> I mean from the degree like hopefully I'll get an understanding of the way the world works and fill out my own arguments. ... I mean, I think it's really important to have a kind of really rounded and thought-out understanding of the world around you.
>
> *Selective* student

The fourth way of seeing sociology was a way of challenging and developing knowledge about the world:

> It has made me query things: 'no, that does not sound logical, that does not sound right'. I think more clearly than I have ever done before. It has changed me. I mean sociology sort of helps to uncover where there is inequality, where there is injustice and it also sometimes, I think, gives ways or possibilities or theories as to how these things could be improved.
>
> *Diversity* student

These four ways of understanding sociology seem to suggest different relations to sociological knowledge. In the first two, sociology is a tool for forming opinions or understanding other people but this knowledge does not seem to have an impact on the student. Whereas, in the third and fourth ways of seeing sociology there is a sense that studying sociology is changing the student and, in the fourth, the sense that this may help them to change the world. Given the differences at the level of the distribution and recontextualising rules, it is interesting that these different ways of seeing sociology were found in all of our four departments.

The similarities in the way that students talked about sociology were also reflected in our focus group data, in which the tutors suggested that assessed work produced by students from across the four institutions contained similar levels and styles of sociological explanation. While there were differences in the types of tasks that students were asked to undertake, the main sources of variation that were discussed, in a focus group between tutors who had commented upon this sample of work, the differences between first year students' and tutors' conceptions of what is meant by description, and disparities in the writing practices of first year sociology students and academics.

The first source of variation discussed was in what first year students and tutors understood by the term 'description'. This was nicely summed up by the tutor from *Selective*:

I was just thinking that because there is the different kind of description. One is just very kind of iterative and reliant on the source. Then there is the kind we want in which the description is quite summative. There is a real paradigm shift. When we say 'describe' we mean 'synthesise' not 'describe'.

Second, the tutors discussed how, for students, writing was, to use Bernstein's term, 'a virtual practice' (Bernstein 1990: 184). This involved writing everything at the last minute for the first time rather than drafting and redrafting an article like an academic does. This process was summarised by our key informant at *Prestige*:

> I think the whole assessment regime encourages doing something to a deadline. It is not about the process of rewriting. It is all about the final mark ... The reality is that they do write everything at the very last minute and that is in part I think why the structure is not very good. It is sort of full of errors but that is exactly what happens if you do something the night before ... And you do a kind of one off, pretty much off the top of your head. It probably does not do any justice to what they know or understand. It is clearly a different process.

In examining a number of texts produced by first year students and tutors using the evaluation rules, the similarity between those produced in each of our four institutions is striking. This suggests that the distribution and recontextualising rules may not be limiting the sociological knowledge that students can gain through their engagement in the first year of their degrees. One possibility is that the practices that we observed in our videos of first year seminars seemed to offer the students in all of our departments a variety of ways of engaging with sociological knowledge. Interestingly, the clearest gap in practices we found at the level of the evaluation rules, again across all of our institutions, seems to be in the gap between the writing practices of academics and the writing practices of students. This has interesting implications for the tribes and territories thesis that we will examine in our conclusion.

Conclusion

So what we have seen across the distribution, recontextualisation and evaluation rules is that while there are clear differences in the distribution rules for our elite and non-elite institutions, these differences becomes less pronounced when looking at the recontextualisation rules, with only one of the elite universities standing out as different; and the differences disappear altogether when we look at the evaluation rules.

There are three caveats that need to be addressed before examining the potential implications of this. First, our data cannot tell us whether the processes we have examined are particular to sociology or might also relate to other disciplines. Second, so far, we have only looked at the first year curriculum and student experience in our four institutions. While students in our four institutions produce remarkably similar texts over the course of their first year, this might change over the second and third years of their undergraduate degrees. We are currently generating and analysing data that will allow us to develop our understanding of what happens in the later years of their degrees. Third, even with our first year data, we are in the early stages of analysis and our analysis should be understood as tentative and provisional, and one that might change as we come to a greater understanding of our data set as a whole.

Our findings here raise questions about Bernstein's (2000) claim that the rules of the pedagogic device are hierarchical, as the distribution and recontextualising rules did not seem to set limits on what could be achieved under the evaluation rules. There are two aspects of this that are worth considering. First, if, as Bernstein (2000) argues, each set of rules is an area of conflict, then it is perhaps not surprising that the hierarchical nature of the pedagogic device may be called into question depending on the outcome of this conflict. Second, this emphasises the productive role that tutors and students can have in overcoming apparent inequalities in the distribution and recontextualising rules. This is something Bernstein (1990: 6) recognised when he emphasised that his work was focused on the systemic level but argued that 'the system does not create copper-etched plates'. Our case study here suggests the practices of students and tutors may act as a challenge to systemic differences, something that Abbas and McLean (2010) also found in relation to sociology lecturers' pedagogic identities.

As well as raising questions about the hierarchy of the rules that make up the pedagogic device, our case study also reinforces the importance of recognising the distinctions between knowledge, curriculum and pedagogic practices. Our findings highlight a huge gap between the practices of academics as researchers and the practices of first year students as learners of sociology, although this gap may decline over the three years of a degree. This reinforces the important message that discipline-as-research cannot be assumed to simply map onto discipline-as-curriculum and discipline-as-pedagogic-text. Overall, this suggests that while disciplinary knowledge practices and the rules of the pedagogic device are significant factors in the shaping of teaching–learning practices, they are not the only factors. Other factors, including the identities of students and tutors, appear to also play a significant role in informing the relations between disciplinary knowledge practices and teaching–learning processes in higher education.

Notes

1 This work was supported by the Economic and Social Research Council [Grant Number: RES-062-23-1438]. We would also like to acknowledge Ourania Filippakou's involvement in generating the data as part of the project team.
2 There are many different ways of characterising the differences between types of university (see Brennan *et al.* 2010 for a discussion). We use the binary of elite/non-elite because this is the characterisation that Bernstein (2000) uses when discussing the differences in curriculum types in higher education.

12

Scene Changes and Key Changes
Disciplines and Identities in HE Dance, Drama and Music

PAUL KLEIMAN

Disciplinarity ... deserves some serious rethinking.

Sperber 2003

Prologue

In *The Shock of the New*, his history of modern art, Robert Hughes (1991) dwells at length on the years either side of the beginning of the twentieth century and on the momentous impact of developments in fields such as science, technology and psychology that occurred at that time. In particular, he focuses on the impact those changes had on art and its production, and on the identities and practices of the artists involved. The classic, single-point perspective that had well served the cause of art since the Renaissance was now considered insufficient to capture the dynamism, speed and multiple perspectives of modern life. The great 'isms' of modern art, for example, cubism, expressionism, futurism, surrealism, developed as direct responses to those changes, and artists – out of necessity – found themselves creating works in different media and frequently collaborating on art projects. Their identities altered, as they became integral parts of a much larger, rapidly shifting 'artsworld'. The notion of the 'pure, dedicated' artist became the – rare – exception in much the same way, a century later and in relation to academics 'the idea of the ivory tower, still current in popular discourse, will today elicit a wry smile from almost every faculty member everywhere' (Becher and Trowler 2001).

Scene Changes and Key Changes

For most of the 20th century, it was plausible to think of academics as members of interconnected communities, notably disciplines and higher education institutions, which afforded them stable and legitimising identities.

Henkel 2005: 155

The disciplines of dance, drama and music[1] comprise what is usually referred to as the 'performing arts' disciplines. However, even that apparently straight-forward statement is somewhat problematic. As Sperber (2003) points out, the current disciplinary system may be becoming brittle, and the notion of clearly defined disciplines is an historical product that, in its present form, goes back to the nineteenth century and to the development of modern universities and research institutions.

The manner in which the disciplines of dance, drama and music have been and are categorised, and the histories of their development in higher educa-tion, are important factors in determining not only how those disciplines are perceived within higher education and beyond but also in determining the identities of the academic practitioners within those disciplines.

The recognition of the three disciplines as appropriate and relevant subjects for undergraduate and post-graduate study is a story that, in the cases of dance and drama, is spread over several decades and, in the case of music, several centuries. Music can trace its academic antecedents to the middle of the fifteenth century and the award of a B. Mus. to Henry Abyngdon at Cambridge in 1464. There is general agreement that the first 'modern' music degree in the UK was established in Edinburgh in 1891, by Professor Fredrick Niecks.

Though Elsie Fogerty, the founder of the Central School of Speech Drama, had been calling for it to be treated as a degree subject in 1906, drama finally separated from English literature and became an academic subject in its own right in 1947. This was due to the pioneering efforts of Glynne Wickham at the University of Bristol who almost single-handedly established drama as a new academic discipline. Most of the early drama departments, similarly, were of English literature descent, and it was a couple of decades later that the new universities of the 1960s and, much later, the post-1992 universities witnessed the development of departments of theatre studies or performing arts that were founded 'from scratch' rather than directly descended from English.

Nicholas (2007), tracing the development of dance in higher education, comments that the discipline had a difficult time in becoming established. Prior to the 1970s, dance had only held a foothold in British institutions of higher education through specialist teacher training courses leading to a Certificate in Education. It was first established as a degree course in combination with other arts subjects or as part of physical education.[2]

> This was the situation until 1976, when the first BA (Hons) in Dance opened at the Laban Centre for Movement and Dance, successor to the Art of Movement Studio. However, it was not until 1984 that the first univer-sity-based, single-honours dance studies BA (Hons) course opened, at the University of Surrey (having been preceded there by post-graduate level dance studies).
>
> Nicholas 2007: 189

Both drama and, particularly, dance, as relatively recent additions to the ever-growing catalogue of degree subjects, have sometimes struggled – within academia itself and also in popular media discourses – to obtain acceptance as bona fide academic subjects. Those struggles have had significant impacts on their developments as subject areas, their attendant discourses and practices, and the identities of their academic practitioners.

In any consideration of the three disciplines in the context of higher education, it is important to note that the dance, drama and music conservatoires – often, but not always, with the word 'Royal' in their title – now play a small but significant role in the trajectory of the development of those subjects in higher education. These institutions have long and distinguished histories as vocationally oriented training grounds for professional performers. While they still perform that primary function, many of the courses these institutions run are now properly validated undergraduate and post-graduate courses. The transition into higher education has, unsurprisingly, not been without its tensions, and there are continuing and often heated debates about how to maintain a 'high-end' vocational/professional training within the 'academic' discourses, practices and regulatory frameworks of higher education.

The manner in which dance, drama and music have been considered and categorised within the wider field of higher education policy also has had an impact on those disciplines. The Quality Assurance Agency (QAA), for example, has always considered dance and drama as the 'performing arts' while music is considered to be a single discipline in its own right. This reflects a prevailing sense of an 'intellectual hierarchy' that perceives music – particularly classical music – as a serious academic discipline in contrast to the somewhat arriviste disciplines of dance and drama. Until 2003, the Higher Education Statistics Agency recognised drama and music as separate categories, but considered dance to be a subset of drama. Thus, before 2003, it is extremely difficult to find separate statistics for dance in higher education in relation to such things as the growth in student numbers, or social class or ethnicity, etc.

In recent years, all three disciplines have experienced significant growth in regard to both the number of subjects that come within the aegis of the disciplines and the number of students studying those subjects (HESA 2010). Music has experienced the rapid development and growth of two 'new' subject areas: music technology[3] and popular music, and what Nightingale (2007: 1) describes as 'the flattening of musical hierarchies, whereby classical music is no longer considered more important than other musical forms'. Drama/theatre studies has seen the development and growth of the field known as performance studies or performance research, and dance has expanded to cover a range of subjects including anthropology, ethnography, documentation and reconstruction, and medicine.

Though the three disciplines are very different, each has been subject to the many shifts and changes that have occurred in UK higher education in recent years. These include:

- the significant impact of the four Research Assessment Exercises (RAE)[4] between 1992 and 2008, and the development of intensive, research-focused cultures in departments and institutions;
- the recent move away from the RAE to the Research Excellence Framework (REF);[5]
- the moves towards the professionalisation of teaching and the requirement, particularly of new teaching staff, to obtain an accredited teaching qualification;
- the requirement to produce standardised, prescriptive programme and module descriptions;
- the increasing requirement to develop and implement detailed, clear and transparent approaches to assessment;
- the emphasis on widening participation in relation to entry to higher education and – at the other end – the emphasis on employability and graduate skills on exiting higher education;
- the impact and use of new technologies.

Though the above apply to all disciplines within higher education, their impact on dance, drama and music – and particularly the first two of those – has been amplified by the nature of the cultures, discourses and practices of those disciplines. For example, in relation to the increased focus on research, there has always been a small but significant group of academics within those disciplines whose identity is defined by and within a research-intensive academic culture. However, for those whose pedagogic discourses and practices reflect a far more performance- and practice-based pedagogic culture, the pressure to undertake and publish 'serious' research has meant that they have had to adopt an academic identity that did not necessarily fit or sit easily with their primary practitioner-teacher identity.

Writing this chapter at the start of 2011, it is impossible to avoid at least mentioning what are likely to be momentous drivers of change not only in the performing arts disciplines, but in the whole of higher education itself. In October 2010, Lord Browne (Browne 2010) published his long-awaited report on the future funding of UK higher education. That was followed closely by the UK Government's announcement of the outcomes of its Comprehensive Spending Review (CSR).

Browne's proposals included:

- doubling and, in some cases, trebling student fees;
- a significant shift from public financing of higher education to private financing;

- a total withdrawal of the financial support for the teaching of arts, humanities and social sciences;
- a strong focus on the STEM subjects – science, technology, engineering and mathematics.

These, and other recommendations that were supported by the government, combined to create a mood of anguish and, in some cases despair, for the future of many arts, humanities and social sciences subjects. A professor of social and political philosophy wrote:

> Even those of us who do survive (and I'm not feeling complacent) are likely to find that the ecology of our subjects will change if students from working-class backgrounds are priced out of degree courses at the most expensive universities and the surviving, cheaper institutions no longer put the humanities on the menu.
>
> Bertram 2010

The likely consequences of the Browne Report and the CSR added to the growing sense that the tectonic plates of higher education were shifting dramatically. There was substantial additional pressure on a sector that had already responded to the shifts and changes already mentioned by taking the first steps toward developing into a 'three-tiered' system of higher education in which higher education institutions fitted into one of the following categories: teaching only, teaching mainly with some research, and research-led. This division occurred not only between institutions but also within institutions with the introduction, on the one hand, of teaching-only contracts and, on the other hand the increasing number of appointments of 'research professors' and the reward of and withdrawal from teaching of institutional 'research stars' (Clegg 2007). One of the consequences of this shift is that academic staff started to negotiate their roles in different phases and in different ways.

So, how have the disciplines of dance, drama and music been affected by these various changes, and what are the implications?

In an attempt to answer that question, and as part of the research for this contribution, I circulated a questionnaire to the discussion lists of the subject associations of dance, drama and music, asking for views on how the disciplines have changed in recent years, and the impact of those changes on academic identities as teachers, researchers and practitioners. The 28 detailed replies I received, from colleagues across a broad range of subjects and institutions, and a number of subsequent emails and conversations with both the respondents and others, revealed the complexities of defining what constitutes the 'discipline'. Rather than a 'tribe' and its 'territory', or even a number of related tribes sharing, ranging over and occasionally contesting a number of linked territories, the landscapes of the three disciplines and their various interlocking and interconnecting communities of practice consists of a complex, multi-faceted, multi-layered network of identities, relationships, values, discourses and practices. As Henkel (2005: 173) describes:

> Academics no longer work in a bounded space. Rather, academic autonomy has become something that must be realised by managing multi-modality and multiple relationships in a context where boundaries have either collapsed or become blurred.

The picture that emerges from all this is of a sector in which all the various parts, from the main structural elements to the many subjects, communities, discourses and practices that occupy it, are in a state of fragmentation and flux. This is particularly noticeable in those disciplines – such as dance, drama and music – that have not only expanded in terms of the number, range and type of subjects they now cover but also have a 'dual identity' as both academic and practice-based disciplines. As disciplines, identities are mutating and transforming, academic identities, too, are shifting and changing, and the question of what or whose identity has become an important and pertinent one. This is exemplified in one of the 'thematic prompts' for a conference on Academic Identities in the 21st Century held in June 2010: 'Fragmentation, specialisation and new work contracts – can we even argue that an "academic identity" still exists?' (University of Strathclyde website 2010).

There is a strong sense that we have moved, or certainly are moving, beyond a period when there was a single identifiable discipline e.g. drama, and a shared understanding of what that discipline was. One senior lecturer in drama, who responded to the questions about changing disciplines, viewed this as an indication of 'a splintering of a shared understanding of what the focus/content/values of a degree programme might be, making it difficult to talk of a single subject area nationally' (Questionnaire response, QR12). A sense of the 'broad spectrum' of themes and subjects and methodological approaches[6] that the discipline of drama/theatre studies now covers can be ascertained from the titles of the eight working groups that currently contribute to the work of the Theatre and Performance Research Association (TaPRA): C20–C21 Performer Training; The Documentation of Performance; Scenography; Directing and Dramaturgy; Applied and Social Theatre; New Technologies for Theatre; Performance, Identity and Community; Performance and the Body; Theatre Performance and Philosophy; Theatre History and Historiography. All this signifies that the 'discipline' now comprises a complex, multi-faceted, boundary crossing, and loosely coupled assortment of academic identities, discourses and practices.

A similar trajectory can be detected in the younger – as an academic subject – discipline of dance. Not only has it grown substantially in terms of the number of courses and students, but also it has matured as a discipline in terms of research and academic robustness. There has been what a Head of Dance described as a 'liberalisation of what is accepted as scholarship – more inclusivity and acceptance of diverse modes, such as practice-based research' (QR5). However, the proliferation of analytical frameworks and the undermining of empirical research have also brought into question the notion of substantial historical knowledge and understanding. A dance historian, in answer to the questions, commented that: 'I feel that dance history is having to fight back in order to establish its identity as a discipline area that may draw on, but does not depend on, theories from other disciplines' (QR1). The problem is particularly acute in dance due to the relatively short time it has been an 'academic' subject. Drama (several decades) and music (several centuries) have had substantial or certainly sufficient periods of time to establish themselves as disciplines with clear identities rooted in established landscapes, for example, historical, philosophical, intellectual. Dance has not had the benefit of such a 'settling in' period. Its academic roots are not as well established and not as deep, and it is therefore, perhaps, rather more susceptible to the 'winds of change' blowing through academia.

In drama/theatre studies, another important factor, particularly in relation to the burgeoning field of performance studies/performance research, is that not only has the discipline 'gone global' (McKenzie et al. 2010: 1) in regard to the number and location of researchers, research centres and transnational collaborations in and between institutions, but also 'there is a growing sense that a profound de-centering' is transpiring':

> Performance studies is no longer only about the West – specifically the United States – studying the 'Rest'. While performance has for some time been recognized as both a contested concept and a practice of potential contestation, the sites and stakes of those contests have both multiplied and entered into new configurations.
>
> McKenzie et al. 2010: 2

Within this complexity (or 'splintering'), some patterns can be discerned, a number of which provide some interesting tensions and counter-balances. In UK drama/theatre studies, these shifts and changes include:

- a move away from the study of the history of drama to the theory of performance;
- far less focus on 'the canon' of playtexts, dramatists, dramatic forms and a related shift from the study and performance of plays to creating devised performance both in and, particularly, outside traditional theatre spaces. 'It is possible to do a Drama degree and not read a play' (QR12, Lecturer in Drama); 'The impact of increased interest in devised theatre, means that particularly "new" universities rarely teach any substantial sort of history or historiography (this is NOT a good thing)' (QR19, Professor of Theatre History);

- a move away from the study of 'plays' as artefacts of interest in themselves – or even in context – and into areas of 'performance', broadly configured. As a consequence, even when studying written texts, new paradigms (see note 2) for understanding the practices involved have been applied;
- an increased separation of research practice from professional practice:[8] 'Students see, study and emulate student work, and the work of those companies touring the academic venue circuit, rather than professional work for general public audiences' (QR13, Lecturer in Drama);
- a much more focused set of research practices, incentives and pressures to create high-quality research outputs, including the increased acceptance and influence of discourses and practices based around practice-as-research;[9]
- in response to developments in the arts world, an increasing amount of crossing of disciplinary boundaries with other creative and performing arts subjects, for example film and visual arts as well as dance and music, and away from traditional humanities subject areas;
- the increased use and integration of information and performance technologies in and into performance.

These shifts and changes have had various and variable levels of impact across the discipline as it is taught in universities. Similar, or parallel shifts can be observed in the disciplines of dance and music, and the 'de-centering' described by McKenzie *et al.* applies as much to those disciplines as it does to drama/theatre studies. That 'de-centering' also applies to the identities of those who work as teachers, researchers and, in a significant number of cases, practitioners in those disciplines.

A recent conversation with a music colleague encapsulated this phenomenon. Originally a professionally trained musician and composer, he is also a musicologist and an acknowledged expert on the work of an early twentieth-century composer. His main teaching specialism is currently in the subject area of music technology, and in recent years he has collaborated with an artist and fellow academic on a series of major art projects and installations that have been exhibited around the world. When we met, he had just returned from a workshop run by biologists that was concerned with the visual and aural representation of biological data, to which they had invited a number of colleagues from the visual arts and music/sound disciplines.

While some, as demonstrated by the music colleague above, embrace the opportunities provided by the de-centering or fragmentation, others find it a rather disconcerting and even threatening phenomenon. One respondent to the questions about changes in the nature of the discipline and identity – a professor of theatre history, specialising in nineteenth-century theatre – wrote, only half-jokingly: 'Oh, I'm becoming a dinosaur!' (QR16). But she then went on to make the serious point that, while only a few years ago there was real concern about the future of theatre history as a discipline, 'There has been extraordinary innovation in my particular corner, with the impact of post-structuralist theory as forming the "new theatre historiography", which I'm lucky to be a part of' (QR16). A similar phenomenon has occurred in dance, where the proliferation of theoretical perspectives on dance studies has, in the words of a dance historian 'been both astounding and sometimes confusing' (QR1).

Among the dance, drama and music conservatoires, there has been relatively little impact in those institutions that have remained as close as they can to their original, skills-based, vocational training ethos, albeit while operating within a framework of validated, academic integrity. However, there has been a significant impact in those instances where institutions have undertaken major changes in curriculum design and delivery or, in some cases, a complete overhaul of their entire higher education provision. As a senior manager in a drama and music conservatoire undergoing profound change commented: 'It's sure as hell scary for teachers in the conservatoire, though, who are not used or suited to change' (QR22). Such changes have been undertaken, in large part, in response to the employability and skills agendas that are now prevalent in higher education, and the consequent recognition that specialist institutions have at least some responsibility to provide a much broader educational experience in preparation for a much greater number and range of career opportunities. This has led to much 'soul-searching' within those institutions. Teaching staff – often with conservatoire training and professional careers themselves – grapple with reconciling the understanding that a wider, more interdisciplinary education will actually benefit the profession, with the widely held perception that pursuing such a path will inevitably result in a dilution of the skills-based training that they value and which they believe the profession demands. Similar tensions exist in the music conservatoires as new technologies and the changing musical marketplace are creating a new and wider range of opportunities for graduates (Nightingale 2007).

There is another aspect in relation to the disciplines of dance, drama and music that might influence the manner in which academic identities are configured – and re-configured – in those disciplines, and the willingness and ability to adapt to the many shifts and changes occurring both internally within those disciplines and in the external environment. Of the three disciplines, drama/theatre studies is possibly the most 'hybrid' discipline in that its discourses and practices range over a particularly wide and varied range of subjects, tools and stimuli. As a senior lecturer in drama commented: 'this mix of skills is far wider in range than in traditional humanities subjects' (QR15). Anyone engaged in drama/theatre studies practice inevitably will have found themselves adopting a plethora of roles and functions in relation to those discourses and practices – in teaching and research, production and performance. Thus, the adoption of multiple, metamorphosing identities within the discipline is a naturally occurring phenomenon, and the 'adapt or die' approach to academic existence is part of the DNA of the discipline.

The phenomenon of a multi-faceted, shifting academic identity also can be discerned in both dance and music as those disciplines expand into new areas of study and work, and as the boundaries between subject areas become increasingly permeable. However, if there is a differentiation between the three disciplines it may be discerned in the extent to which each discipline has become 'de-centred' or detached from the set of discourses and practices that, by general consensus, constituted its core. Drama/theatre studies has experienced a far greater de-centering as a discipline than either dance or music, both of which still retain a distinctive 'core'. In the case of music, the technical element, for example, musical literacy and theory, is very distinctive to music and musical skills. However, as a professor of music wrote, there is a sense that even in music 'there has been an erosion of this, and, as a result, students tend to go for other areas of music such as pure history, philosophy, ethnology, sociology, etc., where, dependency on musical facts derived from musical theory can be avoided' (QR25).

Epilogue

In the course of exploring how academic identity is configured in higher education dance, drama and music it has become clear that academics' narratives are threaded with stories of shifting identities, as they move into, out of, and through communities of practice and located aspects of their professional identities across many contexts (James 2005). One of those contexts, particularly and obviously in relation to learning and teaching – and which has been mentioned only in passing – is the student context. The construction and re-construction of an academic identity occurs in a context in which student identities themselves are being constructed and re-constructed. As higher education in the UK shifts much further towards a student demand-led system driven by bottom-line economics, and as the long-term future of subjects such as dance, drama and music come under increased pressure to prove their worth – to the economy – and their financial viability, it is clear that the academics in those disciplines will continue to adapt to the many and varied changes within and pressures on the environments in which they work. What is less clear, in the face of what appears to be an inexorable process of disciplinary expansion, fragmentation and de-centering, is whether there may be a point at which any notion of an academic identity – in the traditional sense – becomes meaningless.

Acknowledgements

I am indebted to the following dance, drama and music colleagues, in the UK and beyond, for their contributions to this research: Joshua Abrams, Paul Archbold, Tamara Ashley, Jane Bacon, Johannes Birringer, Neil Boynton, Theresa Buckland, Jeremy Dibble, Celia Duffy, Anna Farthing, Nic Fryer, Charlotte

Gompertz, Andrée Grau, Steve Halfyard, Ruth Helier-Tinoco, Michael Huxley, Martin Isherwood, Jennifer Jackson, Peter Johnson, Janet Lansdale, Tom Maguire, Holly Maples, Allan Moore, Robert Penman, Kate Newey, Larraine Nicholas, Sophie Nield, Edel Quin, Michael Russ, Simon Shepherd, Judy Smith, Kathy Smith, Gareth Somers, Bev Stevens, Jayne Stevens, Mark Summers, John Whenham, Lisa Whistlecroft, Martin White, Roger Williams, Noel Witts, Ronald Woodley.

Notes

1   Dance, in its early manifestation as an academic discipline, was concerned mainly with chore-ography, performance, dance history, and the appreciation of contemporary dance. Drama, with its strong link to English literature, was focused mainly around theatre history and the study of plays and their performance. For a considerable period, the study of music was focused on composition, performance, reception, and criticism, particularly in the Western classical tradition. All three disciplines have now expanded considerably to include a wide range of sub-disciplines that range across the arts, humanities, sciences and social sciences. In 2011, PALATINE, the HEA Subject Centre for Dance, Drama and Music, listed 24 sub-disciplines for dance, 49 for drama, 63 for music, and 20 technical/design sub-disciplines.

2   Some dance degree courses are still located in physical education or sports science departments.

3   Boehm (2007), using data from UCAS (the UK's Universities and Colleges Admissions Service) identified 351 degrees in the category of music technology, of which only 131 actually used the phrase 'music technology' in the title. In all Boehm identified 63 different names for music technology courses.

4   The Research Assessment Exercise (RAE) was an exercise undertaken approximately every five years between 1992 and 2008 on behalf of the four UK higher education funding coun-cils to evaluate the quality of research undertaken by British higher education institutions. RAE submissions from each subject area (or *unit of assessment*) were given a rank by a subject specialist peer review panel. The rankings were used to inform the allocation of quality-weighted research funding (QR) each higher education institution received from their national funding council. Top-rated institutions received substantial amounts of money.

5   The Research Excellence Framework (REF) was developed in the light of concerns about the impact of funded university research on the economy, the cost of the RAE, and the 'Government's firm presumption … that after the 2008 RAE the system for assessing research quality and allocating "quality-related" (QR) funding will be mainly metrics-based' (HM Treasury 2006). The first REF is scheduled for 2014.

6   'The breadth of research methods and theoretical frames is as wide as the broad spectrum of subjects studied, being drawn from such fields as anthropology, art history, communication, dance history, history, linguistics, literary studies, philosophy, postcolonial studies, psychology, sociology, and theatre studies. The methods include critical race studies, deconstruction, femi-nism, Marxism, new historicism, phenomenology, psychoanalysis, queer theory, semiotics, and speech act theory' (McKenzie *et al.* 2010: 2).

7   'Decentered: The absence or denial of a particular society's or culture's perspective from which to view the world, usually associated with moving away from a Western or Eurocentric perspective. Could potentially imply the absence of any central perspective' (Eller 2009).

8   The need and requirement for students to see and study performance *in situ* i.e. public performance in public theatres, studios, concert halls, etc. has been replaced to a significant extent by the establishment of a university 'circuit' of performance venues, an unofficial 'list' of preferred companies and performers, and the appointment – from among those companies and performers – of visiting fellows. Consequently, the teaching and research of performance frequently occurs within an academic 'bubble'.

9   Practice-as-research (PaR) is research activity undertaken in-and-through disciplinary artistic
     practice (normally art/media/performance) where the researcher's own practice and critical
     engagement are integral to the research subject, method and outcomes. The outcomes can take
     the form of documented processes and/or products.

13
'We're Engaged'
Mechanical Engineering and the Community

CHRISTINE WINBERG

Introduction and Context

Mechanical engineering programmes, like other professional fields of study, have long been expected to be relevant to the needs of their related industries. In a context like South Africa, university programmes are also expected to contribute to the country's development needs. In an effort to address these new requirements, the coordinator of a mechanical engineering programme invited community-based clients and organisations to set briefs for final (fourth) year engineering students' projects. The community-based clients consulted with students during the process of project development, and were part of an assessment panel that awarded marks for the students' work. The data for this study were obtained from observations of interactions between students, engineering faculty, tutors and clients, as well as pre-programme, mid-programme and post-programme interviews with all participants. The findings of this study indicate that academic–community engagement in an engineering context required the engineering faculty and students to develop new forms of knowledge, adapt existing practices, and build new professional and academic identities. The chapter offers an analysis of the difficulties and possibilities when new requirements are accommodated within existing ways of knowing, doing and being in a mechanical engineering department.

Mechanical engineering is a four-year undergraduate programme in South Africa; traditionally the final year students complete a large project that is intended to integrate several areas of knowledge. Usually such projects are simulated ones, given by faculty to students as a 'high stakes' assessment task. In this case, there were real clients and real projects. The programme coordinator had invited community-based organisations, located in contexts that were familiar to most students, to develop briefs for the final year student projects. Students worked in teams to prototype machines, as specified by their community-based clients. Client 1 was a private client, a disabled cyclist who challenged the students to develop a competitive hand cycle. His intention was to buy the best prototype and to have it professionally manufactured for his own use in cycle races. A non-governmental organisation, Client 2, had two projects: an all terrain trolley – to be used in informal settlements for garbage collection and recycling – and a can crusher – to be used by unemployed people collecting aluminum cans for recycling. Client 3 represented an energy-saving non-governmental organisation that commissioned the students to develop an environmentally friendly generator for use in areas with little or no access to electricity.

The final year project was intended to build students' knowledge and develop their engineering skills. By including community-generated projects, the engineering faculty also hoped to promote students' civic responsibility and encourage reflection on the connections between human, technological and environmental needs. Including real-world projects was a departure from the norm for undergraduate projects, where design, prototype and appraisal cycles were based on closed design problems that were faculty-assigned and usually unrelated to matters of community development.

The Field and Legitimation Claims of Mechanical Engineering

Legitimation code theory (LCT) (Maton 2007; Christie and Maton 2010) is used as a language of description to analyse the collaboration between the academic department and community-based organisations. LCT provides an approach to understanding how different knowledge systems – for example, academic and professional knowledge systems – can be shown to have a relationship to each other. Differences between knowledge types is not necessarily an impediment to collaboration; by analysing academic and professional forms of mechanical engineering knowledge in terms of LCT we are able to understand the different criteria for differing legitimation claims – without necessarily closing off the different knowledge systems from each other. At the same time, LCT enables an awareness of power differentials. Most importantly LCT recognises the importance of the relationship of knowledge claims between and across fields.

LCT is premised on an understanding that every claim to knowledge is a) about something, and b) made by someone. Knowledge claims can thus be located along an epistemic and a social axis. In mechanical engineering the 'epistemic relation' is the relationship between mechanical problems/solutions and the knowledge system that purports to explain it; while the 'social relation' is exemplified by the way in which an engineer mediates engineering knowledge for a client. In the academic world of the mechanical engineer, the epistemic relation is dominant, while in professional practice the social relation increases in importance. LCT can serve to accentuate differences between what, and how, those in universities and those in professional practice know, thereby providing a way in which each may better understand – and critique – the other. From enhanced understanding develops the possibility of mutual, rather than one-sided, recontextualisation, resulting in new insights into knowledge forms.

Mechanical Engineering as an Academic Discipline: the Epistemic Relation

Mechanical engineering is the oldest of the engineering disciplines; it has been part of university structures for about a hundred years (Reid *et al.* 2008). Mechanical engineering is typical of the 'hard applied' disciplines (Biglan 1973) in its application of the 'pure' disciplines of mathematics and physics to the solving of mechanical problems. In the terminology of Bernstein's categorisation of dichotomous ideal types, mechanical engineering has a predominantly 'hierarchical knowledge structure' (Bernstein 2000). The field of mechanical engineering develops through the extrapolation, integration and synthesis of previous engineering knowledge. In mechanical engineering, precision, accuracy, systematic thinking, and orderly processes and procedures are important criteria for the validation of knowledge (Carvalho *et al.* 2009). General engineering skills, such as conceiving models for problems and solutions, setting up and conducting experiments, and applying design and simulation tools, are important for research and knowledge production – for example, rapid prototyping, smart materials and computer simulated machines. In its academic form, mechanical engineering exemplifies what Maton (2007) has called the 'knowledge code': a strong epistemic relation – that is, the importance of physics, mathematics, mechanics and the properties of materials in solving mechanical problems – and a weaker social relation – that is, the personal attributes and qualities of those applying the knowledge base.

Mechanical Engineering as Professional Practice: the Social Relation

As a professional practice, mechanical engineering has significant differences from mechanical engineering as an academic discipline. While the 'knowledge code' remains fundamental to engineering practice, it has to be mediated by what Maton (2007) calls a 'knower code' that requires the professional engineer to mediate knowledge for a particular client within a particular context. Mechanical engineering as a practice thus moves from its hierarchical form toward what Bernstein (2000) calls a horizontal form 'typified as ... context dependent, tacit, multi-layered'. Hierarchical knowledge systems aim 'to bring a broadening base of empirical phenomena within the purview of a decreasing number of axioms and develop through the integration and subsumption of previous knowledge' (Christie and Maton, 2010). Mechanical engineering in practice has developed conventions and procedures that derive their coherence from their contextual effectiveness, rather than from their internal knowledge system. A 'project' is universally understood in professional engineering practice as a 'unit of work', usually defined on the basis of the client (Mills and Treagust 2003). Almost every task undertaken in professional practice by an engineer will be in relation to a project (Baird *et al.* 2000). Work-based projects will have varying timescales, levels of complexity, and will often be done by multidisciplinary teams, including engineers from different specialisations, other professionals as well as non-professional personnel and teams, but all will relate in some way to the contextual coherence of the project.

Teaching and Learning in Mechanical Engineering

The aim of undergraduate mechanical engineering programmes is to graduate mechanical engineers who have a broad knowledge of both the timeless pure disciplines – physics, chemistry and mathematics – and the newer applied disciplines – mechanics, fluid dynamics, and properties of materials – that make up the core curriculum (DeBartolo and Robinson 2007). Learning in mechanical engineering demands the progressive mastery of concepts and techniques in a linear sequence. The 'lecture-demonstration' – also known as a 'demo' – is an important part of undergraduate pedagogy; faculty staff, often with the assistance of a technician, demonstrate problem-solving and show students how to apply knowledge of physics, mathematics and a range of procedures and techniques in the design of machines. Much of engineering problem-solving involves 'translating' engineering problems into mathematical or scientific models. The lecture-demonstration programme introduces students to definitions, concepts and theories; it illustrates related working methods, strategies, algorithms, heuristics and lines of thought and contextualises them. Students usually begin independent work on smaller mathematics- and physics-based problems before they are introduced to the world of machines in the workshop (Mills and Treagust 2003). Thus students both work through problems themselves, and observe expert problem-solving to build their understanding of strategies and heuristics in action (Schoenfeld 1985).

In the engineering disciplines, problem-based and project-based forms of learning are commonly used to encourage students to apply knowledge learned in the lecture-demonstration, or from texts, as well as skills acquired in the workshop, to solve new problems. Project-oriented study, involving the use of small projects within individual courses, progressing to a significant final year project is common in engineering studies (Heitmann 1996). Such projects will usually be combined with the traditional lecture-demonstration method within the same course. Projects thus focus on the application, and possibly the integration, of previously acquired knowledge. Students usually work on their projects in small groups with a project team of tutors and lecturers. Projects are undertaken throughout the length of the course and vary in duration from a few weeks to an entire year. Participation in projects in which they develop a design concept, build a system and test it, prepares students for professional project work. Participation in project work also enables students to practise and integrate the 'soft skills' of communication, teamwork and time management with experimentation and machine design (Perrent *et al.* 2003).

University-based projects tend to be different from work-based projects because they usually involve only one area of engineering specialisation. Faculty-developed problems and projects are selected on the basis of the course material. An important difference between professional engineering and student projects is the timescale of the real-life problem-solving process: designing a machine in real life takes considerably more time than designing a machine as an engineering student project. It is assumed that successful completion of projects requires the integration of all areas of an engineering student's under-graduate training.

From the description above, three basic forms of mechanical engineering can be identified, each with different emphases and areas of focus, although all working within the same knowledge system:

From the concepts developed thus far, we can construct a model of engineering education as striving to balance its vertical, 'academic' form – the 'knowledge code' – with its horizontal expression that is more common in professional practice – the 'knower code': the academic gaze recontextualising specific engineering problems, and practical problems necessitating the recontextualisation of academic engineering knowledge.

Mechanical engineering as an academic discipline	⟺	Teaching and learning practices in mechanical engineering	⟺	Mechanical engineering as a field of professional practice
Epistemic relation 'Knowledge code' Research and knowledge production – nanotechnology, rapid prototyping, smart materials, computer simulated machines Interdisciplinary knowledge production		Epistemic and social relation Curriculum: mathematics, physics, chemistry Applied subjects: mechanics, fluid dynamics Pedagogy: lecture-demonstrations, workshops, problems Assessment: tests and projects		Social relation 'Knower code' Project as a unit of work Mediating engineering knowledge for a client Acting for a client Inter-professional collaboration

Figure 13.1 Relationships between traditional teaching and learning practices, the academic discipline and professional practice in mechanical engineering

In the next section an engineering–community partnership is considered as particular form of recontextualisation.

The Field and Legitimation Claims of Community Engagement

Governments around the world are concerned that universities provide opportunities for students to engage with communities, develop civic and social responsibility and apply what they have learned in their studies to address 'real-world' concerns in partnership with communities. An emerging body of research into community engagement suggests positive outcomes related to student learning, motivation and civic responsibility. At the same time, interest in community engagement and service learning have re-opened debates about higher education for the public good (for example, Benson *et al.* 2000; Chambers 2005).

Community engagement in South African higher education has had a hybrid past, made up of elements of the anti-apartheid struggle, influences from US-based 'service-learning' and volunteerism, and Gibbons and colleagues' (1994) and Nowotny and colleagues' (2001) conceptualisation of a 'Mode 2' society (Muller 2010). For the South African Ministry of Higher Education, community engagement provides universities with opportunities to demonstrate their legitimacy and accountability to communities as a scholarly activity (for example, South African Council on Higher Education 2006). As a means of promoting civic responsibility among students, there has been interest in developing university-based learning that is more situated, participative and community-oriented. Many academics are, however, concerned that both the conceptualisation and practice of community engagement lacks intellectual rigour (Hall 2010). Individual institutional approaches to community engagement vary significantly and the ability of higher education programmes to foster community development is largely dependent on the degree to which disciplinary, curricular, pedagogical and assessment arrangements are compatible with the processes of addressing community needs.

Researching University–Community Interaction

In an effort to address the institutional requirement that all students participate in a 'community engagement' project, the coordinator of a mechanical engineering programme invited community-based organisations to set briefs for final year (fourth year) engineering students' projects. The research study, on which this chapter is based, was built around this intervention for the purpose of evaluating its effectiveness in terms of student learning. The 'community engagement' project was seen to have three phases:

1   a pre-programme planning phase – in which faculty and clients met to negotiate the terms of the client briefs;
2   an implementation phase – in which the students met their community-based clients and addressed the brief; and
3   a post-programme phase in which all project participants met to 'debrief' and suggest improvements for future work.

Observational data, using video- and audio-recordings, were obtained from the interactions between students, their lecturers, tutors and clients throughout the three phases of the project. Semi-structured interviews, based on initial analyses of the observational data, were conducted with engineering faculty, tutors, clients and students at the pre-programme, mid-programme and post-programme phases. In cases where faculty staff or clients were unavailable for interview, they were sent the interview questions via e-mail, and an e-mail archive of responses was included in the data. Also included in the data were the mechanical engineering students' reports and technical drawings that were prepared as part of their assessment. The students' oral presentations that were made to an assessment panel of mechanical engineering faculty and community-based clients were video-recorded. Field notes were made at a post-presentation 'debriefing' between faculty, tutors and students. This research design was intended to provide data from all participants at different stages of the programme, to study the extent to which the participants had similar or different expectations of the project, as well as to determine whether or not the expectations of the different groups were met, and to obtain data from a variety of sources – participants, students' work, e-mails, etc. – to reach multiple views and understandings.

The findings are presented in terms of the three phases of this study: pre-programme, mid-programme and end-of-programme, acknowledging that overlapping concerns were raised by participants at the various stages – for example, during the assessment a number of planning issues were raised.

Pre-Programme: Great Expectations

Before the start of the project, lecturers, tutors, clients and students were asked the question: 'What are you hoping to achieve in the university–community collaboration?' For faculty, the expected benefits had to do with developing students' ability to solve mechanical problems; the primary intention for the project was thus student, rather than community, development. Engineering faculty were concerned that the students should demonstrate their engineering knowledge and abilities:

> Community needs are often fundamental ... but nevertheless [pose] huge challenges for basic quality-of-life issues ... like water accessibility and

treatment that requires technical intervention and 'real' engineering ...
there shouldn't be a problem in finding appropriate projects that will test
students' knowledge of engineering ...

Lecturer 1, pre-programme interview

It would later emerge that 'finding appropriate projects' would prove to be
a key difficulty. For faculty the main purpose of the university–community
projects was the quality of the engineering in the final products produced by
the students.

Tutors were more concerned with the quality of the learning process. They
were particularly concerned about the additional support that students would
require in undertaking client-driven projects:

> My experience in community-based projects can be almost directly trans-
> lated to express the kinds of skills that are needed in the private sector:
> project management, setting specifications, design and implementation,
> cost estimates, etc. Such a complete experience is difficult to achieve within
> a practical university project, in my experience as a student. It's going to be
> a good experience for the students, but difficult for them to manage all the
> elements of the project

Tutor 1, pre-programme e-mail

The clients participated in the collaboration with the understanding that
their organisations would benefit from the project. They hoped for more than
a routine application of engineering knowledge from the students; their expectation of soon-to-be-graduates was that they should be at the cutting edge of
knowledge and innovation in their discipline:

> We can make adjustments from the point of view of usability and practical-
> ity ... what we are looking for is a great idea.

Client 3, pre-programme interview

The students misjudged the extent to which their clients valued innovative
solutions to their technological problems. Students entered into their projects
with enthusiasm, but not with thoughts about meeting specific engineering-
based assessment criteria. Their expectations were that they would be able to
use their existing knowledge and skills to benefit communities.

Mid-Programme: Reality Check

Work on the projects took place over an academic term – approximately six
weeks; during this period the student teams worked with their tutors, under the
supervision of a senior faculty member.

While noting the advantages for students in having an opportunity to apply engineering knowledge in context, faculty expressed concerns about the academic level of the students' work. The difficulties of addressing clients' needs also became more evident as the projects developed. Most of these difficulties had to do with the different aims, practices and structures of academic demands versus clients' requirements. As Lecturer 2, expressed it:

> Even though [the students] are trying to address the client's brief ... it's important that they also include methodical work on problems ... formulating hypotheses for possible solutions ... and ... synthesising partial solutions for ... the original brief ... so that they ... not only test and evaluate the prototype ... but they think about it scientifically.
>
> Lecturer 2, mid-programme interview

The same faculty member remarked that:

> Students are always ready to jump into application ... there is never enough preliminary research.
>
> Lecturer 2, mid-programme interview

Using real clients' briefs for the students' projects in some cases created applications that were extremely complex – such as the generator project – and in others applications that were too simple for the students' level – such as the can crusher. The question asked by one of the members of the assessment panel is indicative of the confusion felt:

> Should the student be awarded marks on the basis of meeting the client's needs ... or on the basis of demonstrating his mechanical engineering knowledge and skills?
>
> Assessment panel, Lecturer 3

Tutors wanted to avoid underestimating students, while acknowledging that some students had little prior experience in working for clients. As one tutor commented:

> It's important to acknowledge what students bring to the course ... and to avoid adopting an 'empty vessel' perspective ... but ... at the same time ... some students are just at the beginning stages of [mechanical engineering] product prototyping ... skills and capabilities ... so how much to assume is a difficult question.
>
> Tutor 2, mid-programme interview

One of the tutors explained the need:

> to do a lot of explicit teaching on a one-to-one basis ... because aspects that apply to some students won't necessarily ... apply to all students.
>
> Tutor 3, mid-programme interview

For clients, an important part of the process was ensuring that there was regular communication between the student team and the community organisation; the clients valued those teams that were committed not only to the problem-solving process, but to ensuring that they addressed the brief:

> Students can know and give the 'right' response ... but in a [community-directed project] you assess what people do ... as opposed to what they know.
>
> Client 2, mid-programme interview

The students' engagement with the clients was greatly assisted by site visits and meetings with client and potential users. These interactions helped them to understand the particular needs of the potential users of their products. One of the students commented that:

> Interviews and meetings with the people affected are essential ... these people need to be 'in the loop' at all times ... so there are no surprises.
>
> Student 1, mid-programme interview

The interactions between students and clients also showed the students that there was a great need for their engineering skills in a developing country like South Africa, and this boosted their confidence in their engineering abilities. Many students reported that the project inspired them to use their skills to create technologies that could enhance communities' quality of life:

> I know for me it has shaped my goals as an engineer and helped me understand the way engineers in the private sector can ... and should interact with disadvantaged communities.
>
> Student 2, mid-programme interview

Post-Assessment Debriefing: Back to the Drawing Board

The client-generated projects provided the students with a clear sense of a product in process, including the fact that the final assessment was not the end of product development. After the assessment panel had judged the student presentations, there were continued interactions between the students and their clients on improvements to the products, as well as collaboration across the design teams. In one case, the best two projects were selected by the client for further development by the students. Such collaboration is common in industry, as one of the tutors writes:

> Because community-oriented projects are inherently about working in teams with other people, including non-engineers, they encourage experimentation and prototyping at an early stage. This benefits students through teamwork, increased development of prototyping skills, and an increased amount of time spent trying ideas instead of relegating them to paper. For many classes … a first prototype will often be made at a smaller scale or with less specific material requirements than a final product, but it is a valuable experience in the design process and often highlights weaknesses or clarifies alternative possibilities. … Community-oriented projects allow students an opportunity to be a part of the full life cycle of a technology or several technologies. Not only are they responsible for mechanical design, but finding and meeting user specifications, doing cost analysis, etc. It seems for many students that this process opens up new ideas of what engineering is and what engineers can do.
>
> Tutor 1, debriefing e-mail

The fact that a project is client-generated does not imply that the client's or product users' needs will be met. In practice, most of the students' designs were practical rather than creative, while the clients had expected product innovation. One of the users of the 'can crusher' claimed that the students had not taken her specific requirements into consideration:

> I would like to crush the cans with my foot … such as with a foot pedal … why didn't any of these students invent a machine that I can work with my foot?
>
> Community member and potential user of the 'can crusher' and observer at the oral presentation, translated from isiXhosa

In the debriefing session the student team claimed that the above user's request came in too late in the development of their prototype and they could not change it. Faculty understood the value of project-based learning lay in meeting clients' needs through frequent meetings with the clients and redesigning as the prototypes progressed – even though in most academic projects there are time constraints on redesign. The faculty member assigned to this group remarked that:

> Re-designing has more to do with attitude than with the project.
>
> Lecturer 1, debriefing

As far as students were concerned, the community projects had been successful; the student groups expressed a strong sense of purpose and motivation; they felt that their reports had been carefully prepared and that they benefited from interaction with community organisations:

> The project method of learning forced us to learn more about our subjects and enabled us to develop solutions to a specific problem ... communicating these ideas to [the client] affected the final solution by combining all the knowledge we had gained into our design ... it was not until the presentation that I realised how much we had learned as a group.
>
> Student 4, debriefing

For faculty, engineering knowledge remained the dominant organisational principle for the assessment of students' knowledge. Students were awarded marks according to the traditional criteria for final year projects. Faculty understood the benefits of project-based learning, but felt that the community-based projects had not been successful in enabling students to demonstrate the solving of engineering problems. They felt that community engagement might be appropriate at an earlier stage of the curriculum, and that complexity of the project should controlled by the lecturer, preferably without real clients. This position is summed up by Lecturer 2:

> Move the community engagement project ... downscale it ... to a smaller project for third years.
>
> Lecturer 2, debriefing

Conclusion

Engineering knowledge is the basis for professional practice, but is different from professional practice. The community engagement project made clear how the professional practice of mechanical engineering is different from the acquisition of engineering knowledge. The community engagement projects initially blurred these distinctions because of the prevalence of project-work in engineering pedagogy; but as the community-based projects progressed, differences between academic-driven and community-driven projects became apparent. At the outset, faculty did not realise how difficult it would be to respond to needs and priorities that were outside of disciplinary and educational concerns, or to change their knowledge-based orientation to one of social and economic relevance. Moore and Maton (2001) point out that:

> The organisation of knowledge within an intellectual field is not simply the way in which previously produced knowledge is arranged into some kind

of order … It is characterised by a principle that also regulates the manner in which new knowledge is produced and its form.

Moore and Maton 2001: 157

Table 13.1 provides a summary analysis of the relationship between the epistemic and the social relation in the community engagement project. Mapping the relation in this way shows the different criteria for the different legitimation claims, and also shows that faculty and tutors' concerns were with the quality of student learning, while students and clients were engaged in addressing community needs – more or less successfully.

The differences between the epistemic and social relation shown in Table 13.1 do not imply that the different knowledge systems should be isolated from each other. Ways of knowing, doing and being in mechanical engineering departments were acquired over many years; in new contexts, and for new purposes, the existing knowledge base – mechanical engineering – and its associated curricular, pedagogical and assessment practices – academic-driven projects, teamwork, demos and academic presentations – are unlikely to be immediately useful in community-based collaboration, nor is community collaboration likely to immediately benefit student learning in engineering. The engineering faculty, in particular, experienced difficulties in crossing the boundaries between academic work and meeting clients' needs. Boundary crossing requires shared meaning-making among groups. Tuomi-Gröhn and Engeström (2003) explain that when different groups work together, common understandings are necessary to ensure reliability across domains. Translation, negotiation, and simplification are required when the academic world and the real world meet.

The difficulties experienced can be expressed in terms of the distance between the existing and the new epistemic and social relation. When the new epistemic relation – the development of socially useful machines – and the associated social relation – service to a developing community – is very different from the existing epistemic – engineering-as-science – and social – engineers-as-professionals – relation, implementation and up-take are unlikely to be successful.

These findings have implications for collaborations between academic departments and the communities they – ultimately – serve. The alignment of engineering expertise and community interests and needs, as well as the extent to which there is compatibility between existing repertoires and new requirements – or the extent to which new requirements can be accommodated within existing practices – would be indicators for successful collaboration. Misalignment of these interests might provide useful learning experiences – as in this study – but the products of students' learning are unlikely to be valued by the academic department or taken up by a community, at least in the short term.

Table 13.1 Dimensions of the epistemic and social relation in the mechanical engineering/community engagement project

EPISTEMIC RELATION: Mechanical engineering in universities			SOCIAL RELATION: Mechanical engineering in professional practice		
Emphasis on	Indicators	Examples from data	Emphasis on	Indicators	Examples from data
Curriculum: engineering knowledge and engineering processes	Lecturers assume projects are similar to traditional engineering projects. Tutors see the benefit in students' exposure to the 'full life cycle' of a project.	There shouldn't be a problem in finding appropriate projects that will test students' knowledge of engineering (Lecturer 1). Community-oriented projects allow students an opportunity to be a part of the 'full life cycle' of a technology or several technologies (Tutor 1).	Professionalism and professional identity	Clients assume they are going to obtain 'cutting edge' ideas from the student teams. Students felt that the projects shaped their identities as professionals-in-training.	We can make adjustments from the point of view of usability and practicality ... what we are looking for is a great idea (Client 3). ... for me it has shaped my goals as an engineer and helped me understand the way engineers in the private sector... should interact with disadvantaged communities (Student 2).
Pedagogy: teaching and learning engineering knowledge and processes	Lecturers are concerned with quality/content of learning. Tutors are concerned with students' different levels, abilities and learning needs.	... it's important [that the students] also include methodical work on problems (Lecturer 2). [I need] to do a lot of explicit teaching on a one-to-one basis ... because aspects that apply to some students won't necessarily... apply to all students (Tutor 1).	Relationship between engineers and clients, acting for a client	Clients valued students' commitment. Students saw the need for regular consultation with clients.	...in a [community directed project] you assess what people do ... as opposed to what they know (Client 2). Interviews and meetings with the people affected are essential ... these people need to be 'in the loop' at all times (Student 1).
Assessment: demonstration of engineering knowledge and engineering processes	Lecturers are concerned that the engineering knowledge applied was not at an appropriate level of difficulty. Tutors understood that students were learning professional skills.	Should the student be awarded marks on the basis of meeting needs ... or on the basis of demonstrating his mechanical engineering knowledge and skills? (Lecturer 1). [Students learned] the kinds of skills that are needed in the private sector: project management, setting specifications, design and implementation, cost estimates, etc. (Tutor 3).	Quality of product, meeting clients'/users' needs	Clients were pleased when their needs were met; disappointed when their needs were not met. Students felt that they had learned both academic content and had represented clients' needs in the final product.	There were useful ideas from all three teams – they now need to work together on the best ideas (Client 1). ... why didn't any of these students invent a machine that I can work with my foot? (Potential user). The project method of learning forced us to learn about our subjects and ... develop solutions to a specific problem ... combining all the knowledge we had gained into our design... it was not until the presentation that I realised how much we had learned (Student 1).

14

Learning and Teaching, Disciplines and Social Practice Theory

VERONICA BAMBER

Introduction

No one doubts the historically significant role of disciplines in shaping some academic practices, and the Biglan typology has been deployed in a number of studies (Neumann 2001: 144). What is in doubt is the extent to which disciplinary explanations help us to understand the messy reality of academic work and practices in the modern university. Fanghanel (2009: 567) points out that Biglan, Becher and others tending toward structuralism 'tend to yield a normalised view of practice, emphasising similarities between disciplinary "tribes" and "territories" while glossing over internal differences' – the influence of other factors such as local context or individual ideology is understated. She reminds us about the tensions between the cognitive and the social, not addressed in these perspectives. For Fanghanel, discipline is both 'a knowledge field and … a sociological object' (Fanghanel 2009: 568), which Becher and Trowler (2001) also acknowledged. In Biglan's terms, the intellectual territory is on a continuum of hard to soft fields, and pure to applied ones. On the social continua are Biglan's convergent, divergent, urban and rural dimensions. However, even the most Biglanesque of writers acknowledge that these dimensions are relative rather than absolute (Kekale 2002: 68), and that boundaries are complex (Becher 1989). Malcolm and Zucas (2009: 498–9) tell us that 'disciplinary boundaries and identities are constantly shifting, contested and dissolving' and 'attempts to divide the "mess" of academic work into essentially artificial categories' can lead to confusion and fragmentation. Like many other current writers, they exhort us to take a more 'nuanced' approach to understanding academic life. Smeby (1996) too suggests that more complex analytical schemes are necessary for consideration of such disciplinary differences.

This is where social practice theory (SPT) comes in. We argued earlier that epistemological essentialism does not reflect the complex nature of higher education (HE), although it has proved to be a useful tool where broad brushstrokes of understanding are sufficient. Moreover 'discipline' is not a straightforward concept for describing what academics think and do. Barnett (2000a) suggests that to cope with the supercomplexity of HE, academics need to work together in 'epistemological pandemonium'. We would suggest, however, that the pandemonium is patterned pandemonium, and SPT helps us to understand some of those patterns. It can help us cope with the 'imponderable and unpredictable' (Strathern 2008: 14) if we anticipate and expect practices and thinking to be just that, but within semi-contained contexts. Disciplinary identities are 'dialogic and emerging through interactions' (Miller 2008: 104), and SPT provides a key to working with those dialogues and interactions.

Having set out our stall about SPT in Chapter 2, we aim in the chapters that conclude each of the Parts to analyse what the contributing authors have said in the light of SPT. There are some key SPT concepts that resonate with what our writers on learning, teaching and the disciplines say. These relate to academic identities, discourse, multiple cultural configurations, and social context. This chapter will consider each of these aspects, and look at what the implications are for learning and teaching.

Academic Identities

Di Napoli and Barnett (2008: 5) talk about 'dislocations of identity' that have happened as academics' traditional sense of identity has been affected by the changing nature of HE, and identity is certainly a key issue for all of the contributing authors in this section. Anne Laiho looks at the development of academic identities in nursing science over time, and the identity of the subject itself. Ashwin *et al.* consider sociological identities in different departments and institutions. Paul Kleiman talks about institutional differences – for example, whether HEIs are teaching only, teaching mainly with some research, or research-led – mirrored in the roles of academic staff. Kleiman perhaps summarises the complexities described by all four authors when he says that: 'the landscape of the [different] disciplines and their various interlocking and interconnecting communities of practice consists of a complex, multi-faceted, multi-layered network of identities, relationships, values, discourses and practices'. This leads to 'the adoption of multiple, metamorphosing identities within the discipline'.

A number of researchers have written about this phenomenon. Di Napoli and Barnett (2008: 4) construe current HE as 'a site of many identities-in-the-making', seen from the perspective of the many groups who make up university life. They remind us that HE has undergone 'seminal changes' in the past 30 years, and institutions have had to rethink their purpose and activities, shaped partly by academics and others who have had to rethink their roles in HE, leading to 'dislocations of identity' (Di Napoli and Barnett 2008: 4). In some cases, this has led to expansions of academic identities, as new opportunities have opened up: 'Processes of identity construction and reconstruction have gone hand in hand in the formulation of the new order. The overall identity of higher education today seems therefore to be a patchwork of *communities of identity* ... These communities are by no means fixed' (Di Napoli and Barnett 2008: 5).

As members of these communities negotiate their place in the new order, and reach 'a better awareness of its members' roles and space' (Di Napoli and Barnett 2008: 6), academic identity continues to be contested and dynamic, with multiple interpretations of academic identity. For Taylor (2008: 29), four types of identities can be distinguished:

- identities taken on through shared practices, accepting given truths;
- identities which are constructed and contested;
- identities which are co-constructed, reflecting non-rational processes;
- identities which are constructed in complex contexts.

Although identity is deeply rooted in an individual's psyche and practices, modern academics are likely to draw on all of these positions in line with their context at any one time, even when the different identity positions seem epistemologically inconsistent (Taylor 2008: 29). Such inconsistencies should be no surprise when we think of the mix of backgrounds from which academics flow into their 'tribe': Shreeve (2009) gives us the example of part-time tutors in art and design who are both professional artists and university academics. Which tribe or community do these individuals belong to? The answer is: several, or different ones at different points in time. Tutors experience multiple identities simultaneously or at different times, with continuous adjustments. Staff either 'drop in' to the academic world; 'move across' to teaching; are – uncomfortably – in both camps; are 'balancing' the best of both worlds; or 'integrating' as an artist educator (Shreeve 2009). As financial pressure on institutions increases, the proportion of fractionally employed staff is likely to rise in academic communities. They bring with them an on-going process of identity construction and reconstruction as they move between the different communities they inhabit, and negotiate to what extent they adopt or reject the practices of each context. But Shreeve's categories do not only apply to fractional staff; full-time staff in mutating environments – like the performing arts lecturers in Paul Kleiman's chapter – also experience such identity reconstruction, learning to accommodate change 'on the job' as they go along.

Identities, then, are continuously under construction, and there may well be a sense of loss as identities mutate (Taylor 2008: 31) and a tendency to blame managerialism, although this may be less helpful than seeing academic identities as 'context-specific assemblages that draw on a shared but open repertoire of traits, beliefs and allegiances' (Taylor 2008: 38). From our SPT perspective, we would add 'practices' to this list, but would wholeheartedly endorse the inseparable mutual influence of context and identities. Taylor (2008: 39) adds that, while research has often been seen as central to academic identities, learning and teaching, and learning about teaching, also need to be included.

What SPT brings to this discussion of identities is the conviction that identities are fluid, constantly (re)negotiated and reconstructed over time within their changing contexts. As we mentioned in Chapter 9, the 'conceptions of teaching' literature of recent decades has value, but does not adequately describe the complexity of this process. For some of the contributing authors in this section, the issue is compounded by staff constantly moving between professional and academic cultures. In each locale, academics and students are positioned in different networks or may have several identities, so they may have several voices (Barnett and Di Napoli 2008: 198). A performing arts lecturer will express their identity differently and deploy different discursive repertoires when working as an artist, or as an educator. An academic sitting on university committees may have a different voice from the one(s) used in their own department. And the voices in their own department will be increasingly varied: according to whether they are discussing research, working with post-graduate students, with undergraduate students or with colleagues on a cross-disciplinary degree programme. On top of this, there is likely to be pressure to adapt to different identities, with an even more attenuated voice, for instance when working – as many of us do – with partner institutions overseas with different educational philosophies, practices and expectations. Barnett and Di Napoli (2008: 202) make the important point that there is, therefore, room for both agency and structure, for individuals to exert their influence and for institutions or disciplinary norms to influence the individuals. Of course, challenges to identity will also be triggered by changes to the mission and strategy of the university, and this will be dealt with in the next part of this book.

Discourse

In SPT, as we have just seen, discourses and identities are intimately connected. Discourses also express and shape social reality and practices. Kapp and Bangeni (2009) looked at how and to what extent students acquire disciplinary discourses. They found that students both resist and absorb the values of their discipline, as they work out how their own identities and discourses intersect with disciplinary discourses. The relationship is not a linear one, as students manifest 'multiple subject positions' (Kapp and Bangeni 2009: 592), as well as gradual acceptance of disciplinary discourses over time. This is interesting because it is yet another manifestation of the fluidity of disciplinary identities and students' absorption of those identities. Shreeve (2009) tells us that students will more easily construct their identities as practitioners in a particular field such as art and design if we pay attention to 'identity work' (Shreeve 2009: 158) and explicitly help students to work between practice and academic contexts. Baxter Magolda (2008) agrees: linking disciplinary learning to students' identities and real-world demands is complex, and can best be achieved via 'learning partnerships'. This was an issue in Chris Winberg's scenario of student engineering projects becoming community projects; the students had learned the 'discourse' of academic work, but this did not sit easily with the different demands of real-life engineering projects. Winberg makes the point that if staff and students are to cross boundaries between academic and field work, common understandings need to be worked at: 'Translation, negotiation, and simplification are required when the academic world and the real world meet'.

Anne Laiho describes the conflicts between different healthcare professionals' perspectives: academicisation, and scholarly discourse, is at odds with clinical practice. The two sides might come closer if effort is put into articulating what the discipline is about 'in ways that are likely to be more meaningful to practitioners, consumers, research funders and the scientific community'. The range of stakeholders Laiho mentions here, each with their own identities and discourses, is a challenge in itself.

Multiple Cultural Configurations

According to SPT, people in universities interact in their various locations, producing different sets of social practices and cultural configurations in each locale. For Barnett and Di Napoli plurality is to be welcomed as a sign of academic freedom, and there is a growing diversity of communities of practice with their own identities – 'even if some of those communities are struggling to establish a coherent identity' (Barnett and Di Napoli 2008: 197). We see this in Anne Laiho's chapter on nursing science, where the relatively youthful discipline of nursing is seeking to establish an academic identity amid varied views on the discipline, and influences of other disciplinary groups. In his chapter, too, Paul Kleiman describes the developing identities of the different subject groups within the performing arts spectrum.

This presents significant challenges, as the university fragments and subgroups find themselves splintered into diverse internal communities which lack common understandings and values to bind them together (Barnett and Di Napoli 2008: 204). So a 'performing arts' department might contain dance, music and drama, all, as Kleiman indicates, with different histories, cultures and aspirations. Similarly, nursing science units may be merged into medical or social science faculties, as Anne Laiho describes, becoming part of bigger units and struggling to assert their cultures and norms in the face of more powerful groups.

The multiple cultural configurations we see in our four contributing authors' chapters are both horizontal and vertical. Vertically, single disciplines can have very different manifestations in different institutions, as Ashwin et al. describe. The 'discipline' of sociology can look very different depending on which angle or university one approaches it from. Similarly, horizontal groupings within institutions mean that disciplines may be bedfellows with cognate subjects, as in the case of nursing and physiotherapy – or not. Economic rationalisations and mergers can lead to strange mixes, where subjects cohabit joint physical spaces and a common organisational location, but very different intellectual and cultural spaces. Laiho makes the point that nursing would not sit comfortably with women's studies, but disciplines may not have a choice as to how they are configured within the organisation. Rather than maintain disciplinary purity, if such a thing ever exists, subjects in any multi-subject institution – and even those in small specialist institutions, such as conservatoires – will rub against each other and be changed in the process.

Another manifestation of multiple cultural configuration lies at the intersection between the academic and professional worlds, as described in Chapter 9. Disciplines which straddle communities – for example, applied subjects such as nursing and engineering – are likely to be constantly challenged to take on ideas and practices from both communities. As professional fields and academic subjects develop over time, whether due to changing economic circumstances, technological innovation or other factors, identities, discourses and practices will all adapt and cross-contaminate across communities. In some cases, as in nursing, academics will have a dual identity, since they practise in both communities, and perhaps experience contradictory demands in each.

In the case of engineering, Chris Winberg talks about the 'academic gaze', which implies that there is also a 'professional gaze'. Winberg uses legitimation code theory to consider power differentials between the two communities, and the relationship of knowledge claims between and across fields. The concept of boundary crossing is important here, since many subjects are operating at such boundaries or intersections, with contradictory demands or expectations, as in the case of Winberg's community engineering projects. This is not necessarily a negative situation, however. Tuomi-Gröhn *et al.* (2003) found that where different cultures meet, new meanings may be formed, and learning opportunities are created within this dynamic discursive space or 'hybrid learning context' (Tuomi-Gröhn *et al.* 2003: 5). In the no man's land of such intersections, elements from each side can combine, freeing different groups from rigid patterns. Students do not find curricular boundary crossing easy (Tuomi-Gröhn *et al.* 2003: 6), but these liminal spaces are sometimes where real learning takes place.

Social Context

Context is an important aspect of SPT, since contextual factors and social practices are intimately intertwined in any location. Context is a key factor in Ashwin *et al.*'s conceptualisation of how sociological knowledge is acquired, by whom, and which influences impinge on the process. They make the point that the tribes and territories notion assumes a semi-universal experience, regardless of the type of institution a student studies in. In contrast, Bernstein's (2000) pedagogic device recognises that there will be inequality between what is offered and experienced at different types of institution. These inequalities are reflected in 'distribution rules' – the contexts in which knowledge is produced;

in 'evaluation rules' – learning and teaching practices; and, to a lesser extent, in 'recontextualising rules' – recontextualising of knowledge into curriculum. It is in the distribution rules that differences are greatest, and Ashwin *et al.* compare elite with non-elite institutions. Interestingly, however, inequalities do not divide neatly down the elite or non-elite institution line.

Institutional type is an important factor in differences found between departments, not only in the case of Ashwin *et al.*'s sociology departments, but also, for example, in engineering (Lattuca *et al.* 2010; Lattuca and Stark 1995). Disciplinary cultures are key factors in academic activity, but are mediated by institutional context, they argue. In other words, local conditions matter (Lattuca *et al.* 2010: 36). In thinking about what affects learning and teaching in any given locale, the institutional and departmental context, as well as sub-field differences, count.

Another aspect of the context within which disciplines operate is the web of external drivers that affect how different subjects develop. For Kleiman, these include research assessment, moves toward the professionalisation of teaching, new technologies and widening access. Kleiman feels that these factors are amplified in particular disciplinary contexts: in research-intensive contexts, academics are funnelled increasingly into research activity, while others may maintain more of a practitioner identity. For arts academics especially, the shifting 'tectonic plates' of HE change – described by Murray Saunders in the next part of this book – are another influence on how they and their disciplines are likely to develop. Both Kleiman and Laiho refer to the 'landscape' of their disciplines as unbounded, complex spaces that academics are constantly renegotiating.

Variations *within* disciplines also matter. Within disciplinary groups, finer-grained categories are needed to capture differences in staff attitudes and behaviours (Lattuca *et al.* 2010: 22), and 'more nuanced understandings of disciplinary and institutional influences on faculty attitudes and behaviours' are needed. Lattuca *et al.* (2010) advocate the use of Holland's typology for sub-discipline analysis, and use this to examine different engineering disciplines in the light of Holland's six personality types. They found that staff in different engineering sub-disciplines 'differ in meaningful ways in the changes they report making in their curriculum, pedagogy and professional development activities' (Lattuca *et al.* 2010: 29). This has implications for classroom practices, for example, the use of active learning pedagogies, the skills emphasised in the curriculum – for example, the extent to which transferable skills are embraced and practised (Lattuca *et al.* 2010: 35–6) – and varied responses to national engineering education guidelines. This raises questions about the generalisability of Chris Winberg's discussion of mechanical engineering; while Chris makes no claims that her analysis extends to other arms of engineering, there are references to 'engineering' as if it were one discipline. So while Lattuca *et al.* (2010) strongly endorse the importance of disciplinary influence, they also look upward and out to the institutional context, and sub-field character-istics. Fields which are treated as a unified field – for example engineering – actually operate at the intersection of disciplinary cultures – and personality types within that culture; institutional context; professional connections; and sub-discipline characteristics. Discipline matters, but so do many other factors, including context.

Impact of Disciplines on Academic Practices

Having established that discipline is only one influence on learning and teaching, we are left with the question of what this means for academic *prac-tices*, since practices are at the centre of SPT. Fitzmaurice (2010) recommends that we conceive of teaching as a practice, to move us:

> ... beyond a narrow and mechanistic view of teaching built around the adoption of effective strategies to one that is broader in scope and takes into account the complexity and contextuality of the work, and the impor-tance of virtuous dispositions and caring endeavour in teaching.
>
> Fitzmaurice 2010: 54

Smeby (1996) looks at whether discipline has a real impact on three learning and teaching practices: time spent on teaching and preparation; distribution of time across different types of instruction; and levels of teaching. He notes that, while teaching content may be discipline-defined, degree structure, curriculum, teaching loads, resources and teaching plans are institutionally framed (Smeby 1996: 69). Then, individual ideological factors that qualify disciplinary manifestations have to be added in to the mix (Fanghanel 2009: 571–2). So, the influence of discipline on teaching and learning practices is constrained.

One way of looking 'beyond a narrow and mechanistic view of teaching' (Fitzmaurice 2010: 54) is to capture the real stories of teachers in practice, rather than glossing over the realities and challenges of practice. And these stories may seem contradictory. Paul Kleiman talks about the 'de-centering' of performing arts academics in the face of change. However, in their study of sociology lecturers, McLean and Abbas (2009) found that lecturers' disci-plinary identities were not fragmenting, in spite of the pedagogical challenges of adapting to managerialism and marketisation. In fact, the lecturers did not see changes to the discipline as a great threat, although they did wish to retain the 'sacred knowledge' of the discipline in their core curriculum (McLean and Abbas 2009: 531). In order to do this, academics seemed prepared to change their methods of learning and teaching – their practices; Chris Winberg's example of engineering lecturers trying out a different approach to student projects is a case in point.

Conclusions

Returning to the concept of 'tribes and territories', what I think we have seen in the preceding chapters is a web of complexities that is not easily readable through the 'tribes' lens. For academics who are weaving their way through academic life, over-simplifying the realities of that life is not helpful. For example, Poyas and Smith (2007) describe the struggle of clinical faculty teacher educators to construct identities, when their identities are confused in 'a professionally blurred context' (Poyas and Smith 2007: 332). Problems – such as those experienced by clinicians who become faculty – are compounded by the failure to acknowledge identity clashes.

Neither is it doing any favours to the students entering today's much more complex world if we try to corral them into disciplinary boxes. Students struggle with what can be mysterious 'ways of knowing' (Tynan and New 2009) if what they bring to the learning situation – their individual beliefs and backgrounds – is ignored. Baxter Magolda (2008: 11) talks about the need for students to learn 'self-authorship' and epistemological complexity, rather than 'externally-derived formulas for what to believe, how to be and how to relate to others'. Students need to be able 'to translate their disciplinary learning into supercomplex, transdisciplinary contexts' (Baxter Magolda 2008: 19). Poyas and Smith (2007) found that cultural factors are also important, if students are to mesh with the educational experience that is on offer. The fit between student identities and institutional cultures is a key issue if learning is to take place.

As we said in Chapter 2, in SPT academics and students are not cultural dopes who simply enact social roles. Academics are not passive victims of a tribal hierarchy, but educators who are motivated to do well by their students in an increasingly demanding HE sector – and those demands are increasingly demanding. Hardy (2010), in his study of teaching conditions in an Australian university, uses Kemmis and Grootenboer's (2008) concept of 'practice architectures' to analyse teachers' experiences. Three sets of factors – socio-political, cultural-discursive and material-economic – influence teachers' work, within conditions that are increasingly economic-, resource- and audit-driven. Academics were aware that what they could do with their students, and how, was conditioned by these elements. In other words, teaching practices were affected not simply by disciplinary norms, but by complex, inter-related factors external to the discipline, which constitute 'practice architectures'. The importance of this thinking is that it highlights the need to work on the 'conditions of practice' (Hardy 2010: 402), so that academic practices can be supported.

This requires us to take what a number of writers (for example, Fanghanel 2009; Lattuca et al. 2010; Malcolm and Zucas 2009) exhort us to take: a more nuanced view of how discipline influences learning and teaching. Smeby (1996) suggests that more complex analytical schemes are necessary for consideration of different practices between disciplines. Smeby found that lecturers in different disciplines spent different amounts of time on different types of teaching activity – for example, seminars as opposed to lectures or laboratory work – on preparing for teaching, and on the levels they taught at. However, not all of these differences were attributed to disciplinary norms. For example, citing Kyvik (1991) and Kuhn (1970), Smeby (1996: 70) notes that disciplines are likely to be multi-paradigmatic rather than having a single paradigm, and that this also applies, to some extent, to the range of teaching activities. Other explanations of difference are communication language and degree of dependence; for instance, in the humanities and social sciences students doing research normally choose their own topics, while those in the natural sciences are more likely to have topics allocated by supervisors. These practical results of different disciplinary practices cannot simply be explained by an 'epistemological determination of work' (Clark 1987).

Malcolm and Zucas (2009: 504) encourage us to look at the actors in the disciplines themselves, so we can better 'understand interdisciplinary practices, particularly in relation to the growth, transformation and withering of disciplines over time and space'. This will shed more light than focusing on boundary constructions. Boyer (1990) also recommended that we reconceptualise academic work to better reflect the four scholarships of academic activity. One of these, the scholarship of integration, connects ideas across disciplinary boundaries. Working with interdisciplinarity has its challenges, for example if it is management-imposed, to rationalise and merge subjects, rather than pedagogically or intellectually driven by academic communities which see the point of working together. One way forward might be the development of 'mindful disciplinarity' as part of an academic apprenticeship, so that teachers develop a critical awareness of the discipline as 'a site of intellectual and social practice' (Malcolm and Zucas 2009: 505).

What this part of the book has established is that the extent and nature of disciplinary differences in learning and teaching has been relatively under-researched (Neumann 2001; Middendorf and Pace 2004). American Association of Higher Education research in the early 1990s looked at the complexities of teaching in different disciplinary contexts (Neumann 2001: 136), and some studies (for example, Lattuca et al. 2010) have also focused on variation within disciplines – although this is often swept aside in the bigger brush strokes of interdisciplinary analysis. Studies usually focus on the hard–soft, pure–applied dichotomies, such as the use of essays in soft, pure subjects and examinations in hard applied fields. I would conjecture that research in the near future will concentrate increasingly on another 'hard' factor: the effects of staff workload allocation, class size, research pressure, limited contact hours, rather than on the fine points of disciplinary difference in itself. The tone might change to:

... yes, we do have distinctive ways of thinking and practising in our subject, and my students need to learn these. But that will happen in the light of the resource we have been allocated, not just because in the social sciences we like to have seminars.

The next section of the book explores some of these catalysts for change.

4

Catalysts for Changing Disciplinary Practices

15

Imperatives for Academic Practices
Catalysts for Sustained Change

MURRAY SAUNDERS

Education either functions as an instrument which is used to facilitate integration of the younger generation into the logic of the present system and bring about conformity or it becomes the practice of freedom, the means by which men and women deal critically and creatively with reality and discover how to participate in the transformation of their world.

Paulo Freire 1970: 23

This part of the book looks outside the cultures that inhabit disciplines themselves to identify emerging forces shaping academic practices. Metaphors matter, as we know, and alternative metaphors we might deploy here are 'catalysts' on the one hand and 'driver' on the other. The 'driver' metaphor suggests a fairly straightforward causal link between a new set of circumstances or 'affordances' and a change in higher education practices.

By contrast the 'catalyst' metaphor suggests a feature or a set of features that hasten or bring into being new practices. The changes in practice or new emphases in practice are created because of the convergence of catalytic factors resulting in the perception that there is a compelling need for a response. This compulsion is not some kind of reductive force determining action – as is the case with the 'driver' idea – but is a mix of complicity and compliance on the part of higher education actors who identify, often in a competitive way, a powerful set of reasons for new actions. These reasons may or may not be logically or technically derived but are based on a socially sourced shift in what seems strategically required in order to continue to survive.

For these reasons the idea of a 'catalyst' is metaphorically richer than other possibilities in the context of the complex congruencies the contributors to this section outline.

Our social practice approach characterises people working within universities as carriers of practices who enact reservoirs of ways of behaving, understanding and responding in individualised repertoires that are to a certain extent particular to them. However, in this section we identify elements in the professional, social and political environment of higher education that configure the 'reservoirs' and 'repertoires' of practice in the process of individuation from structural characteristics.

The configuration of the 'repertoires of recognizable practices', as Reckwitz (2002: 250) has it, involves routinised ways of understanding, knowing and behaving. The focus in analysis is therefore best located in the practices, not the individuals involved. We argue that any useful theory of knowledge and of disciplines needs to see them as being to some extent socially constructed, but at the same time recognising that knowledge is objective in ways which transcend the historical conditions of its production.

We do not claim that the themes our contributors address are definitive or comprehensive. In a way, there is arbitrariness about them and another group of editors might have identified an alternative list. That said, we feel this group of themes form an agenda that most interested commentators and observers of higher education will recognise and agree have resonance as catalysts of new practices in higher education worldwide. In the light of our definition of a 'catalyst', we suggest the themes have the following characteristics in common:

- They have become associated with changes in academic practices worldwide and not confined to one national or regional system.
- They represent a powerful set of considerations that stakeholders within higher education and those charged with managing it institutionally and nationally feel obliged to respond to.
- They have a sustained and resilient quality and have permeated higher education systems at a variety of levels.
- They are not confined to any one discipline and have a meta- or transdisciplinary character.
- They signal competing explanatory paradigms for how academics behave and suggest a dilution of the explanatory power of disciplinary cultures for the emergent configurations of academic practices.

The section begins with Ray Land's focus on the emergence of interdisciplinarity as a troublesome concept for the retention of clear boundaries between disciplines that can be taken for granted. He understands this new dynamic in terms of the threshold concepts associated with the conceptual integration of different perspectives, a letting go of a previous stance, an ontological shift, and acquisition of a new shared discourse and argues that it suggests a primarily personal change in subjectivity. The impetus is provided by the interdisciplinary imperative, which is concerned, for example, with issues that do not fit easily under the lens of one discipline, and which are generated increasingly by society and distinguished by relatively short-time courses calling in some cases for a policy action. While the themes that characterise our preoccupations are overwhelmingly interdisciplinary in nature, he argues that barriers remain within and between tribal communities. He notes that interdisciplinarity remains difficult, and often fails. It requires mutual deconstruction of each other's terminologies, and mutual discourses or frameworks remain in short supply. Existing organisational structures usually get in the way. Academic incentives certainly still point the other way. He argues that the jury is still out on the capacity we have currently to change modes of knowledge generation and exchange in the globalised and digitised world of the present, but he argues strongly that the academic incentives which currently predispose academics to keep within their disciplinary territories, both conceptually and socially, may need to be rethought in order to engineer such a shift.

The chapter by Kerri-Lee Krause focuses on the influence of higher education policy drivers, including graduate capabilities and generic skills, and their increasing role in shaping the nature of academic practices within disciplinary cultures and identities. Using the example from the emerging tourism domain, she provides a lens through which to examine some of the practices academic staff deploy as they engage with what she terms 'vectors'. This metaphor is interesting in that it denotes both a 'carrier' or shaping influence as well as a direction. A change vector might be seen to imply both meanings. Her chapter analyses the interplay of change vectors within disciplinary territories and the higher education policy landscape and considers the implications for university policy and management. She adopts the Schuster and Finkelstein (2006) perspective in which demographic changes in the population; technological changes; market forces; the ageing academic workforce and associated implications for the workforce of the future; and the quality and performativity agenda, constitute the main shaping influences. She identifies other policy drivers including research assessment exercises, performance-based funding for learning and teaching, and economic imperatives to prepare work-ready graduates who will contribute to the knowledge economy.

The contested field of tourism is used in this chapter to illustrate a domain of study in flux. Krause argues that this kind of example is apt for the illustration of ways in which academic staff might manage themselves, their tribal affiliations and their sense of place in a contested environment. Confronting and working with the grain of ambiguity, reconfigured workloads and empowerment are among the possible responses to the 'vectors' of change she identifies. She understands these vectors as having the potential to dissipate and fragment academic communities but also, if academics can harness such fluidity, it may lead to reinforced bonds and encourage intellectual partnerships across traditional disciplinary boundaries and innovative approaches to inquiry and knowledge production. The threshold concepts Ray Land discusses in his chapter might be useful in combination with such analyses.

Valerie Clifford's focus is on the internationalisation of higher education, but not just on market share in terms of international students and supporting them to be successful in their studies. She argues that universities are realising that to become 'international universities' in reality, rather than just in rhetoric, then internationalisation needs to pervade every aspect of the institution and should include the 'internationalisation' of the education of the majority, non-mobile home students.

She argues that a reformed curriculum is central to the enterprise of internationalism at home, yet she notes that the curriculum has figured minimally in university internationalisation strategies. While reforming the curriculum for internationalisation is embraced in some disciplines it is resisted in others. She analyses the differences that emanate from practices associated with the hard, pure disciplines on the one hand and the 'soft' disciplines on the other with less secure boundaries. The focus she promotes within internationalisation is not on knowledge as in subject content, but on the student and their future needs, and society's needs for them, as global citizens. These roles require skills of criticality, creativity, and intercultural communication, and the ability to articulate and engage with different value systems. The chapter exemplifies this stance by reference to a recent study that highlighted the resistance of the hard, pure disciplines to such an orientation. The study was carried out in an Australian university. She shows how the internationalisation agenda foregrounds the enculturated nature of higher education and focuses attention on the cultural values and beliefs underlying curricula and pedagogy. She notes how internationalisation requires that academics look at their personal and professional values, at their way of interacting with cultural others and broaden their understanding of knowledge systems, values, behaviours and embedded practices.

Clifford suggests that these discussions need to focus on the students rather than the discipline. A factor discussed by many of the staff in the study was their own level of 'internationalisation' and, therefore, their ability to internationalise the curriculum. She argues that internationalisation offers universities a new ethos in which academics can reconceptualise their epistemology and pedagogy based on constructivist and situated perspectives. Many disciplines have embraced the perspectives of internationalisation and are exploring the exciting possibilities of interdisciplinarity. Internationalisation may offer the disciplines a new lease of life rather than threaten their way of organising knowledge.

The chapter by Susan Lea and Lynne Callaghan is informed by a study originating in 2002, with a second follow-up study conducted in 2010 focusing on what they term supercomplexity. This notion, originally developed by Ronald Barnett in the early part of the last decade, points to the multiple frameworks of understanding, action and self-identity which now characterise the higher education landscape. They argue that this concept is particularly apt for the analysis of how the participants in their research were experiencing the changing context of higher education and its impacts upon their teaching. Their work suggests that research which over-emphasises disciplinary culture and its effects on teaching practices should be read rather more critically and that a rather more inconsistent and uncertain relationship exists between disciplines and practices. In their work, differences between academic cultures and their disciplinary epistemologies did not emerge very strongly, but common concerns and themes emerged relevant to all lecturers and took precedence over their 'tribal' differences.

They argue that the complexity of the social, economic and political context within which higher education is practised is often reduced to single variable effects. Following Barnett, they conceive of a supercomplex world that is characterised by a multiplicity of frameworks. In earlier work, they found that lecturers and managers clearly articulated the impact of the challenging nature of higher education upon their teaching and learning activity, and their responses to it. Respondents in the follow-up study suggested that the solution was that a more collegiate, multidisciplinary style of working might be the way to cope with a supercomplex environment.

With Martin Oliver's chapter, we turn to a feature of twenty-first-century life embedded in all areas of social practice, that of the 'new technologies' but, in particular, the digital technologies and how these developments are shaping academic practices. This chapter explores claims that technology is changing the academic practices associated with teaching and learning. First, examples of this kind of claim are drawn from the literature, and a professional 'tribe' involved in this process is identified. Then, two examples are offered that look at the process of change from the perspective of activity theory. The chapter concludes by reframing technology as an opportunity for encouraging or resisting change, rather than a simple cause.

Oliver notes that technology is often written about as a 'driver' for change in education. Sometimes it is positioned as a simple cause. Less extreme, but nonetheless widespread, is the 'softer' kind of technological determinism. This suggests that there will be an evolution in learning and teaching, with technology as a catalyst, if not a simple cause. He notes that claims are made for the power of technology to transform higher education. It is positioned as an all but unstoppable force, poised to sweep away existing structures and practices. As the examples in his chapter show, however, the relationship between technology and change is not nearly so simple.

Rather than being the sole explanatory cause of change, technology is implicated in change in complex and political ways. Technologies do not so much overwhelm the practices of 'tribes'. Instead, they can be understood as something that particular groups can take up because they help with some wider problem – such as offering more flexible courses so as to address flagging student recruitment – or because they can be used to influence the practice of others, as is the case with the digitised resource collection to which Oliver refers in his chapter. It may be better therefore to understand teaching technologies as producing new practices – because they are constituted using different tools and, at a micro level, in pursuit of different purposes – but not new disciplinary cultures. He notes that academics find ways to use technologies to protect the roles and principles that they value, preserving the practices they value, even if these may be enacted in very different ways. In an important sense, therefore,

Oliver argues that the determining power of the new technologies may be overstated and that while new practices have certainly developed because of their use, they tend still to be shaped by the cultural assumptions associated with the tribe.

In summary, the following chapters explore, by the use of different perspectives and foci, the way in which academic practices are increasingly shaped by forces outside the cultures associated with the disciplines themselves. These forces reflect the permeable determining processes that indicate the radical shift of academic practice from relative insularity to relative responsiveness to societal and global pressures. Practices have moved from being very loosely coupled to relatively tightly coupled to outside determinants in which external changes and imperatives increasingly exert influence on how academics behave and what they think is important.

16
Crossing Tribal Boundaries
Interdisciplinarity as a Threshold Concept

RAY LAND

The chains of habit are generally too small to be felt until they are too strong to be broken.

Dr Samuel Johnson 1709–1784

Introduction

It is generally accepted that the training and acculturation involved in becoming a professional scholar, and in gaining entry to an academic tribe, is concerned principally with acquiring deep knowledge in a specialised field. The disciplines within which the majority of these specialised fields are organised serve not just as sources of knowledge and expertise but as bases of personal identity (Henkel 2000). If all learning can be construed in one way or another as 'a change in subjectivity' (Pelletier 2007), then disciplinarity can be seen as one key determinant of academic identity. Disciplines have developed their own conceptual worlds, with their own robust 'ways of thinking and practising' (McCune and Hounsell 2005: 255) and 'knowledge practices' (Strathern 2008: 11). Immersion within these worlds and practices constitutes the process of academic formation. We are what we know and do. Perkins has characterised these distinctive modes of reasoning and explanation as 'games of enquiry' or 'epistemes':

> a system of ideas or way of understanding that allows us to establish knowledge. ... the importance of students understanding the structure of the disciplines they are studying. 'Ways of knowing' is another phrase in the same spirit. As used here, epistemes are manners of justifying, explaining, solving problems, conducting enquiries, and designing and validating various kinds of products or outcomes.
>
> Perkins 2006: 42

This formative strength and generative social context in which to practise has traditionally served as the foundation of an academic career. The established scholarship on academic tribes and territories has amply demonstrated this (Becher 1989; Becher and Trowler 2001). However, as we increasingly find ourselves in an age of globalisation, uncertainty, risk and speed, the pressing scientific, social and economic problems of our times – climate change, sustainability, terrorism, national debt, health, ageing populations – seem to demand more than one disciplinary lens to bring them more clearly into view. As the quotation from Dr Johnson above implies, the previously useful and strong chains of disciplinary habit may imperceptibly become what his English contemporary and fellow poet William Blake termed 'mind forg'd manacles', and a potential impediment to interdisciplinary practice. We will return to this issue in greater depth later but it is worth noting at this point the observation by Lowham and Schilla in their study of collaboration and interdisciplinarity in graduate education, that:

> [p]erhaps what is most remarkable about the long history of interdiscipli-nary research in the United States is that, despite considerable funding, support with nearly religious fervour, and much practice, interdisciplinary research and education often fell short of genuine integration and the results were stymied 'by disciplinary chauvinism and the psychological, social, and epistemological problems of working across disciplines' (Klein 1990: 35).
>
> Lowham and Schilla 2008: 2

An earlier study by Frodeman *et al.* (2001) found that interdisciplinary research often resulted in identifying and pursuing new fields of specialisation as opposed to the conceptual integration and shared insight to which interdisci-plinary practice often aspires.

Threshold Concepts

Meyer and Land (2003b), in their work on threshold concepts and troublesome knowledge, have shown how threshold concepts serve to map and limit concep-tual territories and disciplinary boundaries. Disciplinary subjectivity, they maintain, is to a degree determined by these boundaries, as urban and national identities are comparably constructed within geographical and cultural bound-aries. Their studies of disciplinary learning across various subjects (Meyer and Land 2006; Land *et al.* 2008; Meyer *et al.* 2010) indicate how acquisition of a threshold concept within a particular discipline operates in the manner of 'a portal, a liminal space, opening up a new and previously inaccessible way of thinking about something' (Meyer and Land 2003b: 412). This leads to a trans-formed way of understanding, or interpreting, or viewing something without which the learner finds it difficult to progress. As a consequence of compre-hending a threshold concept there may thus be:

> a transformed internal view of subject matter, subject landscape, or even world view. Such a transformed view or landscape may represent how

people 'think' in a particular discipline, or how they perceive, apprehend, or experience particular phenomena within that discipline.

Meyer and Land 2003b: 412

The notion of a learning threshold can be used to analyse the ontological shift required, not just within academic learning but in other forms of professional, social and cultural development. In this respect it offers a useful conceptual tool through which to consider the nature of interdisciplinarity and the challenges it presents. It is proposed here that, for many discipline-minded 'tribal' academics, interdisciplinarity presents many, if not all, of the characteristics of a threshold concept. If interdisciplinarity is valued as both a personal and common good, for the reasons intimated earlier, then it might be deemed desirable for more academics to become more interdisciplinary-minded. In terms of threshold theory, this would entail their passing through a liminal phase of transformation into new conceptual territory, crossing both conceptual and disciplinary boundaries into an untravelled world in which previously inaccessible perspectives are brought into view.

The journey toward a more interdisciplinary mode of thinking and practising is likely to be instigated or provoked, as is the acquisition of other threshold concepts, by an encounter in the preliminal state with a form of 'troublesome knowledge'. According to threshold theory, the troublesome knowledge inherent within the threshold concept serves to unsettle prior understanding or habituated practice, rendering it fluid, and provoking a state of liminality:

> Within the liminal state an integration of new knowledge occurs which requires a reconfiguring of the learner's prior conceptual schema and a letting go or discarding of any earlier conceptual stance. This reconfiguration occasions an ontological and an epistemic shift. The integration/reconfiguration and accompanying ontological/epistemic shift can be seen as *reconstitutive* features of the threshold concept. Together these features bring about the required new understanding.
>
> Meyer *et al.* 2010: xi

The reconfiguring discussed here will involve the integration of new conceptual material at the same time as the letting go of prevailing conceptual schemata. Herein lies much of the troublesomeness of the transformation. For reasons discussed later, the ontological shift experienced within the liminal space will also incur – and require – a loosening or weakening of disciplinary identity. The liminal process [Latin *limen* – 'threshold'] of gaining the new understanding is likely to lead the learner across conceptual boundaries into new conceptual space. Both learning and learner are irreversibly transformed, producing a postliminal state marked by a changed use of discourse. All of these dimensions of threshold concepts – the encounter with troublesome knowledge, integration of new understandings, letting go of a prior stance, ontological shift, the crossing of conceptual boundaries, irreversible transformation, changed discourse – would seem to characterise the process of adopting interdisciplinary practice.

A Spectrum of Collaboration

Of course collaboration between members of disciplinary tribes can take on a number of complexions. Colleagues can work on joint projects in a complementary fashion with little interaction between disciplines. This is often characterised as 'multidisciplinarity'. Interdisciplinarity is more generally acknowledged as a situation where disciplines interact and learn from each other, and members of different academic tribes work 'at the crossroads of several disciplines and sets of practical demands' (Gasper 2010: 59). Blackmore (2010: 10) defines this level of collaboration as 'an encounter with knowledge sets, methodologies and skills from more than one established academic discipline, combined with reflection on the relationships between the sets of knowledges, skills and methodologies explored.' Within this area of collaboration Klein (1990: 64) defines four types of interdisciplinary activities: borrowing, problem-solving, increasing consistency of methods and concepts, and establishing an inter-discipline. The other end of the spectrum, often termed 'transdisciplinarity', entails individual academics adopting the perspectives and ways of seeing and practising more familiarly used in other tribal territory. This requires the ability to connect fields, to integrate 'foreign knowledge', to tolerate high levels of uncertainty and risk and to cross boundaries, though without seeking 'a unified super-formulation' (Gasper 2010: 60). An example might be that of ecological economics, where economists view phenomena from ecological perspectives, as opposed to say environmental economics where economists bring their existing conceptual lenses and ways of thinking and practising to bear on the phenomenon of the environment. The former will require a substantial shift in subjectivity, the latter probably no shift.

The Case for Interdisciplinarity

A number of voices have challenged the uses of interdisciplinarity, questioning the degree of innovation that is claimed or the creative value that is added by such engagements (Frodeman *et al.* 2001). Gasper (2010: 52), however, advocating more widespread adoption of interdisciplinary practices, has spoken of a 'problematique of interdisciplinarity'. He suggests that, within an interdisciplinary field and practice such as public policy and administration, '(t)he complexity of policy cases frequently exceeds the grasp of discipline-based knowledge, even when brought together from different disciplines' (Gasper 2010: 53). He argues that a field like this has to draw on various types of knowledge and understanding in order to tackle the various kinds of 'pressing and interconnected real issues' besetting our current society that were typified earlier, and suggests that thinking and practice within a field like public policy 'links material from different fields without unifying them' (Gasper 2010: 53):

> Whereas disciplines can attain a high degree of enclosure around self-defined concepts, methods and questions, and leave aside matters not convenient for … [a] disciplinary matrix, a practically oriented public servant enterprise like public administration should never adopt such a prioritisation of tidiness above usefulness.'
>
> Ibid

He also indicates that the temporalities of disciplinarity and interdisciplinarity are different, with the latter often expecting a faster pace:

> Much interdisciplinarity arises in response to practical and immediate life problem situations, where we cannot wait for discipline-gained knowledge that is not yet available. Such work, oriented to life problems, might not be conventionally scientifically elegant, but it draws on sophisticated craft skills of selection, synthesis and judgement.
>
> Ibid

Klein (2000: 13) similarly identifies issues that do not fit easily under the lens of one discipline, and which are 'generated increasingly by society and distinguished by relatively short-time courses calling in some cases for a policy action result and in other cases for a technological quick fix.' The 'practical and immediate life problem situations' to which Gasper refers might take the form of, say, forensics, where in the normal course of a criminal investigation it would be necessary to have close co-operation among forensic chemists, medics, police scene of crime officers, lawyers, journalists, politicians, media officers, civil administrators, criminologists, counsellors and psychologists. Another situation might be public energy utilities, such as the use of tidal barrier technologies, where electrical engineers and civil engineers could find themselves working in collaboration with ecologists, biologists, zoologists, financiers, economists, computer modellers, politicians, media officers, lawyers, urban planners, rural and community development specialists, tourism consultants, journalists, policy analysts, management scientists and sociologists. Another currently topical scenario is that of climate change, particularly in relation to global warming, in which environmental scientists, physicists, meteorologists and geologists work together and share perspectives with geographers, economists, statisticians, computer scientists, politicians, journalists, civil servants, policy analysts and sociologists. Hall's (2011) detailed empirical study of uncertainty as a threshold concept in climate change science demonstrates the difficulty of establishing a common discourse in this field, let alone consensus or shared perspectives. Work oriented to life problems, Gasper (2010: 52) suggests, might not be 'conventionally scientifically elegant'. In the case of the last scenario, climate change, the interdisciplinary debates have occasionally led to knowledge of a much more troublesome kind, including the positing of new paradigms, such as that of post-normal science:

> Philosophers and practitioners of science have identified this particular mode of scientific activity as one that occurs where the stakes are high, uncertainties large and decisions urgent, and where values are embedded in the way science is done and spoken. It has been labelled 'post-normal' science ... The danger of a 'normal' reading of science is that it assumes science can first find truth, then speak truth to power, and that truth-based policy will then follow.
>
> Hulme 2007: 1

Hulme provoked further controversy by iconoclastically challenging traditional disciplinary practices, contending that: 'Climate change is too important to be left to scientists – least of all the normal ones' (ibid).

Venturing into Strange Places

Barnett (1999: 43) has characterised the world facing twenty-first-century higher education as a 'radically unknowable world'. In a recent seminar in which I asked a group of academics from varied disciplinary backgrounds to identify the salient characteristics of their society over the next decade they identified the characteristics listed in Figure 16.1.

Moreover these features were seen not as characterising a futurological possibility but rather as an intensification of already established trends. The supercomplexity included in the list is another term coined by Barnett to depict a condition in which, unlike mere complexity, 'interactions between the elements are unclear, uncertain and unpredictable' (Barnett 2004: 249) and where challenges are never resolved because 'it produces a multiplication of incompatible differences of interpretation' (ibid). This is a state in which 'our ignorance expands in all kinds of directions' (ibid: 250) and in which there arises a 'need for imagination and creative "knowing-in-situ". Mode 3 knowledge where all our knowledge – of the world, of our situations, of ourselves – is contested.' Barnett has spoken elsewhere of the need for modern academics to 'venture into strange places' with their students (Barnett 2007: 147) and of the need for a new pedagogy to address a supercomplex world which 'must be founded on openness, mutual disclosure, personal risk and disturbance' (Barnett 2004: 258).

Uncertainty	Unpredictability
Speed and acceleration	Risk
Complexity	Need for flexibility and agility
Supercomplexity	Entitlement versus responsibility
Multiculturalism	Scarcity of resources
Mobility of the population	Austerity
Conflict (social, military)	Sustainability
Inter-generational tension	Need for prudence
Need for ethical citizenship	Transparency and accountability
Information saturation	Discontinuity and rupture
Proliferation of knowledge	Shifting paradigms
Globalisation	Poverty versus affluence
Internationalisation	Outsourcing of jobs
Increasing panic	Youthfulness
Private/public sector tension	

Figure 16.1 Perceived characteristics of the twenty-first century

Interdisciplinarity as Troublesome Knowledge: the Gaze of the Cyclops

A pedagogy based on radical contestability is a tall order. Similarly, for academics whose professional training has emphasised deep immersion within a largely monodisciplinary community of practice – and for whom all the career rewards have to date largely been dependent on production and performance of outputs geared to that community – it is not surprising that a somewhat Cyclops-like application of a single disciplinary lens is retained as the most reliable guarantee of future career success. Such immersion in the literature and practice of a specific tribe becomes a source of expertise, rigour and renown. Regarding an interdiscplinary pedagogy, Lowham and Schilla report that:

> the major obstacle to ensuring sincere investment from programme participants was the fact that these types of interdisciplinary programs are largely still add-ons to conventional degree programs. No matter how tolerant any department is of unconventional coursework, departments, for the most part, eventually judge researchers on what they produce in the conventional sense.
>
> Lowham and Schilla (2008: 1)

This is probably even more true of research practices within a disciplinary community where many forms of official evaluation of personal and institutional research output discourage ventures across disciplinary boundaries or into interdisciplinary collaboration. Recognition of such work is often still deemed risky and consequently best avoided.

Hence interdisciplinarity and its more rarefied variant transdisciplinarity present an encounter with troublesome knowledge. Such practice is alien and counter-intuitive in Perkins' typology. Recognition and understanding of the value and purpose of interdisciplinarity constitutes a threshold concept insofar as it requires a significant ontological shift at the same time as a conceptual integration of new perspectives and the letting go of some prevailing conceptual schemata. It will require, too, a changed use of discourse (Meyer and Land 2005). The paradox here of course is that crossing into new conceptual territory, making shifts in subjectivity and acquiring a changed discourse is how we became disciplinarily-minded and adept at ways of thinking and practising in the first place. This was how our disciplinary identity was originally constituted. To work effectively in interdisciplinary or *trans*disciplinary contexts, however, our disciplinary subjectivity needs to be reconstituted. Our disciplinary identity needs to be not abandoned – far from it – but loosened, perhaps weakened to an extent. Not surprisingly this can be experienced as a sense of loss and hence resisted.

Espousing such possibilities provokes a liminal state of transformation which the works of Klein (1990, 1996), Lowham and Schilla (2008) and Gasper (2010) show is uncomfortable. As Schwartzman (2010: 38) maintains, '[r]eal learning requires stepping into the unknown, which initiates a rupture in knowing … By definition, all TC [threshold concept] scholarship is concerned (directly or indirectly) with encountering the unknown'. O'Sullivan *et al.* (2002: 11) suggest that transformative learning requires the experiencing of 'a deep, structural shift in the basic premises of thought, feelings, and actions'. This shift of consciousness 'dramatically and irreversibly alters our way of being in the world'. Erica McWilliam, an established Australian professor of education working mainly through qualitative methodologies, talks frankly of such a personal transformation that was triggered through working with one of her doctoral students, Jen Tan, who was more confident than herself in the use of quantitative methodologies. She acknowledges also her behaviour as a 'defended subject' using scholarly critique as a form of identity maintenance:

> I realised that I had missed an opportunity to round out my understanding of methodology by coming to grips with measurement as a valuable means of enquiry … My scholarly critiques of 'white coat' objectivism had allowed me to step around the judicious use of quantitative enquiry and I came to regret that gap in my knowledge, however much I was able to generate publications about the nature of knowledge and its politicisation

... This is not written as a confessional, but a simple acknowledgement that critique is a very useful means for maintaining blind spots in our learning.

McWilliam and Tan 2010: 45

Wagner (2010: 33) points out that whereas academics are adept at identifying the blank spots of research not yet undertaken within their disciplinary field, they are much less adept at recognising and acknowledging, as McWilliam does here, the blind spots of methodologies or topics that are never employed and which interdisciplinary collaboration might bring into view. Like Adam and Eve, disciplinary specialists tend to find it difficult to leave the comforting Eden of their discipline, to cross the boundary into interdisciplinarity. As with the McWilliam and Tan anecdote, an encounter with the wise and provocative serpent of troublesome knowledge might be required to occasion the ontological shift required, though the price of transformation may well be a degree of 'ontological insecurity' (Giddens 1991) or 'boundariless anxiety' (Bergquist 1995: 11). Giri (1998) suggests that the kind of shift that is needed is one 'from a nest of identity as an academic or professional of type T to a self-conception as pilgrim or seeker'. Rather than one's initial disciplinary training taking on the character of a caste-mark for life, Gasper argues that '[i]nterdisciplinarity is more achievable when people act not as representatives of disciplines but of themselves, their experiences, values and insights' (Gasper 2010: 55).

Conclusion: Overcoming Barriers to Interdisciplinarity

Interdisciplinarity would seem to be a strong candidate for a threshold concept. It requires troubling conceptual integration of different perspectives, a letting go of a previous stance, an ontological shift, and acquisition of a new shared discourse. This would suggest a primarily personal change in subjectivity. As Kothari (1988) argues, '[f]or true interdisciplinarity to develop, it is the *individual* that has to become interdisciplinary, not the group'. Hanks, however, argues differently, and for a social learning model:

Learning is a process that takes place in a participation framework, not in an individual mind. This means, among other things, that it is mediated by differences of perspective among the co-participants. It is the community, or at least those participating in the learning context, who 'learn' under this definition. Learning is, as it were, distributed, distributed among co-participants, not a one-person act.

Hanks 1991: 15

Nonetheless barriers remain within and between tribal communities. The history of disciplinary relations in universities has not noticeably been one of harmony, falling more commonly on a scale between at best distant and cautious trade, through ignorance, antagonism, ridicule and competition to at worst imperial conquest, with disciplines in close cognate proximity within faculties often the most territorial, often for reasons of competition for limited shared resource (Gasper 2010: 58). Interdisciplinarity remains difficult, and often fails. It requires mutual deconstruction of each other's terminologies, and mutual discourses or frameworks remain in short supply. Existing organisational structures usually get in the way. Academic incentives certainly still point the other way. The cultures of disciplinary communities of practice draw on strong bonding capital. As a way out of this, Gasper advocates the formation of new networks – inter-organisational linkages, meeting places, patterns of informal contact; new roles within interdisciplinary groupings – for example, as 'bridgers' or 'synthesisers'; the idea of bridging capital, to counter the bonding capital of tightly-coupled disciplinary communities ('Inferior theories might sometimes function better as bridges', Gasper 2010: 57); the forging of shared discourses, mutually accessible and acceptable intellectual frameworks – a complex system of concepts and models something like an 'eco-system of enquiry', he suggests. Nussbaum characterises the latter as 'narrative imagination' which brings about 'the capability to imagine the lives of others and to respond positively' (Nussbaum 1997, cited in Thomson and Walker 2010: 13). The goal of this is not necessarily consensus. As Boulding (1986) has pointed out, interdisciplinarity and the shared perspectives it might bring does not always culminate in agreement, which might in some circumstances prove counter-productive anyway. The point is shared respect and reciprocity rather than mutual ignorance.

Carmichael's (2010, 2011) work on the Economic and Social Research Council's 'Transforming Perspectives' project at the University of Cambridge offers an interesting way forward in this regard. This interdisciplinary initiative used the threshold concepts framework itself 'as a means of initiating cross-disciplinary discourse' and to challenge teachers 'to consider what is distinctive about their own disciplinary "ways of thinking and practising" and invite reflection' (2010: 53). This was found to open up a productive space for 'the articulation of difference' (Carmichael 2010: 59; 2011: 11).

> This kind of working across disciplines differs from more established approaches to cross-disciplinary and interdisciplinary work, which characteristically involves a team being deliberately constructed to solve some pre-existing and well-defined problem.
>
> Carmichael 2010: 58–9

Carmichael (2010: 59) points to Strathern's call for cross-disciplinary work 'to speak of possibilities that lie in being captured by another's concerns ... for it also makes visible the interest of those who are identifiably "other" to the discipline in hand' (Strathern 2006: 203).

It remains to be seen whether the changing modes of knowledge generation and exchange in a fast, globalised and digitised world will accelerate the rate of adoption of interdisciplinary and even transdisciplinary ways of thinking and practising among academic tribes, or whether the academic incentives which currently predispose academics to keep within their disciplinary territories, both conceptually and socially, may need to be rethought in order to engineer such a shift.

17

Change Vectors and Academic Identities
Evolving Tribes and Territories

KERRI-LEE KRAUSE

Introduction

This chapter examines the evolving nature of discipline-based tribal groups and the territories they occupy in the twenty-first century. Discussion focuses on the influence of higher education policy drivers, including graduate capabilities and generic skills, and their role in shaping disciplinary cultures and identities. Interpretation of the issues is underpinned by social theories of identity and a socio-constructivist approach to analysing the interplay between academics and the higher education policy environment. The narrative of the emerging tourism domain provides an enlightening lens through which to examine some of the strategies academic staff might deploy as they engage with the complex interplay of change vectors within disciplinary territories and the higher education policy landscape. Implications for university policy and management are considered by way of conclusion.

Vectors of Change in the Higher Education Landscape

The vector metaphor is a useful interpretive tool for understanding the mechanism and impact of change in the higher education sector. Schuster and Finkelstein (2006: 12–16) use the metaphor to depict five change vectors influencing the nature of academic work. These are: demographic changes in the population; technological changes; market forces; the ageing academic workforce and associated implications for the workforce of the future; and the quality and performativity agenda. Beyond the quality assurance issues identified by these researchers is the broader policy environment comprising political and socio-economic drivers that significantly affect higher education institutions and their communities. Policy drivers include research assessment exercises, performance-based funding for learning and teaching, and economic imperatives to prepare work-ready graduates who will contribute to the knowledge economy. Associated drivers include expectations that universities will explicitly demonstrate their value-added contributions to society, including community engagement, service learning and a range of co- and extra-curricular activities for students.

Change vectors do not necessarily move synergistically in the same direction. On the contrary, in higher education these vectors typically propel the sector in diverse, often conflicting, directions that sometimes result in irreconcilable tensions. For many academic staff, the disciplinary context represents a site of considerable friction as powerful higher education change vectors in the form of diversification in the higher education workforce and massification, with its incumbent pressures, come head to head with quality imperatives. This combination of external pressures, combined with institutional and disciplinary tensions, is interpreted by some as a potential threat to the fundamental issues of what it means to be an academic, to belong to a disciplinary tribe, to inhabit familiar intellectual territory.

The shortcomings of the vector metaphor are acknowledged. For instance, vectors tend to denote straight lines, whereas the nature of change is typically recursive and non-linear. Nevertheless, the connotations of magnitude and direction associated with vectors effectively capture the considerable scope of challenges facing academics who increasingly find themselves confronting tensions between the deeply held values and beliefs of their disciplinary community (Henkel and Vabo 2006) and externally imposed policy imperatives.

Theoretical Underpinnings

The theoretical framework for this consideration of evolving tribes and territories is informed by social theories of identity and a socio-constructivist approach to analysing the interplay between academics and the policy environment. It draws on social learning theories that focus on the importance of agency, self-efficacy, locus of control and self-regulation in identity development (Bandura 1977, 1997). Interpersonal theories concerning social and cultural influences on self-perceptions and the shaping of identities (Leary and Tangney 2003) also inform the thinking in this chapter. As communities develop, social practices, values and attitudes are reinforced and become routinised (Reckwitz 2002). Use of a common discourse is integral to reinforcing social practices, shaping identities (Taylor 1989), uniting tribal members and delineating community territory (Pahre 1996).

While languages and shared social practices represent powerful uniting forces in disciplinary communities, so too does a sense of place and territory. Phenomenological approaches contribute to our understanding of the role of place in shaping communities, their values and identities (Twigger-Ross et al. 2003; Walker 2007). In this paradigm, place may be depicted as a situated practice made up of social interactions (Massey 1994). It is a locale where relationships and unique identities are created. Place or territory arguably plays a key role in shaping identities in academic disciplinary communities. The disciplinary territory represents a familiar place – or 'shelter' (Freidson 1994) – where disciplinary epistemologies are debated and where disciplinary cultures, practices, knowledges and understandings (Reckwitz 2002) are perpetuated through curriculum and inquiry.

What happens, however, when those familiar disciplinary places are threatened, or their very existence contested? How do academic staff manage in a twenty-first-century higher education environment where government policy drivers, funding mechanisms and regulatory frameworks exert increasingly powerful influences on academic practices in the disciplines? These are some of the questions to be explored in this chapter.

Competing Tensions in Twenty-first-Century Disciplinary Contexts

The construction of identity is depicted as a continuous and reflexive process (Jenkins 1996). Henkel (2010) contends that academic staff in the twenty-first century experience perpetual 'construction, deconstruction, and reconstruction in the context of multiple and shifting collectivities and relationships'. A less optimistic interpretation of the uncertainty experienced by the postmodern academic workforce is that of Bauman (2000: 14) who refers to the 'falling apart, the friability, the brittleness, the transience, the until-further-noticeness of human bonds and networks' characterising the liquidity of the postmodern era. Despite the fluidity of communities, academic staff continue to attest to the power of the discipline as a unifying force in shaping academic identity and providing a familiar place for sharing ideas and inducting new generations of scholars (Krause 2009a, b; Malcolm and Zukas 2009; Musselin 2005; Parry 2007). These apparently conflicting views exemplify higher education change vectors in action. In one respect, disciplinary tribes remain a significant force with magnitude and power in the eyes of academic staff. A competing vector is evident in the strength of higher education change forces and the blurring of traditional boundaries between academic and professional roles and between disciplines. Added to this is the dynamic of the external policy environment and the changes it brings to bear through regulatory frameworks in a rapidly changing market environment.

Given these multiple change forces within and beyond disciplinary contexts, how does the academic workforce juggle competing priorities and tensions in a constantly evolving higher education terrain? This section of the chapter argues the need for academic communities to develop a critical awareness of the change vectors in their environment, along with the capacity to engage with these changes in productive, proactive ways. The contested domain of tourism represents an instructive vehicle for exploring how contestations about disciplinarity co-exist with external policy drivers and accountability measures.

Tourism: a Case of Challenging Tribal Identities and Disciplinary Territories

Tourism is a disputed field of study. Some argue that it is a discipline, albeit embryonic and emerging (Leiper 1981, 2000); others argue that it is a domain of study that will never constitute a discipline by virtue of its pluralistic nature and lack of a cohesive theoretical framework (Echtner and Jamal 1997; Tribe 2009). It is beyond the scope of this chapter to explore these arguments in detail; suffice to say that the territory is contested and the existence of a homogeneous tribe questionable. Despite these debates, tourism continues as a viable domain of study in higher education. The tourism narrative includes several worthwhile lessons for the sector on how scholars across disciplines might manage themselves and their sense of place and identity in the twenty-first century. Of particular interest are the implications for dealing with contested policy environments which increasingly seek to shape the curriculum and disciplinary inquiry. Policy issues relating to generic skills and graduate capabilities will be used by way of example in this chapter.

To explore the tourism narrative, whether conceptualised as a field or a discipline, four academic staff from Australian public universities were interviewed as part of a larger investigation of eight disciplines (Krause 2009a). The broader study compared the perspectives of 55 academic staff in traditional disciplines, including mathematics and history, as well as those in newer fields of study such as tourism and environmental science across four Australian public universities. Interviewees were asked about their views on how disciplinary cultures shape the approaches and practices of teachers and students. Themes for exploration included: academic identities and communities in the respective disciplines; the changing student body and associated curriculum and assessment reforms; and policy issues pertaining to the place of generic skills in the discipline. The discussion that follows is informed by findings pertaining to academic staff perceptions of disciplinary knowledge and methods, along with perspectives on the place of generic skills in the curriculum, particularly in the tourism domain. Given the small sample size in this empirical study, no claim for generalisability is made. Rather, the data and cogent literature in the field are used as the basis for proposing three guiding principles for engaging productively in evolving higher education settings.

As the tourism narrative unfolds, it is evident that this is a tribe of academics reconciled with the ambiguity of their domain of study. The field has roots in such subject areas and disciplines as economics, management, geography, ecology, sociology and anthropology. There is no doubt that tourism as a field of study stems from a rich combination of inter- and multidisciplinary strands of inquiry (Coles *et al.* 2006). Academics teaching in the field have wide-ranging stories to tell about how they came to teach and conduct research in tourism, including:

> I was originally an economic historian ... nine years ago X university received a great deal of industry money in order to set up a Tourism course. We had nobody who could teach Tourism and so I volunteered.
>
> Tourism interviewee 1

> My PhD was in economics. I regard myself as a public policy analyst ... about a decade ago I was shifted, not necessarily voluntarily, to set this school up ... we saw it essentially as a multidisciplinary school that would cover not just business disciplines, but disciplines from the social sciences.
>
> Tourism interviewee 2

> My background is arts and culture ... If somebody asks me what my job is I say I'm a lecturer in Tourism. People say, 'what does that mean?' I say 'it's a Bachelor of Business degree ... and then we apply it to the tourism industry'.
>
> Tourism interviewee 3

These narratives illustrate some of the ways in which academic staff have managed the ambiguity of the territory they inhabit. This ambiguity has led members of the tourism tribe to explore theoretical frameworks to help them understand and interpret who they are and where they belong in the higher education community. A review of the literature suggests that academic members of the tourism community have used the often-disputed territorial debates as the basis for engaging productively with the international policy imperative to prepare graduates for the knowledge economy of the future. While it may be argued that such engagement is much easier for those in vocationally oriented fields and disciplines such as business or tourism, this example nonetheless represents a useful illustration of how one field is taking steps to engage proactively with the policy environment in which it operates.

Each of the three guiding principles for engaging productively in evolving higher education settings will be elaborated in turn by way of exploring strategies for managing tribal ambiguities and fuzzy territorial boundaries in times of change. Implications for university policy and management are then considered.

Engaging with Ambiguity

Academic staff in the field of tourism present a salutary case study of tribal members who face ambiguity on several levels. Their status as a disciplinary tribe is contested (Tribe 2009), their multidisciplinary roots are eclectic and their structural location in universities varies significantly. Some tourism programmes are located in Faculties of Business and Commerce, others in Departments of Management, and yet others in Faculties of Arts and Social Sciences. In other words, it would appear that there is relatively little to keep this heterogeneous group together – whether as a discipline or a field of study. Some have suggested that a common language for this domain of study might strengthen cohesive ties in the field, arguing that the disciplinary status and legitimacy of tourism in universities would be supported through the use of an appropriate discipline label such as 'tourism science' or 'tourismology' (Jovicic 1988).

In the face of such ambiguity, rather than distancing themselves from the challenges, tourism scholars have proposed various ways forward. These include the need to reconceptualise tourism (Farrel and Twining-Ward 2004) by shifting away from traditional linear approaches to problem solving to more integrative, nonlinear frameworks that encourage a systems approach to investigating tourism-related issues. Another means of engaging with ambiguity is evident in the recognition of complexity inherent in dealing with wicked problems of the domain of study. Some commentators in the field have proposed the possibility of the 'post-disciplinary' lens as a way to depict the tourism territory – or territories (Coles *et al.* 2006; Goodwin 2004). Despite the contested nature of the field, Coles and colleagues contend that tourism knowledges should not be pursued by academic staff working in 'disciplinary isolation' (2006: 295). Instead, they propose post-disciplinarity as an alternative paradigm for organising intellectual endeavours and academic work.

Post-disciplinarity challenges the received understanding of disciplinarity (Hellstrom *et al.* 2003: 251), providing new territory for the production of knowledge among academic peers who form communities that transcend traditional disciplinary boundaries. Hellstrom and colleagues draw connections between Mode 2 knowledge production (Gibbons *et al.* 1994) and post-disciplinarity. Sayer (1999: 5) defines post-disciplinary studies as those that evolve when 'scholars forget about disciplines' and 'identify with learning rather than with disciplines'. Extending beyond the paradigms of multi- and transdisciplinarity, post-disciplinarity transcends traditional notions of discipline to address complex multi-level issues that extend beyond 'discipline-bound straitjackets' (Coles *et al.* 2006: 313). Proponents of the post-disciplinary approach contend that it does not signify the disappearance of traditional disciplinary tribes and territories; rather it offers an additional, parallel space for scholars to build community beyond disciplines. It is instructive to consider how academic communities are exploring the possibilities of post-disciplinary perspectives for creating and legitimating new problem-solving spaces for the future. Considerations such as these may well extend to other disciplinary communities.

Theorising Contested Space

A second principle characterising the ways in which some tourism scholars are seeking to come to terms with the contested space in which they operate is that of theorising the multiplicity of competing perspectives and conditioning factors inherent in their field. One means of capturing the state of flux in which they find themselves as a community is actor–network theory (ANT). ANT has been applied in a range of social science contexts (Law 2004) including to depict the messiness that characterises academic work (Malcolm and Zukas 2009). The actor–network approach has been deployed by some researchers to investigate tourism problems in the field (Johannesson 2005; Rodgera *et al.* 2009). It is particularly useful for this purpose, given its capacity for facilitating investigation of concatenated actors. These actors may be human or non-human. For instance they may include interconnections among people, objects (for example, cars, hotels), information (for example, travel brochures) and technologies (for example, websites) (Paget *et al.* 2010).

Some researchers have gone one step further, applying ANT at a meta-level to investigate the field of tourism itself (van der Duim 2007). This has proven to be a constructive theoretical resource for understanding the heterogeneous network of interacting actors – human as well as non-human – involved in shaping the tourism community of scholars and the territories they inhabit (Latour 1999; Law 1999; Ren *et al.* 2010). ANT facilitates analysis of the interplay of social, technical and natural objects within networks that frame human interactions, shape activities and direct movements (Murdoch 1998: 367).

In the context of this chapter, ANT is educative as a means of depicting the relational aspects and complex interlinking of heterogeneous entities within the tourism space. These include academic staff, their original disciplinary backgrounds, and their structural location in university departments. Actors might also include external drivers shaping the field, such as higher education policy, environmental, technological and economic factors. The use of theoretical frames such as ANT to analyse actor networks and interchanges is yet another example of how scholars in an evolving field of study are actively trying to come to terms with how their community is constituted, potential sources of contention and implications for the intellectual spaces they inhabit.

Engaging with the Policy Environment

A third principle illustrating ways in which the international tourism community of scholars is coming to terms with its place in higher education is evident in responses to the external policy environment in relation to the generic skills movement in higher education.

In the empirical study of 55 academic staff across eight discipline areas (Krause 2009a), interviewees were asked to comment on their views of the place of generic skills in the curriculum. Tourism academics were distinguished by being the only group of interviewees who were unanimous about critical thinking being the most important generic skill for tourism graduates. Critical thinking, problem solving and analytical skills were among the three most highly ranked skills across the disciplines, but no other academic groups in the sample, apart from the tourism group, rated critical thinking as being of highest importance. These findings provide an exploratory account only, given the limited sample size. Nevertheless, they represent useful insights into the field.

For instance one interviewee extended the discussion about critical thinking skills, adding that they also wanted students to be able to make 'autonomous judgements ... we want our students to be independent and autonomous thinkers' (Interviewee 2). Elsewhere the same interviewee emphasised the importance of 'leadership' and 'morals and ethics' as important graduate capabilities for tourism graduates. One Tourism academic also drew attention to the importance of 'industry and community engagement' (Interviewee 4). Neither of the latter two skills was specified by any of the interviewees across the other seven discipline areas.

This is a noteworthy finding that is supported by the international Tourism Education Futures 2010–2030 consortium of 45 senior tourism educators and industry experts (2009). The latter came together for a summit to discuss the implications of social and industry changes for tourism curricula of the future. Among other outcomes, summit representatives from 13 nations identified a set of values intended to form the foundation for future tourism education programmes. Five sets of generic skills, underpinned by values, were identified by this group, namely: stewardship, ethics, knowledge, professionalism and mutuality (TEFI 2009). The authors of the draft white paper acknowledge the dynamic nature of the initiative, which is future-focused and recognises the need to fundamentally 'retool and redesign' tourism education as part of a redefinition of tourism knowledge sets, structures and assumptions (Sheldon et al. 2008: 63).

This recognition of the importance of reviewing and potentially repositioning tourism education for the future arguably reflects the result of reciprocal changes between international scholars and a policy environment that attaches value to generic skills (Barrie 2006; Bath et al. 2004), employability (Yorke 2009) and the articulation of graduate outcomes in higher education. The Tourism Education Futures summit illustrates one way in which an academic tribe has proactively engaged with the policy environment by identifying a suite of graduate capabilities for future tourism graduates. Another example of tourism academics engaging with the policy context is evident in the work of Zehrer and Mossenlechner (2009) who consulted employers to gauge their perceptions of employability skills and competencies. This research illustrates the impact of employability imperatives (Knight and Yorke 2004) on disciplinary research and associated curriculum design.

Regardless of one's views of the merits or otherwise of the employability agenda and the 'de-disciplined' (Jones 2009) generic skills movement, the attention drawn to graduate attributes and capabilities has had a significant impact on the ways in which disciplines and fields of study organise themselves and their activities. A case in point is the Australian Learning and Teaching Council's (ALTC) Discipline Standards initiative. In response to government imperatives and the introduction of a new regulatory environment for quality and standards in the tertiary sector, the ALTC repositioned its discipline-based Learning Networks to place a greater emphasis on discipline-based academic standards and the articulation of threshold learning outcomes. The Australian initiative has been cognisant of the European Tuning project and the OECD Assessment of Higher Education Learning Outcomes (AHELO) project, as well as the UK subject benchmark statements. All of these developments represent powerful examples of change vectors in the higher education policy arena that have noteworthy implications for disciplinary communities, their members, the nature of their interactions within and across traditional disciplinary territories, and their future. The next section explores implications of these developments in institutional contexts.

Implications and Conclusions

This chapter has explored some of the notable change vectors in higher education, particularly those relating to the external policy environment. Implications for institution-level policy and management are significant, for this is where academic work is defined, communities shaped, territories explored and identities formed. While the literature continues to attest to the significance of the disciplinary unit as a key determinant of how academics organise their work and engage in knowledge production, this is not the only factor involved. Churchman's findings are a pertinent reminder that universities comprise 'shifting narratives of academia' (Churchman 2006: 13) held by various academic subcultures and groups of staff in whom an array of perceptions of the academic role reside. For instance, Churchman identifies three main clusters of academic staff with distinctive discourses: the 'making a difference' cluster focuses on the 'right' role of universities in educating youth and contributing to disciplinary communities; the 'social interaction' cluster emphasises the value of human relations, trust and comradeship in academia; while the third 'corporate' group are expedient and pragmatic in their approach to academia by aligning their work practices with institutional missions and reward structures. Churchman recognises that memberships of these various clusters overlap and that identities may be reconstructed over time. Nevertheless, this framework serves as an apt reminder to universities that disciplinary tribes and territories are but one way of understanding the complexity that characterises academic work and identities.

Institutional policymakers and managers need to be mindful of the various motivating factors, allegiances and discourses shaping academic staff perceptions of their roles and communities. This awareness requires regular consultation with a cross-section of staff at all levels of the organisation. It involves creating spaces for dialogue, particularly at department level, but also across departments and at whole-of-institution level. University policymaking needs to be informed by academic voices and regularly reviewed to ensure that it reflects the changing realities of the academic landscape. The powerful nexus between academic and professional staff also needs to be recognised in these conversations (Gordon and Whitchurch 2010). Dialogue may include debate and contestation. These are all important dimensions of responsive university policymaking that can and should be managed on the basis of mutual respect and a desire to work together in the context of rapidly evolving higher education landscapes.

The contested field of tourism has been used in this chapter by way of a case study illustrating a domain of study in flux. Various sources of contestation have been explored, including challenges over its relative disciplinary status, where it belongs structurally in universities, and how it defines itself epistemologically and ontologically (Pernecky 2010). A somewhat extreme example was chosen to illustrate ways in which academic staff might manage themselves, their tribal affiliations and their sense of place in a contested environment. Three action principles are identified in the chapter to guide academic communities confronted with powerful external policy drivers that challenge them to reconceptualise their notion of discipline-based communities and spaces. These principles apply to university communities just as they do to those who belong to fields of study or discipline groups. Proactive engagement with ambiguities and uncertainties is an important guiding principle for those seeking to make sense of uncertainty. Universities should ensure that their policies in such areas as workload allocation and systems for reward and recognition are underpinned by a strongly theorised evidence base that recognises the evolutionary nature of academic work and the complex network of actors in operation within and across disciplinary territories. In order to engage productively with policy environments, academic staff need to be empowered to do so. University managers should actively pursue opportunities to involve staff in policymaking and in articulating and enacting the strategic directions of the institution. This may be achieved within and beyond disciplinary communities, but should always be mindful of the range of cultures they represent.

As vectors of change continue to move forcefully through the sector, it seems we are facing a key fork in the higher education road, with at least two ways of interpreting the evolutionary process among academic tribes. The liquidity of postmodern communities has the potential to dissipate and fragment academic communities, creating transient nomads who have no sense of disciplinary connection and are easily swayed by external winds of change in the higher education policy arena. On the other hand, such fluidity may also lead to reinforced bonds, strengthened intellectual partnerships across traditional disciplinary boundaries and innovative approaches to inquiry and knowledge production. Successful universities of the future will actively foster the evolution of academic tribes and territories as they capitalise on a combination of fluid agility in academic networks, along with the power that comes from identifying with disciplinary communities who speak a common language and share similar cultural and epistemological values.

18

Internationalisation
Troublesome Knowledge for the Disciplines

VALERIE A. CLIFFORD

Introduction

The focus of internationalisation in higher education has, until recently, been on market share in terms of international students and supporting them to be successful in their studies in a foreign environment. Cross-border education has further developed to include mobility, not just of persons, but also of programmes and institutions (Stella 2006). Universities are slowly realising that to become 'international universities' in reality, rather than just in rhetoric, then internationalisation needs to pervade every aspect of the institution and needs to include the 'internationalisation' of the education of the majority non-mobile home students.

The term 'Internationalisation at Home' was first mooted by Nilsson in 1999, his focus being the needs of the 80–85 per cent of students who do not have the experience of living and studying abroad and yet need to be prepared for living and working successfully and sustainably in an interdependent, globalised, multi-cultural world. A reformed curriculum is central to this enterprise, yet the curriculum has figured minimally in university internationalisation strategies until recently (Harman 2005), and even now is usually understood as referring to inducting international students into 'how the west is done' (Doherty and Singh 2005) and adding international case studies to the curriculum (De Vita 2007). While reforming the curriculum for internationalisation is embraced in some disciplines, it is resisted in others: the hard pure disciplines (Becher 1989; Becher and Trowler 2001) such as science, maths and information technology finding it more difficult to accommodate than the soft pure and all the applied disciplines (Clifford 2009).

The disciplines have provided a framework for organising knowledge for several centuries and Becher (1989) described the academic tribes that have formed around the disciplines, each having their own culture and academic orientations including epistemological and pedagogical beliefs and practices. Subsequent work has shown that disciplinary boundaries are becoming more fluid (Becher and Trowler 2001) and that interdisciplinarity is increasing. However, the disciplines are still our major academic reference point, contact with our disciplines being figural in the formation of our academic identities (Hegarty 2008).

In the science and maths areas – Becher's hard pure category – knowledge is considered to be objective, measurable, impersonal and value-free and based on logical deduction and reasoning. Knowledge is built incrementally, new knowledge being integrated into existing knowledge leading to new conclusions. Mathematical modelling is used to break down complex ideas and search for universal 'truths'. Pedagogically these areas are seen traditionally to favour the lecture mode of delivery, with problem-based seminars using case studies and simulations (Lindblom-Ylänne et al. 2006; Neumann et al. 2002).

In contrast soft disciplines, such as the humanities, are seen to offer a more discursive engagement with a body of knowledge, where personal experiences and ideas are valued, knowledge is seen to be value-laden, and analysis is complex and disputed. Pedagogically the humanities and social sciences favour face-to-face tutorials with discussions and debates, students being encouraged to consider many possible 'answers' to scenarios (Lindblom-Ylänne et al. 2006; Neumann et al. 2002).

The focus of internationalisation, per se, is not on knowledge as in subject content, but on the student and their future needs, and society's needs for them, as global citizens. These roles require skills of criticality, creativity and intercultural communication, and the ability to articulate and engage with different value systems. It is immediately apparent, from the above descriptions, that the response of the disciplines to internationalising the curriculum will be varied. This was exemplified in a recent study that highlighted the resistance of the hard pure disciplines (Clifford 2009).

Disciplinary Reactions to Internationalisation

The study was carried out at all eight campuses of a large Australian university, including a campus in South Africa and one in Malaysia – details of the study are in Clifford 2009. Curricula for all the campuses, and for the many partnership arrangements, were designed by the staff at the Australian campuses and passed to staff overseas to deliver in a set mode. Assessments were also set and marked in Australia, the main concern of the university being quality assurance of their market brand. The university considered that, by holding the content and delivery of courses constant and having all assessment dealt with in Australia, they were offering students all over the world the 'same' student learning experience (Schapper and Mayson 2004). The challenge to this concept of quality by lecturers on and offshore is discussed below.

The study showed that in the hard pure disciplines there was a strong belief that their disciplines by nature were already international, being based on value-free universal principles, and that they did not need to engage in the debate around internationalisation of the curriculum (IoC):[1]

Chemistry covers all cultures, there's no way it is culturally differentiating between chemistry here and chemistry in the US, or chemistry in Britain, in China, in Nigeria, in Columbia.

Science, TA

I don't think for technical and Computer Science subjects there is any IoC involved. It is just a matter of updating your field or your discipline ... People are learning the same thing irrespective of their environment irrespective of their country – IT is the same IT all over the world.

IT, TA

Similarly, Bond *et al*'s (2003) review indicated that resistance to IoC was mostly found among male scientists who had never lived outside the United States. However, Martinez Alemán and Salkever (2004), in an American study, found that no discipline groups claimed 'multiculturalism' to be inappropriate for their discipline, but that it did fit more naturally into certain disciplines, and that the hard pure disciplines did not view it as a priority or a significant educational matter.

In the hard applied subjects, such as pharmacy and medicine, there was also a belief in 'international science', but it was recognised that the students would be working in different systems, with different regulations, belief systems and ethical standards, and that this would affect the outcome. The staff gave examples of this in action:

Trying to break down the view of doctors as god-like figures. Sometime this is difficult, sometimes it is not even worth trying, it's not even appropriate to try.

Medicine, TA

In the soft disciplines, no distinctions were apparent between the views of staff in the pure and applied areas. Mostly these disciplines did not claim any privileged knowledge – except for geography and psychology – 'what I am striving to do is to create materials or create a curriculum where no one perspective is privileged' (Education, TA) and all saw education as 'about opening up people's ideas and different ways of looking at things, a different way of thinking, of talking about things' (History, TA). While education was seen as important for its own sake it was acknowledged that students needed to be employable. Clarifying who their students were, what their needs were and the goals of the courses was the starting point for many of the lecturers.

Centering the Periphery

This picture is complicated when we consider the different geographical-cultural positionings of staff and students, and what, for them, is the centre and what is the periphery. With the exception of staff in hard, pure disciplines, all staff in all locations advocated the need for global perspectives:

> Make sure that students understand what is the theory and who developed it, when did they develop it, what was the thinking at the time, and then think about how can this be applied to different contexts or not ...
>
> BusEco TA

But there was also a concern for engagement with the local:

> The 'Science' is about universal principles, taught the same over the world, they also saw ... but local environments and cultures lead to different curriculum and practices.
>
> Medicine, TA

Offshore campuses staff especially wanted to adapt curriculum content to reflect the local environment:

> Like climatology, the climate is the same, the concept is the same so you might teach about the climate of South Africa or the climate of Australia or Europe but the principles are basically the same ... we have localised our syllabi, a lot of our syllabi, about 50–60 per cent.
>
> Geography, TSA

> Local situations are important ... [the students] come from so many different backgrounds. Maybe a tenth of them are going to go out into the local South African context. So I think there needs to be balance ... they need to learn the South African way. But then I think they need to be exposed to another set of ethics and another set of laws ... we must have a very international focus because we have so many international students and they are going back to very different environments.
>
> IT, TSA

> They should be able to place all their studies in the context of their cultural background that they brought into the university when they first arrived.
>
> IT, TA

A Malaysian-based lecturer was concerned about teaching a unit in Malaysia based on Australian political, governmental and industrial situations when the context in Malaysia was so different. Similarly a unit on the health of Australian Aboriginals delivered by distance education to Hong Kong had to be replaced by one on health of the local communities. It was also commented that it was unfortunate that the Australian students could not learn about the Malaysian systems. Staff in South Africa saw an imperative for curricula to address issues of development, arguing that if the students did not receive such an education then it was of no relevance to the country.

Cross-border education particularly highlights the tensions between the universal and the local as not only are students from other cultures sitting in Australian classrooms, but the university is 'providing its services in a different social and political climate altogether' (Communication, TM). This lecturer, in Malaysia, described the cultural clashes in teaching concepts from the Australian curriculum such as social class and pornography, which caused offence and led to complaints among her students. She asked: 'how are you going to impart those values of liberalism and humanism and still fall in line with Islamic views and perspectives?' She went on to describe:

> The paradox of trying to maintain your internal [university] identity and its integrity, and trying to accommodate international differences and cultural differences. Where do you draw the line? When does your burger stop being a burger?
>
> Communication, TM

Cultural Diversity and Pedagogical Practice

Attending to cultural diversity was resisted in the hard pure disciplines, the scientists seeing their work as 'culturally neutral':

> The scientific principles are not ones confined to particular parts of the world as such. The principles are international and the principles are such that it is hard for me to see how I can teach differently ... It is culturally neutral. Cultural diversity among students would not make a difference because 'that is the nature of science'.
>
> Science, TA

One IT lecturer described as 'pedagogical imperialism' the 'beaming in' of courses into China, Indonesia, Australia and other places, with diverse students participating in one virtual classroom, where the university had not yet worked through the issues of diverse pedagogies (IT, TA).

In other areas staff showed a high level of awareness of cultural difference among students and of cultural difference in professional practice. In the hard applied disciplines they saw that the graduates needed to be able to problem solve, and to be culturally sensitive and flexible:

> Flexibility, I suppose, of mind but that is hard to get that ... an ability to be able to interact and get out in the world and move around, interact with people in a way that's productive, respectful and, as I say, being prepared

to take on board interesting and new ways of dealing with things and not having a view that the way things are done in Australia is the way things should be done.

Medicine, TA

Make students more sensitive to cultural differences and values. Don't have to accept other values but need to open up to other ideas and let them 'judge for themselves'.

Engineering, TM

Teaching values was another difficult area for those in the hard pure disciplines. While for a law lecturer in Australia 'internationalisation of the curriculum has to mean greater access to value explicit education ... by value explicit ... is the notion of fairness in all things', many staff in the hard disciplines hold beliefs in the objectivity of knowledge and do not see their job as teaching about values. This is also a disturbing prospect if you have had no training in dealing with sensitive issues in the classroom.

So while academics in the hard pure disciplines, the hard applied and some soft applied disciplines believed in universal, objective knowledge, they had their views tempered by issues of the background of the students, the context in which the curriculum is delivered and the possible context of students' future lives. Similarly academics in the soft disciplines saw the importance of the students' past and future lives in the construction of the current educational experience of the students.

To address the differing experiences and needs of students, some local staff at the overseas campuses re-authored materials and adapted the delivery to make it relevant to the local environment and the teaching styles more familiar to the students:

The interaction in the classes differs depending on the location and the culture. ... in some of the Arabic countries they're very free with their views. They're very open and talkative and in fact, will often argue with each other if there are differences of opinion, you get quite an interesting debate going on in the classroom. It is much more difficult to generate that in some of the Asian countries.

Medicine, TA

In Australia staff were becoming increasingly aware of the differentiated needs of their students:

You have to be sensitive to the fact that some people are uncomfortable being here, they're away from home, they're in a different cultural environment, different teachers will have greater or less of a clear sensitivity to them, they'll have English language difficulties, we may or may not be giving them appropriate support ... And many people are scared to speak out in class. And again, Australian culture is not that different, it's not a natural Australian thing to speak out in class ... so I'm encouraging my Australian students to get engaged in the same way.

Law, TA

Staff in the overseas campuses were particularly sensitive to the backgrounds of their students, recognising that some came from areas of political instability, students sitting in class next to students from 'enemy' tribes. The staff in the overseas campuses were also frequently multi-lingual and worked with students from different cultures all the time. A Malaysian lecturer described the staff in Malaysia as 'hybrids', working all the time in three major cultures, usually having been overseas for part of their education, and with the mass media beaming in western culture to their country. They did not need to be taught how to teach IoC but felt that that Australian lecturers could learn from their experience 'but they were not listening'.

In the non-hard-pure disciplines there was an awareness of the complexity of diversity beyond the cultural, to include ethnicity, gender, sexuality, religion, age, social class and disability. There was a belief in the need for an interactive pedagogy, but also a recognition that some students would be uncomfortable with this. An IT lecturer in Australia questioned whether it was appropriate to try and get some groups of students to speak in class, especially if they were Muslim women having to speak in front of males. The staff were aware of their own need for skills in facilitating discussion groups and creating safe environments for all students to participate.

An IT lecturer in South Africa saw the need for staff to be 'internationalised' and the need for the curriculum to be jointly developed by staff involved in delivering the units in different cultures so that the curriculum fitted into different educational structures. The lack of joint curriculum development was interpreted by an Australian IT lecturer as an issue of control, the Australian university feeling a need to keep control of curriculum, and the maintenance of standards across all campuses being seen as an imperative above any consideration of student or local needs.

Discussion

The internationalisation agenda is foregrounding the enculturated nature of higher education and focusing attention on the cultural values and beliefs underlying curricula and pedagogy. Post-colonial writers have often added an ideological stance to this debate, making the area particularly troublesome knowledge (Meyer and Land 2003b) to 'epistemological absolutists' (Turner and Robson 2008: 20).

Turner and Robson (2008) describe internationalisation in terms of a continuum moving from 'symbolic' to 'transformative', the symbolic being something the institution does, while the transformative is what the institution is. This moves internationalisation from being a business deliverable for managers to being about academics' personal world views and values and needing to feel that their values align with those of the institution.

Internationalisation is requiring academics to look at their personal and professional values, at their way of interacting with cultural others and to broaden their understanding of knowledge systems, values, behaviours and embedded practices. The underlying question is whether it is best to address internationalisation within the academic context of the disciplines or outside these discourse communities. To answer this we need to consider academic development practices in higher education.

Although disciplinary boundaries are becoming more fluid and interdisciplinarity increasing, academics' intellectual and professional identities still appear to be centred on their disciplines (Hegarty 2008; Beck and Young 2005; Becher and Trowler 2001; Mestenhauser and Ellingboe 1998). Asking academics to fundamentally question their intellectual and social frames of reference is a threat to their identities and their sense of self-integrity (Carson, 2005) and raises the possibility of resistance in the form of compliance to university dictums rather than personal commitment.

Creating the conditions for a critique of deeply entrenched intellectual traditions can be difficult (Mestenhauser and Ellingboe 1998). Becher and Trowler (2001) illustrated how this resistance is reinforced by professional identification with the discipline, making it difficult to a take a view in opposition to one's colleagues. Academics who do question the discipline are often censured by their colleagues (Gibbs and Coffey 2001; Becher 1989; Dobbert 1998). As the basis of academic thought is critical thinking, which encourages openness, divergence and respect for opposing views, such resistance to new ideas can be viewed as strange. There is also a history of divergent thinking in science and maths. In 1986 Sandra Harding was writing about multicultural science, a science that takes into consideration the influence of culture on what is studied, how it is studied and by whom, and critical mathematics and ethnomathematics study traditional maths through cultural context and perspectives (Kitano 1997; Rosenthal 1997). However, addressing the cultural assumptions of their disciplines appears to be particularly difficult in the hard pure disciplines.

Challenging academics to rethink their beliefs about knowledge and pedagogy may best be approached by centering discussions in discipline-based communities of practice (Wenger 1998) in partnership with academic developers and researchers, the latter providing cross-discipline and cross-cultural facilitation, to bring theory and practice together (Blackmore et al. 2010; Trowler et al. 2005; Neumann et al. 2002). This partnership may also assist academics to learn the language necessary for the development of cross-disciplinary communities of practice to explore the implications of internationalisation in different contexts (Turner and Robson 2008).

Part of these discussions needs to focus on the students rather than the discipline canon. We need to ask why students are engaging in higher education, what do they want/need to get out of it? (Jenkins 1999). The answers to this question will reflect the previous experiences of the students and their perceptions of their future lives. Both of these need to be taken into account when developing curricula. This is now exemplified by some universities in their 'Graduate Attributes' such as that written by the University of South Australia (2001):

> Graduate Attribute No 7 – to develop graduates who demonstrate international perspectives as professionals and as citizens through: broadening the scope of the course to include international content and/or contact, and ... development of cross-cultural communication skills.

Another example is provided by Queen Mary's, London (2010) which has seven graduate attribute themes that include 'engage critically with knowledge', 'learn continuously in a changing world' and 'have a global perspective' (which includes 'accept responsibilities that come from taking a global perspective').

Blackmore et al. (2010) argue that approaching curriculum change through disciplines/departments and work groups is most productive; and work at Oxford Brookes University bringing together programme teams for two days in 'Course Design Intensives', along with academic developers and specialists in the areas under discussion, has been found to increase understanding of what internationalisation means and the possibilities for fundamental redevelopment of the curriculum.

A factor discussed by many of the staff in the study was their own level of 'internationalisation' and, therefore, their ability to internationalise the curriculum. The need for staff to move from ethnocentrism to ethnorelativism is also seen as problematic in much of the literature (Sanderson 2011; Turner and Robson 2008; Bond et al. 2003; Teekens 2003). While some staff, especially overseas staff at the Australian campuses and offshore staff, were very aware of their own global knowledge and inter-cultural competence, there was a feeling that there needed to be more provision for other staff to work overseas to widen their own horizons and capabilities and for collecting valuable resources. At the university in the study, the presence of the offshore campuses and the willingness of the staff at those campuses to work with the Australian staff offered a unique opportunity for collaborative teaching, research and curriculum development. Staff development opportunities for staff to work with colleagues from overseas, to learn about the backgrounds of their students, to see examples of IoC in action, and the availability of international resources are all essential ingredients of a change programme that senior management could be encouraging and facilitating.

Resistance to change has been reinforced by the concern of the tertiary sector with quality assurance and a belief that this can best be achieved through a standardised curriculum (Schapper and Mayson 2004). Quality assurance here is being used as a proxy for standards and this stance needs to be challenged as the educational experiences of students in transnational education situations is not regarded as comparable to the experience of students at the university's home campus (Doorbar 2004). There is an extensive literature on quality in higher education and an approach of 'fitness for purpose' where the service meets the customer needs or requirements is a useful approach to consider with regard to internationalisation. In higher education, a wide range of customers can be identified: students; staff; professional bodies; employers; funding agencies; government; and society at large. These groups may hold different views of 'purpose' and 'fitness' in higher education (Campbell and Rozsnyai 2002; Council For Higher Education Accreditation (CHEA) 2001). In this chapter I am arguing that the needs of the learners in preparing them for their future lives is paramount, so applying a 'fitness for purpose' approach to quality would be appropriate and could provide the flexibility required to deal with different cultural contexts. Van Damme (2002) argued that models of 'fitness for purpose' may be more appropriate so that 'the risks of cultural intrusion and 'imperialism' already inherent in international delivery' are not further intensified (p.18). Ideas of quality enhancement are also currently favoured but difficulties in measuring improvement probably make this impractical in the transnational education scenario.

Standardisation was also identified by staff in the survey as a mechanism of control and a perception that Australia was the 'centre' in terms of intellectual knowledge and rigour and pedagogical expertise. This concept was challenged by staff on- and offshore, some of the latter taking the initiative in shifting the centre to the periphery, foregrounding local knowledge and pedagogy for their students, seeing education that dealt with issues of development as vital to the future of their students and their countries.

Conclusion

Internationalisation offers universities a new ethos, a new way of being, and the disciplines the opportunity to reconceptualise their epistemology and pedagogy based on constructivist and situated perspectives. The challenge to contextualise their knowledge and focus on student learning needs may provide the stimulus to, particularly, the science and maths disciplines that have been losing student numbers for a number of years, to reinvent themselves in a form more relevant to today's students. Many disciplines have embraced the perspectives of internationalisation and are exploring the exciting possibilities of the shifting of centre and periphery and of interdisciplinarity. Internationalisation may offer the disciplines a new lease of life rather than threaten their way of organising knowledge.

Note

1   Quotes from interview scripts for staff are referenced with the discipline of the person followed by their campus location e.g. BusEco, TSA; Arts, TA. The campuses indicated are TM = Malaysia, TSA = South Africa, TA = Australia.

19

Teaching in an Age of 'Supercomplexity'
Lecturer Conceptions in Context

SUSAN J. LEA AND LYNNE CALLAGHAN

Introduction

The past two decades have seen the development of a prolific body of research examining student conceptions of learning, perceptions of the learning environment and approaches to learning augmented by similar research pertaining to lecturers and their teaching. This parallel work is essential, as findings suggest a relationship between the way that lecturers approach their teaching and students approach their learning in higher education (HE) (Prosser *et al.* 2003; Trigwell *et al.* 1999). Moreover, since the evidence suggests that learning outcomes are influenced by the approach taken by students to their learning (Trigwell and Prosser 1991; Lizzio *et al.* 2002), examining lecturers' experiences of teaching is an important area of study and one that forms the focus of this chapter.

In 2002, we conducted qualitative research into lecturers' perceptions and experiences of teaching (Lea and Callaghan 2008).[1] In interpreting our findings we found Barnett's (2000a) concept of supercomplexity useful. A situation of supercomplexity involves multiple frameworks of understanding, action and self-identity and it seemed an apt way to capture how our participants were experiencing the changing context and climate of HE and its impacts upon their teaching. The invitation to contribute to this book offered us the opportunity to gather further data to compare lecturers' conceptions of teaching in the fast-changing context of HE from 2002 with those of 2010, and in particular, to test the supercomplexity notion further.

Researching Approaches to Teaching

Although most authors summarise extant literature as distinguishing between just two approaches to teaching – a teacher-centred or transmission approach and a student-centred or facilitation approach (Lindblom-Ylänne *et al.* 2006) – a range of models of conceptualising lecturers' teaching have been proposed. For example, in an early study, Dall'Alba (1991) identified seven ways in which teachers conceived of their teaching, ranging from teaching as simply presenting information through to teaching as bringing about conceptual change. Such taxonomies of teaching classify how lecturers conceive of, or approach, their teaching, and theoretically order the range of possible positions along a continuum from more teacher-centred to more learner-centred. Thus, while researchers use different terms – for example, approaches, orientations, conceptions – different definitions of these terms and identify different numbers of possible approaches to teaching, their work is generally unified by this continuum approach.

The use of different terms, which variously conceptualise teaching, remains further complicated by a lack of precision in many authors' use of terminology. Thus, while 'orientations' are usually seen as more stable and 'approaches' are usually seen as relations between the teacher and the teaching situation, this difference is not always discernible in the literature. Indeed, the concept of a teaching 'approach' is diversely used with some researchers seeing teaching approach as relatively stable (for example, Kember and Kwan 2002) and others acknowledging that context may affect approach to teaching (Prosser and Trigwell 1999). Even so, many papers are underpinned, implicitly or explicitly, by the notion that the individual lecturer is more or less fixed at a point on the teacher-centred/learner-centred continuum, thereby ultimately seeing teaching approach as static over time and contexts. Like Lecouteur and Delfabbro (2001), therefore, we argue that the theoretical model associated with deriving taxonomies of teaching is too crude to adequately describe, understand or explain the complexities of teaching in HE today.

The influential models put forward by Biggs (1999) and Prosser and Trigwell (1999) offer more scope. Biggs proposes three 'levels of thinking about teaching' moving from a transmission-dominated position (level one), through an increased focus on 'what the teacher does' (level two) to a more interactive third level where teaching is seen to support learning. The strength of Biggs' model is that the level three conceptualisation sees the teacher as operating in the learning and teaching context. However, as a three-stage linear model, the possibility does not exist that the teacher may operate at different levels depending on the context within which they find themselves. Prosser and Trigwell's (1999) model of teaching parallels Biggs' (1999) 3P – presage, process, product – model of student learning. They argue that teachers, like learners, enter HE with prior conceptions of teaching based in their own personal experience. These are then influenced by teachers' perceptions of the teaching context and, as a consequence, teachers will adopt different approaches to teaching that will lead to different teaching outcomes. This focus on the lecturer in context represents a constructive theoretical move away from the lecturer as displaying a fixed approach to his/her teaching more or less regardless of context.

Quantitative instruments (for example, Prosser and Trigwell 1999) have been developed to measure approaches to teaching quickly and with large samples. Studies have shown that student-focused 'conceptual change' approaches to teaching are associated with deep approaches to learning; and that teacher-focused 'information transfer' approaches to teaching are associated with surface approaches to learning (Trigwell *et al.* 1999). Some studies have attempted to identify socio-demographic and contextual factors that may influence lecturers' approaches to teaching. Gender, nationality (Nevgi *et al.* 2004) and educational training (Gibbs and Coffey 2004) have been shown to be relevant. A discipline effect has also been found (for example, Lueddeke 2003; Lindblom-Ylänne *et al.* 2006), with lecturers in the 'hard' disciplines – for example, science and engineering – adopting a teacher-centred approach to teaching and lecturers from 'soft' disciplines– for example, social science and humanities – taking a more student-centred approach. It is proposed that such differences are rooted in the cultural and epistemological differences associated with different academic 'tribes' (Becher and Trowler 2001). However, findings are inconsistent and in a recent study (Stes *et al.* 2008) no association between approaches to teaching and subject/discipline was found, although the authors caution that there were methodological challenges associated with the research.

One of the difficulties associated with research on lecturer teaching to date is that studies have tended to examine a single and specific teaching situation, although 'the same teachers may well have different conceptions, perceive their teaching situation in different ways and adopt different approaches to teaching in different teaching contexts' (Prosser and Trigwell 1999: 156–7). The field is characterised by individual–social dualism. Thus, the complexity of the social, economic and political context within which higher education is practised is overlooked, or reduced to single variable effects. This 'messiness' of the HE world is precisely what emerged, unexpectedly, in our earlier research (Lea and Callaghan 2008) and led us to frame those results within Barnett's (2000a, 2000b, 2000c) concept of supercomplexity. A supercomplex world is characterised by a multiplicity of frameworks; by 'fragility' in relation to the way that we understand the world and ourselves and therefore 'in the ways in which we feel secure about acting in the world' (Barnett 2000a: 257) – by uncertainty, unpredictability, challengeability and contestability (Barnett 1999). In our earlier work, lecturers and managers clearly articulated the impact of the confused, contradictory and challenging nature of HE upon their teaching and learning activity, and their responses to it. Indeed, as social psychologists we were surprised to find that little research has explored the pressures faced by academics in HE today – with the exception of Trowler's (1998) study of NewU and Becher's (1989) earlier seminal work. Consequently, our interest is in lecturers' perceptions and experiences of teaching, located within the changing context and climate of HE in England.

The Studies

The original study was conducted in 2002, with a second small study conducted in 2010. Both studies utilised a qualitative design of interviews and focus groups (see Table 19.1) in order to achieve a rich corpus of data.

Table 19.1 Research design

	Study 1: 2002		Study 2: 2010	
Participant role	Manager	Lecturer	Manager	Lecturer
Data collection method	Focus group	Interview	Focus group	Focus group
Participant number	13	9	4	6

Participants in both studies included lecturers from a range of disciplines – subjects within the humanities, science and engineering, arts, business studies, and food, land use and leisure – as well as key learning and teaching staff – for example, chairs of Faculty learning and teaching committees; associate deans teaching and learning – from a university in the south-west of England.

Study one's interviews and focus groups were guided by semi-structured schedules, derived from the research literature and findings of the researchers' earlier studies. Interviews focused on lecturers' personal experiences of teaching and learning. Focus groups centred on key discussion points that echoed the areas addressed in the individual interviews. These were: conceptions of learners and how students learn; conceptions of HE lecturers and the activity of teaching; and the learning and teaching environment. The aim of the small-scale 2010 study was to update knowledge specifically of the contextual issues that arose in our first study. Therefore, the semi-structured focus group schedule was informed by the two main themes that emerged from the 2002 data and specifically addressed the contextual issues perceived to be impacting on higher education, the nature of that impact, and strategies for managing these effects.

Lecturers participating in study one and managers participating in focus groups in 2002 and 2010 were recruited purposively. Lecturers participating in study two were randomly selected using staff lists and a random number table. Both studies were approved by the university's human ethics subcommittee. Interviews took the form of a 'conversation with a purpose' (Willig 2002) enabling the establishment of rapport and a relaxed interaction. They were usually conducted in participants' offices and lasted between 45 minutes and one-and-a-half hours. 'Light touch' facilitation of focus group discussion was offered by the researchers when participants discussed issues outside the parameters of the research, and to move discussion along to enable all topics to be considered within the time allotted (cf. Morgan 1988; Krueger 1997). Focus groups were run in a quiet room on the main campus and lasted between one and one-and-a-half hours.

The interviews and focus group discussions were recorded and transcribed using the light Jeffersonian method (Jefferson 1985). Data were analysed using grounded theory (Strauss and Corbin 1997). The researchers analysed the data independently and then compared their findings. Overall, there was considerable agreement between the researchers on the codes, categories and elements of a grounded theory. Where there was disagreement, the data were returned for further independent analysis, and discussion took place until consensus could be achieved. A key issue in relation to the second study was that the analysis had independent analytic integrity, particularly since the second study sought to focus on the issue of context that arose in the first. For this reason, the researchers did not consult the detailed findings of their 2002 study and only compared the 2002 and 2010 data at the end of the analytic process.

Findings

Data analysis of the 2002 data generated a grounded theory comprising two main themes, 'Understanding the HE context' and 'Dealing with the HE context' – each involving a number of sub-themes. The notion of 'supercomplexity' seemed apposite to describe participants' experiences within HE; with competing and contested frameworks of understanding being felt at the level of classroom interactions with students. Consequently, the aim of our small 2010 study was to explore explicitly the impact of the fast-changing HE context on lecturers and managers. The two original main themes thus structured our 2010 findings but differences transpired between the two samples in terms of sub-themes.

Understanding the HE Context

Table 19.2 below presents the contextual issues that participants in both 2002 and 2010 identified as impacting on their teaching.

In 2002, the first sub-theme pertained to the perceived low value associated with teaching and learning activity, as compared to the perceived high value placed on research in HE. The pressure to research and a belief that research contributed most significantly to promotion left lecturers feeling that they

Table 19.2 Contextual issues identified by participants

2002 Sub-themes	2010 Sub-themes
Research agenda and the Research Assessment Exercise (RAE)	Research agenda and the Research Excellence Framework (REF)
Erosion of state funding for HE	Economic recession and erosion of state funding for HE
External control over curricula	External control over curricula
Widening participation	Employability and the role of HE
Nature of secondary education	

should 'always be doing the other' (P4 2002);[2] that is, when they were engaged in teaching activity, they should be doing research, and vice versa. This sub-theme emerged again in 2010 with lecturers describing a very similar set of perceptions and experiences. Further, it was not simply the research–teaching dilemma that was apparent in the 2010 sample, but also the pressure to increase research output and related impact, particularly in relation to the forthcoming Research Excellence Framework – despite state efforts to enhance equality in status between research and teaching (Barnett, 2000a). For example, one participant commented:

> This kind of corporate culture. We need to produce papers, research, what-ever, instead of being really creative, doing something which makes sense ...
>
> FG2 2010

The second sub-theme identified in 2002, the erosion of state funding for HE, attracted considerably more discussion in 2010. The economic recession coupled with the new Conservative/Liberal Democrat coalition government made this particular sub-theme a substantial focus of lecturer talk. In partic-ular, lecturers described a context of uncertainty and insecurity manifested in concerns about potential redundancy, the freezing of posts when staff left resulting in an ever-increasing workload for those remaining, and the possi-bility of some programmes no longer being commissioned or being terminated. Thus, compared to our 2002 sample, where the talk centred on top slice and the lack of resources to update equipment, the nature of the issues discussed in 2010 struck more forcibly at the ontological and epistemological heart of HE. Discussion revealed anxieties about what is expected of universities, with the perceived demise of their traditional function and increasing focus on new knowledges, performativity (Lyotard 1984), employability and enterprise.

> The feeling that the change of economic climate is changing our teaching.
>
> FG2 2010

> I think there's quite a lot of uncertainty at the moment, and we're all a bit concerned about our future, and where it will be. And what effect that has on teaching, well who knows?
>
> FG2 2010

In 2002, participants were concerned with the issue of widening participa-tion. However, our 2010 participants did not mention this initiative but instead spoke fairly extensively about the impact of 'employability', a concept that was largely absent in our earlier sample. Discussion returned to the purpose of HE, and was characterised by contradiction and dilemma. Participants contrasted a desire to educate with the demand to train, talking about education versus employability. A set of bipolar opposites was used to contrast traditional education – involving critical intellectual inquiry, questioning and theory – with educating for the employability agenda – seen as the teaching of skills, the demonstration of standards through evidence and a focus on practice or the development of 'the tools of the trade'. While lecturers were not arguing for an exclusive focus on 'traditional' education, they were articulating a concern about balance – as defined by what they understood employability to mean and the subsequent effect on their role:

> I guess the difference is, are we training people or are we educating people? We would probably rather be educators than trainers, um, if we had to put our eggs in one basket. It's not possible to do that, if it ever was. I guess it was.
>
> FG3 2010

Discipline differences emerged in both samples with lecturers in disciplines regulated by professional bodies feeling particularly constrained in terms of the curricula. These lecturers felt that they were simply transmitting information and teaching skills that students would require upon leaving university, rather than truly educating students through enhancing theoretical knowledge and understanding. Thus, although there was a common theme around the purpose of HE, lecturers discovered disciplinary differences through conversation:

> It's only when you meet people at a similar level in other disciplines, or other faculties, or other places, the tribes, you find actually how different practice can be across one institution.
>
> FG3 2010

> I mean it sounds like we have different disciplines … and some of those comments, perhaps are driven by things that are not universal for all of us.
>
> FG1 2010

Interestingly, the solution put forward by a number of the 2010 participants was that a more collegiate, multidisciplinary style of working might be the way to cope with a supercomplex environment. For example, one lecturer talked about the need for people to start 'crossing borders' (FG3 2010) in order to survive, echoing Barnett's (2000b) assertion that it is unlikely that any knowledge fields will be able to remain pure in the contemporary world.

The final sub-theme that only emerged in our 2002 study, the nature of secondary education, related to lecturers' frustration at students' lack of independent learning and critical thinking on entering HE and the need for them to front load programmes to facilitate students' progression to the HE context. In 2010, lecturers seemed more concerned about what they were educating students for, than where they had come from.

Dealing with the HE context

This theme concerned how lecturers attempt to deal with the perceived impact of the HE context on their practice. In the 2002 study, three sub-themes emerged which described a dynamic teaching process comprising: an awareness of students' needs and experiences; responsiveness and flexibility in relation to balancing external factors and students' needs; and a reflective approach to teaching practice. Analysis of the 2010 data found that this analytic framework was again relevant. However, due to the political and economic climate at the time of the 2010 data collection – with the imminent publication of the Browne Review of HE funding – participants' discussion was characterised by a pervasive sense of insecurity and uncertainty.

The 2002 participants ranged from having a basic awareness of contextual issues and just having a 'good moan' about academic life, to utilising this awareness to embark on a more conscious and dynamic process to attempt to resolve some of the issues they raised. The managers in the 2010 sample also perceived some teaching staff as having limited awareness of the potential impact of contextual issues on teaching and learning, despite their perception that the world of HE has become significantly more complex in recent years:

> I think there'll be a variety of different responses ... I think the people who will be bothered are the people like us, who can see the sort of writing on the wall ... my guess is that there may be plenty of staff who are not feeling any different.
>
> FG1 2010

However, for most staff in both samples, this awareness of teaching context led them to engage in responsive and flexible behaviour in order to minimise the impact of such issues on students' learning. Thus, lecturers anticipated and reacted to factors they perceived as potentially affecting the teaching and learning process, demonstrating flexibility in approach both within a teaching situation, between different classes and in longer-term planning. As with the 2002 sample, the 2010 findings revealed that lecturers often responded to external pressures by changing the teaching environment and method of delivery. Following Barnett (2000b) these lecturers could be seen to be responding to the competing demands of the HE world:

> This kind of external force or condition is changing my teaching, demanding a different style – more practical, less practical, depends.
>
> FG2 2010

Further, in response to the economic downturn, 2010 managers viewed the development of continuing professional development (CPD) courses as a constructive longer-term response to the funding crisis for HE institutions, although some staff noted that directing teaching efforts down this route could potentially diminish the quality of 'traditional' teaching avenues, again echoing 'the purpose of HE' debate:

> Now, if we go down that route, because we're pushed financially, that'll clearly take a lot of our efforts. Because we're going to have to start thinking about different ways of doing things, than what we're used to in the mainstream. But as a consequence, that's going to have direct knock-on effects for the way we're teaching our undergraduate students.
>
> FG1 2010

Moreover, while lecturers described being responsive and adaptable, they noted that their attempts at enhancing teaching at an institutional level could be thwarted by inflexible and detached institutional processes:

> One comment I had is that the process to go through to be really innovative with your teaching can be quite long winded. And I find that sometimes that prevents me from saying 'right I'll try something totally new this time'.
>
> FG2 2010

Finally, some 2010 lecturers perceived the climate of HE as mirroring the environment that students will face upon leaving university and entering the job market. As such, these lecturers attempted to turn the impact of contextual factors into positive drivers to explicitly encourage students to exploit learning opportunities:

> So, in fact, I'm using the external economic pressure to force my students to, to work hard. Just to show them that, you know, you should be prepared. So, I don't really feel it as a problem, rather an opportunity. To some extent, it helps.
>
> FG3 2010

As in 2002, in 2010 some participants indicated that while responsiveness and flexibility are necessary to deal with the supercomplexity of the HE context, it is also crucial to be reflective to maximise student learning. Some lecturers believed that their teaching could be enhanced but that this was difficult to achieve within current constraints:

> I'm quite frustrated, actually. And I think I could do quite a lot better. But there are too many other things that get in the way of me doing that.
>
> FG3 2010

Both cohorts gave examples of the involvement of others in this reflection process. For example, one lecturer in the 2002 sample used group brainstorming to evaluate student needs. Some of the 2010 sample extolled the virtues of peer review of teaching and obtaining feedback from students. The latter was viewed by lecturers as the most valuable medium to initiate their reflection on their teaching. This was particularly the case where lecturers engaged in informal dialogue with students to inform both the current teaching situation and future planned provision:

> I think that informal feedback is much more valuable than the formal feedback. And to be honest, I find the formal university processes for feedback of very little value to me.
>
> FG3 2010

In summary, lecturers in both 2002 and 2010 articulated a detailed understanding of the supercomplexity of the HE context, and described a dynamic process of engaging in teaching in relation to the uncertainty, unpredictability, challengeability and contestability (Barnett 1999) of that world. Perhaps not surprisingly, the 2010 data were more directly oriented to the fractured and fragile function of HE and the subsequent implications for identity and action. In both cohorts, tribal or territorial differences were somewhat overshadowed by shared issues and concerns.

Discussion and Conclusions

This chapter has explored lecturers' perceptions and experiences of teaching in the current HE context. Literature in this area tends to be dominated by 'taxonomies' of teaching, which give limited consideration to the influence of context and see lecturers as being more or less defined by a specific approach or orientation to teaching. Yet, our original study (Lea and Callaghan 2008) conducted in 2002 revealed that, given the opportunity, lecturers raised a wide range of issues that they felt impacted on their teaching. These issues extended beyond the classroom, the academic department and institution to government policy and practice, and to social, economic and political drivers. To mitigate the impact of context upon teaching and learning, lecturers engaged in a dynamic process of awareness, responsiveness and reflection. These original findings resonated with Barnett's (2000a) concept of 'supercomplexity'.

When we were approached to contribute to this book, we took the opportunity to gather a little more data in relation to the supercomplexity thesis. We undertook a very small-scale study, which is limited in its generalisability, and therefore our findings need to be viewed with considerable caution. Nevertheless, as with our 2002 study, lecturers were keen to discuss their efforts to deliver an excellent educational experience to students while managing the impact of competing and contradictory drivers and influences. Barnett's (2000a) concept of supercomplexity appeared even more relevant in 2010; insecurity and uncertainty pervaded participants' talk and they actively discussed competing notions of HE and their teaching practice.

Interestingly, differences between academic cultures and their disciplinary epistemologies (Becher and Trowler 2001) did not emerge very strongly – with the exception of courses leading to professional registration versus those that did not – arguably because in both cohorts, but especially in 2010, the nature of HE was itself at issue. Thus, common concerns and themes emerged relevant to all lecturers and took precedence over tribal differences.

It is unsurprising, perhaps, that lecturers raised a host of contextual issues affecting HE, given substantial changes within the sector (Sikes 2006). What surprised us was the way in which our participants connected these issues to their teaching. It is our contention, therefore, that future research needs to explore more rigorously the impact of context on teaching and learning. Although there has been some appreciation of its influence on teaching (for example, Biggs 1999; Prosser and Trigwell 1999; Lindblom-Ylänne et al. 2006), context has usually been defined in terms of the immediate teaching environment or institutional context. The impact of the broader social, economic and political context, in all its supercomplexity, is largely ignored.

The theoretical shift to a broader conceptualisation of teaching is important for two reasons. First, it acknowledges the impact of supercomplexity on HE, and on teaching practice. Second, it facilitates a more sophisticated understanding of teaching and teachers – not simply as 'rote teachers', firmly rooted in an approach irrespective of time or context, but as flexible, malleable and adaptable beings in interaction and dialogue with their students and each other. Our research has revealed lecturers attempting to facilitate learning and prepare students for the world beyond the university while managing the fractured nature of HE. Indeed, we would assert that lecturers and managers – across tribes and territories – need to be adaptable and flexible if they are to cope with the multiple frameworks of understanding, action and self-identity that define the current context of HE, and if they are to be effective teachers of students. We would agree with Barnett (2000b: 265) that 'a new responsibility is falling on universities to demonstrate that the education they offer is likely to be adequate to the challenges of the supercomplex world'. Similarly, we would argue that a new responsibility is falling on scholars of HE to demonstrate that the theory and research they offer is adequate to the challenges of the supercomplex world. An exciting project lies ahead, of generating new frameworks of knowledge and understanding, or to paraphrase Barnett (2000c: 209) 'an epistemology of (teaching) amid uncertainty'.

Notes

1   The original 2002 research was funded by a National Teaching Fellowship awarded to the first author. The authors wish to thank Ursula Lanvers, Lauren Mutton and Susan Eick for assisting in the 2002 and 2010 data collection respectively, and the participants who gave up their time to attend focus groups and interviews.

2   Quotations are annotated as follows: For focus groups, focus group number (FG1 for example), followed by the year; for individual interviews, participant number (P1 for example), followed by the year.

20
Technology and Change in Academic Practice

MARTIN OLIVER

Introduction

This chapter explores claims that technology is changing academic practice. First, examples of this kind of claim are drawn from the literature, and a professional 'tribe' involved in this process is identified. Then, two examples are offered that look at the process of change from the perspective of activity theory. The chapter concludes by reframing technology as an opportunity for encouraging or resisting change, rather than a simple cause.

Background

Technology is often written about as a 'driver' for change in education. Sometimes it is positioned as a simple cause – for example, Presnky (2001) has argued that because young people now make such extensive use of digital technologies, generational differences have arisen that apply not only to how they learn, work and play, but even to how their brains are structured.

Less extreme, but nonetheless widespread, is the 'softer' kind of technological determinism. This suggests that there will be an evolution in learning and teaching, with technology as a catalyst, if not a simple cause. This can be seen in UK higher education policy, for example:

> E-learning exploits interactive technologies and communication systems to improve the learning experience. It has the potential to transform the way we teach and learn across the board. It can raise standards, and widen participation in lifelong learning. ... It can enable every learner to achieve his or her potential, and help to build an educational workforce empowered to change. It makes possible a truly ambitious education system for a future learning society.
>
> DfES 2003

Dire consequences are threatened if universities fail to engage with this problem. For example:

In an expert roundtable conducted by Demos, one participant used a telling analogy to describe the current predicament of the higher education sector: 'This seminar feels a bit like sitting with a group of record industry executives in 1999.' Technology undermined certain business models that sustained the music industry, but the threat was not to music itself, only to the way that current business models worked.

Bradwell 2009: 11

This idea is not new. Since at least 1992, the use of technology has been described first as a 'Trojan horse' (Hammond and Trapp 1992) and later as a 'Trojan mouse' (Soloway 1997) that either causes, or at least invites, reconsideration of learning and teaching.

> E-learning is often talked about as a 'trojan mouse', which teachers let into their practice without realizing that it will require them to rethink not just how they use particular hardware or software, but all of what they do.
>
> Sharpe and Oliver 2007: 49

This happens, at least in part, because processes that could once be governed by tacit knowledge need to be specified and formalised to allow technical systems to operate – as Cornford describes it, 'the virtual university is the university made concrete' (2000).

Yet this apparently inexorable force for change seems unable to deliver on its promises. Tracing more than 40 years of UK policies on technology and higher education, Conole *et al.* (2007) are able to chart some developments. There was, for example, an initial focus on mainframe computers for scientific research; a phase in which desktop PCs predominated and practitioner developments were promoted; and a period focusing on developing a shared infrastructure and integration into mainstream learning and teaching. However they also conclude, 'sadly there has been too much evidence of knee-jerk policy' (p. 54), and echo the experiences summarised by Mayes (1995) over a decade earlier:

> People who have been involved over any length of time with educational technology will recognise this experience, which seems characterised by a cyclical failure to learn from the past. We are frequently excited by the promise of a revolution in education, through the implementation of technology. We have the technology today, and tomorrow we confidently expect to see the widespread effects of its implementation. Yet, curiously, tomorrow never comes. We can point to several previous cycles of high expectation about an emerging technology, followed by proportionate disappointment, with radio, film, television, teaching machines and artificial intelligence.

While there are many individual case studies of success, literature reviews tend to be more equivocal; Russell (1999), for example, has a book and associated website dedicated to the 'no significant difference' phenomenon, documenting a consistent lack of evidence across radio, television, video and online learning to support any claims that any of these media improve students' chances of success on a course. Nevertheless, expectations continue to run high for each new technology that is introduced, and research still follows these familiar cycles of hope and disappointment (Gouseti 2010).

Interestingly, the same strange mix of revolution and 'business as usual' can be seen in relation to the emergence of a new 'tribe' associated with the use of technology in education. In 1999, Gornall pointed to the emergence of a group of 'new professionals', some of whom are described as learning technologists. This group were marginal yet influential, often linked to strategic initiatives but equally often outside of existing institutional structures. Their role was to cross the boundaries of disciplinary 'tribes', to share and develop learning and teaching through the use of technology (Oliver 2002). This role is fairly well documented in the UK, but is also visible in universities in Europe (Oliver *et al.* 2005), the U.S. (Oliver 2002) and South Africa (Hodgkinson-Williams and Czerniewicz 2007), for example. Interestingly, however, it is also possible to trace very similar discussions of this 'new' group as far back as 1976 (Lawless and Kirkwood). Their identity as a 'tribe' may be relatively diffuse and is rarely recognised, but it has proved persistent nonetheless.

This is, of course, not the only 'tribe' for whom technology is a consideration. Arguably, technological developments have affected every academic field, although perhaps in different ways. One useful lens through which this can be described is the idea of 'technical pedagogic content knowledge' or TPCK (Mishra and Koehler 2006). Developed in the context of teacher education, this is a development of Shulman's idea of pedagogic content knowledge – the idea that an academic needs to know about their discipline – 'content knowledge' or CK; about learning and teaching –'pedagogic knowledge' or PK; and about the overlap between these: the specificity of how to teach this particular discipline – 'pedagogic content knowledge' or PCK. Shulman's framework has been widely criticised (e.g. as an oversimplified account of 'knowledge' – 2005b); however, it was developed in order to critique teacher training by pointing out topics that were neglected – how to teach this topic rather than just teach in general. Mishra and Koehler (2006) added technology to this framework, allowing them to analyse educational practices and training courses in four further ways: in terms of knowledge about technology (TK); about the technologies of teaching – for example, virtual learning environments (TPK); about the technologies used in the discipline – for example, computer-based concordances or electron microscopes (TCK); and finally about the knowledge of how to use technology to teach that specific topic (TPCK).

This analytic distinction is helpful in disambiguating different kinds of technology and the varying degrees to which they influence practice in a disciplinary area. While particular technologies may effectively redefine what scholars in an area can study (Latour and Woolgar 1979), others that are primarily thought about in terms of teaching may have little or no impact at all on disciplinary practices. Both categories of technology may need to be brought together, however, when actually teaching.

This may help to explain why many of the technologies that are discussed within education seem to have little purchase on the practices of disciplinary 'tribes'; however it does not explain why there seems to be so little evidence in general for the promised impact of technology on learning and teaching. How has this pattern of hope and disappointment managed to persist for so long? How can the sense of constant expectation and revolution be reconciled with the body of research that consistently undermines claims to progress? Part of the answer to this lies with challenges to the determinist account of the relationship between technology and education and, with it, to the notion of media comparison studies.

Methodology

To illustrate the points made above, two case studies have been chosen. These demonstrate the complexities of how technology can be implicated in changes in higher education, without having to view it as the 'cause'. The first concerns the adoption of a virtual learning environment (VLE); the second, the replacement of a physical resource collection with a digital one. Each describes changes in practice, but also provides an insight into the management of professional identities.

For each, interviews were undertaken with the staff involved – an academic in the first case, two members of support staff in the second. The interviews were analysed using activity theory (Engeström 2001). This focuses on purposeful action as the unit of analysis, understood in terms of activity systems (Kuutti 1996). The actors in activity systems are referred to as 'subjects'; their intentions as 'objects' – in the sense of an objective to be achieved. Tools in this tradition are broadly understood, including: embodied tools – artefacts such as computers, hammers, and so on; symbolic tools – such as writing and language; and conceptual tools – such as theories.

Contextualising this triad are three concepts that describe the social framing of the activity, described in terms of communities, their rules and the division of labour (Kuutti 1996). 'Rules' are understood to be tacit as well as explicit. The 'community' represents the social grouping within which the activity takes place. In order to achieve the object, a complex activity may be undertaken in a distributed manner. This distribution is referred to as the 'division of labour'.

These concepts, taken together, are referred to as an activity system (see Figure 20.1; solid lines represent relationships between concepts and the dashed lines represent relationships that are implied).

Another important distinction is between three levels of activity. The most general is the activity itself – a strategic-level description of intentional tool use in context; more specific are the series of actions that constitute it – specific deliberate uses of tools, in context, to achieve tactical components of the overall task; and finally there are the operations that constitute each action – each so simple and routine that, unless a problem occurs, they are performed automatically. This distinction allows the creation of nested accounts of practice that encompass both strategic and 'automatic' acts.

Of particular importance in this kind of analysis are 'contradictions' within the system – points at which the system breaks down. These are understood as arising from the relationship between at least two elements of the system. This permits a fine-grained analysis of cases and the suggestion of potential solutions.

The interview transcripts were reviewed to identify passages where disruptions, breakdowns or problems were mentioned. These were listed, and duplicated topics were ignored. Each remaining theme was analysed in terms of activity theory. For the purposes of this chapter, individual themes have been chosen that relate directly to questions of changing practice and professional identity.

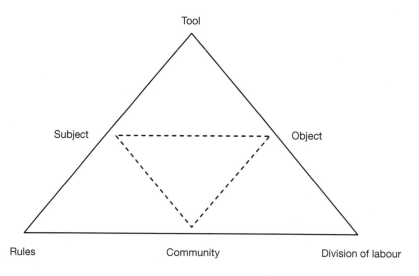

Figure 20.1 Activity theory triangle

Case Study One: VLE Adoption

This study involved interviews with a lecturer before and after the introduction of a VLE into their teaching (Price and Oliver 2007). Discussions – particularly, forms of peer support – formed an important part of the course, and much of the interview data concerned the process that the participant described as 'moving' discussion online. This change in practice is quite widely discussed in the research literature, and various models have been proposed for how this ought to be achieved (for example, Salmon 2000). An important question in the analysis was whether the 'move' the participant described really could be understood as transferring existing practice into a new context, or whether the use of a VLE required practice to change.

There were certainly indications that a simple 'transfer' account failed to explain the problems that the staff and students experienced with online discussion – for example, the interviewee discussed the absence of conventional cues, including facial expression and tone of voice, and the anxieties that this could produce.

> That illustrates the complexity of what is going on here and what people feel when they're typing something in about, well what is this going to say about me, what will other people say, how will they judge me?

Interestingly, however, the participant attributed more importance to the teacher than the technology in influencing discussions.

> I think ... the role of the facilitator is key. And I think the role of the facilitator in any learning event is key, and the stance that they take and the way in which they take up either the new technology, or any change in classroom practice in a face-to-face situation, will determine the response of the participants.

Specific important features of the role included planning and designing the activities, modelling the kinds of behaviour they wanted from their students and ensuring that the discussions were perceived as 'safe', avoiding anxiety that might impede participation.

One aspect of the teacher's role, which will be the focus here, is the importance the participant placed on monitoring students, both in terms of supporting their motivation and learning, and in terms of attendance. This was seen as particularly important, and was described as being the same within a VLE as in a conventional setting. In this case, the participant had used tools available within the VLE to monitor student interaction, allowing intervention where they felt it was needed. Several of these were considered to have been successful, which the participant took as evidence that face-to-face practices had been transferred to online teaching.

I'm looking for some kind of contribution, any contribution, I look for basically and if I don't get that then I know there's probably something wrong. It's when people are chipping in their bits and then all of a sudden it goes quiet. That's the danger sign. You do pick up on odd stuff like that – it's just transferring what you normally do in normal situations to a virtual environment.

Activity theory was used to analyse this participant's account of intervening in discussions. At a strategic level, the analysis was consistent with the participant's 'just transferring' explanation; technology, in this account, was not driving any meaningful change in academic practices. The tool used changed, but the other analytic categories – subject, object, division of labour, and so on – did not. The role of the tutor remains the same: to monitor, look for categories of behaviour such as non-contribution, to intervene where this happened. There was no change to the role of the tutor as the result of the introduction of the new technology.

At the level of action, the account of change as 'just transferring' started to become more problematic. Specifically, the tools used by the tutor to enact their role were different. For example, rather than watching people in a room, student monitoring functions were used to generate participation lists for specific discussions. Analytically, the subject, community and rules remained the same, while the rules were changed – for example, to 'ensure presence on a list' rather than 'ensure presence in class' as a marker of participation. The status of the object and the division of labour are debatable. The purpose (object) is still to encourage student engagement, but speaking no longer counts towards this; the nature of the engagement that is sought is different. Responsibility for tasks is also subtly different: while students are still expected to contribute and the tutor still has responsibility for monitoring this, the tutor will need to undertake this periodically – since contributions could come in over a period of days or weeks – rather than continuously throughout a short time-bound period. So, while the object and outcome of the activity system were preserved – or 'just transferred' – the system as a whole had been re-worked to incorporate the VLE.

Operationally, the fine-grained analysis of this account is inconsistent with the 'just transferring' explanation. Operations from the face-to-face setting, such as 'scan the room', 'listen for things to go quiet', are now replaced by operations such as 'click this link to generate a list of contributors' and 'click this link to reveal students' patterns of reading the online materials'. The subjects and community remain the same, but the tools used are different – posting through the VLE rather than speaking; the object has changed – create a list, review the list, etc., rather than listen, look for signs of disengagement, etc.; the rules have changed – in terms of what 'counts' as engagement; and the division of labour is different – the production and monitoring of contributions take place as part of separate tasks, not as integrated parts. At this level, the previous practice is almost unrecognisable in the new system.

> What this reveals is how the move to teaching online renders the role of the teacher both the same and different simultaneously. The purpose and strategic direction may remain unchanged, but the methods of achieving this alter in significant ways.
>
> Price and Oliver 2007: 24

This inconsistency, in which the perception of change depends fundamentally on the way in which the data are analysed, offers an explanation for the tension identified above between claims of transformation and evidence suggesting no progress with technology. Successful teaching was not transformed; the participant was still able to teach successfully. Their educational values were unchanged, and they perceived their role to be 'transferred'. However, the way in which this success was achieved was transformed: the practices of learning and teaching are different, with those using the VLE consisting of reading, composition, contribution and generating lists to check whereas classroom practices consisted of listening, speaking and observing. They leave more enduring traces – text records, tallies in a database – than the ephemeral, unrecorded conversations in classrooms. The practices of learning and teaching are disaggregated, allowing them to be undertaken more flexibly in terms of timing and location; they are different, but they still constitute an educational conversation and they still support learning.

Case Study Two: Digitising a Slide Collection

This second study builds on the previous one. Having shown how successful transformation can also be understood as preservation of the things that matter to an educator – role, values and so on – this next example shows how technology can be used to engender changes in practice.

This study involved staff maintaining a well-established and generally successful resource collection for use in teaching. There were, however, some recurrent problems. For example, when academics searched for teaching resources, they were not always able to find something appropriate. If this was because there was no suitable resource, the collection staff could intervene either to suggest an alternative or, if time permitted, create something. (Analytically, this involved changes in the rules and division of labour to involve them in the activity of preparing for teaching.) At other times, academics simply failed to understand the way the collection was structured – the system rules. This was resolved by asking the support staff for help – a change in the division of labour – creating duplicate resources – a change to the tool, but one that was seen as costly in terms of staff time and storage space – or by the academic concerned learning more about the rules of resource classification.

This kind of learning by academics was perceived to be relatively rare, however. Generally, breakdowns in resource selection were resolved by the support staff developing the tool or changing how they worked, not by the academics changing their practice. For example, the support staff set up the projection equipment needed to use the resources during teaching, because the academics had found this difficult; they also fixed these when they broke. In effect, each new development in the service represented an expansion of the set of practices the support staff undertook, leaving the academics' practices untouched. The support staff preserved the efficiency of academic practice by taking on and solving the problems that arose themselves.

Throughout the interview, the support staff kept returning to the problem of how to help staff and students to make best use of the collection. Just explaining the system was not sufficient to enable users to understand it; instead, the system needed to be learnt through use – ideally, with the service staff on hand for support. This was relatively easy with students, for whom assessment could be used to force them to engage with the use of resources from the collection:

> When first year students come in there's a presentation they have to do in their first term where they are advised to come to the [resource collection], and it has to be [resources] from here, and as they come in we've individually helped them to find the [resources].

However, the same process was harder with academic staff, who were perceived as reluctant to change how they worked.

> I think they're concerned about speed and ease of access, and I think they're also concerned that they'd have to learn something new, in terms of how to use it, because it's a system that works very smoothly, and I think also they feel slightly uneasy that it might increase their workload.

At the time of the interviews, the support staff were digitising parts of the collection to make the archiving and sharing of resources more efficient and effective. As with other developments, this added to their workload. The academics did not engage with this, relying instead upon the support staff to deal with any changes for them. However, at the time of the interview, this situation was about to change:

> At the moment, we're fulfilling a very particular task with the digitisation, we're digitising a particular course and that's going to be expanded. We've got a plan of how we're going to expand that. But staff members will have to be a bit more active in how they select [resources] to be digitised and how they provide information for us to attach to those [resources].

Previously, filing resources had been a job for support staff. Indeed, as noted, some academics' understanding of the system was insufficient to guarantee they could access the resources they needed. However, in this new context, the provision of information used to classify resources (metadata) was discussed as an academic activity, not a support one, because it relies upon disciplinary expertise and an appreciation of the pedagogic role the resource will have.

Perhaps surprisingly, given that this was previously considered to be an administrative task and so might be seen as an additional and routine burden, some academics had chosen to engage in this process and had responded positively to it. One reason was that this helped avoid other time-consuming problems for them.

> When they are providing this information it's coming from a … list that they've provided anyway for students, and all they have to do is come in and talk to us for five minutes … and it'll help their teaching, because it'll mean they're not constantly bombarded with students asking the same questions when they could actually have it as part of the information attached to [a resource], and students have no excuse not to sort of go and find it out themselves.

Additionally, this development could facilitate other areas of their work, such as research.

> They're realising that it's becoming an increasingly important part of academic life, they're going to more conferences now where there are PowerPoint presentations using digital [resources], and they see it working better and better as the technology gets better. And I think they want to be involved in it themselves. Because certainly the travelling's much more convenient. Or if they're having particular [resources] made for something that they might not ever use to project in a classroom again, they can digitise them and use them for that.

In activity theoretic terms, this new tool could be used to resolve conflicts within several activity systems.

A related problem concerned projection equipment. The digital projection equipment was simpler and more reliable than older technologies, but the service staff had to support both. The support staff had tried to reduce this burden by helping academics learn how to do this themselves – a change in the division of labour.

> It's easier to use the new equipment. Much easier for people to fix themselves if any problems happen in classrooms, rather than having to call us, because that's occasionally a real disruption, having to go into classrooms

in the middle of a working day to fix a [broken resource] or something. But we do now try and educate the staff as to how to use the equipment as well. We get them all in and show them how to change a bulb and so on so that they can do it themselves.

This training did not guarantee that academics would take this work on. While it was easy for them to call out the support staff, they did this. This presented a dilemma for support staff, who had to reconcile their professional commitment to minimising disruption to academics' practices with the long-term sustainability of the service and the ongoing disruption to teaching.

The solution proposed was to allow the older projection equipment to break. They recognised that this would cause short-term problems for all concerned, but believed that in the longer term it would make the established practice of using the older technology undesirable, so that it would be less effort for the academics to swap to using the newer projection equipment instead. This would allow the support staff to phase out the time-consuming work of setting up and maintaining projection equipment.

This reveals two points. First, that the introduction of technology can result in changes in practice, even where this requires more work, where there are benefits in other related activities. Second, successful systems do not provide a strong reason to change practice – or for people to learn. When a change was necessary – in this case, to ensure that a service remained viable – a breakdown had to be engineered that made change desirable. Technology does not 'cause' either change; it is more plausible to attribute the motivation to concerns about practicality. Nevertheless, technology remains an important part of the explanation for each of these kinds of change.

Conclusions

Great claims are made for the power of technology to transform higher education. It is positioned as an all but unstoppable force, poised to sweep away existing structures and practices. As these examples have shown, however, the relationship between technology and change is not nearly so simple.

First, neither 'technology' nor 'change' should be thought of as simple, unified categories. There are many examples of both, and a more nuanced account is helpful in explaining historical patterns of use and non-use. Differentiating between the tools of the discipline and those of teaching, for example, clarifies that we should not expect to see consistent changes across all communities. For some, it will simply be easier to integrate the kinds of tools already used in disciplinary practices with the tools being introduced into learning and teaching. Examples of this would be disciplines such as English literature or art history in which the same databases might be used for teaching as for research; computing, where the development of teaching tools would be a credible learning activity; or architecture, where familiarity with professional computer-aided design tools would be expected from courses. Other disciplines may have the additional work of having to use entirely separate technologies for teaching.

This differentiation between using technology for what might be seen as 'core' disciplinary work and using it for more peripheral concerns, such as teaching, may help to explain some of the 'surface level' interdisciplinary work that takes place around technology (Conole *et al.* 2010). Academics from many disciplines may use technology for teaching in similar ways, but even if the technology has the potential to mediate their work, there is no guarantee that they will understand it in the same ways, have a shared language to talk about it, or consider it important enough to try to have a conversation about it at all.

Moreover, rather than being the sole explanatory cause of change, technology is implicated in change in complex and political ways. Successful technologies can be allowed to break in order to force people to change their practice; they can form a nexus that brings together several related activities; and new technologies can be adopted so as to preserve practices or roles that academics feel are important. Technologies do not so much overwhelm the practices of 'tribes', nor even sneak in and subvert those practices from within – the 'Trojan mouse'. Instead, they can be understood as something that particular groups can take up because they help with some wider problem – such as offering more flexible courses so as to address flagging student recruitment – or because they can be used to influence the practice of others, as was the case with the digitised resource collection. It may be better therefore to understand teaching technologies as producing new practices – because they are constituted using different tools and, at a micro level, in pursuit of different purposes – but not new disciplinary cultures. Rather, they act as a marker or a weathervane that shows which way the wind is blowing for a discipline: something that people choose to use to understand and respond to changes, rather than their 'driver'.

This analysis echoes Cousin's analysis (2005) of metaphors in VLEs. In that work, these environments are designed to convey a familiar sense of conventional classroom teaching to ensure 'a stable transition' (p. 121) for teachers new to teaching in this way. However, this analysis emphasises why this may be so desirable: academics find ways to use technologies to protect the roles and principles that they value, preserving the practices they value, even if these may be enacted in very different ways.

21

Transformations from Without and Within the Disciplines
The Emerging Practice Landscape

MURRAY SAUNDERS

Introduction

The contributions in this section have provided insight into the way in which the determining influences of disciplinary cultures on academic practice are being mediated and in some cases eclipsed by other features of the global higher education landscape. These catalysts for change are becoming increasingly important in explaining the emphases in practice that contemporary higher education now has.

The way practice is shaped by features of the physical and socio-political environment is a critical issue. We have been using a consistent notion of practice within this text that understands it as routine behaviours derived from a personal or collective knowledge base. This knowledge base of the social, technical and political environment yields the basis on which decisions about priorities, actions and compliances are made. We explore these dimensions in more detail in our last chapter.

The notions of compliance and complicity are important here. We do not depict higher education actors as robotic dupes, whose actions are devoid of agency and understanding; the way in which leadership from the universities were complicit in the UK design of an individualised and differentiated funding model for UK universities is a case in point. Our analyses require that we often need fine-grained and situated distinctions between actors at different points in the system and in different national systems in order to make sense of why it is that academic practice may have the profile it does at a particular point in time and place. We talk of the 'congruence' of features that result in catalysing new practices.

While we signal the agentic as well as the structural quality of determinants of academic practice, there is an implication in which recognition of these catalysts, and acting upon their repercussions, has a hegemonic quality. There is a sense of the irresistible about them, of inevitability. It is simply 'the way the world works now' and we, in higher education, either become adept at manoeuvring and managing this environment or we will be 'left behind'. The idea of 'externality' is important here because a 'catalyst' is within the ontological basket of social realism which depicts the 'derivation of behaviours' in the form of practice, as both *outside* one's self, but *of* one's self and, in this case, perceived as a required or overriding imperative for action. This non-dualist position is important in explaining the way in which imperatives for action derive both from outside a higher education actor's mind and body yet become integrated into individual and 'social' cognition and are colonised by them in order to provide meaningful frameworks for action. The catalysts provide us with a new '*logics*' in which certain decisions now provide advantages or disadvantages personally, institutionally and systemically which are broadly accepted as being a winner or loser in the 'new order'. This is how hegemony works.

What our contributions suggest is that there are transformative forces at work which are becoming increasingly important in explaining why academics are doing what they are doing, giving importance to certain practices over others and enthusiastically pursuing policies that embody new priorities. We note that our contributions include changes that are prompted from outside and within the cultures of disciplines themselves and which may transcend and cross traditional cultures of disciplines.

The contributions in this section have identified some key imperatives of the catalytic environment that can be condensed into three categories: the imperative to engage in new curricular practices; the imperative to respond to managerial control and performativity; and national policy imperatives.

The Imperative to Engage in New Curricular Practices

This imperative has become an important catalyst because of the nature of knowledge building and its purpose has shifted. Ontologically, the nature of academic practice has been influenced by a shift in what counts as knowledge in the context of the global challenges that form policy agendas.

Knowing what our world is has increasingly involved recognising the integrated rather than atomised nature of most of its features. Ray Land's chapter suggests the need for new concepts to enable the interdisciplinary imperative for change emanating from a view on the nature of knowledge which is increasingly thematically or problem-centred on a global scale.

Bhaskar's (2010) perspective, for example, is a persuasive statement of intent that argues that an interdisciplinary approach is required to deal with the issue of climate change and the multitude of linked phenomena which both constitute and connect to it. In an important sense, what Bhaskar offers us in critical realism is a 'threshold concept' of the kind Ray Land suggests in his chapter to address the imperative of interdisciplinarity. Bhaskar goes some way toward developing the new ontology by using critical realism to articulate a framework for reconfiguring the relationships between disciplines. This imperative moves the focus for academic practice away from the conventions that might have developed within mono-disciplinary discourse.

> Transdisciplinarity in creative interdisciplinary work has seemed to some writers as to involve breaking with the very notion of a discipline, to the extent that there has been talk of postdisciplinarity.
>
> Bhaskar 2010: 5

He goes on to describe some work in the research of disability to illustrate this imperative in which he: 'used the concept of a laminated system to ontologically underpin a critique of the history of disability studies as involving successively three forms of reductionism' (p. 5).

Bhaskar identifies contributions of some eight 'disciplines' in the 'over-determination' (Althusser 2008) of explanation of phenomena in this domain. He uses a similar approach to address issues associated with climate change. Similarly, at Lancaster University in the UK, the theme of food security acts as a new ontology to construct research and teaching agendas (Lancaster University 2010).

Val Clifford offers another perspective on this new ontology by focusing on the internationalisation of curricular practice that involves academics in new knowledge building of personal and professional values concerning how they interact with learners and colleagues from other cultures and how they construct identities as global citizens. The challenge she poses is whether it is best to address internationalisation within disciplines or outside these discourse communities. In pursuing the argument concerning convergence outside the power of disciplines to shape academic practice, new ontologies are not particularly associated with the new technologies. Martin Oliver makes the important point that there are many new practices associated with the use of new technologies in teaching and research but not new disciplinary cultures. Academic practices are changing rapidly because of new technologies, but, he argues, this has a neutral effect as far as disciplinary cultures are concerned.

The Imperative to Respond to Managerial Control and Performativity

Two of our contributions refer to the growth in the practices associated with competitive positioning. The practices associated with this process have always been a part of academic life and have conventionally been associated with knowledge building and tensions between different research-based theories or explanations in competition with one another. The race to publish discoveries has been the stuff of academic legend within the sciences, in particular, and with some perverse effects as Anderson *et al.* testify (2007). While there was a sense in which the excellence and influence of individual researchers has always cast their institutional homes in a positive light, it is with the initiation of the national research excellence assessments (Paul 2008) that we have a shift not just in competition between researchers in similar fields, but systemically between one higher education institution and another both within and between nation states. In other words, performativity is now systemic and procedural with many imperatives for practices. Moed (2008), on the basis of a detailed analysis of the publishing practices associated with research assessment exercises over 20 years, shows us that these practices characterise behaviour across all areas of the disciplinary canon at both departmental and institutional levels. We have identified elsewhere (Saunders *et al.* 2011) the way in which mechanisms designed to differentiate between institutions, in terms of the attribution of value to what they do, have become increasingly important in prompting practices, from individual academics to national systems. It can be argued that the managerial cultures and the way they form a systemic imperative have become all pervasive and prompt common concerns, impulses and strategies between disciplines rather than emphasise differences (see Beckmann and Cooper 2004). Rosemary Deem (1998), using research undertaken in the mid-1990s, identifies the practices that have now become commonplace but, more importantly from the perspective of this book, have created continuities and commonalities in academic practice which are eclipsing disciplinary cultures as determining influences. What is interesting is that differences in disciplinary cultures have not been a dominant mediating mechanism through which managerial practice has been situated in university departments. More important has been the congruence of practices across departmental boundaries, between institutions and between countries. Deem, notes that:

> 'new managerialist' theorists include the use of internal cost centres, the fostering of competition between employees, the marketisation of public sector services and the monitoring of efficiency and effectiveness through measurement of outcomes and individual staff performances. Other features include attempting to change the regimes and cultures of organisations and to alter the values of public sector employees to more closely resemble those found in the private 'for profit' sector.
>
> Deem 1998: 50

These practices now include a much more resonant understanding of global positioning associated with research excellence and recruitment (see Hazelkorn 2009). What is important, however, is that the international rankings have embedded within them a disciplinary bias based on publishing practices and the way value is attributed to academic outputs. We are experiencing a convergence of practices associated with the way value is attributed. This convergence, however, privileges a particular tradition. Common practices now include a reductive approach to value attributed on the basis of high impact journals, bibliometrics and citation indexes. The cultural differences between disciplines

– the more heterogeneous outlet and output profiles associated with the humanities and social sciences in comparison with the physical sciences – are now converging in terms of global estimations of value.

The National and International Policy Imperatives

Earlier we noted that practices have moved from being very loosely coupled to relatively tightly coupled to outside determinants; external imperatives that exert influence academics' behaviour. Very significant among these are national and supra-national policy. It always was a caricature that academic practices were determined by global disciplinary communities with the uncomplicated mission of pushing back the 'frontiers of knowledge' inculcating a new generation of academics into disciplinary ways of behaving. Certainly, higher education is now inextricably linked to nation states which mediate global issues and themes. The adoption of a common framework of 'readable and comparable degrees' in Europe via the Bologna Declaration (see the Leuven Communiqué 2009 for examples of frequent updates) signal a range of extra-disciplinary imperatives which shape important and cross disciplinary themes, not least global competitiveness (Keeling 2006).

A case in point involves the recent global trend by governments to shift the burden of cost of the higher education system away from the state and onto the individual (Altbach *et al.* 2009). The ideas underlying the UK government position on the relationship between higher education as a public and private good are based largely on the recommendations and arguments in the Browne Report (2010) which was tasked to explore funding models for higher education. In this report we have a paradigm shift from analogous policy historically and internationally. It is the first time that distinctions are made in the social value placed on different disciplines via differential funding mechanisms. It is congruent with the idea of a degree in the arts, social sciences and humanities as a commodity in the true sense of the word, that is, its use and value is in its exchange, to be bought at a good price by individuals who should be charged for it. It is tempting to understand this position, in part, as a seductive justification for deriving extra resources as western liberal/centre governments struggle to justify payment for a 'massified' sector from public funds. However, I think there is more to it than that. Relevant to this chapter is the basis for deciding what might be in the higher education curriculum from the Browne Report point of view. The report is clear about the basis for the disciplinary mix. It has a two dimensional rationale. Both are heavily imbued with an economic or marketised discourse. The first is student choice:

> In our proposals, we are relying on student choice to drive up quality. Students will control a much larger proportion of the investment in higher

education. They will decide where the funding should go; and institutions will compete to get it. As students will be paying more than in the current system, they will demand more in return.

Browne Report 2010: 29

'Deciding where funding should go' means, in effect, that the higher education curriculum will be decided mainly by the consumer. It is significant that this perspective has several underlying messages. It privileges the here and now, and has an unrealistic faith in the authenticity and efficacy of 'consumer want' as the main curricular design principle. Most other considerations are absent, like, for example, those embedded in the ideals of cultural and knowledge development across a wide range of disciplinary practices and knowledge forms. To acknowledge that there may be other considerations is not to deny that what students might want is an important dimension. But, there is a clear circularity in this argument. Once the decision to individualise or privatise higher education as a 'good' in which the individual invests for personal gain, then prioritising their 'wants' as a distributive or design mechanism above social or cultural considerations makes perfect sense. Take that away, and then it does not make much sense at all. Students' 'needs' become more important and the onus moves to exciting, engaging teaching and learning practices rather than the disciplines themselves.

The second basis on which the curriculum might be designed lies with the interests of the economy. Two issues are especially relevant here. Whatever the analysis of how the economy might best be served by higher education, should that be the only other determinant apart from consumer choice? First, there are arguments that suggest that a direct correspondence between the needs of the economy – whatever they might be – at any particular time and what goes on in higher education is to be eschewed. It is precisely the lack of a direct link, its systemic independence, in form, time and place, that gives higher education one of its greatest strengths (see for example Saunders 2006, and Little and Arthur 2010). Secondly, the Browne Report's view on the relationship between the economy and the curriculum, or put another way, which disciplines are particularly pertinent to the economy, is extremely one dimensional and simplistic. They are called 'priority subjects'. Only these will be 'socially' funded as a public good and the public good is inherently 'economic':

we envisage a large reduction in the funding available to institutions through HEFCE. That reduction may be equivalent to removing all funding from anything other than priority subjects. This contributes to wider reductions in public spending. Government continues though to have a vital role in providing public investment for priority subjects ...

Browne Report 2010: 42

The report suggests that these 'priority subjects' are:

> courses that deliver significant social returns such as to provide skills and knowledge currently in shortage or predicted to be in the future. Students may not choose these courses because the private returns are not as high as other courses, the costs are higher and there are cheaper courses on offer, or simply because these courses are perceived as more difficult. *Typically the courses that may fall into this category are courses in science and technology subjects, clinical medicine, nursing and other healthcare degrees, as well as strategically important language courses.*
>
> Ibid: 42

Notwithstanding the reductionism inherent in the primacy of a solely economic rationale for higher education, the assumption that only science and technology have direct 'economic' benefits in comparison with the other disciplines might be challenged in the light of the complex requirements of twenty-first-century survival and growth.

There are interrelated dimensions in the way the emerging economic drivers impact upon the disciplines. The first is the direct influence of differential funding of students, teaching and general research on differential attribution of value to disciplines. Put simply and reductively, it argues that social good is presented as 'economic' or serving employability. In turn, however, even that representation is flawed and is simplistically associated with science and technology. The potential implications are that the arts, humanities and social sciences will be subject solely to the exigencies of the educational marketplace.

The second refers to a more fundamental question concerning the status of different kinds of knowledge within the higher education canon if undertaking research or teaching or study is differentially funded. The context of this consideration is that the practices associated with knowledge production – research; circulation – teaching and learning; and uses – impact or effects – within and beyond higher education can be understood in terms of public and private 'goods'. If we take the Browne Report as a proxy for UK government policy in the absence of a white paper – which, in the light of the Department for Business, Innovation and Skills briefings, it is reasonable to do – then the depiction of higher education as a private good for funding purposes does have implications. These implications are in three interrelated propositions. First, 'real' social good resides in certain disciplines and not others indicated by the direction of public resources allocated by government. Second, if researchers and students wish to engage in activity outside the disciplines designated as a social good – non-priority subjects – then they cannot expect resources from the public purse. Third, students engaged in learning within universities accrue individual 'goods' through this process if they achieve a qualification – that is, they accrue big social and economic advantages over those who have not achieved a degree qualification. This individual 'graduate premium' will also accrue a 'social premium' if it is within a designated discipline and will thus be funded 'socially'. If it is not, then the cost of this premium will be paid by the student.

The implication is that whole swathes of the current higher education curriculum in the UK and, by default, the disciplines, will no longer count as a 'social good'. This perspective fails to see the bigger, unintended effects on the balance and shape of the higher education curriculum for generations of students to come and, in turn, on future populations as a whole.

Mary Henkel (2007) argues that this imperative, embodied in the funding debate, is strongly associated with the relationship between conceptions of the primacy of the knowledge society and new conceptions of the state and involves a shift away from the relative freedoms of disciplinary cultures. She argues that this shift signifies the breaking down of boundaries that have been critical for the 'justification of academic rights to self-government and freedom of inquiry' (p. 87). She notes that the ideal of academe as a sovereign, bounded territory has been 'superseded by ideals of engagement with societies in which academic institutions are "axial structures"' (p. 87):

> Changing conceptions of knowledge and of its place in late modern societies have impelled governments and their citizens to demand continuing expansion and change in higher education, as knowledge is seen as a private and a public good, the key to individual as well as national economic advance and social inclusion. Knowledge and its acquisition are increasingly valued in instrumental terms, and understood not as the discovery of truths so much as regulated practices and the exercise, at different levels, of cognitive skills.
>
> Henkel 2007: 89

Henkel synthesises the emerging contours of this policy environment and demonstrates why it is has become so important in shaping academic practice. The contributions from Kerri-Lee Krauss, Susan Lea and Lynne Callaghan all provide perspectives on the way in which the resourcing of higher education and the imperatives of policy provide the new frameworks for action for front line academics and their organisational settings. Building on the developments Henkel identifies, we can suggest the following.

- The responsibility for quality and the attribution of value to higher education practice now lies mainly with the state. Regulation is shared between higher education institutions and the academics. However, reliance on independent institutions or individual professionals to ensure their own quality and standards has been replaced by national standardisation. This signals the breakdown of the 'social contract' between academics and society that enabled them to 'police' themselves.

- There has been a process, well exemplified in the UK, of externalising functions that 'lie at the heart of academic autonomy, namely peer review and self-evaluation, so that they become "instruments of external oversight"' (Neave and Tight 1988: 46, quoted in Henkel 2007)
- Research funding is increasingly tied to those assessed as achieving outputs of international quality. The consequence of this exercise has been severely to restrict individual academic freedom in some universities to continue to research in specific, scientific areas and to shape the choices of universities as to the research agendas they will support (Henkel 2007: 91).
- Academic autonomy or freedom has become conditional and negotiated with agencies of government through the funding councils and research bodies. As government policies change, they use these agencies to assess how far higher education institutions are implementing them – the policies. They provide a framework by which academics measure legitimate action and decide on priorities.
- In the UK at least, higher education is being increasingly depicted as a private good with an array of knock-on effects for the disciplinary structures of the higher education curriculum and their funding.

Conclusion

These catalysts for change for individual and group professional identities within higher education are beginning to reshape what counts as academic practices. These practices occur on a global stage and are creating effects on what counts as the higher education curriculum and on the choices for research and its dissemination. What is considered legitimate knowledge is changing; their emphases now on new syntheses and integrative practices driven by ideas about global needs and concerns. As Ronald Barnett (1994) observed in the early 1990s, knowledge itself is now contingent on use and usability with a more direct connection between knowledge utilisation and production.

Judgements on how academics perform and on the value of what they do are multi-faceted and often involve complicity between internal and external actors. How curricular practice is resourced and the role of the state in mediating and legitimating priorities for higher education is reconfigured in a more tightly coupled and interventionist relationship.

In policy terms, we have the shift toward the individualisation of benefits of higher education and the relative invisibility of its social benefits. In the UK, the differential funding model which privileges only part of the higher education curriculum, while at the same time continuing with the policy rhetoric on the importance of the knowledge economy and global competitiveness, leaves academics with a confusing and contradictory context for action. These tensions and the uneven territory we are beginning to inhabit will be the focus of our final chapter.

22

Conclusion

Academic Practices and the Disciplines in the 21st Century

PAUL TROWLER, MURRAY SAUNDERS, VERONICA BAMBER

In previous chapters we laid out our theoretical position, and captured some of the lived examples of academics dealing with the changing nature of academic work. In this final chapter we draw together our ideas, and provide vignettes, scenarios in which the phenomena we describe are played out day-to-day. These vignettes take the form of composite 'scenes' in which a recognisable and familiar embodiment of a practice is presented to illustrate the shifts in the priorities, decision-making, strategic thinking and tone behind what academics are now doing and why they are doing it. Of course we are not suggesting that all academics are thinking in the same way. Nonetheless academics are required to negotiate and respond to a range of features of the higher education landscape that they experience in common. The purpose of the vignettes – in some cases captures of real conversations – is to create resonance and recognition of these commonalities. They are not intended to be exhaustive but are intended to be evocative.

First we will recapitulate our ontological perspective.

We have depicted universities as dynamic constellations of clusters of social practices. These constellations are made up of clusters of practices that are 'linked' by their association with a particular aspect of university life. As Alvesson (2002) says, universities have multiple cultural configurations, largely generated in departmental contexts as groups of colleagues work together on common projects over extended periods of time. These projects concern teaching, research, quality assurance, income generation, and so on. In working on these, individuals and groups draw on practice resources: common understandings of how things should be done, as well as sets of associations, meanings and tacit assumptions about priorities and values. To all intents and purposes, the practice resources we are referring to constitute a knowledge base of individual, environmental, social, political, technical and physical features which provides personal and collective imperatives for acting, communicating and thinking in particular ways. These practice resources condition dominant or hegemonic conventions of behaviour, structure decision-making and shape discursive use – our thinking here is influenced by Giddens' (1984) notion that social structures comprise both rules and resources which condition and legitimise behaviour.

Some resources are derived from disciplinary roots, for example understandings of 'normal' practices associated with different aspects of doing research on particular topics that were learned during undergraduate and postgraduate study. As well as enacting these resources, individuals and groups are also generating, in an agentic way, situated sets of understanding and practices. This process can be conflictual and often involves the operation of power of different sorts (Trowler 2008b). The way practices are shaped by features of the physical and socio-political environment is a critical issue. Here, the interaction of humans operating in practice clusters, and the tools they use, lead to changes in practices, which in turn shape tool-use.

So higher education institutions comprise practice clusters enacted and re-shaped in specific contexts which, for the outsider, will usually feel both familiar and strange: there will be aspects of what they see that have common features in other universities, but there will be situated aspects generated locally, too. From the perspective of the insiders working in a university, professional life will involve moving between practice clusters and, because practices in these clusters have become 'normalised', their situatedness remains largely invisible to insiders. There may be teaching in the morning, supervising students in the early afternoon and attending committee meetings later on. At different points in the year, or even in the day, activities and priorities change. Student assessment, quality audit and enhancement, course development, student recruitment all have a cyclical quality. This characteristic is the case for most professional roles in universities, though, of course, the nature of the practice clusters will be different. During the working week the pattern of each day will usually be diverse, too. Everyone experiences days that they are really not looking forward to, perhaps filled with committee meetings of limited interest or with difficult meetings with colleagues or students. Other days are less testing.

The first vignette is a composite internal conversation about events that really happened within an education department in the UK, but in reality over a period of time. It illustrates the intersection between an interpretation of the environment and the generation of practices.

Vignette 1: Shaping a Teaching Strategy: Notes to Self

I have been asked by my head of department (HOD) to do a bit of 'horizon scanning' in order to help shape our teaching strategy. We have a need to develop a reliable income stream to offset the increasingly competitive research grant-getting opportunities. The strategic decision was made that, relatively speaking, teaching offered reliable income-generating possibilities and we should think about new courses.

Although I am not entirely sure just what all this means, I know that my colleagues in Belgium and France in education departments had been asked to do the same kind of thing and had come up with a Master's design that fitted with the emerging Bologna Process. I am not too sure what the implications are for us but I do think it means that we should be thinking of widening our recruitment base so that EU students can relatively easily slot into our courses in terms of content, timing and assessment.

My European colleagues also mentioned to me that they had included in their curriculum designs a much wider group of colleagues, so that issues associated with the 'big global challenges', as Maria put it, could be genuinely reflected in what and how students learned.

If we are to make any headway on this then we have to start doing things a bit differently. First of all, we cannot just rely on repackaging what we do already but have to start talking to people from other departments, and we need to see how our validation processes and servicing costs will help or hinder cross-departmental collaboration, especially between departments in different faculties. At the moment all course validation begins within faculties. We also need to see how flexible we can be with students attending whole modules, units, individual lectures, and all that. The modules need to appeal on a thematic rather than subject basis and be 'marketable' to European universities in flexible arrangements. The content will have to be internationalised to appeal across the European board.

But, how do we go about this? What on earth are the 'big challenges' – is there a consensus on that? Probably not, let alone how we should construct what counts as a course of some kind. What would a curriculum on say, 'world poverty' look like? What would be an appropriate knowledge base for students, and who decides? Does it make sense to talk about it like this?

Perhaps the world poverty network is where I should start. Who is the prime mover behind it? Now just let me Google …

Commentary

This composite of an internal conversation is an authentic construction of a series of real discussions. It shows the way an interpretation of salient environmental features – *construction of a knowledge base* – yields some imperatives for action. In this case, contracting resources for higher education prompts a response to look for reliable income streams – *practice clusters associated with income generation*. In turn, these practices involve yet other new clusters associated with the design of university curricula which are not bound together by the logic of a discipline but by the ontological logic of a strategic 'big challenge'. This new ontology requires practices that involve collaborations across departments, with people who are not normal 'curricular bedfellows'. It also requires the rethinking of the systems and protocols – *reified practices or tools* – which make cross-faculty working difficult or cumbersome.

The significance of disciplines

The question this book asks is: 'What is the salience of disciplinary power in the constellation of academic practice clusters?' To help map this we developed Table 1.1 in Chapter 1, which depicted the literature in terms of authors' approaches to three issues on three axes. Axes B and C concerned views on the scope and extent of disciplinary power, in other words the range of areas of professional life it impinged on and its strength. Our argument contradicts many of the writers we discussed there: we do *not* consider it possible to make a general statement about the scope and strength of influence of disciplinary power. Instead, seen at the quotidian level, the salience and power of disciplines increases or decreases – or is sometimes completely absent – according to the context of practice. So, for any given individual, their disciplinary background might be of significance in some contexts of their practice at some times. Moreover, exactly what the significance of discipline is will shift for that same individual. In developing a research proposal they will deploy discipline-based understandings of research methodology and methods, epistemological and ontological assumptions, and so on. In suggesting this we are developing Bernstein's notion that the *site of practice* conditions the nature of the discipline. While Bernstein examined the recontextualisation of disciplines from discipline-as-research to discipline-as-teaching, we suggest that in multiple sites of practice a similar recontextualisation process occurs.

To ground this, we turn to a meeting in a South African university where we see a head of department of media studies consciously 'working the discipline' for strategic purposes.

Vignette 2: Meeting with the HR Advisor

Author: Vicki Trowler

HOD: We seem to have a bit of a problem here. When this new system was implemented, the Senate was assured by the HR Director that HODs would be notified in good time about staff whose probation period was nearing an end, so that we could do the necessary review and take the necessary actions. I asked for a report the other day, as I'd heard nothing and I had a sneaky suspicion that Kevin's probation was running out – and I see that not only Kevin, but Janet and Nazeema too, have all snuck through the system with no notification. Nazeema's a star, she absolutely deserves to be permanent, but I would have wanted to extend Janet's probation for another year as she still hasn't completed her PhD, which was part of the agreement on appointment, and Kevin has been a complete disaster and we need to start processes to terminate.

HUMAN RESOURCES ADVISOR (HRA): Are you sure you didn't receive an email? The system is set up to notify the HOD three months before probation ends ...

HOD: I didn't get any &^%$ email! I don't want to know what the system is supposed to do – we were told that and agreed to its implementation on the assurance it would work. It hasn't. I want to know what *you are* going to do to fix this – to confirm Nazeema's appointment, extend Janet's probation and get rid of Kevin.

HRA: We can't do that. If their probation period has lapsed and they've not been warned in good time, it is deemed that their appointments have been confirmed and they are now permanent staff. You'll have to retrench them [make them redundant] or follow the procedure for performance improvement ...

HOD: This is not my problem – it's *your* system that *&^%ed up! I can't retrench anyone – that would suggest I had too many staff and I don't. I just have the wrong staff member – he can't teach what I need him to teach, he's published nothing and his PhD was sent back with major corrections that will require almost an entire rewrite. I've got a brilliant young guy on a contract who's been doing some exciting work on black kids' use of social media but I'm going to lose him if I can't offer him a permanent post – he's been brilliant with the black students. He's come up with wonderful ideas for a research collaboration with Scandinavia and we've looked at restructuring Media and Society for first years to reflect more of what's going on in New Media but I need him to teach it. None of the others has his insights ...

HRA: They're all Media Studies specialists, surely they could read up on it ...

HOD: You're missing the point. Having a young black guy who grew up where those kids are now, who speaks their language and understands their slang and relates to their priorities as an insider is very different to briefing some white, middle-class expert on reality television and expecting them to be as good. It's not just about knowing the content; it's about all kinds of life experience he brings to bear on his understanding because of his background.

HRA: You can't have another permanent post. You already have more SLEs [Senior Lecturer Equivalents] than your FTE [Full-time Equivalent] ratio dictates. You'll have to make do with what you have.

HOD: There's no point discussing this with you! It's *your* problem, *your* system failed so now *I'm* stuck with a staff member I can't use who's blocking me appointing a staff member I desperately need in order to address a *huge* area that's unfolding in the discipline, who also happens to be black which is better for our demographic profile, *and* he's really good with our black students which is great in all sorts of ways ... And you think I can fix this all by telling Kevin to stop staring at *Big Brother* and learn isiXhosa and start hanging out on Facebook with kids from the townships? Do you not understand a single thing I've told you? I'm going to the Dean ...

Commentary

The Head of Department in this vignette finds herself caught between two conflicting prerogatives – her role as manager, overseeing the human resources processes involved in the appointment of new staff, the review of their probation and the confirmation of their appointments on satisfactory performance on the one hand, and her role as academic leader, directing the development of the academic project and providing disciplinary leadership within her department, on the other. The tools – the new HR system – have let her down, and the Human Resource Advisor to whom she turns for assistance is stuck within the management paradigm and cannot understand the complexity of the problem.

The HOD attempts to invoke her disciplinary authority – using the discipline as warrant – to convince the HRA, whose monocular view remains fixed, and when that fails she resorts to invoking other strategic discourses – transformation of the staff demographics to a more racially representative profile, improving the student experience, and improving organisational culture through increasing diversity – which she hopes will have greater resonance. Defensively, the HRA counter-invokes management norms about staffing ratios – replete with TLAs (Three Letter Acronyms) for greater authority – effectively signalling an unwillingness to engage. The HOD's initial constructive and collegial approach – "we seem to have a bit of a problem" – has now been replaced by blame – "it's your problem" – and turning to higher authority – the Dean – in an attempt to put the obstructive support staff member back in his place – invoking the hidden hierarchy between academic and non-academic staff in the process.

In thinking about the nature of disciplines, (and situating ourselves on axis A of Table 1.1 in Chapter 1 – the cause of disciplinary influence), we subscribe to a social realist approach. In other words, we acknowledge that disciplines have 'real' epistemological characteristics, that knowledge structures do condition practices in quite real ways. Physics is different from sociology, and physicists need to do things in different ways from sociologists. At the same time there are social processes going on, narratives being developed about the nature of the discipline, its history and its special features. Sometimes there are multiple narratives and contestation about what the discipline is and what it requires, even within the discipline itself. As Kuhn noted years ago, from time to time paradigms break down and internecine warfare breaks out.

It is in the "social" side of social realism that social practice theory (SPT) comes in, when the characteristics of practices engage with 'disciplines' and with communal reservoirs and individual repertoires of behaviours, assumptions, feelings and motivations. These combine to 'create' disciplinary differences layered above 'real' differences founded in epistemological differences.

The shift we are indicating refers to the practice resources academics use to determine what they think they should be doing, what they value and to what they should give priority. The congruence between what academics may value and to what they give priority has become fractured and has taken on a different hue. The following vignette illustrates this in the context of the overseas partnerships which many universities across the world are pursuing as a means of increasing student numbers and, specifically, high-paying overseas student numbers.

Vignette 3: Diary of an Academic Link Person – Overseas Partnerships

OMG – I've just been briefed by the Head of School about my new role as Academic Link Person (ALP) for Overseas Partnerships. What on earth have I taken on? Not that there was much choice. It was that or admissions for all our undergraduate programmes, a real poisoned chalice. It seems I'm going to have to coordinate the School's partnerships with institutions in India, Malaysia, China and Switzerland. And there are new partnerships being planned with Turkey and Greece. I've got more than a few worries about this:

- At the Exam Board in Delhi, the Indian staff were aghast when the external examiner and UK course leader re-marked all scripts in the lead-up to the Board, they were so concerned about plagiarism. The Indian people thought these were pretty good students who worked hard and attended all classes (9am–4pm each day). It became clear that their expectations of what the students would produce are very different from ours. It looks like there's a big job needing done to make sure we're all on the same page about what students need to do to get a UK degree.
- One of our course leaders has been talking with his Chinese counterpart about 'domesticating the curriculum' – reframing it within the Chinese context. Sounds great, but who's going to do it? Really don't think our colleagues out there have tuned in yet to how our educational levels – qualifications framework etc. – work. Who's going to support them with all of that? Not me. I simply don't have the time.
- The Malaysian staff are all full-time professionals who are teaching our programmes part-time in the evenings. We – the course leader and I – are meant to be doing 'staff development' with them. As if we didn't have enough with teaching the students. What do I know about staff development?
- We've got student recruitment problems as well: looks like some of our partners are recruiting students with inadequate levels of English. So when they come to the UK to do the final year of their programme, they are really struggling and we get lots of fails. We've had calls – and even visits – from angry parents who've paid mega-bucks for their kids' education and are not happy. Not their fault, it's really an admissions problem with our partner

institution. But it's not our fault either – why should I have to pick up the cost for some other institution's mistakes?

- And what about the basic logistics of trying to work with all these partners ... Communicating with my own colleagues in the department is hard enough – and getting harder by the minute as nobody has time for pleasantries any more – so how am I going to keep in touch with people thousands of miles away with very different cultures and educational philosophies? Easy to say 'video conference', but that's yet another job to do.
- Apparently, I need to get our partner staff 'working as a programme team'. Huh.
- And then there's all the 'student experience' stuff: sounds fine in our little world, but how many of these partners have personal tutors, careers officers, disability provision, staff–student committees, not to mention programme monitoring?
- Not only do I have to work out how to get all these undergraduate arrangements working, but the SMT is now talking postgraduate collaborations – apparently there's a vast market in PG courses. I'm not sure our partners are quite up to PG provision.
- I suppose I'll need to check through the contracts our VP has signed with all these institutions and see what he's committed us to. I don't know where to start, and it's just been shovelled onto my desk since Freda left. I had no idea she'd been doing all this. No wonder she was never around.

Commentary

In this vignette, what academics do is being reconstructed, or recontextualised in Bernstein's language, to fit other, commercial needs; the marketisation of education offers opportunities, but also many challenges to educational standards and aspirations, and to academic practices. For instance, the notion of discipline-based communities of practice fits poorly when colleagues are not local or subject-based. This renders the notion of 'being an academic' elastic in many ways; overseas colleagues may not be full-time academics, and are certain to have different educational philosophies from what we would expect in our own contexts – even if they work within the same discipline. Nonetheless, although we have said that there is no one disciplinary norm, there are certainly epistemological and behavioural characteristics in each discipline. Home academics are working cross-culturally, perhaps finding that they have to dilute the values, practices and norms they would normally espouse.

Differences of thinking and practice are compounded by educational provision in partner institutions not having the same support systems as UK academics would expect; this means UK academics may have to take on additional roles, such as quality monitoring, staff development, curriculum advice and team development. Academic work is no longer simply teaching, administration and research.

Raising the level of analysis above the quotidian to look at higher education systems allows us to make more general statements about the salience of disciplines than is possible at the fine-grained level of daily life. Over the past 30 years, in most countries, disciplines have been steadily eclipsed as the driving force of academic practices (Halsey 1992). Other forces, values and priorities have come to the fore, but disciplines are still of significance in some areas of academic practice and in many different ways.

The use of the metaphor 'eclipse' here is apt because it denotes a sense of the determining power of disciplines being overshadowed, overwhelmed or concealed by other sources. These may be conventions of appropriateness, discourses and other knowledge resources used to shape practices. It does not mean that discipline has disappeared. In many ways, it still shapes what might be considered an idealistic or romantic view of the disciplinary effect, which has been overtaken by the evolution of the socio-economic policy environment of the past 40 years or so. It often takes the form of a discourse of resistance to what academics feel they now have to give priority. We could depict this feature of contemporary academic life as 'romancing the discipline' as it denotes an idealised, allegoric set of practices associated with the immersion in research and thinking unsullied or contaminated by worldly contexts. 'I managed to get away and do some real work' is often the discursive way this romance of the discipline is counterpointed with the trials of everyday academic life.

The following vignette takes the form of data from the recent evaluation of the Scottish Quality Enhancement Framework (2010) in which the expanded reference points for academics can create some dissonance and, indeed, feelings of disempowerment and alienation.

Vignette 4: Discussion with a Lecturer in a Scottish University

> Certainly, [it is] true that our university [staff are] scared of outside bodies that assess them, evaluate what they do ... This university is scared of control and even its obsession with structures at the moment, with how many departments should there be, is actually all about anxiety, about control. Wanting to monitor what we do and wanting to have units that are cost effective or initiative effective. Come up with an idea and want to make sure that we carry it out, because they're worried about external funding and what might happen elsewhere.

It was suggested that this particular institution's lack of confidence means that teaching practitioners can become distanced from the university's goals:

> One example is that we went through a reorganisation and got rid of faculties some years ago and, as a result of that, instead of three management tiers, we now have five. So, what it's done is it's got us further away from

understanding the decision-making process ... The way I see it is that it's because the university's so worried about the outside world that it is obsessed with structures and organisation which becomes increasingly opaque to people ... So, there is a kind of sense in which there's a sort of lack of transparency which goes on. We're tempted to invest in many ideas that are clearly vital to the university without fully understanding what they're about, which I find quite difficult sometimes.

Commentary

The experience of this lecturer of the way the institution had adopted the 'outward facing' agenda to conform to the new imperatives suggests this academic perceived a fractured sense of institutional identity and an individual uncertainty about the legitimacy and degree of externality of the new 'conventions' shaping practice. In the view of this academic, the institution was 'colluding' with these external demands and not just allowing them to shape priorities, structure systems and organisational forms, but enthusiastically embracing their logic and providing strong agency.

It is perhaps not surprising that some of the early work on the significance of discipline, such as Becher's 1989 edition of *Tribes and Territories*, found that disciplines were very significant. This is not just because disciplines had not yet been eclipsed by other forces, but because such studies tended to focus on elite institutions, disciplines and individuals. They also focused on a narrower range of academic practices than we have done in this book. Becher's 1989 book only looked at research, and we would agree, of course, that discipline is of most salience there. Top professors in top universities are most likely to spend most of their time doing exactly that, but even in the late 1980s academics in lower status institutions would have had a range of tasks in multiple clusters of social practice. In some of these, disciplines would not have been significant, even then. With the development of research assessment frameworks in a number of countries – the Research Excellence Framework in the UK – the predominance of discipline in research has been attenuated, as the following vignette shows.

Vignette 5: Email from the Dean – Research Excellence Framework

Dear Mike
So glad that you've agreed to be Theme Leader for our Research Excellence Framework submission to the 'Allied Health Professions' Unit of Assessment. As we discussed when we met, it's really urgent that you get moving on this, as we have to have our submission ready by 2013 – all too close. I said I would type up a few notes from our meeting: hopefully this will be a good starting point for you.

As we both know, the REF will decide our allocation of research funding 'on the basis of excellence' – God knows what 'excellence' means, it's so open to interpretation. What we do know is that we'll be assessed according to our research outputs – the main factor – as well as the wider impact of research and the vitality of the research environment. No pressure here then ... We might be the new kid on the block in making this submission, but we can't afford to get it wrong. We really need to raise our research profile if we're going to compete in the research game – and we know some of the big players have already put enormous effort into this. We don't have their resources, but we can't stand still. Move up the league tables or die. It's not just for research, either; if we can raise the research stakes, it will really help our Chinese student recruitment effort.

We need an Action Plan!

Regarding who's in the Theme, we're looking at a grouping under the tentative Theme of 'Ethical Practice in Health Care'. We spoke about a group of staff from our own faculty, i.e. Nursing, Physiotherapy, Dietetics, Occupational Therapy and Podiatry. They are likely to be joined by staff from outside the faculty – Psychology and Sociology are possibles. One of your jobs is to work out who to include – this could be a bit sensitive since a number of staff are borderline. As usual, we're going to be scratching about to make it look like a decent research effort – no mean task when we're up to our ears in teaching. We need a decision about who will be submitted quite soon, once you've done the detailed analysis of their outputs, impact etc.

Some thoughts on what needs to happen next:

We discussed the need to call together everyone who might be included in the Theme, to discuss:

- What's required. They all need to understand what the Theme is about, and start to manoeuvre their research accordingly.
- Your production of the strategic narrative. A first stage would be for you to outline the rationale for this grouping, and an indication of how the decisions about who's included will be made.
- Any support that is needed/available for colleagues who need to 'up the ante' a bit. There's not much resource available, but we could look at mentoring – although our professorial colleagues could be a bit resistant to spending their time looking after the interests of junior staff. There's a job to be done in helping them appreciate the interests of the wider group – not quite sure how you're going to manage that, but I'll be behind you all the way.
- Get everyone aligned around the Theme. Ask everyone to give you a list of publications in progress, and which journals they're planning to submit to. We need to make sure that they don't submit to the wrong journals. They can publish till the cows come home, but if it doesn't line up with the Theme it's useless. No more 'but I've been researching this topic for years'.

- Start thinking about the case studies we'll be putting together to demonstrate our Impact – looks like Impact will be 20 per cent of the REF judgement this time round. Can you get people to consider how they're having social, economic or cultural impact? They need to be able to evidence this – and just disseminating their research outputs won't wash. We need to demonstrate 'reach and significance'. Might need a bit of imagination stretching.
- You need to give some thought to how we get individual members of staff working collaboratively on this – surely they can find some interdisciplinary work that they can hang some of their research on? Might be more of a chance of getting outputs if we get some of them working together.
- Anyone we could put forward for the national panel of this Unit of Assessment? It would be great to have some insider information, but I don't really think we've got anyone who's up to the job, do you?

You are as aware as I am, Mike, that this is – excuse the phrase – 'mission critical': no research funding, no research. If all these people don't want to be on teaching-only contracts from 2015 onwards, they really need to get their act together. Otherwise, we're all going to be in one big FE college.
Good luck!
Brian

Commentary

The vexed question of how much autonomy academics have – as opposed to the romantic vision of how much they are nostalgically thought to have had – is played out in this vignette. Managerial discourse supplants a collegial one, as league tables and competitiveness become part of the vocabulary of academics. Strategic narrative shapes behaviours, or simulates the direction of travel of research. Research is probably the area of practice in which academics have enjoyed most autonomy, although, as mentioned above, this has been much more the case in elite, research-intensive institutions.

In the vignette, the instrumentality of research is exposed – research is not about creating new knowledge, but has been distorted by now being mediated through competitiveness, positioning and presence in the market. Staff interests are subjugated to institutional strategic positioning, and individual staff could be seen as – reluctant – passengers on a journey not of their own making. They have lost ownership of their research, as it is rebranded for other purposes. Identities are forced into different shapes, to suit potential research strengths and weaknesses. For individual academics, this can mean contractual change – for example, teaching-only contracts – or a change of direction in research focus. For subject groups, it can mean the demise of the group, or its reincarnation in other forms. Disciplinary allegiances may be broken and formed. Although previous thinking was that research assessment reinforced the significance of discipline

communities, with increased collaboration and dialogue within those communities (Henkel 2002: 141), we would suggest that the dynamic has changed, and
dialogue is also taking place across disciplinary groups as cross-disciplinary
research is encouraged. For institutions, it is part of the struggle to improve their
position, perhaps to become part of a more elite university grouping.

The shifting territories of academic practices

The argument made throughout this book about the use of the metaphor of
tribes and territories has centred on the primacy and importance of the cultures
associated with the forms of knowledge embedded in the disciplines. This was
the lexicon. The analytical assumptions were based on the view that academic
life was dominated by the production of knowledge by academics, its circulation
by academics through teaching and its potential or latent use by others in the
fields of application in business, industry or public policy. What is important in
this stance is that, broadly speaking, the work of academics was undertaken in
an 'inward facing' way. Its social and intellectual references were overwhelmingly drawn from other academics and their output.

Putting our argument in another way, the 'tribes' that we are looking at are
much more dispersed across a wider vista than was the case in Becher's original
book. Our understanding of 'territories' is a much wider one too than in the
original work. For Becher (1989) and those who followed that book, the concept
of territories related to disciplinary boundaries, to the map of knowledge. These
different territories largely conditioned tribal practices. Our conspectus in this
book is wider and the 'territories' that we see conditioning practices go far
beyond the map of knowledge creation, circulation and use. The territories of
concern now include the demands of business and international competition,
of the evaluative state and of students as consumers, as well as other catalysts of
practice, as we have described in Part 4 of this book.

The widened nature of the academic territory is embodied in the following
extract from a discussion with a university manager about the employability
theme within the Scottish higher education system and about what counts as
'quality practice' within the sector. It illustrates the way academics, particularly
those who manage institutions, are now 'outward facing' in their consideration
of priorities for action.

Vignette 6: Response to the Employability Agenda

The Economic Development Agencies in Scotland have now been re-organ-
ised into something called Skills Development Scotland and I guess that
what we hope is that what we do joins up as much as possible with these
things – more so perhaps than it did in the past. It's probably more relevant
for what goes on in colleges because it's clearly linked to employer needs

but increasingly I think the rhetoric of higher education – they've bought into the sense of employability as 'a good thing', and that brings benefits in that they are recognised as a major contributor to the knowledge economy and economic growth and hence a good return on public investment. But that does bring in a whole new range of stakeholders, like employers, who then say 'well, these students aren't ready for work', and so on. A rather sterile debate sometimes but, nevertheless, there are new stakeholders out there who I think would say 'my definition of quality includes those notions about fitness for purpose and employability'.

Commentary

We can see in this manager's perspective the adoption of a quintessentially instrumental view of the territory that higher education now inhabits. Quality or good practice in higher education is defined in terms of outward-facing considerations concerning the 'new stakeholders'.

We do not want to overstate the shift in the territories that academics inhabit. We are not arguing that the cultures associated with different disciplines no longer have any potency at all in shaping what academics do. They clearly do and there are important differences in the ways in which academics in different disciplines undertake their research, teach and connect with outside stakeholders. Our position is that these differences are present within an environmental matrix that all academics share and it is this new territory that we are endeavouring to explore. In the next vignette, the scenario relates to the curriculum development process.

Vignette 7: Conversations about Programme Development

PAT: I need to pick your brain, Roy. I've been told we need to develop a new postgraduate taught (PGT) programme – apparently the existing PG programmes in the School are 'in decline' and we need something new and shiny to attract international postgrads. I've never developed a new programme before. Any hints on where to start?

ROY: Oh, yes. Talk to the Quality Unit. They'll sort you out. Of course, in the good old days you'd just go off and write up what you wanted to teach, but that's all gone now. That would never wash with the Faculty Portfolio Group.

Some time later, in the Quality Unit …

PAT: Maria, I've been told we need to develop a new PGT programme, and Roy tells me you'll put me on the right track. What do I need to do?

MARIA: Here's the quality manual, Pat. That will give you the guidelines for programme development, leading up to validation. When are you aiming to run the programme?

PAT: Next September.

MARIA: Oh, dear, that's a bit of a challenge, given that it's March now. You need to get going.

PAT: I've not been given any workload allocation to do this. It's on top of my normal teaching and research, not to mention course admin. Where should I start?

MARIA: The first step is market research: what are other universities doing in this area, i.e. what's the competition? What demand will there be for the programme, and from whom? Then there are professional body requirements: make sure you're following their standards and competency framework. And have you talked to the external examiners of your existing programmes about this?

PAT: Eh, no.

MARIA: And then there are various university strategies to consider. For example, can you demonstrate that the new proposal has been equality- and diversity-tested? And there are some institutional strategies – for example, sustainability, employability – that will need to be acknowledged. There will be questions from the validation panel as to how you're responding to those.

PAT: I know nothing about all of that.

MARIA: Well, there are training sessions on programme validation and curriculum design that I'm sure you'll find helpful. That will help you cover issues of level of delivery – are you at the right level for the Qualifications Framework, for example? And then there are Employer Views and Alumni Views, so you're not just working in a vacuum. Are you offering the programme in traditional face-to-face mode, blended or distance learning?

PAT: No idea! I'll get back to you on that one.

Some time later...

PAT: Roy, any idea what mode of delivery we should be offering this new programme in?

ROY: Good question. Let's discuss it with the team. I suppose it will depend how the programme fits with other courses in the faculty – we could have some conjoint teaching, so that would help with costings. I think Law have a module that we could plug into.

PAT: Oh, no. That service teaching was a nightmare last time.

ROY: No choice, Pat. You know it makes sense. And if we can plug in to the Research Methods teaching to all students across the faculty, that's another cost saving. Who do you think might teach on the programme?

PAT: I can't face asking them. They're all going to say they've already got too much on, especially with the REF coming up. Every time you ask anyone to do anything these days, they take a step backward ...

Commentary

This vignette is an interesting depiction of the diminishing power of the disciplines: disciplinary norms or curricula have a minor role in the conversation. The major dynamic comes from administrative, policy-driven and income-generation agendas. Even in an apparently 'academic' activity like programme development, disciplinary discourses have been supplanted by managerialist discourses, relating to quality assurance and commercialisation. Education is conceived of as a business, with customers who pay fees. Technology may be harnessed to facilitate the 'delivery' of education and training to a wider market. In this scenario, the discretion of the individual academic is limited. Academic staff, even in the learning and teaching development process, may again be reluctant passengers. Staff from different discipline groups may find themselves thrown together in a market-driven endeavour. Boundaries between disciplinary groups are eroded by a drive towards interdisciplinarity or multidisciplinarity, perhaps responding to the interests of external professional groups, rather than academic ones.

Of course, this is a simplistic analysis of what will be a complex process of course development, in which academic conversations will naturally follow. But at this stage of development, the impetus is entrepreneurial rather than academic.

Conclusions

The challenges and changes to constellations of social practice clusters we have described in this chapter help us answer the question of what the salience of disciplinary power is in our universities. We have seen in the chapters throughout the book that drivers and forces beyond the discipline have increasingly influenced academic practices and catalysed new ones. If we were to use this device to track the power of territorial factors over time, in our broader definition of territories, it would be clear that these territorial factors have assumed greater force compared to that of disciplines. This varies, as we have said, according to context of practice, but there is no doubt as to the direction of travel.

This trajectory has meant that, increasingly, disciplinary groups are involved in multiple narratives and contestation about what the discipline is and what it requires; Kuhn's paradigm wars (Kuhn 1962) are being fought in often small ways on the battleground of daily practices, as academics work between what they value and what they give priority to. This is not new (for example, Henkel

2002), but is probably escalating. It is, increasingly, some distance from the world described by McNay (1995: 106) in which the main activities of universities were teaching and research, and most developments sprang from these two activities; decisions were taken within the structures that organised the activities, mainly discipline-based departments, within the framework of peer scholars in the international community. Hannan and Silver (2002) also describe the department as the main loyalty base of institutions, where academics feel they 'belong'. There is still truth in these statements, but the chapters in this book have illustrated the more complex higher education terrain we all currently inhabit.

In the light of all this, we repeat that the metaphor of tribes and territories has possibly outlived its usefulness. That metaphor does remind us of the ritualistic nature of some practices, of the notion of tribal leaders, of the power of traditions and other features of tribes – at least as stereotyped. 'Tribal' as applied to political parties has become a derogatory term in the UK, suggesting sectarianism and inflexibility. Klein (2000) points out that territorial metaphors abound in daily use in universities, and the use of tribes and territories matches that: 'fields', 'turf', 'boundary', 'domain', and so on. Thus boundaries are redrawn and there are turf wars. Other related ideas have been developed, she notes: trading zone, creole zone, pidgin zone, borderland. But all of this suggests something too fixed, too closed and too monolithic. Not only is the metaphor rooted in a suspect historical and ideological legacy, as Manathunga and Brew point out in Chapter 4, but its heuristic power is now limited.

Barnett (2011), like Manathunga and Brew, draws on watery metaphors to describe contemporary higher education. He talks of 'the liquid university' (p. 32) where knowledges (for him they are now plural) have also become liquid, jostling and competing with each other. Boundaries between disciplines 'dissolve in this epistemic freneticism', he says (p. 113). But this may be overstating the chaotic character of the situation. In a personal communication, Chris Rust has suggested that a better metaphor for disciplines and their practitioners is *nations*, which suggests more structure than oceans but is less rigid than tribes. The idea of disciplines as nations is perhaps more fecund in terms of suggesting inner complexity, dynamism, conflict and change as well as coherence. The comparisons between disciplines, their institutional articulation and their location within policy, on the one hand, and nations' relationship with state structures are also powerful ones.

What does this mean for the academics we have been portraying? Being an effective academic in the twenty-first century means possessing repertoires of practice that balance the demands of multiple competing imperatives. These repertoires involve being environmentally savvy. Being 'epistemically fluent' in the new environment requires much more than inward-facing knowledge of the practices associated with a discipline. It also means understanding and working with the tensions between institutional drivers and personal identities which are individual, disciplinary and constantly mutating. Delanty (2008: 124) makes the point that an academic's identity has traditionally been separate from institutional context – though in fact there are 'locals' as well as these 'cosmopolitans' (Gouldner 1957). In this argument, being cosmopolitan or local is a state that academics could opt into or out of, and in which academics enjoy a relatively high level of independence from their institutions. But the rise in the power of multiple external catalysts of practice means that opting into or out of some of the activities we have described may no longer be possible. The normative space in which academics work has become a site for struggle, around academic issues such as the organisation of knowledge production and transmission, and where authority lies in situations of competing values.

However the word 'struggle' obscures the reality that academics are not victims of gladiatorial combat, but are party to reshaping their work scenarios. Delanty (2008: 133) claims that 'the changing institutional frameworks contain many social spaces in which identities are being shaped and where many identity projects are emerging'. Whether academics oppose, accommodate, reinterpret or embrace non-disciplinary influences, the effect is a continual ebb and flow of power and dialogue between institution, individual, and stakeholder groups. The romantic conception of 'tribes and territories' entrenched in elite, research-led institutions was probably never a good reflection of the broader academic reality – perhaps characterised by 'contrived collegiality' and a nostalgic wish for community. Now, it is certainly out of date, and needs to be replaced by a conception that adequately captures the complexities and intricacies of contemporary academic practices. Rather than tribes inhabiting territories, we see in this book's pages academics responding to imperatives to reshape their practices – sometimes in complicity, sometimes in collusion, often with resistance. Determined in part by where they are located in terms of career, role and biography, they make moment-by-moment choices in the flux of professional life, developing new repertoires, and yet still maintaining some disciplinary stabilities within an environmental matrix whose fluidity is ubiquitous.

References

(All websites last accessed 11 March 2011)

Abbas, A. and McLean, M. (2010) Tackling Inequality through Quality: A comparative study using Bernsteinian concepts. In E. Unterhalter, and V. Carpentier (Eds) *Global Inequalities in Higher Education: Whose interests are we serving?* Houndmills, Basingstoke: Palgrave Macmillan, pp. 241–67.

Abel-Smith, B. and Stevens, R. (1967) *Lawyers and the Courts: A sociological study of the English legal system 1750–1965*. London: Heinemann.

Aboriginal and Torres Strait Islander (ATSI) Commission and Council for Aboriginal Reconciliation. (1992) *Indigenous Australia Kit.* Canberra: AGPS.

Academy of Finland (1997) Suomen Tieteen Tila Ja Taso 1997. Terveyden Tutkimus. Suomen Akatemian Julkaisuja 11/97.

Academy of Finland (2000) Suomen Tieteen Tila Ja Taso. Katsaus Tutkimukseen Ja Sen Toimintaympäristöön Suomessa 1990-Luvun Lopulla. Suomen Akatemian Julkaisuja 6/00.

Academy of Finland (2003a) Nursing and Caring Sciences. Evaluation report. Publication of the Academy of Finland 12/03.

Academy of Finland (2003b) Suomen Tieteen Tila Ja Taso 2003. Katsaus Tutkimustoimintaan Ja Tutkimuksen Vaikutuksiin 2000-Luvun Alussa. Suomen Akatemian Julkaisuja 9/03.

Academy of Finland (2009) Suomen Tieteen Tila Ja Taso. Suomen akatemian julkaisuja 9/09.

Adams, C. (2006) PowerPoint, Habits of Mind and Classroom Culture. *Journal of Curriculum Studies*, 38, 4, 389–411.

Ahonen, P.P., Hjelt, M., Kaukonen, E., and Vuolanto, P. (Eds) (2009) *Internationalisation of Finnish Scientific Research*. Publications of Academy of Finland 7/09.

Aikenhead, G. (2007) Expanding the Research Agenda for Scientific Literacy. Paper presented to the Linnaeus Tercentenary 2007 Symposium Promoting Scientific Literacy: Science education research in transaction. Uppsala University, Sweden, 28–29 May 2007. http://www.usask.ca/education/people/aikenhead/expand-sl-res-agenda.pdf

Akerlind, G.S. (2008) An Academic Perspective on Research and Being a Researcher: An integration of the literature. *Studies in Higher Education*, 33, 1, 17–31.

Allen-Collinson, J. (2007) Get Yourself Some Nice Neat Matching Box Files! Administrators and occupational identity work. *Studies in Higher Education*, 32, 3, 295–309.

Altbach, P., Reisberg, and Rumbley, L. (2009) *Trends in Global HE: Tracking an Academic Revolution.* A Report Prepared for the UNESCO 2009 World Conference on Higher Education: UNESCO.

Althusser, L. (2008) *On Ideology.* London: Verso.

Alvesson, M. (2002) *Understanding Organizational Culture.* London: Sage.

Anderson, J. (2008) Mapping Academic Resistance in the Managerial University. *Organization,* 15, 2, 251–70.

Anderson, M., Ronning, E., De Vries, R. and Martinson, B. (2007) The Perverse Effects of Competition on Scientists' Work and Relationships. *Science and Engineering Ethics,* 13, 4, 437–61.

Archer, M. (2000) *Being Human: The problem of agency.* Cambridge: Cambridge University Press.

Archer, M. (2007) *Making our Way through the World.* Cambridge: Cambridge University Press.

Ashwin, P. (2009) *Analysing Teaching–Learning Interactions in Higher Education.* London: Continuum.

Atkins, S. and Hoggett, B. (1984) *Women and the Law.* London: Weidenfeld and Nicolson.

Austin, A. (1998) *The Empire Strikes Back: Outsiders and the struggle over legal education.* New York and London: New York University Press.

Bailey, F. (1977) *Morality and Expediency: The folklore of academic politics.* Chicago: Aldine Publishing Company.

Bain, J.D., McNaught, C., Mills, C. and Lueckenhausen, G. (1998) Understanding CFL Practices In Higher Education in Terms of Academics' Educational Beliefs: Enhancing Reeves' analysis. In R. Corderoy (Ed.) *Flexibility: The next wave.* Proceedings of the 15th annual conference of the Australasian Society for Computers in Learning in Tertiary Education. Wollongong, NSW: University of Wollongong, pp. 417–24.

Baird, F., Moore, C.J. and Jagodzinski, A.P. (2000) An Ethnographic Study of Engineering Design Teams at Rolls-Royce Aerospace, *Design Studies,* 21, 4, 333–55.

Baldwin, S. (2010) Teachers' and Students' 'Relationship with Knowledge': An exploration of the organisation of knowledge within disciplinary and educational contexts. PhD Thesis, Lancaster University.

Ball, S. (2008) *The Education Debate.* Bristol: Policy Press.

Bandura, A. (1977) *Social Learning Theory.* New York: General Learning Press.

Bandura, A. (1997) *Self-Efficacy: The exercise of control.* New York: W.H. Freeman.

Barnett, R. (1994) *The Limits of Competence: Knowledge, higher education and society.* Buckingham: SRHE and Open University Press.

Barnett, R. (1999) *Realizing the University in an Age of Supercomplexity.* Buckingham, SRHE and Open University Press.

Barnett, R. (2000a) Supercomplexity and the Curriculum. *Studies in Higher Education,* 25, 255–65.

Barnett, R. (2000b) University Knowledge in an Age of Supercomplexity *Higher Education* 40: 409–22.

Barnett, R. (2000c) *Realizing the University in an Age of Supercomplexity.* London: McGraw-Hill, p. 200.

Barnett, R. (2004) Learning for an Unknown Future, *Higher Education Research and Development,* 23, 3, 247–60.

Barnett, R. (2007) *A Will to Learn: Being a student in an age of uncertainty.* Buckingham: SRHE and Open University Press.

Barnett, R. (2011) *Being a University.* London: Routledge.

Barnett, R. and Di Napoli, R. (2008) Identity and Voice in Higher Education: Making connections. In Di Napoli, R. and Barnett, R. (Eds) *Changing Identities in Higher Education: Voicing Perspectives.* London and New York: Routledge.

Barrie, S. (2006) Understanding What We Mean By The Generic Attributes of Graduates. *Higher Education,* 51, 215–41.

Barry, A., Born, G. and Weszkalnys, G. (2008) The Logics of Inter-disciplinarity. *Economy and Society,* 37, 1, 20–49.

Bath, D., Smith, C., Stein, S., and Swann, R. (2004) Beyond Mapping and Embedding Graduate Attributes: Bringing together quality assurance and action learning to create a validated and living curriculum. *Higher Education Research and Development,* 23, 313–28.

Bauman, Z. (2000) *Liquid Modernity.* Oxford: Blackwell.

Bauman, Z. (2006) *Liquid Life.* Cambridge: Polity Press.

Baxter Magolda, M.B. (2008) Three Elements of Self-Authorship. *Journal of College Student Development,* 49, 4. http://muse.jhu.edu/journals/journal_of_college_student_development/v049/49.4.baxter-magolda.html

Bayer, A. (1991) Book review: Academic Tribes and Territories: Intellectual enquiry and the culture of disciplines by Tony Becher. *The Journal of Higher Education,* 62, 2, 223–5.

Becher, T. (1987a) Academic Discourse. *Studies in Higher Education,* 12, 3, 261–74.

Becher, T. (1987b) The Disciplinary Shaping of the Profession. In B.R. Clark (Ed.) *The Academic Profession: National, disciplinary, and institutional setting.* Berkeley and Los Angeles: University of California Press.

Becher, T. (1989) *Academic Tribes and Territories: Intellectual enquiry and the culture of disciplines.* Buckingham: Open University Press.

Becher, T. (1990) Professional Education in a Comparative Context. In Torstendahl, R. and Burrage, M. (Eds) *The Formation of Professions: Knowledge, state and strategy.* London: Sage Publications, pp. 134–50.

Becher, T. and Trowler, P. (2001) *Academic Tribes and Territories: Intellectual enquiry and the culture of disciplines* (2nd edn). Buckingham: Open University Press/SRHE.

Beck, J. and Young, M.F.D. (2005) The Assault on the Professions and the Restructuring of Academic and Professional Identities: A Bernsteinian analysis. *British Journal of Sociology of Education,* 26, 2, 183–97.

Beck, U. and Beck-Gernsheim, E. (2002) *Individualization.* London: Sage.

Beckmann, A. and Cooper, C. (2004) 'Globalisation', the New Managerialism and Education: Rethinking the purpose of education in Britain. *Journal of Critical Education Policy Studies,* 2, 2, September. http://www.jceps.com/print.php?articleID=31

Benson, L., Harkavy, I. and Puckett, J. (2000) An Implementation Revolution as a Strategy for Fulfilling the Democratic Promise of University-Community Partnerships: Penn-West Philadelphia as an experiment in progress. *Nonprofit and Voluntary Sector Quarterly,* 29, 1, 24–45.

Berger, G. (1970) *Introduction. OECD-CERI indisciplinarity – Problems of teaching and research in universities.* Nice: CERI/French Ministry of Education.

Bergquist, W.H. (1995) *Quality through Access, Access with Quality: The new imperative for higher education.* San Francisco: Jossey-Bass.

Bernstein, B. (1990) *The Structuring of Pedagogic Discourse: Volume IV Class, codes and control*. London: Routledge.

Bernstein, B. (1999) Vertical and Horizontal Discourse: An essay. *British Journal of Sociology of Education* 20, 2, 157–73.

Bernstein, B. (2000) *Pedagogy, Symbolic Control and Identity: Theory, research, critique* (revised edition). New York: Rowman and Little.

Bertram, C. (2010) Finishing Schools for Gilded Youth? *New Statesman*, 13 October 2010. http://www.newstatesman.com/blogs/cultural-capital/2010/10/arts-humanities-browne-support

Bhabha, H. (1994) *The Location of Culture*. London: Routledge.

Bhaskar, R. (2010) Contexts of Interdisciplinarity: Interdisciplinarity and climate change. In R. Bhaskar, C. Frank, K. Hoyer, P. Naess, and J. Parker (Eds) *Interdisciplinarity and Climate Change: Transforming knowledge and practice for our global future*. London: Routledge.

Bibbings, L. (2003) The Future of Higher Education: 'Sustainable research businesses' and 'exploitable knowledge'. *Socio-Legal Newsletter*, 40, 1–3.

Biggs, J.B. (1999) *Teaching for Quality Learning at University*. Milton Keynes: Society for Research in Higher Education and Open University Press.

Biggs, J. (2003) *Teaching for Quality Learning at University* (2nd edition). Maidenhead: Open University Press.

Biglan, A. (1973) The Characteristics of Subject Matter in Different Academic Areas. *Journal of Applied Psychology*, 57, 3, 195–203.

Birks, P. (1998) The Academic and the Practitioner. *Legal Studies*, 18, 397–414.

Blackmore, P. (2010) *The King's-Warwick Project: Creating a 21st Century Curriculum*. London: HEFCE.

Blackmore, P., Chambers, J., Huxley, L. and Thackwray, B. (2010) Tribalism and Territoriality in the Staff and Educational Development World. *Journal of Further and Higher Education*, 34, 1, 105–17.

Boehm, C. (2007) The Discipline that Never Was: Current developments in music technology in higher education in Britain. *Journal of Music, Technology and Education*, 1, 1, 7–21.

Bond, S.L., Qian, J. and Huang, J. (2003) *Role of Faculty in Internationalizing the Undergraduate Curriculum and Classroom Experience*. Ottawa: Canadian Bureau for International Education.

Boulding, K. (1986) Foreword. In G.L. Johnson (Ed.) *Research Methodology for Economists – Philosophy and Practice*. New York: Macmillan.

Bourdieu, P. (1977) *Outline of a Theory of Practice*. Cambridge: Cambridge University Press.

Bourdieu, P. (1986) The Forms of Capital. In J. Richardson (Ed.) *Handbook of Theory and Research for the Sociology of Education*. New York: Greenwood. 241–58. http://www.marxists.org/reference/subject/philosophy/works/fr/bourdieu-forms-capital.htm

Bourdieu, P. (1988) *Homo Academicus*. Translated by P. Collier. Cambridge: Polity Press.

Bourdieu, P. (2000) *Pascalian Meditations*. Translated by R. Nice. Cambridge: Polity Press.

Boyer, E., L. (1990) *Scholarship Reconsidered: Priorities of the professoriate*. Princeton: Carnegie Foundation for the Advancement of Teaching.

Bradney, A. (1998) Law as a Parasitic Discipline. *Journal of Law and Society*, 25, 71.

Bradney, A. (2003) *Conversations, Choices and Chances: The liberal law school in the twenty first century.* Oxford: Hart Publishing.

Bradney, A. and Cownie, F. (2000) British University Law Schools. In D. Hayton (Ed.) *Law's Future(s).* Oxford: Hart Publishing, pp. 1–18.

Bradwell, P. (2009) *The Edgeless University.* London: Demos. http://www.demos.co.uk/files/Edgeless_University_-_web.pdf

Brayne, H. (2000) A Case for Getting Law Students Involved in the Real Thing: The challenge to the saber-tooth curriculum. *The Law Teacher,* 34, 17.

Brennan, J., Edmunds, R., Houston, M., Jary, D., Lebeau, Y., Osborne, M., and Richardson, J. (2010) *Improving What is Learning at University. Improving Learning Series.* London: Routledge.

Brew, A. (1999) Research and Teaching: Changing relationships in a changing context. *Studies in Higher Education,* 24, 3, 291–301.

Brew, A. (2001) *The Nature of Research: Inquiry in academic contexts.* London: RoutledgeFalmer.

Brew, A. (2002) Book review of Nowotny, H., Scott, P. and Gibbons, M. (2001). Re-thinking Science: Knowledge and the public in an age of uncertainty. Cambridge, Polity Press. *Studies in Higher Education,* 27, 3, 353–4.

Brew, A. (2003) Teaching and Research: New relationships and their implications for inquiry-based teaching and learning in higher education. *Higher Education Research and Development,* 22, 1, 3–18.

Brew, A. (2008) Disciplinary and Interdisciplinary Affiliations of Experienced Researchers. *Higher Education,* 56, 423–38.

Brew, A. and Lucas, L. (Eds) (2009) *Academic Research And Researchers.* London: Open University Press/SRHE.

Browne Report (2010) *Securing a Sustainable Future for HE: An independent review of HE funding & student finance* 12 October 2010 http://www.bis.gov.uk/assets/biscore/corporate/docs/s/10-1208-securing-sustainable-higher-education-browne-report.pdf or www.independent.gov.uk/browne-report

Brownsword, R. (1999) Law Schools for Lawyers, Citizens and People. In F. Cownie (Ed.) *The Law School: global issues, local questions.* Aldershot: Ashgate, pp. 26–40.

Bruce, C. and Gerber, R. (1995) Towards University Lecturers' Conceptions of Student Learning. *Higher Education,* 29, 443–58.

Brunila, K. (2009) Sukupuolten TASA Arvo Korkeakoulutuksessa Ja Tutkimuksessa. Sosiaali-Ja Tervesministeriön Selvityksiä 2009:51. Helsinki.

Bulmer, M. (Ed.) (1985) *Essays on the History of British Sociological Research.* Cambridge: Cambridge University Press.

Campbell, C. and Rozsnyai, C. (2002) Quality Assurance and the Development of Course Programmes. *Papers on Higher Education Regional University Network on Governance and Management of Higher Education in South East Europe.* Bucharest: UNESCO.

Campbell, C. and Wiles, P. (1975) The Study of Law in Society in Britain. *Law and Society Review,* 10, 547.

Carmichael, P. (2010) Threshold Concepts, Disciplinary Differences and Cross-Disciplinary Discourse. *Learning and Teaching in Higher Education: Gulf Perspectives,* 7, 2, 53–71.

Carmichael, P. (2011) Tribes, Territories and Threshold Concepts: Educational materialisms at work in higher education. *Educational Philosophy and Theory.* Published online at: http://onlinelibrary.wiley.com/doi/10.1111/j.1469-5812.2010.00743.x/abstract.

Carson, T. (2005) Becoming Somebody Different: Teacher identity and implementing socially transformative curriculum. In R. Golz (Ed.) *Internationalization, Cultural Difference and Migration: Challenges and perspectives of intercultural education.* London: Transaction Publishers, 153–8.

Carvalho, L., Dong, A. and Maton, K. (2009) Legitimating Design: A sociology of knowledge account of the field, *Design Studies*, 30, 5, 483–502.

Chambers, T.C. (2005) The Special Role of Higher Education in Society: As a public good for the public good. In A.J. Kezar, A.C. Chambers and J.C. Burkhardt (Eds), *Higher Education for the Public Good: Emerging Voices from a National Movement.* New York: Jossey-Bass.

Cheek, J., and Jones, J. (2003) What Nurses Say They Do and Need: Implications for the educational preparation of nurses. *Nurse Education Today*, 23, 1, 40–50.

Christie, F. and Maton, K. (Eds) (2010) *Disciplinarity: Systemic functional and sociological perspectives.* London: Continuum.

Churchman, D. (2006) Institutional Commitments, Individual Compromises: Identity-related responses to compromise in an Australian university. *Journal of Higher Education Policy and Management*, 28, 1, 3–15.

Churchman, D. and King, S. (2009) Academic Practice in Transition: Hidden stories of academic identities. *Teaching in Higher Education*, 14, 5, 507–16.

Clark, B.R. (1987) Conclusions. In B.R. Clark (Ed.) *The American Academic Profession.* Berkeley: University of California Press.

Clark, B. (1998) *Creating Entrepreneurial Universities: Organizational pathways of transformation.* London: Pergamon.

Clark, B. (1993) The Problem of Complexity in Modern Higher Education. In S. Rothblatt and B. Wittrock (Eds) *The European and American University since 1800: Historical and sociological essays.* Cambridge: Cambridge University Press, 263–79.

Clegg, S. (2007) Academic Identity and Intellectual Enquiry: Breaking the research/teaching dualism? Paper presented at the International Colloquium: International policies and practices for academic enquiry. Southampton Solent University, 19–21 April 2007.

Clifford, V. A. (2009) Engaging the Disciplines in Internationalising the Curriculum. *International Journal of Academic Development*, 14, 2, 133–43.

Coles, T., Hall, J., and Duval, D. (2006) Tourism and Post-Disciplinary Enquiry. *Current Issues in Tourism*, 9, 4, 293–319.

Collier, R. (1991) Masculinism, Law and Law Teaching. *International Journal of the Sociology of Law*, 19, 427.

Collier, R. (2003) 'Useful Knowledge' and the 'New Economy': An uncertain future for (critical) socio-legal studies? *Socio-Legal Newsletter*, 39, 3–4.

Collier, R. (2005) The Liberal Law School, the Restructured University and the Paradox of Socio-Legal Studies. *Modern Law Review*, 68, 475.

Commission on the Social Sciences (2003) *Great Expectations: The social sciences in Britain.* Academy of the Learned Societies for the Social Sciences. www.acss.org. uk/docs/GtExpectations.pdf

Conaghan, J. (2002) Reassessing the Feminist Theoretical Project in Law. *Journal of Law and Society*, 27, 351.

Conole, G., Scanlon, E., Mundin, P. and Farrow, R. (2010) *Interdisciplinary Research: Findings from the technology enhanced learning research programme.* London: Teaching and Learning Research Programme. http://www.tlrp.org/docs/ TELInterdisciplinarity.pdf

Conole, G., Smith, J., and White, S. (2007) A critique of the Impact of Policy and Funding. In G. Conole and M. Oliver (Eds) *Contemporary Perspectives in e-Learning Research*. London: Routledge, pp. 38–54.

Corlett, J. (2000) The Perceptions of Nurse Teachers, Student Nurses and Preceptors of the Theory Practice Gap in Nurse Education. *Nurse Education Today*, 20, 6, 499–505.

Cornford, J. (2000) The Virtual University is … the University Made Concrete? *Information, Communication and Society*, 3, 4, 508–25.

Cotterell, R. (1995) *Law's Community: Legal theory in sociological perspective*. Oxford: Clarendon Press.

Council For Higher Education Accreditation (CHEA) (2001) *Glossary of Key Terms in Quality Assurance and Accreditation*. http://www.chea.org/international/inter_glossary01.html

Cousin, G. (2005) Learning from Cyberspace. In R. Land and S. Bayne (Eds) *Education in Cyberspace*. London: RoutledgeFalmer, pp. 117–29.

Cownie, F. (2000) Women in the Law School: Shoals of fish, star fish or fish out of water? In P. Thomas (Ed.) *Discriminating Lawyers*. London: Cavendish Publishing.

Cownie, F. (2004) *Legal Academics: Culture and identities*. Oxford and Portland: Hart Publishing.

Cownie, F. (2010) Introduction: Contextualising Stakeholders in the Law School. In F. Cownie (Ed.) *Stakeholders in the Law School*. Oxford: Hart Publishing.

Crane, D. (1972) *Invisible Colleges: Diffusion of knowledge in scientific communities*. Chicago: University of Chicago Press.

Dall'Alba, G. (1991) Foreshadowing Conceptions of Teaching. Paper presented at the 16th Annual Conference of the Higher Education and Development Society of Australia, Brisbane, Queensland, Australia. Internationalizing Higher Education. Critical explorations of pedagogy and policy. Hong Kong: Springer.

Davidson, G. (1994) *Credit Accumulation and Transfer in the British Universities 1990–1993*. Canterbury: University of Kent.

Davies, C. (1995) *Gender and the Professional Predicament of Nursing*. Buckingham: Open University Press.

Davies, W.M. (2006) An 'Infusion' Approach to Critical Thinking: Moore on the critical thinking debate. *Higher Education Research and Development*, 25, 2, 179–93.

De Vita, G. (2007) Taking Stock: An appraisal of the literature on internationalising higher education learning. In E. Jones and S. Brown (Eds) *Internationalising Higher Education*. London: Routledge.

DeBartolo, E. and Robinson, R. (2007) A Freshman Engineering Curriculum Integrating Design and Experimentation. *The International Journal of Mechanical Engineering Education*, 35, 2, 91–107.

Deem R., (1998) 'New Managerialism' and Higher Education: The management of performances and cultures in universities in the United Kingdom. *International Studies in Sociology of Education*, 8, 1, 34–51.

Deem, R., Hillyard, S. and Reed, M. (2007) *Knowledge, Higher Education and the New Managerialism: The changing management of UK universities*. Oxford: Oxford University Press.

Delanty, G. (2008) Academic identities and institutional change. In R. Di Napoli and R. Barnett *Changing Identities in Higher Education: Voicing perspectives*. London and New York: Routledge.

Department for Education and Skills (DfES) (2003) *Towards a Unified e-Learning Strategy.* http://www.dfes.gov.uk/highereducation/hestrategy/pdfs/DfES-Higher Education.pdf

Di Napoli, R. and Barnett, R. (2008) *Changing Identities in Higher Education: Voicing perspectives.* London and New York: Routledge.

Dicey, A.V. (1883) *Can English Law be taught at the Universities?* London: Macmillan.

Dobbert, M. (1998) The Impossibility Of Internationalizing Students by Adding Materials to Courses. In J. Mestenhauser and B. Ellingboe (Eds) *Reforming the Higher Education Curriculum: Internationalizing the campus.* Phoenix: Oryx Press.

Doherty, C and Singh, M. (2005) How the West is Done: Simulating Western pedagogy in a curriculum for Asian international students. In P. Ninnes and M. Hellsten, M (Eds) *Internationalizing Higher Education. CERC Studies in Comparative Education,* 16, 1–8.

Donald, J. (1995) Disciplinary Differences In Knowledge Validation. In N. Hativa and M. Marincovich (Eds) *Disciplinary Differences in Teaching and Learning: Implications for practice.* San Francisco: Jossey-Bass.

Donald, J. (2002) *Learning to Think: Disciplinary perspectives.* San Francisco: Jossey-Bass.

Doorbar, A. (2004) British Council Transnational Education: Qualitative market research findings. Paper presented to Going Global Conference, Edinburgh.

Dunkin M.J. and Precians, R.P. (1992) Award-Winning University Teachers' Concepts of Teaching. *Higher Education,* 24, 483–502.

Duxbury, N. (2001) *Jurists and Judges.* Oxford: Hart Publishing.

Echtner, C.M. and Jamal, T.B. (1997) The Disciplinary Dilemma of Tourism Studies. *Annals of Tourism Research,* 24, 4, 868–83.

Economic and Social Research Council (ESRC) (1994) *Review of Socio-Legal Studies: Final Report.* ESRC: Swindon.

Nature (2010) Editorial: Save Our Cities, 467, 883–4, 21 October.

Eller, J. D. (2009) *Cultural Anthropology: Global forces, local lives.* London: Routledge.

Ellis, R. J. (2009) Problems May Cut Right Across the Borders. In B. Chandramohan and S. Fallows *Interdisciplinary Learning and Teaching in Higher Education.* London: Routledge, pp. 3–17.

Elzinga, A. (1990) The Knowledge Aspect of Professionalisation: The case of science-based education in Sweden. In R. Torstendahl and M. Burrage (Eds) *The Formation of Professions.* London: Sage Publications, pp. 151–73.

Engeström, Y. (2001) Expansive Learning at Work: Toward an activity theoretical reconceptualization. *Journal of Education and Work,* 14, 1, 133–56.

Entwistle, N. and Walker, P. (2000) Strategic Alertness and Expanded Awareness within Sophisticated Conceptions of Teaching. *Instructional Science,* 28, 5/6, 335–61.

Evans, C. (1995) Choosing People: Recruitment and selection as leverage on subjects and disciplines. *Studies in Higher Education,* 20, 3, 253–65.

Fanghanel, J. (2009) The Role of Ideology in Shaping Academics' Conceptions of Their Disciplines. *Teaching in Higher Education,* 14, 5, 565–77.

Farrel B. and Twining-Ward L. (2004) Reconceptualizing tourism. *Annals of Tourism Research,* 31, 2 (April), 274–95.

Fenwick, T. and Edwards, R. (2010) *Actor-Network Theory in Education.* London: Routledge.

Fitzmaurice, M. (2010) Considering Teaching in Higher Education as a Practice. *Teaching in Higher Education.* 15, 1, 45–55.

Fitzpatrick, P. and Hunt, A. (1987) (Eds) *Critical Legal Studies*. Oxford: Basil Blackwell.

Foucault, M. (1975) *Discipline and Punish*. Harmondsworth: Penguin.

Foucault, M. (1984) *Le souci de soi. L'histoire de la sexualité, Vol. III*. Paris: Gallimard.

Freidson, E. (1994) *Professionalism Reborn: Theory, prophecy and policy*. Chicago: University of Chicago Press.

Freire, P. (1970) *Pedagogy of the Oppressed*. London: Penguin.

Friesen, N. and Cressman, D. (2010) *Media Theory, Education and the University: A response to Kittler's history of the university as a media system*. http://cjms.fims. uwo.ca/issues/07-01/Friesen%20and%20Cressman.pdf

Frodeman, R., Mitcham, C. and Sacks, A. B. (2001) Questioning Interdisciplinarity. *Science, Technology and Society Newsletter*, 126/127, 1–5.

Fuller,S.(2002)*KnowledgeManagementFoundations*.Oxford:Butterworth-Heinemann.

Fulton, O. (1996) Which Academic Profession Are You In? In R. Cuthbert (Ed.) *Working in Higher Education*. Buckingham: SRHE and Open University Press.

Gallagher, P. (2004) How The Metaphor of a Gap between Theory and Practice has Influenced Nursing Education. *Nurse Education Today*, 24, 4, 263–8.

Gasper, D. (2010) Interdisciplinarity and Transdisciplinarity. Diverse purposes of research: Theory-oriented, situation-oriented, policy-oriented. In P. Thomson and M. Walker (Eds) *The Routledge Doctoral Student's Companion*. London and New York: Routledge.

Geertz, C. (1976) *Toward an Ethnography of the Disciplines*. Princeton: Princeton Institute for Advanced Study (mimeo).

Genn, H., Partington, M. and Wheeler, S. (2006) *Law in the Real World: Improving our understanding of how law works (The Nuffield Inquiry on Empirical Legal Research)*. London: Nuffield Foundation.

Gibbons, M., Limoges, C., Nowotny, H., Schwartzman, S., Scott, P. and Trow, M. (1994) *The New Production of Knowledge: The dynamics of science and research in contemporary societies*. London: Sage.

Gibbs, G. and Coffey, M. (2001) The Impact of Training on University Teachers' Approaches to Teaching and on the Way Their Students Learn. Paper presented at the EARLI Symposium 2001. Training University Teachers to Improve Student Learning.

Gibbs, G. and Coffey, M. (2004) The Impact of Training of University Teachers on Their Teaching Skills, Their Approach to Teaching and the Approach to Learning of Their Students. *Active Learning in Higher Education*, 5, 87–100.

Giddens, A. (1979) *Central Problems in Social Theory: Action, structure and contradiction in social analysis*. London: Macmillan.

Giddens, A. (1984) *The Constitution of Society*. Cambridge: Polity Press.

Giddens, A. (1991) *Modernity and Self-Identity: Self and society in the late modern age*. Cambridge: Polity.

Giddens, A. (1999) *Runaway World: How globalisation is reshaping our lives*. London: Profile Books.

Gilbert, N.G. and Mulkay, M. (1984) *Opening Pandora's Box: A sociological analysis of scientists' discourse*. Cambridge: Cambridge University Press.

Giri, A.K. (1998) Transcending Disciplinary Boundaries. *Critique of Anthropology*, 18, 4, 379–404.

Glassick, C. E., Huber, M. T. and Maeroff, G. I. (1997) *Scholarship Assessed: Evaluation of the professoriate. An Ernest L Boyer Project of the Carnegie Foundation for the Advancement of Teaching*. San Franscisco: Jossey-Bass.

Goff, R. (1983) *The Search for Principle*. Proceedings of the British Academy 169.

Goodrich, P. (1996) Of Blackstone's Tower: Metaphors of distance and histories of the English law school. In P. Birks (Ed.) *Pressing Problems in the Law Volume Two: What Are Law Schools For?* Oxford: Oxford University Press, chapter 5.

Goodwin, M. (2004) Recovering the Future: A post-disciplinary perspective on geography and political economy. In P. Cloke, M. Goodwin and P. Crang (Eds) *Envisioning Human Geography*. London: Arnold, pp. 65–80.

Gordon, G. and Whitchurch, C. (2010) *Academic and Professional Identities in Higher Education: the Challenges of a Diversifying Workforce*. Abingdon: Routledge.

Gornall, L (1999) 'New Professionals': Change and occupational roles in higher education. *Perspectives*, 3, 2, 44–49.

Gouldner, A.W. (1957) Cosmopolitans and Locals: Toward an analysis of latent social roles (I and II). *Administrative Science Quarterly*, 2, 281–306 and 444–80.

Gouseti, A. (2010) Web 2.0 and Education: Not just another case of hype, hope and disappointment? *Learning, Media and Technology*, 35, 3, 351–6.

Gow, L. and Kember, D. (1993) Conceptions of Teaching and Their Relationship to Student Learning. *British Journal of Educational Psychology*, 63, 20–33.

Gower, L.C.B. (1950) English Legal Training: A critical survey. *Modern Law Review*, 13, 137.

Greed, C. (1991) *Surveying Sisters*. London: Routledge.

Gregg, P. (1996) Modularisation: What academics think. In Higher Education Quality Council, *In Focus: Modular Higher Education in the UK*. London: HEQC.

Grindle, N., and Dallat, J. (2000) Nurse Education: From casualty to scapegoat? *Teaching in Higher Education*, 5, 2, 205–18.

Hall, B.M (2011) Teaching Uncertainty: The case of climate change. Unpublished PhD thesis. Cheltenham: University of Gloucestershire.

Hall, M. (2010) Community Engagement in South African Higher Education. Kagisano 6. Retrieved 22 February 2011 from http://www.che.ac.za/documents/d000204/Kagisano_No_6_January2010.pdf

Halsey, A.H. (1992) *Decline of Donnish Dominion*. Oxford: Oxford University Press.

Halsey, A. (2004) *A History of Sociology in Britain*. Oxford: Oxford University Press.

Halsey, A. (2005) The history of sociology in Britain. In A. Halsey and W. Runciman (Eds) *British Sociology: Seen from without and within*. Oxford: Oxford University Press.

Halsey, A. and Runciman, W. (Eds) (2005) *British Sociology: Seen from without and within*. Oxford: Oxford University Press.

Hammond, N. and Trapp, A. (1992) CAL as a Trojan Horse for Educational Change: The case of psychology. *Computers and Education*, 19, 87–95.

Hanks, W.F. (1991) Foreword. In J. Lave and E. Wenger (Eds) *Situated Learning: Legitimate peripheral participation*. New York: Cambridge University Press, pp. 13–24.

Hannan and Silver (2002) Guide to Innovation in Teaching and Learning. Available at: http://www.heacademy.ac.uk/resources/detail/resource_database/id192_Guide_to_Innovation_in_Teaching_and_Learning

Harding, S. (1986) *The Science Question in Feminism*. Ithaca: Cornell University Press.

Hardy, I. (2010) Academic Architectures: Academic perceptions of teaching conditions in an Australian university. *Studies in Higher Education*, 35, 4, 391–404.

Harman, G. (2005) Internationalisation of Australian Higher Education: Critical review of literature. In P. Ninnes and M. Hellsten (Eds) *Internationalizing Higher Education. Critical explorations of pedagogy and policy*. Hong Kong: Springer.

Harman, G. (2009) Prince of Networks: Bruno Latour and metaphysics. http://www.re-press.org/book-files/OA_Version_780980544060_Prince_of_Networks.pdf.

Hartley, A. (1983) Ideology and Organisational Behaviour. *International Studies of Management and Organisation*, 13, 3, 26–7.

Hativa, N. and Goodyear, P. (2002) *Teacher Thinking, Beliefs and Knowledge in Higher Education*. Dordrecht: Kluwer.

Hayles, N. (1999) *How We Became Posthuman: Virtual bodies in cybernetics, literature and informatics*. Chicago: University of Chicago Press.

Hayles, N. (2006) Unfinished Work: From cyborg to cognisphere. *Theory, Culture, Society*, 23, 7–8.

Hayward, C.R. (2000) *De-facing Power*. Cambridge: Cambridge University Press.

Hazelkorn, E. (2009) The Impact of Global Rankings on Higher Education Research and the Production of Knowledge. *UNESCO Forum on Higher Education, Research and Knowledge Occasional Paper N°16*. http://unesdoc.unesco.org/images/0018/001816/181653e.pdf

Hegarty, K. (2008) Shaping the Self to Sustain the Other: Mapping impacts of academic identity in education for sustainability. *Environmental Education Research*, 14, 6, 681–92.

Heitmann, G. (1996) Project-Oriented Study and Project-Organised Curricula: A brief review of intentions and solutions. *European Journal of Engineering Education*, 21, 2, 121–31.

Hellstrom, T., Jacob, M. and Wenneberg, S. (2003) The 'Discipline' of Post-Academic Science: Reconstructing the paradigmatic foundations of a virtual research institute. *Science and Public Policy*, 30, 4, 251–60.

Henkel, M. (2000) *Academic Identities and Policy Change in Higher Education*. London and Philadelphia: Jessica Kingsley Publishers.

Henkel, M. (2002) Academic Identity in Transformation? The case of the United Kingdom. *Higher Education Management and Policy*, 14, 3, 137–47.

Henkel, M. (2005) Academic identity and autonomy in a changing policy environment. *Higher Education*, 49, 1–2, 155–76.

Henkel, M. (2007) Can Academic Autonomy Survive in the Knowledge Society? A perspective from Britain. *Higher Education Research & Development*, 26, 1, 87–99.

Henkel, M. (2010) Introduction: Change and continuity in academic and professional identities. In G. Gordon and C. Whitchurch (Eds) *Academic and Professional Identities in Higher Education: The challenges of a diversifying workforce*. London: Routledge, pp. 3–12.

Henkel, M. and Vabo, A. (2006) Academic Identities. In M. Kogan, M. Bauer, I. Bleiklie and M. Henkel (Eds) *Transforming Higher Education: A comparative study*. London: Jessica Kingsley Publishers, pp. 127–59.

Hepple, B. (1996) The Renewal of the Liberal Law Degree. *Cambridge Law Journal*, 55, 470.

HESA (2010) *Online Students and Qualifiers Data Tables: Subject of Study*. Higher Education Statistics Agency, UK. www.hesa.ac.uk

Hicks, A. (1995) Legal Practice is an Academic Matter. *SPTL Reporter* (Spring) 6.

Hirst, P.H. (1974) *Knowledge and the Curriculum*. London, Routledge.

Hirst, P.H. (1993) Education, Knowledge and Practices. In P. Hirst, R. Barrow and P. White (Eds) *Beyond Liberal Education: Essays in honour of Paul H. Hirst*. New York: Routledge.

HM Treasury (2006) *Science and Innovation Investment Framework 2004–2014: Next steps*. HMSO: London.

Hockey, J. and Allen-Collinson, J. (2009) Occupational Knowledge and Practice amongst UK University Research Administrators. *Higher Education Quarterly*, 63, 2, 141–59.

Hodgkinson-Williams. C. and Czerniewicz, L. (2007) Educational Technologists in Higher Education Institutions in South Africa: Moving beyond random acts of progress. *ReBel Symposium 12–14/11/2007.*

Huber, M. (2002) *Disciplines and the Development of a Scholarship of Teaching and Learning in the United States of America.* Discussion paper for the Learning and Teaching Support Network. York: LTSN.

Hughes, R. (1991, revised edition) *The Shock of the New.* New York: Knopf.

Hulme, M. (2007) The Appliance of Science. *The Guardian*, Wednesday 14 March 2007. http://www.guardian.co.uk/society/2007/mar/14/scienceofclimatechange.climatechange

Hunt, A. (1987) The Critique of Law: What is 'critical' about Critical Legal Studies? In P. Fitzpatrick and A. Hunt (Eds) *Critical Legal Studies.* Oxford: Basil Blackwell.

James, N. (2005) Academic identity development: Narratives of shifting experiences. Paper presented at British Sociological Association Annual conference, 21–23 March 2005, University of York, UK. Available at: http://www.britsoc.co.uk/user_doc/05BSAConfJamesNalita.pdf

Jauhiainen, A., Jauhiainen, A., and Laiho, A. (2009) The Dilemmas of the 'Efficiency University' and the Everyday Life of University Teachers. *Teaching in Higher Education*, 14, 4, 417–28.

Jefferson, G. (1985) An Exercise in the Transcription and Analysis of Laughter. In: T. Van Dijk (Ed.) *Handbook of Discourse Analysis: Discourse and dialogue.* London: Academic Press, pp. 25–34.

Jenkins, A. (1999) Discipline-Based Educational Development. *International Journal of Academic Development*, 1, 1, 50–62.

Jenkins, R. (1996) *Social Identity.* London: Routledge.

Johannesson, G. (2005) Tourism translations: Actor–Network Theory and tourism research. *Tourist Studies*, 5, 2, 133–50.

Jones, A. (2009) Redisciplining Generic Attributes: The disciplinary context in focus. *Studies in Higher Education*, 34, 1, 85–100.

Jones, A. (2010) Generic Attributes in Accounting: The significance of disciplinary context. *Accounting Education*, 19, 1–2, 5–21.

Jovicic Z. (1988) A plea for tourismological theory and methodology. *Tourism Review*, 43, 3, 2–5.

Kapp, R. and Bangeni, B. (2009) Positioning (in) the Discipline: Undergraduate students' negotiations of disciplinary discourses. *Teaching in Higher Education*, 14, 6, 587–96.

Keeling, R. (2006) The Bologna Process and the Lisbon Research Agenda: the European Commission's expanding role in higher education discourse. *European Journal of Higher Education*, 41, 2, 203–23.

Kekale, J. (2002) Conceptions of Quality in Four Different Disciplines. *Tertiary Education and Management*, 8, 65–80.

Kember, D. and Kwan, K. (2002) Lecturers' Approaches to Teaching and their Relationship to Conceptions of Good Teaching. In N. Hativa and P. Goodyear (Eds) *Teacher Thinking, Beliefs and Knowledge in Higher Education.* Dordrecht: Kluwer, pp. 219–40.

Kember, D. and Kwan, K.P. (2000) Lecturers' Approaches to Their Teaching and Their Relationship to Conceptions of Good Teaching. *Instructional Science.* 28, 469–90.

Kember, D. and Leung, D.Y.P. (2011) Disciplinary Differences in Student Ratings of Teaching Quality. *Research in Higher Education*, 52, 278–99.

Kemmis, S. and Grootenboer, P. (2008) Situating Praxis in Practice: Practice architectures and the cultural, social and material conditions for practice. In S. Kemmis and T. Smith (Eds) *Enabling Praxis: Challenges for education.* Amsterdam: Sense Publishers, pp. 37–62.

Kilpiäinen, S. (2003) Odotetaan Käytäntöä Ja Saadaan Teoriaa. Tutkimus Kemi-Tornion Ammattikorkeakoulun Terveysalan Opiskelijoiden Käsityksistä Ja Kokemuksista Opetuksesta Ja Ohjauksesta Vuosina 1995–1997 Ja 2000–2001. Lapin Yliopisto. *Acta Universitatis Lapponiensis*, 59.

Kinnunen, J. (1999) Onko Suomalainen Hoitotieteen Tutkimus Ja Opetus Sivuraiteella? *Hoitotiede*, 11, 4, 183–5.

Kitano, M.K. (1997) A Rationale and Framework for Course Change. In M.K. Kitano and A.I. Morey (Eds) *Multicultural Course Transformation in Higher Education: A broader truth.* Needham Heights, MA: Allyn and Bacon.

Klein, J. T. (1990) *Interdisciplinarity: History, theory, and practice.* Detroit: Wayne State Press, p. 331.

Klein, J. T. (1996) *Crossing Boundaries: Knowledge, disciplinarities and interdisciplinarities.* Charlottesville, VA: University Press of Virginia.

Klein, J, T, (2000) A conceptual vocabulary of interdisciplinary science. In P. Weingart and N. Stehr (Eds) *Practising Interdisciplinarity.* Toronto: University of Toronto Press, pp. 3–24.

Knight, P. and Yorke, M. (2004) *Learning, Curriculum and Employability in Higher Education.* London: RoutledgeFalmer.

Kogan, M. and Henkel, M. (1983) *Government and Research.* London: Heinemann.

Koivula, J., Rinne, R. and Niukko, S. (2009) Yliopistot Yrityksinä? Merkkejä Ja Merkityksiä Suomessa Ja Euroopassa. *Kasvatus*, 40, 1, 7–27.

Kolb, D. (1981) Learning Styles and Disciplinary Differences. In A. Chickering (Ed.) *The Modern American College.* San Francisco: Jossey-Bass, pp. 232–55.

Kolb, D. (1984) *Experiential Learning: Experience as the source of learning and development.* NJ: Prentice-Hall.

Kothari, U. (1988) *Rethinking Development: In search of humane alternatives.* Delhi: Ajanta.

Krause, K. (2009a) Interpreting Changing Academic Roles and Identities in Higher Education. In. M. Tight, K.H. Mok, J. Huisman, and C.C. Morphew (Eds) *The Routledge International Handbook of Higher Education.* Oxon: Routledge, pp. 413–26.

Krause, K. (2009b) *Challenging Perspectives on Learning and Teaching in the Disciplines: The academic voice.* Paper presented at SRHE Conference, December 2009, South Wales, UK.

Kreber, C. (Ed.) (2009) *The University and its Disciplines: Teaching and learning within and beyond disciplinary boundaries.* London: Routledge.

Krishnan, A. (2009) *What are Academic Disciplines? Some observations on the disciplinary vs. interdisciplinarity debate.* ESRC National Centre for Research Methods Working Paper 03/09 http://eprints.ncrm.ac.uk/783/

Krueger, R. (1997) *Moderating Focus Groups.* Thousand Oaks: CA: Sage Publications.

Kuhn, T.S. (1962) *The Structure of Scientific Revolutions.* Chicago: University of Chicago Press.

Kuhn, T.S. (1970) *The Structure of Scientific Revolutions*, 2nd. Edition. Chicago: University of Chicago Press.

Kuuppelomäki, M. and Tuomi, J. (2005) Finnish Nurses' Attitudes Towards Nursing Research and Related Factors. *International Journal of Nursing Studies*, 42, 2, 187–96.

Kuutti, K. (1996) Activity Theory as a Potential Framework for Human Computer Interaction Research. In B. Nardi (Ed.) *Context and Consciousness: Activity theory and human-computer interaction*. Cambridge, MA: The MIT Press, pp. 17–44.

Kyvik, S. (1991) *Productivity in Academia*. Oslo: Norwegian University Press.

Lahtinen, M. and Heikkinen, M. (2003) Työistä Kokonaisiksi. Vastine Katri Ryttyläisen Artikkeliin "Kilttien Tyttöjen Tiede – Naisnäkökulma Hoitotieteelliseen Tutkimukseen. *Hoitotiede*, 15, 5, 244–6.

Laiho, A. (2005) Sisar Tieteen Saloissa – Sairaanhoitajien Akatemisoimisprojekti Pohjoismaissa 1900-luvulla. Turun yliopisto, Kasvatustieteiden laitos.

Laiho, A. (2010) Academicisation of Nursing Education in the Nordic Countries. *Higher Education*, 60, 6, 641–56.

Laiho, A., and Ruoholinna, T. (2008) Terveysalan Ammattilaisten Koulutuspuhe: Erontekoja, Nostalgiaa Sekä Koulutuksen Ja Työn Epäsuhtaa. *Yhteiskuntapolitiikka*, 73, 1, 36–51.

Laird, T.F.N., Shoup, R., Kuh, G. D. and Schwarz, M. J. (2008) The Effects of Discipline on Deep Approaches to Student Learning and College Outcomes. *Research in Higher Education*, 49, 469–94.

Lancaster University (2010) *Feeding the World: A global challenge*. www.foodsecurity-lancaster.net.

Land, R. Meyer, J.H.F. and Smith, J. (Eds) (2008) *Threshold Concepts within the Disciplines*. Rotterdam and Taipei: Sense Publishing.

Latour, B. (1999) *Pandora's Hope*. Cambridge, MA: Harvard University Press.

Latour, B. (2000) When Things Strike Back: A possible contribution of 'science studies' to the social sciences. *British Journal of Sociology*, 51, 1, 107–23.

Latour, B. and Woolgar, S. (1979) *Laboratory Life: The social construction of scientific facts*. Beverly Hills, US: Sage.

Lattuca, L. and Stark, J. (1995) Will Disciplinary Perspectives Impede Curricular Reform? *Journal of Higher Education*, 65, 4, 401–26.

Lattuca, L.R., Terenzini, P.T., Harper, B.J. and Yin, A.C. (2010) Academic Environments in Detail: Holland's theory at the subdiscipline level. *Research in Higher Education*, 51, 21–39.

Law, J. (2004) *After Method: Mess in social science research*. London: Routledge.

Lawless, C. and Kirkwood, A. (1976) Training the Educational Technologist. *British Journal of Educational Technology*, 1, 7, 54–60.

Lawson. F.H. (1968) *The Oxford Law School 1850–1965*. Oxford: Clarendon Press.

Lea, M. and Stierer, B. (2009) Lecturers' Everyday Writing as Professional Practice in the University as Workplace: New insights into academic identities. *Studies in Higher Education*, 34, 4, 417–28.

Lea, S..J and Callaghan, L. (2008) Investigating Lecturer's Perceptions of Teaching in the Supercomplexity of Higher Education. *Higher Education*, 55, 171–88.

Leary, M.R. and Tangney, J.P. (2003) *Handbook of Self and Identity*. New York: Guilford Press.

Lecouter, A. and Delfabbro, P.H. (2001) Repertoires of Teaching and Learning: A comparison of university teachers and students using Q methodology. *Higher Education*, 42, 205–35.

Lefebvre, H. (1984) *Everyday Life in the Modern World*. New Brunswick: Transaction Books.

Leino-Kilpi, H., and Suominen, L. (1997) Suomalainen Hoitotieteellinen Tutkimus 1950-Luvulta Nykypäivään. *Hoitotiede*, 9, 2, 55–65.

Leiper, N. (1981) Towards a Cohesive Curriculum in Tourism: The case for a distinct discipline. *Annals of Tourism Research*, 8, 69–84.

Leiper, N. (2000) An Emerging Discipline. *Annals of Tourism Research*, 27, 3, 805–9.

Leuven Comuniqué (2009) *The Bologna Press 2020 – The European Higher Education Area in the New Decade*. Communiqué of the Conference of European Ministers Responsible for Higher Education. Leuven and Louvain-la-Neuve.

Lindblom-Ylänne, S., Trigwell, K., Nevgi, A. and Ashwin, P. (2006) How Approaches to Teaching are Affected by Discipline and Teaching Context. *Studies in Higher Education*, 31, 3, 285–98.

Lingard, L., Schryer, C.F., Spafford, M. and Campbell, S.L. (2007) Negotiating the Politics of Identity in an Interdisciplinary Research Team. *Qualitative Research*, 7, 501–19.

Little, B. and Lore, A. (2010) Less Time to Study, Less Well Prepared for Work, Yet Satisfied with Higher Education: A UK perspective on links between higher education and the labour market. *Journal of Education and Work*, 23, 3, 275–96.

Lizzio, A., Wilson, K. and Simons, R. (2002). University Students' Perceptions of the Learning Environment and Academic Outcomes: Implications for theory and practice. *Studies in Higher Education*, 27, 27–50.

Lodahl, J.B. and Gordon, G. (1972) The Structure of Scientific Fields and the Functioning of University Graduate Departments, *American Sociological Review*, 37, 57–72.

Löw, M. (2008) The Constitution of Space: The structuration of spaces through the simultaneity of effects and perception. *European Journal of Social Theory*, 1, 11, 25–49.

Lowham, E. and Schilla, A (2008) Buzzwords, Jargon, Both or Neither? Collaboration and interdisciplinarity in graduate education. Paper presented at the annual meeting of the APSA Teaching and Learning Conference, San Jose Marriott, San Jose, California, Feb 22, 2008 http://www.allacademic.com/meta/p245586_index.html

Lucas, L. (2006) *The Research Game in Academic Life*. Maidenhead: Open University Press/SRHE.

Lueddeke, G. R. (2003) Professionalising Teaching Practice in Higher Education: A study of disciplinary variation and teaching-scholarship. *Studies in Higher Education*, 28, 2, 213–28.

Lukes, S. (2005) *Power: A radical view*. Second edition. London: Palgrave Macmillan.

Lyotard, J.F. (1984) *The Postmodern Condition: A report on knowledge*. Manchester: Manchester University Press.

McCune, V. and Hounsell, D. (2005) The Development of Students' Ways of Thinking And Practising in Three Final-Year Biology Courses. *Higher Education*, 49, 3, 255–89.

McGlynn, C. (1998) *The Woman Lawyer: Making the difference*. London: Butterworths.

MacIntyre, A. (1981) *After Virtue: A study in moral theory*, 2nd edition. London: Duckworth.

Mackay, L. (1990) Nursing: Just Another Job? In P. Abbot and C. Wallace (Eds), *The Sociology of the Caring Professions*. London: Falmer Press. pp. 29–39.

McKenzie, J., Roms, H. and Wee, C.J.W-L. (Eds) (2010) *Contesting Performance: Global sites of research performance interventions*. London: Palgrave Macmillan.

McLean, M. and Abbas, A. (2009) The 'Biographical Turn' in University Sociology Teaching: A Bernsteinian analysis. *Teaching in Higher Education*, 14, 5, 529–39.

McNay, I. (1995) From the Collegial Academy to Corporate Enterprise: The changing cultures of universities. In T. Schuller (Ed.) *The Changing University?* Buckingham: SRHE and Open University Press.

McNay, I. (2009) Research Quality Assessment Objectives, Approaches, Responses and Consequences. In A. Brew and L. Lucas (Eds) *Academic Research and Researchers*. Maidenhead: Open University Press/SRHE, 35–53.

McWilliam, E. and Tan, J. (2010) When Qualitative Meets Quantitative: Conversations about the nature of knowledge. In P. Thomson and M. Walker, (Eds) *The Routledge Doctoral Student's Companion*. London and New York: Routledge.

Maharg, P. (2007) *Transforming Legal Education: Learning and teaching law in the early twenty-first century*. Aldershot: Ashgate.

Malcolm, J. and Zukas, M. (2009) Making a Mess of Academic Work: Experience, purpose and identity. *Teaching in Higher Education*, 14, 5, 495–506.

Manathunga, C. (2009) Postcolonial Perspectives on Interdisciplinary Researcher Identities. In A. Brew and L. Lucas, (Eds). *Academic Research and Researchers*. London: Open University Press, 131–45.

Martinez Alemán, A.M. and Salkever, K. (2004) Multiculturalism and the American Liberal Arts College: Faculty perceptions of the role of pedagogy. *Studies in Higher Education*, 29, 1, 39–58.

Massey, D. (1994) *Space, Place, and Gender*. Minneapolis: University of Minnesota Press.

Maton, K and Muller, J. (2007) A Sociology for the Transmission of Knowledges. In F. Christie and J.R. Martin (Eds) *Language, Knowledge and Pedagogy: Functional linguistic and sociological approaches*. London: Continuum.

Maton, K. (2007) Knowledge-Knower Structures in Intellectual and Educational Fields. In F. Christie and J.R. Martin (Eds) *Language, Knowledge and Pedagogy: Functional Linguistic and Sociological Perspectives*. London: Continuum.

Mayes, J. (1995) Learning Technology and Groundhog Day. In W. Strang, V.B. Simpson and D. Slater (Eds), *Hypermedia at Work: Practice and Theory in Higher Education*. Canterbury: University of kent Press.

Mestenhauser, J. and Ellingboe, B. (1998) *Reforming Higher Education Curriculum: Internationalizing the campus*. Phoenix: American Council on Education and Oryx Press.

Meyer, J. and Land, R. (2003a). *Threshold Concepts and Troublesome Knowledge: Linkages to ways of thinking and practising within the disciplines*. ETL Project Occasional Report 4. Edinburgh: University of Edinburgh. http://www.etl.tla.ed.ac.uk/docs/ETLreport4.pdf

Meyer, J.H.F. and Land, R. (2003b) Threshold Concepts and Troublesome Knowledge (1): Linkages to ways of thinking and practising. In: C. Rust (Ed.) *Improving Student Learning: Ten years on*. Oxford: OCSLD.

Meyer, J.H.F. and Land, R. (2005) Threshold Concepts and Troublesome Knowledge (2): Epistemological considerations and a conceptual framework for teaching and learning. *Higher Education*, 49, 373–88.

Meyer, J.H.F. and Land, R. (2006) (Eds) *Overcoming Barriers to Student Understanding: Threshold concepts and troublesome knowledge*. London and New York: Routledge.

Meyer, J.H.F., Land, R. and Baillie, C. (Eds) (2010) *Threshold Concepts and Transformational Learning.* Rotterdam and Taipei: Sense Publishing.

Middendorf, J. and Pace, D. (2004) Decoding the Disciplines: A model for helping students learn disciplinary ways of thinking. *New Directions for Teaching and Learning,* 98, 1–12

Miers, M. (2002) Nurse Education in Higher Education: Understanding cultural barriers to progress. *Nurse Education Today,* 22, 3, 212–19.

Miller, L. (2008) Scenes in a University: Performing academic identities in shifting contexts. In R. Di Napoli and R. Barnett (Eds) *Changing Identities in Higher Education: Voicing perspectives.* London and New York: Routledge.

Mills, J.E. and Treagust, D.F. (2003) Engineering Education: Is problem-based or project-based learning the answer? *Australasian Journal of Engineering Education,* online publication 2003–04. Retrieved March 24, 2009 from http://www.aaee.com.au/journal/2003/mills_treagust03.pdf

Milner, A. (1963) On the University Teaching of Criminal Law. *Journal of the Society of Public Teachers of Law (New Series),* 7, 192.

Mishra, P. and Koehler, M.J. (2006) Technological Pedagogical Content Knowledge: A new framework for teacher knowledge. *Teachers College Record,* 108, 6, 1017–54.

Moed, H.F. (2008) UK Research Assessment Exercises: Informed judgments on research quality or quantity? *Scientometrics,* 74, 1, 153–61.

Mol, A. and Law, J. (1994) Regions, Networks and Fluids: Anaemia and social topology. *Social Studies of Science,* 24, 4, 641–71.

Moore, R. and Maton, K. (2001) Founding the Sociology of Knowledge: Basil Bernstein, intellectual fields and the epistemic device. In A. Morais, I. Neves, B. Davies, and H. Daniels (Eds) *Towards a Sociology Of Pedagogy.* New York: Peter Lang, pp. 153–82.

Moore, R. and Muller, J. (1999) The Discourse of 'Voice' and the Problem of Knowledge and Identity in the Sociology of Education, *British Journal of Sociology of Education,* 2, 2, 189–206.

Morgan, D.L. (1988) *Focus Groups as Qualitative Research.* London: Sage.

Mouffe, C. (1992) Feminism, Citizenship, and Radical Democratic Politics. In J. Butler and J. Scott (Eds) *Feminists Theorize the Political.* London: Routledge, 369–84.

Mulcahy, L. (2007) A Crisis in Socio-Legal Studies? *Socio-Legal Newsletter,* 51, 1.

Muller, J. (2007) On Splitting Hairs: Hierarchy, knowledge and the school curriculum. In F. Christie and J. R. Martin (Eds) *Language, Knowledge and Pedagogy: Functional linguistic and sociological perspectives.* London and New York: Continuum Press, pp. 65–86.

Muller, J. (2010) Engagements with Engagement: A response to Martin Hall on community engagement in South African higher education. *Kagisano* 6. http://www.che.ac.za/documents/d000204/Kagisano_No_6_January2010.pdf

Muller, J. and Subotzky, G. (2001) What Knowledge is Needed in the New Millennium? *Organization,* 8, 2, 163–82.

Murdoch, J. (1998) The Spaces of Actor-Network Theory. *Geoforum,* 29, 357–74.

Musselin, C. (2005) European Academic Labor Markets in Transition. *Higher Education,* 49, 135–54.

Naffine, N. (1993) Assimilating Feminist Jurisprudence. *Law in Context,* 11, 78.

Neave, G. and Tight, M. (Eds) (1988) *On Being Economical with University Autonomy: Being an account of the retrospective joys of a written constitution. Academic Freedom and Responsibility.* SRHE/Open University Press, Milton Keynes, pp. 31–48.

Nelson Laird, T.F., Shoup, N., Kuh, G.D. and Schwarz, M.J. (2008) The Effects of Discipline on Deep Approaches to Student Learning and College Outcomes. *Research in Higher Education*, 49, 469–94.

Nespor, J. (2003) Undergraduate Curricula as Networks and Trajectories. In R. Edwards and J. Usher *Space, Curriculum and Learning*. Greenwich: Information Age Publishing, pp. 93–122.

Nespor, J. (2007) Curriculum Charts and Time in Undergraduate Education. *British Journal of Sociology of Education*, 28, 6, 753–66.

Neumann, R. (1996) Researching the Teaching-Research Nexus: A critical review. *Australian Journal of Education*, 40, 1, 5–18.

Neumann, R. (2001) Disciplinary Differences and University Teaching. *Studies in Higher Education*, 26, 2, 135–46.

Neumann, R., Parry, S. and Becher, T. (2002) Teaching and Learning in their Disciplinary Contexts: A conceptual analysis. *Studies in Higher Education*, 27, 4, 405–17.

Nevgi, A., Postareff, L. and Lindblom-Ylänne, S. (2004) The Effect of Discipline on Motivational and Self-Efficacy Beliefs and on Approaches to Teaching of Finnish and English University Teachers. A paper presented at the EARLI SIG save Higher Education Conference, June 18–21, 2004.

Newman, J. (1853) Discourses on University Education and (1857) Lectures and Essays on University Subjects. Reprinted in J.H. Newman (1976) *The Idea of the University*. Oxford: Oxford University Press.

Nicholas, L. (2007) *Dancing in Utopia: Dartington Hall and its dancers*. Alton, Hampshire: Dance Books.

Nieminen, P. (2008) Caught in the Science Trap? A case study of the relationship between nurses and "their" science. In J. Välimaa and O.-H. Ylijoki (Eds), *Cultural Perspectives On Higher Education* New York: Springer, pp. 127–41.

Nightingale, J. (2007) Reframing The Musical Landscape: Music networks and creative industry in Australia. Paper for NACTMUS - Music in Australian Tertiary Institutions. http://www.nactmus.org.au/PDF/Nightingale.pdf

Nilsson, B. (1999) Internationalisation at Home: Theory and praxis. *Forum*, Spring, Netherlands: European Association of International Education.

Nowotny, H., Scott, P. and Gibbons, M. (2001). *Re-thinking Science: Knowledge and the public in an age of uncertainty*. Cambridge: Polity Press.

Nussbaum, M. (1997) *Cultivating Humanity. A classical defence of reform in liberal education*. Cambridge MA: Harvard University Press.

O'Donovan, K. (1985) *Sexual Divisions in Law*. London: Weidenfeld and Nicolson.

O'Siochru, C. (2010) Where the Difference Lies: Predicting inter-disciplinary differences in epistemological beliefs. *Psychology Teaching Review*, 15, 2, 12–24.

O'Sullivan, E.V., Morrell, A. and O'Connor, M.A. (2002) *Expanding the Boundaries of Transformative Learning: Essays on theory and praxis*. New York: Palgrave.

Oliver, M. (2002) What Do Learning Technologists Do? *Innovations in Education and Training International*, 39, 4, 245–52.

Oliver, M., Price, S., Boycheva, S., Dugstad Wake, J., Jones, C., Mjelstad, S., Kemp, B., Nikolov, R. and van der Meij, H. (2005) *Empirical Studies of the Impact of Technology-Enhanced Learning on Roles and Practices in Higher Education*, Kaleidoscope project deliverable 30-03-01-F. www.noe-kaleidoscope.org/intra/docs/full_deliverables/D30-03-01-F.pdf

Paget, E., Dimanche, F. and Mounet, J.P. (2010) A Tourism Innovation Case: An actor-network approach. *Annals of Tourism Research*, 37, 3, 828–47.

Pahre, R. (1996) Mathematical Discourse and Cross-Disciplinary Communities: The case of political economy. *Social Epistemology*, 10, 1, 55–73.

PALATINE (2010) *Research Excellence Framework: Workshops on the impacts of research in the practice-based creative and performing arts, the humanities and social sciences.* http://www.palatine.ac.uk/briefings/2024/#ref

Parker, J. (2002) A New Disciplinarity: Communities of knowledge, learning and practice. *Teaching in Higher Education*, 7, 4, 373–86.

Parpala, A., Lindblom-Ylänne, S., Komulainen, E., Litmanen, T. and Hirsto, L. (2010) Students' Aproaches to Learning and their Experiences of the Teaching-Learning Environment in Different Disciplines. *British Journal of Educational Psychology*, 80, 2, 269–82.

Parry, S. (2007) *Disciplines and Doctorates*. Dordrecht: Springer.

Paul, R.J. (2008) Measuring Research Quality: The United Kingdom Government's Research Assessment Exercise. *European Journal of Information Systems*, 17, 324–9.

Pelletier, C. (2007) Learning Through Design: Subjectivity and meaning in young people's computer game production work. Unpublished PhD Thesis. London: Institute of Education.

Perälä, M.-L. and Ponkala, O. (1999) Tietoa Ja Taitoa Terveysalalle. Terveysalan Korkeakoulutuksen Arviointi. Korkeakoulujen Arviointineuvoston Julkaisuja 8.

Perkins, D. (2006) Constructivism and Troublesome Knowledge. In J.H.F. Meyerand and J.H.F. Land (Eds) *Overcoming Barriers to Student Understanding: Threshold concepts and troublesome knowledge.* London and New York: Routledge.

Pernecky, T. (2010) The Being of Tourism. *The Journal of Tourism and Peace Research*, 1, 1, 1–15.

Perrent, J.C., Bouhuijs, P.A.J. and Smits, J.G.M.M. (2003) The Suitability of Problem-Based Learning for Engineering Education: Theory and practice. *Teaching in Higher Education*, 5, 3, 345–58.

Pinch, T. (1990) The Culture of Scientists and Disciplinary Rhetoric. *European Journal of Education*, 25, 3, 295–304.

Poyas, Y. and Smith, K. (2007) Becoming a Community of Practice: The blurred identity of clinical faculty teacher educators. *Teacher Development*, 11, 3, 313–34.

Prensky, M. (2001) *Digital Natives, Digital Immigrants, Part II: Do they really think differently?* http://www.marcprensky.com/writing/Prensky%20-%20Digital%20 Natives,%20Digital%20Immigrants%20-%20Part2.pdf

Price, S. and Oliver, M. (2007) A Framework for Conceptualising the Impact of Technology on Teaching and Learning. *Educational Technology & Society*, 10, 1, 16–27.

Prosser, M. and Trigwell, K. (1999) *Understanding Learning and Teaching: The experience in higher education.* Milton Keynes: The Society for Research into Higher Education and Open University Press.

Prosser, M., Ramsden, P., Trigwell, K. and Martin, E. (2003) Dissonance in the Experience of Teaching and its Relation to the Quality of Student Learning. *Studies in Higher Education*, 28, 37–48.

Queen Mary's, London (2010) *Academic Principles and Regulations, Section A1: General Statements of Principle August 2010.* http://www.esd.qmul.ac.uk/sande/projGA/docs/QMGA%20Statement%20DEC%202009.pdf

Quinlan, K.M. (1996) Collaboration and cultures of teaching in university departments: Faculty beliefs about teaching and learning in history and engineering. Unpublished dissertation, Stanford University.

Quinlan, K.M. (1999) Commonalities and Controversy in Context: A study of academic historians' educational beliefs. *Teaching and Teacher Education*, 15, 4, 447–63.

Rambur, B. (2009) Creating Collaboration: An exploration of multinational research partnerships. In A. Brew and L. Lucas (Eds) *Academic Research and Researchers.* Open University Press/SRHE, 80–95.

Reckwitz, A. (2002) Toward a Theory of Social Practices: A development in culturalist theorising. *European Journal of Social Theory*, 5, 2, 243–63.

Reid, A., Dahlgren, O., Petocz, P. and Dahlgren, A. (2008) Identity and engagement For Professional Formation. *Studies in Higher Education*, 33, 6, 729–42.

Ren, C., Pritchard, A. and Morgan, N. (2010) Constructing Tourism Research: A critical inquiry. *Annals of Tourism Research*, 37, 4, 885–904.

Reynolds, J. (2010) Writing in the Discipline of Anthropology: Theoretical, thematic and geographical spaces. *Studies in Higher Education*, 35, 1, 11–24.

Rhoades, G. (1998) *Managed Professionals: Unionized faculty and restructuring academic labour.* Albany: State University of New York Press.

Rhoades, G. (2007) Technology-Oriented Courses and a Mode III Organization of Instructional Work. *Tertiary Education and Management*, 13, 1, 1–17

Rhoades, G. (2010) Envisioning Invisible Workforces: Enhancing intellectual capital. In G. Gordon and C. Whitchurch (Eds) *Academic and Professional Identities in Higher Education: The challenges of a diversifying workforce.* London: Routledge, 35–53.

Rhoades, G. and Sporn, B. (2002) New Modes of Management and Shifting Modes and Costs of Production: Europe and the United States. *Tertiary Education and Management*, 8, 3–28.

Rinne, R. (2004) Searching for the Rainbow: Changing the course of Finnish higher education. In I. Fägerlind and G. Strömqvist (Eds) *Reforming Higher Education in the Nordic Countries: Studies of change in Denmark, Finland, Iceland, Norway and Sweden.* International Institute for Educational Planning. UNESCO, pp. 89–135.

Rinne, R. and Koivula, J. (2007) The Dilemmas of the Changing University. In M. Shattoch and G. Williams (Eds) *Univerisities and the Knowledge Economy: Entrepreneuralism and organisational change.* Paris: IIEP, UNESCO.

Rip, A. (2004) Strategic Research, Post-Modern Universities and Research Training. *Higher Education Policy*, 17, 153–66.

Robertson, J. and Bond, C. (2001) Experiences of the Relation between Teaching and Research: What do academics value? *Higher Education Research and Development*, 20, 1, 5–19.

Rodger, K., Moore, S. and Newsome, D. (2009) Wildlife Tourism, Science and Actor-Network Theory. *Annals of Tourism Research*, 36, 3, 645–66.

Rosenthal, J.M. (1997) Multicultural Science: Focus on the biological and environmental sciences. In M.K. Kitano and A.I. Morey (Eds) *Multicultural Course Transformation in Higher Education: A broader truth.* Needham Heights, MA: Allyn and Bacon.

Ruscio, K.P. (1987) Many Sectors, Many Professions. In B. Clark *The Academic Profession.* Berkeley: University of California Press.

Russell, T. (1999) *The No Significant Difference Phenomenon.* Montgomery, AL: International Distance Education Certification Center.

Ryle, G. (1949) *The Concept of Mind.* Harmondsworth: Penguin.

Ryttyläinen, K. (2003) Kilttien Tyttöjen Tiede - Naisnäkökulmaa Hoitotieteelliseen Tutkimukseen. *Hoitotiede*, 15, 4, 198–200.

SA 794/2004. (2004) Government Decree on University Degrees.

Sabri, D. (2010) Absence of the Academic from Higher Education Policy. *Journal of Education Policy*, 25, 2, 191–205.

Salmon, G. (2000) *E-Moderating: The key to teaching and online learning*. London: Kogan Page.

Sampson, A. and Komer, K. (2010) When Government Tail Wags the Disciplinary Dog: Some consequences of national funding policy on doctoral research in New Zealand. *Higher Education Research and Development*, 29, 3, 275–89.

Sanderson, G. (2011) Internationalisation and Teaching in Higher Education. Special Issue: Internationalising the home student. *Higher Education Research and Development*, 30, 5, 661–76.

Saunders, M. (2006) From 'Organisms' to 'Boundaries': The uneven development of theory narratives in education, learning and work connections. *Journal of Education and Work*, 19, 1, 1–27.

Saunders, M., Trowler, P. and Bamber, V. (2010) *Reconceptualising Evaluative Practices in Higher Education*. London: Open University Press.

Savage, N. and Watt, G. (1996) A House of Intellect for the Profession. In P. Birks (Ed.) *Pressing Problems in the Law Volume 2*. Oxford: Oxford University Press, chapter 4.

Sayer, A. (1999) *Long Live Postdisciplinary Studies! Sociology and the curse of disciplinary parochialism/imperialism.* http://www.comp.lanc.ac.uk/sociology/papers/Sayer-Long-Live-Postdisciplinary-Studies.pdf

Sayer, A. (2005) *The Moral Significance of Class*. Cambridge: Cambridge University Press.

Sayer, A. (2008) Essentialism, Social Constructionism, and Beyond. *The Sociological Review*, 45, 3, 454–87.

Schapper, J. and Mayson, S. E. (2004) Internationalisation of Curricula: An alternative to the Taylorism of academic work. *Journal of Higher Education Policy and Management*, 26, 2, 189–205.

Schatzki, T.R. (1996) *Social Practices: A Wittgensteinian approach to human activity and the social*. Cambridge: Cambridge University Press.

Schatzki, T.R., K. Knorr-Cetina and E. von Savigny (Eds) (2001) *The Practice Turn in Contemporary Theory*. London: Routledge.

Schoenfeld, A.H. (1985) *Mathematical Problem Solving*. New York: Academic Press.

Schuster, M. and Finkelstein, M. (2006) *The Restructuring of Academic Work and Careers: The American faculty*. Baltimore: The Johns Hopkins University Press.

Schwartzman, Roy (2010) *Fundamentals of Oral Communication*. 2nd edition. Dubuque, IA: Kendall Hunt.

Scott, P. (2006) The Academic Profession in a Knowledge Society: In U. Teichler (Ed.) *The Formative Years of Scholars*. London: Portland Press.

Select Committee on Legal Education (1846) Report from the Select Committee on Legal Education. 25th August 1846, *House of Commons Sessional Papers 1846*, vol X.

Sharpe, R. and Oliver, M. (2007) Designing Courses for E-Learning. In H. Beetham and R. Sharpe (Eds) *Rethinking Pedagogy for a Digital Age: Designing and delivering e-learning*. London: Routledge, pp. 41–51.

Sheldon, P., Fesenmaier, D., Woeber, K., Cooper, C. and Antonioli, M. (2008) Tourism Education Futures, 2010–2030: Building the capacity to lead. *Journal of Teaching in Travel and Tourism*, 7, 3, 61–8.

Shinn, T. (1982) Scientific disciplines and organizational specificity. In Elias, N., Martins, H. and Whitley, R. D. (Eds) *Scientific Establishments and Hierarchies*. Dordrecht, Reidel.

Shore, C. and Wright, S. (1999) Audit Culture and Anthropology: Neo-liberalism in British higher education. *Journal of the Royal Anthropological Institute*, 5, 557–75.

Shreeve, A. (2009) 'I'd Rather be seen as a Practitioner, Come In To Teach My Subject': Identity work in part-time art and design tutors. *International Journal of Art and Design Education*, 28: 151–9.

Shreeve, A., Simms, E. and Trowler, P. (2010) A Kind of Exchange: Learning from art and design teaching. *Journal of Higher Education Research and Development*, 29, 2, 12–150

Shulman, L. (2005a) Signature Pedagogies in the Professions. *Daedalus*, 134, 3, 52–9.

Shulman, L. (2005b) *The Signature Pedagogies of the Professions of Law, Medicine, Engineering, and the Clergy: Potential Lessons for the Education of Teachers.* http://hub.mspnet.org/index.cfm/11172

Sibeon, R. (2007) *Contemporary Sociology and Policy Analysis.* Eastham: Tudor Business Publishing.

Sikes, P. (2006) Working in a 'New' University: In the shadow of the Research Assessment Exercise. *Studies in Higher Education*, 31, 555–68.

Singh, P. (2002) Pedagogising Knowledge: Bernstein's theory of the pedagogic device. *British Journal of Sociology of Education*, 23, 4, 571–82.

Slaughter, S. and Leslie, L.L (1997) *Academic Capitalism. Politics, policies and the entrepreneurial university.* Baltimore/London: Johns Hopkins University Press.

Smeby, J.-C. (1996) Disciplinary Differences in University Teaching. *Studies in Higher Education*, 21, 1, 69–79.

Smith, L.T. (1999) *Decolonising Methodologies: Research and Indigenous peoples.* London and New York: Zed Books Ltd.

Soloway, E. (1997) Scaffolding Learnings and Addressing Diversity: Technology as the Trojan mouse. In *Proceedings of CHI 1996.* New York: ACM Press.

South African Council on Higher Education (2006) Community Engagement in Higher Education, Proceedings of the Conference Hosted by the Higher Education Quality Committee of the Council on Higher Education and the Community–Higher Education–Service Partnerships Initiative of Jet Education Services. Cape Town, South Africa: 3–5 September 2006. http://www.che.ac.za/documents/d000153/HEQC_Conference_Community_Engagement_HE_2007.pdf

Southall, A. (1996) *Tribes: Encyclopedia of cultural anthropology. Vol. 4.* New York: Henry Holt and Company.

Sperber, D. (2003) 'Why Rethink Interdisciplinarity?' http://www.dan.sperber.fr/?p=101 (English version of 'Pourquoi repenser l'interdisciplinarité?' Text discussed in the virtual seminar Rethinking Interdisciplinarity / Repenser l'interdisciplinarité on www.interdisciplines.org 2003 (where the whole discussion is available).

Spitzer, A., and Perrenoud, B. (2006) Reforms in Nursing Education across Western Europe: Implementation processes and current status. *Journal of Professional Nursing*, 22, 3, 162–71.

Stanley, L. (2005) A Child of its Time: Perspectives on 'othering' in sociology. *Sociological Research Online*, 10, 3. http://www.socresonline.org.uk/10/3/stanley.html

Stella, A. (2006) Quality Assurance of Cross-Border Higher Education. *Quality in Higher Education*, 12, 3, 257–76.

Stes, A., Gijbels, D. and Van Petegem, P. (2007). Student-Focused Approaches to Teaching in Relation to Context and Teacher Characteristics. *Higher Education*, 55, 255–67.

Stevenson, K. and Sander, P. (2002) Medical Students are from Mars – Business and Psychology Students are from Venus – University Teachers are from Pluto? *Medical Teacher*, 24, 2, 27–31.

Strathern, M. (2000) The Tyranny of Transparency. *British Educational Research Journal*, 26, 3, 309–21.

Strathern, M. (2006) A Community of Critics: Thoughts on new knowledge. *Journal of the Royal Anthropological Institute*, 12, 1, 191–209.

Strathern, M. (2007) Interdisciplinarity: Some models from the human sciences. *Interdisciplinary Science Reviews*, 32, 2, 123–34.

Strathern, M. (2008) Knowledge Identities. In R. Di Napoli and R. Barnett (Eds) *Changing Identities in Higher Education: Voicing perspectives*. London and New York: Routledge.

Strauss, A.L. and Corbin, J.M. (1997) *Grounded Theory in Practice*. Thousand Oaks, CA: Sage.

Sugarman, D. (1991) A Hatred of Disorder: Legal science, liberalism and imperialism. In P. Fitzpatrick (Ed.) *Dangerous Supplements: Resistance and Renewal in Jurisprudence*. London: Pluto Press, pp. 34–67.

Taylor, C. (1989) *Sources of the Self: The making of the modern identity*. Cambridge: Cambridge University Press.

Taylor, P. (2008) Being an Academic Today. In Di Napoli, R. and Barnett, R. (Eds) *Changing Identities in Higher Education: Voicing perspectives*. London and New York: Routledge.

Teekens, H. (2003) The Requirement to Develop Specific Skills for Teaching in an Intercultural Setting. *Journal of Studies in International Education*, 7, 1, 108–19.

Thomas, P. (1997) Socio-Legal Studies: The case of disappearing fleas and bustards. In P.A. Thomas (Ed.) *Socio-Legal Studies*. Aldershot: Ashgate, chapter 1.

Thomson, P. and Walker, M. (Eds) (2010) *The Routledge Doctoral Student's Companion*. London and New York: Routledge.

Thornton, M. (1998) Technocentrism in the Law School: Why the gender and colour of law remain the same. *Osgoode Hall Law Journal*, 36, 369.

Tight, M. (2008) Higher Education Research as Tribe, Territory and/or Community: A co-citation analysis. *Higher Education*, 55, 593–605.

Tissen, R. and Deprez, F. L. (2008) *Towards a Spatial Theory of Organizations*. Working NRG Working Paper 08–04. http://www.zerospaceadvies.nl/publicaties/pdf/SpatialOrganizayions080304.pdf

Tourism Education Futures Initiative (TEFI) (2009) *A Values-Based Framework For Tourism Education: Building the capacity to lead: White Paper*. uovadis.wu-wien.ac.at/drupal/files/White%20Paper%20May22_0.pdf

Tribe, J. (2009) Tribes, Territories and Networks in the Tourism Academy. *Annals of Tourism Research*, 37, 1, 7–33.

Trigwell, K. (2002) Approaches to Teaching Design Subjects: A quantitative analysis. *Art, Design and Communication in Higher Education*, 1, 2, 69–80.

Trigwell, K. and Prosser, M. (1991) Improving the Quality of Student Learning: The influence of learning context and student approaches to learning on learning outcomes. *Higher Education*, 22, 251–66.

Trigwell, K. and Prosser, M. (1996) Changing Approaches to Teaching: A Relational perspective. *Studies in Higher Education*, 21, 3, 275–84.

Trigwell, K., Prosser, M. and Waterhouse, F. (1999) Relations between Teachers' Approaches to Teaching and Students' Approaches to Learning. *Higher Education*, 37, 57–70.

Trist, E. (1972) Types of Output Mix in Research Organisations and their Complementarity. In A.B. Cherns, R. Sinclair and W.I. Jenkins (Eds) *Social Science and Government: Politics and Problems*. London: Tavistock.

Trowler, P. (1998) *Academics Responding to Change: New higher education frameworks and academic cultures*. Buckingham: Open University Press/SRHE.

Trowler, P. (2001) Captured by the Discourse? The Socially Constitutive Power of New Higher Education Discourse in the UK. *Organization*, 8, 2, 183–201.

Trowler, P. (2008a) *Cultures and Change in Higher Education*. London: Palgrave Macmillan.

Trowler, P. (2008b) Beyond Epistemological Essentialism: Academic tribes in the 21st century. In C. Kreber (Ed.) *The University and its Disciplines: Teaching and learning within and beyond disciplinary boundaries*. London: Routledge.

Trowler, P. and Cooper, A. (2002) Teaching and Learning Regimes: Implicit theories and recurrent practices in the enhancement of teaching and learning through educational development programmes. *Higher Education Research and Development*, 21, 3, 221–40.

Trowler, P. and Turner, G. (2002) Exploring the Hermeneutic Foundations of University Life: Deaf academics in a hybrid community of practice. *Higher Education*, 43, 227–56.

Trowler, P. and Wareham, T. (2007) Reconceptualising the 'Teaching-Research Nexus'. In HERDSA Proceedings of the Annual HERDSA Conference 2007: *Enhancing Higher Education Theory and Scholarship*. 8–11 July 2007, Adelaide Australia. http://www.herdsa.org.au/wp-content/uploads/conference/2007/papers/p53.pdf

Trowler, P. and Wareham, T. (2008) Tribes, Territories, Research and Teaching: Enhancing the 'teaching-research nexus'. http://www.heacademy.ac.uk/assets/York/Trowler_Final_Report.pdf

Trowler, P., Fanghanel, J. and Wareham, T. (2005) Freeing the Chi of Change: The higher education academy and enhancing teaching and learning in higher education. *Studies in Higher Education*, 30, 4, 427–44.

Tuomi, J. (1997) Suomalainen Hoitotiedekeskustelu. Jyväskylän Yliopisto. *Studies in Sport, Physical Education and Health*, 51 (monograph of doctoral thesis).

Tuomi-Gröhn, T. and Engeström, Y. (Eds) (2003) *Between School and Work: New perspectives on transfer and boundary-crossing*. Amsterdam: Pergamon.

Tuomi-Gröhn, T., Engeström, Y. and Young, M. (2003) From Transfer to Boundary-crossing Between School and Work as a Tool for Developing Vocational Education: An Introduction. In Tuomi-Gröhn, T. and Engeström, Y. (Eds) *Between School and Work: New perspectives on transfer and boundary-crossing*, Amsterdam: Pergamon

Turner, S. (2000) What are Disciplines? And how is interdisciplinarity different? In P. Weingart and N. Stehr *Practising Interdisciplinarity*. Toronto: University of Toronto Press, pp. 46–65.

Turner, Y. and Robson, S. (2008) *Internationalizing the University*. London: Continuum.

Turpin, T. and Garrett-Jones, S. (2000) Mapping the New Cultures and Organization of Research in Australia. In P. Weingart and N. Stehr (Eds) *Practising Interdisciplinarity*. Toronto: University of Toronto Press, pp. 79–109.

Twigger-Ross, C.L., Bonaiuto, M. and Breakwell, G. (2003) Identity Theories and Environmental Psychology. In M. Bonnes, T. Lee and M. Bonaiuto (Eds) *Psychological Theories for Environmental Issues*. Aldershot, England: Ashgate, pp. 203–33.

Twining, W. (1994) *Blackstone's Tower: The English law school*. London: Sweet and Maxwell.

Twining, W. (1998) Thinking about Law Schools: Rutland reviewed. *Journal of Law and Society*, 25, 1.

Tynan, J. and New, C. (2009) Creativity and Conflict: How theory and practice shape student identities in design education. *Arts and Humanities in Higher Education*, 8, 3, 295–308.

University of Åbo Akademi. Caring Science. https://www.abo.fi/student/en/vardvetenskap

University of Kuopio. Department of Nursing Science. http://www.uku.fi/hoitot/english/

University of Oulu. Terveystieteiden Laitos. http://www.oulu.fi/hoitotiede/

University of South Australia, (2001) Strategies for Internationalisation of the Curriculum. Graduate Qualities. (Only available on staff intranet).

University of Strathclyde (2010) Conference: Academic Identities for the 21st Century, 16–18 June 2010: http://ewds.strath.ac.uk/aic/ThemesPrompts.aspx

University of Tampere. Hoitotieteen Laitos. http://www.uta.fi/laitokset/hoito/

University of Turku. Department of Nursing Science. http://www.med.utu.fi/hoitotiede/en/

Van Damme, D. (2002) Trends and Models in International Quality Assurance and Accreditation in Higher Education in Relation to Trade in Education Services. Paper presented at OECD/US Forum on Trade in Educational Services, p.18.

Van der Duim, R. (2007) Tourismscapes: An actor-network perspective. *Annals of Tourism Research*, 34, 4, 961–76.

van Heerden, A. (2005) Articulating the Cognitive Processes at the Heart of Chemistry. In T. Riordan and J. Roth (Eds) *Disciplines as Frameworks for Student Learning*. Sterling VA: Stylus, pp. 95–120.

Vick, D.W., Murray, A.D., Little, G.F. and Campbell, K. (1998) The Perceptions of Academic Lawyers Concerning the Effect of the United Kingdom Research Assessment Exercise. *Journal of Law and Society*, 25, 536.

Virtanen, P. and Nevgi, A. (2010) Disciplinary and Gender Differences among Higher Education Students in Self-Regulated Learning Strategies. *Educational Psychology*, 30, 3, 323–47.

Vuolanto, P. (2004) Hoitotieteen Rakentuminen Hoitotiede-Lehden Menetelmä- Ja Keskusteluartikkeleissa Vuosina 1989-2002. Pro gradu -tutkielma. Tampereen yliopisto.

Wagner, J. (2010) Ignorance in Educational Research: How not knowing shapes our knowledge. In P. Thomson and M. Walker (Eds) *The Routledge Doctoral Student's Companion*. London and New York: Routledge.

Walker, R. (2007) An Alternative Construction of Identity: A study of place-based identity and its implications. Paper presented at the American Communication Conference annual meeting, Taos, New Mexico, Oct. 3–7, 2007: http://www.acjournal.org/holdings/vol9/fall/articles/identity.html

Warde, A. (2005) Consumption and Theories of Practice. *Journal of Consumer Culture*, 5, 2, 131–53.

Wareing, S. (2006) How Students Learn in Their Subjects; Identifying models. Paper presented at SEDA Spring Conference Advancing Evidence-Informed Practice in HE Learning, Teaching and Educational Development. Liverpool, UK: 8–9 June.

Weingart, P. and Stehr, N. (Eds) (2000) *Practising Interdisciplinarity*. Toronto: University of Toronto Press.

Wenger, E. (1998) *Communities of Practice. Learning, meaning and identity.* Cambridge: Cambridge University Press.

Wertsch, J., Del Rio, P. and Alvarez, A. (Eds) (1995) *Sociocultural Studies of Mind*. Cambridge: Cambridge University Press.

Whitchurch, C. (2010a) Convergence and Divergence in Professional Identities. In G. Gordon and C. Whitchurch (Eds) *Academic and Professional Identities in Higher Education: The challenges of a diversifying workforce.* London: Routledge, pp. 167–84.

Whitchurch, C. (2010b) The Challenges of a Diversifying Workforce. In G. Gordon and C. Whitchurch (Eds), *Academic and Professional Identities in Higher Education: The challenges of a diversifying workforce.* London: Routledge, pp. 245–56.

Willig, C. (2002) A Discourse Dynamic Approach to the Study of Subjectivity. In D. Marks (Ed.) *The Health Psychology Reader.* London: Sage.

Wilson, G. (1987) English Legal Scholarship. *Modern Law Review*, 50, 6, 818–54.

Wolfe, S. and Flewitt, R. (2010) New Technologies, New Multimodal Literacy Practices and Young Children's Metacognitive Development. *Cambridge Journal of Education*, 40, 4, 387–99.

Ylijoki, O.-H. (2008) A Clash of Academic Cultures: The Case of Dr. X. In J. Välimaa and O.-H. Ylijoki (Eds) *Cultural Perspectives on Higher Education* New York: Springer, pp. 75–89.

Ylijoki, O-H. (2000) Disciplinary Cultures and the Moral Order of Studying. *Higher Education*, 39, 339–62.

Yorke, M. (2009) Assessment for Career and Citizenship. In C. Kreber (Ed.) *The University and its Disciplines.* New York: Routledge, pp. 221–30.

Young, M.F.D. (2000) Rescuing the Sociology of Educational Knowledge from the Extremes of Voice Discourse: Towards a new theoretical basis for the sociology of the curriculum. *British Journal of Sociology of Education*, 21, 4, 523–36.

Young, M.F.D. (2008) Bringing Knowledge Back. In *From Social Constructivism to Social Realism in the Sociology of Education.* London: Routledge.

Young, P. (2010) Generic or Disciplinary Specific? An exploration of the significance of discipline-specific issues in researching teaching and learning in higher education. *Innovations in Education and Teaching International*, 47, 1, 115–24.

Zehrer, A. and Mossenlechner, C. (2009) Key Competencies in Tourism Graduates: The employers' point of view. *Journal of Teaching in Travel and Tourism*, 9, 3, 266–87.

Index

academic affiliation, complexity in 47
academic practices, definition 15
academicisation of the nursing profession 115
academics as cosmopolitans 103
academics as locals 103
activity systems 30, 223, 229
actor network theory 31, 192
agency 25, 31, 91
approaches to teaching 208

black-letter law 59, 63–4
blended professionals 27, 28
Browne Report 133, 236–8

capital accumulation 79
capitals and the role array 86
catalysts for change 169, 232
classification and framing 122
colonialism 48
community engagement 147
compliance and complicity 232
conceptions of teaching 159, 208–9
contextual concerns 34, 37, 42
critical legal studies 13, 22, 42, 61–2
critical realism 8
curriculum knowledge and pedagogic practices, 128

de-centering of disciplines 104, 137, 163
de-centering of identities 137
de-centering the subject 29
decontextualising 33
dignification of disciplines 43
disciplinary discourse 123
disciplinary knowledge practices and the curriculum 118
disciplinary metaphors 94
discipline as bastion 35
discipline as curriculum 5, 35

discipline as research 5, 35
discipline as warrant 35
disciplines, definition 5, 9
disciplines and research, conceptualising 76
discourse 159
discursive capture 36
discursive repertoires 159
distribution rules 12, 119, 121, 127–8
doctrinal approach to academic law 57, 58, 59, 60, 67
domains of study 11
donnish dominion 7
dual identity of academics 104

educational ideologies 42, 74, 76, 105, 163
emotionality 31
employability 253
enterprise ideology 74
epistemes 175
epistemic and social relations 154
epistemological essentialism 18, 99, 101
epistemological paradigms 100
evaluation rules 12, 119, 124, 127, 128
externalist influence on sciences 110

feminism and academic law 61, 65
feminism and nursing studies 113
filters and pedagogical constructs 93, 105
fluidity as metaphor 51
forms and fields of knowledge 10

global policy ensemble 29

hierarchical knowledge structure 144
hierarchical knowledge systems 144
history and practices 33

identities 47, 78, 91, 93, 130, 135, 138, 139, 157–8

interdisciplinarity 13–15, 165, 170, 178–9, 182–3, 207, 233, 256
internalist influence on sciences 110
internationalisation 171–2, 181, 197
invisible college 38

'knower code' 144, 146
knowledge code 144, 146
knowledge practices 175
knowledge resources 34
knowledgeability 31

legitimation code theory 143, 161
liminality 177
liquid modernity 46, 52, 55, 94
liquidity in academic communities 195
loosely coupled practices 236

managed professionals 27
managerialism 28, 33, 42, 163
marketisation 163
metaphor 106
micropolitics 34
mindful disciplinarity 165
Mode 1 14, 45
Mode 2 14, 15, 45, 51, 55
Mode 3 180
moral order of studying 19
multidisciplinarity 14, 178, 256
multiple cultural configurations 32, 160, 241
multiple subject positioning 159

new managerialism 78, 235
new public management 110
nomothetic models 13

ocean as metaphor 51, 53
orientations to teaching 209

paradigm wars 42, 256
pedagogic content knowledge 222
pedagogic device 12, 100, 118–20, 128; definition 119
pedagogic discourses 133
pedagogical imperialism 201
performativity 15, 213
PhD degree, shaping research practices 70
phenomenography 26
playfulness in art and design 69
post-colonial theory 203
post-disciplinary studies 191
poststructuralism 7

power 34, 37
practice architectures 164
practice clusters 32
practice resources 241
practice-based pedagogic culture 133
producer capture 14
program affiliation 43
progressivism 74

RAE 66, 71, 84, 133, 140
recontextualisation 33, 35, 244, 248
recontextualisation of knowledge 119
recontextualisation rules 12–13, 119, 122, 124, 127–8
reflexive deliberation 36
repertoires of practice 32, 34
repertoires of recognizable practices 170
research, definition of 69, 71, 77; formalisation of 70, 77; orientations to 73–4
Research Assessment Exercise 11, 42, 55, 65–6, 71, 72, 76, 78, 80–86, 89, 118, 121, 133, 140, 212, 276
Research Excellence Framework 42, 65, 72, 133, 140, 213, 250, 276
reservoirs of practice 32–3
restless disciplines 6
rivers as metaphor 52
role array 82–4

socio-legal studies 61
sensitising theory 30
service learning 147
shifting territories of academic practices 253
signature pedagogies 24–5, 31, 99, 101
sites of practice 12–13, 244
situated cognition 31
situational contingency 31
social constructionism 22
social hydraulics 35
social practice theory 9, 10, 30, 76, 91, 99, 156, 246
social practices, definition 10, 31
social realism 233, 246
social reconstructionism 74
socio-legal approach 64, 67
Socio-Legal Studies Association 66
sociology as situated practice 79
socio-material theory 31
structure 35, 42
structured dispositions 35
structures 36
subjectivity 33

subjects 11, 12
supercomplexity 156, 164, 172–3, 180–81, 208, 210
sustainability 33

teaching-research nexus 68
technological determinism 173
technology and academic practices 220
territories, and the atomisation of knowledge 56; as conditioning practices 253; as confining 171; as metaphor 50, 51; contested 103; epistemological nature of 18; facilitating supervision and control 50, 51; shifting 253
Third Space 28
threshold concepts 24, 99, 101, 170–71, 176, 177, 183–4
tightly coupled practices 236
tourism and tribal identities 189
traditionalism as ideology 74
transaction spaces 45
transdisciplinarity 14, 164, 182
tribes, and boundary crossing professionals 222; and colonialism 56; and communities of practice 93; and moral orders 21; and neo-liberalism 46; and technologies 231; as metaphor 11, 41, 43–4, 48, 50–51, 53, 55, 100, 102, 105, 253, 257; as multicultural 28; colonial inheritance of 48–9, 50; dissolution of 27; neo-liberal attack on 14
tribes and territories, evolution of 196; preditions from the thesis 121
Trojan mouse 221, 231
troublesome knowledge 24, 170, 176–7, 181–3, 203, 274, 276

unhomeliness and interdisciplinarity 53
universities as axial structures 239

vectors of change 171, 186, 187
virtual learning environment adoption 225
virtual practice 127
vocational culture and academic practices 117
voice discourse 8, 9

ways of knowing 164
ways of thinking and practising 24, 99, 101, 175